LIVING LANGUAGE®
ULTIMATE
SPANISH
ADVANCED

ULTIMATE

SPANISH

ADVANCED

WRITTEN BY

DANIEL HOLODYK,

RENNERT BILINGUAL

EDITED BY

ANA SUFFREDINI AND

HELGA SCHIER, PH.D.

LIVING LANGUAGE®
A Random House Company

Published by Living Language, A Random House Company,
201 East 50th Street, New York, New York 10022.

Random House, Inc. New York, Toronto, London, Sydney, Auckland
www.livinglanguage.com

Living Language is a registered trademark of Crown Publishers, Inc.

Printed in the United States of America

Library of Congress Cataloging-in-Publication Data is available upon request.

ISBN 0-609-80253-4

10 9 8 7 6 5 4 3 2 1

First Edition

ACKNOWLEDGMENTS

Many thanks to Crown's Living Language™ staff: Kathryn Mintz, Jessica Frankel, Christopher Warnasch, Julie Lewis, Jim Walsh, Jessica Allan, Lenny Henderson, Eleuteria Hernandez, Christian Viveros, Ronald Cere, Carmen Vega-Carney, and Mario Castro Cid. Special thanks to *El Diario*, Atilio Jorge Castelpoggi, and the U.S. Chamber of Commerce for providing essential materials.

CONTENTS

INTRODUCTION

Living Language™ *Ultimate Spanish Advanced* is a continuation of the beginner–intermediate *Ultimate Spanish* program. If you have already mastered the basics of Spanish in school, while traveling abroad, or with other *Living Language*™ courses, then *Ultimate Spanish Advanced* is right for you.

The complete course includes this text, along with eight hours of recordings. However, if you are confident of your pronunciation, you can also use this manual on its own.

With *Ultimate Spanish Advanced* you'll continue to learn how to speak, understand, read, and write idiomatic Spanish. The program will also introduce you to some of the more interesting aspects of Latin American and Spanish culture and business. You'll be able to participate in engaging conversations about a variety of topics, as well as recognize and respond to several styles of formal and informal speech.

The course will take you everywhere, from coffee plantations to ancient ruins to book fairs, while teaching useful vocabulary and expressions. You'll practice deciphering newspaper articles and economic reports. You'll also learn about subtle cultural distinctions in personal interaction, such as when to insist on paying for dinner and when to stop, that will help smooth your way abroad.

COURSE MATERIALS

THE MANUAL

Living Language™ *Ultimate Spanish Advanced* consists of twenty lessons, four reading passages, and two review sections. The reading passages appear after every five lessons. There are review sections after Lesson 10 and Lesson 20. It's best to read and study each lesson in the manual before listening to it on the recordings.

DIALOGO (DIALOGUE): Each lesson begins with a dialogue in standard, idiomatic Spanish presenting a realistic situation—a job interview, searching for an apartment, buying a car—set in various locales. All dialogues are translated into colloquial English.

APUNTES (NOTES): The notes in this section refer to specific expressions and phrases in the dialogue. They'll introduce you to the cultural and historical background relevant to a particular expression, and allow you to see grammar rules and vocabulary "in action."

1

GRAMATICA Y USOS (GRAMMAR AND USAGE): After a brief review of basic Spanish grammar, you'll concentrate on the more advanced grammatical forms and their usage. You'll learn how to express yourself more accurately and appropriately by using idiomatic Spanish. For easy reference, the heading of each topic corresponds to its listing in the table of contents.

ESTUDIO IDIOMATICO (WORD STUDY): This section focuses on idiomatic expressions in Spanish. You'll learn how to express anger in Spanish the way a native speaker would, to be more precise about time, and even how to show off a little. You'll also learn some of the more colorful Spanish idioms and maxims. This in-depth vocabulary study will improve your idiomatic usage of Spanish and help you avoid common linguistic pitfalls.

HABLEMOS DE NEGOCIOS (LET'S TALK BUSINESS): In this section you'll explore different areas of the Latin American and Spanish economies, as well as cultural and historical information relevant to business etiquette and procedures. Discussing topics such as dress codes, import and export, and advertising, this section will enable you to conduct business in Latin America and Spain with confidence.

EXAMEN (QUIZ): This section allows you to review the grammar and vocabulary covered in the lessons. You can check your answers in the *Respuestas* (Answers) section appearing after Lesson 20.

LECTURA (READING): The four reading passages—appearing after Lessons 5, 10, 15, and 20—are not translated. The material covered in the preceding lessons, along with the vocabulary notes on the more difficult words and phrases will enable you to infer the meaning, just as you would when reading a newspaper article or business report abroad.

REPASO (REVIEW): The two review sections appear after Lessons 10 and 20. Similar in structure to the *Examen,* these sections will allow you to integrate and test your mastery of the material covered in the preceding lessons.

APPENDIXES: There are eight appendixes: a guide to pronunciation, verb charts, irregular past and present participles, a dictionary of grammatical terms, a grammar summary, cardinal and ordinal numbers, and a section on letter writing.

GLOSSARY: The extensive two-way glossary will provide an invaluable reference as you work through this program and as you apply your knowledge when communicating with Spanish speakers and traveling abroad.

INDEX: The manual ends with an index of the major grammar points covered in the lessons.

The appendixes, glossary, and index make this manual an excellent source for future reference and study.

RECORDINGS (SETS A & B)

This program provides you with eight hours of audio instruction and practice. There are two sets of complementary recordings: the first is designed for use with the manual, while the second may be used independently. By listening to and imitating the native speakers, you'll improve your pronunciation and comprehension while learning to use new phrases and structures.

RECORDINGS FOR USE WITH THE MANUAL (SET A)

This set of recordings gives you four hours of audio practice in Spanish only, featuring the complete dialogues of all twenty lessons. The recorded material appears in **boldface** in your manual. You'll first hear native Spanish speakers read the complete dialogue without interruption at normal conversational speed. Then you'll have a chance to listen to the dialogue a second time and repeat each phrase in the pauses provided.

If you wish to practice your comprehension, first listen to the recordings of the dialogue without consulting the translations in the manual. Write down a summary of what you think the dialogue was about, and then listen to the recordings a second time, checking how much you understood with the translations in the manual.

After you study each lesson and practice with Set A, go on to the second set of recordings (Set B), which can be used on the go—while driving, jogging, traveling, or doing housework.

RECORDINGS FOR USE ON THE GO (SET B)

This set of recordings gives you four hours of audio instruction and practice in Spanish and English. Because they are bilingual, the Set B recordings may be used on the go without the manual, wherever it's convenient to learn.

The twenty lessons on Set B correspond to those in the manual. A bilingual narrator leads you through the four sections of each lesson.

The first section presents the most important phrases from the original dialogue. You will first hear the abridged dialogue without interruption at normal conversational speed. You'll then hear it again, phrase by phrase, with English translations and pauses for you to repeat after the native Spanish speakers.

The second section reviews and expands upon the most important vocabulary introduced in the lesson. You will practice words and phrases collected from the *Diálogo* (Dialogue), *Apuntes* (Notes), *Estudio idiomático* (Word Study), and *Hablemos de negocios* (Let's Talk Business). Additional expressions show how the words may be used in other contexts. Again, you are given time to repeat the Spanish phrases after the native speakers.

In the third section you will explore the lesson's most important grammatical structures. After a quick review of the rules, you can practice with illustrative phrases and sentences.

The conversational exercises in the last section integrate what you've learned and help you generate sentences in Spanish on your own. You'll take part in brief conversations, ask and respond to questions, transform sentences, and occasionally translate from English into Spanish. After you respond, you'll hear the correct answer from a native Spanish speaker.

The interactive approach on this set of recordings focuses on the idiomatic spoken word and will teach you to speak, understand, and *think* in Spanish.

Now let's begin.

LECCION 1

A. DIALOGO (Dialogue)

¡BIENVENIDO AL SUR!

El Sr. Michael Thompson, un hombre de negocios de los EE.UU.[1] acaba de aterrizar en el Aeropuerto Internacional Arturo Merino Benítez en Santiago, Chile.[2] Al salir por la puerta de llegada, oye:

ALTOPARLANTE: **Pasajeros del vuelo 345 proveniente de Los Ángeles, favor de[3] dirigirse a Control de pasaportes.**

De pronto, un hombre le toca el hombro al Sr. Thompson.

SR. ROJAS: **Disculpe señor, ¿me podría[4] decir la hora?**

SR. THOMPSON: **¡Cómo no![5] Son las . . . ¡pero! Todavía tengo la hora de Los Ángeles. ¿Cuál es[6] la diferencia de horas?**

SR. ROJAS: **A ver . . . creo que es de cuatro horas.[7]**

SR. THOMPSON: **¡Bueno! Entonces son las diez menos cuarto.**

SR. ROJAS: **¡Muchas gracias! Tengo que hacer una conexión para[8] Montevideo y estoy apurado.[9]**

SR. THOMPSON: **¡Entiendo! Yo también tengo apuro.[9] Vamos a ver cómo nos va[10] en Inmigración.**

Después de esperar su turno en la fila, el Sr. Thompson se acerca al oficial de inmigración.

OFICIAL DE INMIGRACION: **¡Buenos días, Señor! Su pasaporte, por favor . . .**

SR. THOMPSON: **¡Cómo no! Aquí lo tiene.**

OFICIAL DE INMIGRACION: **¿Viene Vd. como turista o en viaje de negocios?**

SR. THOMPSON: **En viaje de negocios.**

OFICIAL DE INMIGRACION: **¿Cuánto tiempo piensa quedarse en el país?**

SR. THOMPSON: **Unos[11] dos meses.**

OFICIAL DE INMIGRACION: **Aquí tiene sus documentos. Por favor, presente este formulario[12] al salir del país. Espero que disfrute de su estadía.**

En "Reclamación de Equipaje," el Sr. Thompson ve al[13] Sr. Rojas nuevamente.

SR. THOMPSON: **Parece que tuvimos suerte. Pasamos**[14] **bastante rápido.**

SR. ROJAS *(riendo):* **Sí, pero aún me falta pasar por**[15] **otro aeropuerto más. ¿Viaja a Chile por**[16] **primera vez?**

SR. THOMPSON: **Así es. Vengo para familiarizarme con los productos locales. Trabajo para una empresa de importación y exportación en los EE.UU.**

SR. ROJAS: **¡Ah, qué interesante! Pienso que va a encontrar muchos productos originales.**

SR. THOMPSON: **Así espero, pero por ahora tengo el problema de cómo llegar hasta el centro.**

SR. ROJAS: **En eso puedo aconsejarle. Le conviene**[17] **tomar un taxi si tiene maletas. También hay un bus,**[18] **pero el centro no está lejos y los taxis no son tan caros. Además lo llevan hasta la puerta del hotel.**

SR. THOMPSON: **Gracias por el consejo. ¡Ah! por fin llegan las maletas.**

Ambos viajeros juntan sus valijas, pasan por la Aduana y por fin salen a la terminal de Llegadas Internacionales.

SR. THOMPSON *(jadeando):* **¡Qué calor sofocante!**

SR. ROJAS *(tratando de no reír):* **¡No se preocupe! Por la tarde va a hacer más calor todavía.**[19]

SR. THOMPSON: **¡Ya veo que voy a tener que acostumbrarme al clima!**

ALTOPARLANTE: **Atención pasajeros: PLUNA anuncia la apertura del embarco para el vuelo 542 con destino a Montevideo por la puerta 19.**

SR. ROJAS: **¡Bueno, ése es mi vuelo! ¡Ah! Y la boletería del micro queda**[20] **al otro lado de la terminal. ¡Buena suerte en lo suyo!**[21]

SR. THOMPSON: **Igualmente, y ¡muchas gracias por su ayuda! ¡Feliz viaje!**

WELCOME TO THE SOUTH.

Mr. Michael Thompson, a businessman from the U.S., has just landed at Arturo Merino Benítez International Airport in Santiago, Chile. Upon leaving the arrival gate, he hears:

LOUDSPEAKER: Passengers from flight 345 arriving from Los Angeles, please proceed to Passport Control.

Suddenly, a man taps him on the shoulder.

MR. ROJAS: Excuse me, sir. Could you please tell me the time?

MR. THOMPSON: Of course! It's . . . Oh! My watch is still on Los Angeles time. What's the time difference?

MR. ROJAS: Let's see . . . I think it's four hours.

MR. THOMPSON: Okay! In that case, it's a quarter to ten.

MR. ROJAS: Thank you very much! I have to make a connection to Montevideo, and I'm in a hurry.

MR. THOMPSON: I know! I'm in a rush myself. Let's see how we do at Immigration.

After waiting in line for fifteen minutes, Mr. Thompson walks up to the Immigration Officer.

IMMIGRATION OFFICER: Good morning, sir! Your passport, please . . .

MR. THOMPSON: Of course! Here it is!

IMMIGRATION OFFICER: Are you here as a tourist or on business?

MR. THOMPSON: On business.

IMMIGRATION OFFICER: How long do you plan to stay in the country?

MR. THOMPSON: About two months.

IMMIGRATION OFFICER: Here are your documents. Please show this form upon leaving the country. Hope you enjoy your stay!

At Baggage Claim, Mr. Thompson sees Mr. Rojas again.

MR. THOMPSON: It looks like we were lucky. We went through pretty fast.

MR. ROJAS (laughing): Yes, but I still have to go through another airport. Is this your first trip to Chile?

MR. THOMPSON: Yes, it is. I'm here to familiarize myself with the local products. I work for an import/export company in the U.S.

MR. ROJAS: Oh, how interesting! I think you'll find many original products.

MR. THOMPSON: I hope so! But for now, I have another problem: how to get downtown.

MR. ROJAS: I can help you with that. If you have luggage you'd better take a taxi. There is an airport bus, but downtown isn't far, and taxis aren't expensive. Besides, they'll take you right to the hotel door.

MR. THOMPSON: Thanks for the advice. Oh! Here's our luggage, at last!

Both travelers get their luggage, pass through Customs, and finally exit into the International Arrivals Terminal.

MR. THOMPSON (panting): It's unbearably hot!

MR. ROJAS (trying not to laugh): Don't worry! It'll get even hotter in the afternoon.

MR. THOMPSON: I see that I'll have to get used to the weather!

LOUDSPEAKER: Attention passengers: PLUNA flight 542 to Montevideo is now boarding at gate 19.

MR. ROJAS: Well, that's my flight! Oh, and the ticket window is on the other end of the terminal. Good luck with your business!

MR. THOMPSON: The same to you, and thanks for your help! Have a good flight!

B. APUNTES (Notes)

1. Notice that the acronym of *Estados Unidos* contains two double letters to indicate plural nouns. Another way of marking plural nouns in Spanish acronyms is with a lowercase *-s* following the capital letter. There is no way to know which form should be used for a particular acronym; they must simply be memorized. For example, *Buenos Aires* can only be abbreviated as *Bs.As.*, and not with two double letters.

2. Chile is located on the Pacific coast of South America, and its culture is heavily influenced by Europe. After decades of military dictatorship under General Pinochet, Chile returned to democratic rule in 1989 and now has a growing economy, thanks to its hard-working population. It is trying to further stimulate its economy by adopting a free market system.

3. *Favor de,* a shortened form of *Haga(n) Vd(s) el favor de,* is generally used in public announcements.

4. Note the use of the conditional tense *(¿podría Vd.?)* instead of the indicative *(¿puede Vd.?)* to make the sentence more polite. This usage is most common in Latin America. Another way of asking the time is *Disculpe, ¿tiene/tendría Vd. la hora?*

5. *¡Cómo no!, ¡Por supuesto!,* and *¡Con gusto!* are polite ways of saying *Sí.* In a more casual setting, you could say: *¡Está bien!, ¡Bueno!,* or *¡Vale!* (in Spain).

6. Although both *¿qué?* and *¿cuál?* can mean *"what?,"* *¿qué?* is used only when asking for the definition of a word. Compare: *¿Qué es una capital?* (What is a capital?) *¿Cuál es la capital de Venezuela?* (What's the capital of Venezuela?) For more on the uses of *¿qué?* and *¿cuál?*, see *Gramática y usos, Lección 11.*

7. In English, compound adjectives and adverbs are common. In Spanish, however, use *de* + a descriptive phrase to give more detailed descriptions of nouns or verbs. For example: *un cuento de nunca acabar* (a never-ending story); *una muchacha de veinte años* (a twenty-year-old girl); *comer de buena gana* (to eat wholeheartedly).

8. Note the use of *para* instead of *a* with destinations.

9. Although *tener* + a noun is generally used to express emotions and states of being, you can also use the verb *estar* + an adjective, as long as the adjective is not too cumbersome. Thus, "I'm hungry" can be expressed by both *tengo hambre* and *estoy hambriento,* and "I'm thirsty" with both *tengo sed* and *estoy sediento.* The expressions with *tener,* however, are much more common and widely accepted.

10. The verb *ir(le) a uno* is used to express how things are going for someone. *Las cosas nos van bien.* (Things are going well for us.)

11. When used before a unit of measure, the plural indefinite articles *unos* and *unas* indicate an approximate amount. *La ciudad está a unos veinte kilómetros.* (The city is about twenty kilometers away). *Estuve en Nueva York unas dos semanas.* (I was in New York for about two weeks.)

12. Be sure not to confuse *el formulario* (the legal form) and *la forma* (the form, the shape).

13. Note the use of the word *a* (in the contraction *al*) when the direct object is a person. For more on *a personal,* see *Gramática y usos, Lección 2.*

14. Be careful not to confuse tenses in the *nosotros* form of *-ar* verbs. Their present indicative and preterite forms are the same, so the tense must be derived from context. *Ayer cantamos mucho.* (Yesterday we sang a lot.) *Cantamos todos los días.* (We sing every day.)

15. Here, *por* means "through."

16. Here, *por* means "for."

17. The verb *convenir* (to suit, to be appropriate) is also used in the idiomatic expression *conviene a saber* (that is to say), and its reflexive form *convenirse* means "to reach an agreement."

18. *El microómnibus* (often abbreviated to just *micro* or *ómnibus*) refers to a tour bus. A city bus is *un autobús,* although many countries have their own local terms, such as *el colectivo* in Argentina, *la micro* in Chile, *el camión* in Mexico, and *la guagua* in Puerto Rico.

19. *Todavía* and *aún* (still, yet) are most commonly used in reference to time. *Todavía/Aún estoy aquí.* (I'm still here.) But, they can also be used to mean "even more." *Juan es muy alto, pero Pedro es aún más alto.* (Juan is tall, but Pedro is taller still). For more on comparatives, see *Gramática y usos, Lección 11.*

20. The verb *quedar* means "to remain; to be located." It can be used instead of the verb *estar* to indicate location, especially when asking for directions. *¿Dónde queda el Banco Central?* (Where is the Central Bank?) *¿Dónde quedan los baños?* (Where are the restrooms located?)

21. *¡Buena suerte en lo suyo!* literally means "Good luck with that which is yours!" It is a common phrase used to wish someone luck politely. In a more informal setting, you can use *¡Que te vaya bien!*

C. GRAMATICA Y USOS
(Grammar and Usage)

---

1. *EL PRESENTE DEL INDICATIVO* (THE PRESENT INDICATIVE)

Spanish verbs are classified according to their infinitive endings: *-ar, -er,* and *-ir.* These groups are called first, second, and third conjugations (in alphabetical order). To form the present indicative of regular verbs,[1] simply drop the infinitive ending, and replace it with the appropriate personal ending *(hablar → habl- → hablo).* The personal endings for *-ar* verbs are: *-o, -as, -a, -amos, -áis, -an;* for *-er* verbs: *-o, -es, -e, -emos, -éis, -en;* and for *-ir* verbs: *-o, -es, -e, -imos, -ís, -en.*

	HABLAR TO SPEAK	TEMER TO FEAR	PARTIR TO LEAVE
yo	hablo	temo	parto
tú	hablas	temes	partes
él/ella/Vd.	habla	teme	parte
nosotros	hablamos	tememos	partimos
vosotros	habláis	teméis	partís
ellos/ellas/Vds.	hablan	temen	parten

---

1. For the conjugation of irregular verbs, refer to the verb charts in the Appendix (p. 306).

Some verbs, known as stem-changing verbs, undergo vowel changes in the stem of all but the first and second person plural forms. There are three possible changes: *o→ue, e→ie,* and *e→i.* The first two are the most common.[2]

	CONTAR TO COUNT ON	*PERDER* TO LOSE	*PEDIR* TO ASK FOR
yo	*cuento*	*pierdo*	*pido*
tú	*cuentas*	*pierdes*	*pides*
él/ella/Vd.	*cuenta*	*pierde*	*pide*
nosotros	*contamos*	*perdemos*	*pedimos*
vosotros	*contáis*	*perdéis*	*pedís*
ellos/ellas/Vds.	*cuentan*	*pierden*	*piden*

Note that the stem vowel is softened only if it occurs in a stressed syllable. This simple phonetic rule will help you keep track of the vowels in stem-changing verbs.

The present indicative is used to make general statements, and to describe ongoing or habitual actions in the present.

El Sr. Thompson es un hombre de negocios próspero.
Mr. Thompson is a successful businessman.

¿Qué haces?—Busco mis maletas.
What are you doing?—I'm looking for my luggage.

Viajamos a Sudamérica a menudo.
We travel to South America often.

In addition to its basic usage, the present indicative can also be used:

a) To describe past events more dramatically (this is known as the historical present).

El General San Martín cruza los Andes.
General San Martín crossed the Andes mountains.

b) To speak about future events informally (as in English).

Los Thompson vienen a casa mañana.
The Thompsons are coming over tomorrow.

---

2. Note that this changing or softening of the stem vowel is a basic phonetic characteristic of the Spanish language. It affects not only verbs, but many other word stems as well. For example, *bondad—bueno, fortaleza—fuerte, feroz—fiera.*

c) To talk about actions that began in the past, but continue in the present.

Hace tres meses que estoy en Colombia.
I've been in Colombia for three months.

2. EL PASADO Y FUTURO INMEDIATO: "ACABAR DE" Y "ESTAR POR" (THE IMMEDIATE PAST AND FUTURE: ACABAR DE AND ESTAR POR)

To describe an action that has just been completed, use *acabar de* (in the present indicative) followed by a verb in the infinitive.

Acabo de ver un programa muy interesante.
I've just seen a very interesting program.

Juan acaba de llegar del trabajo.
Juan just arrived from work.

To express an action that is about to take place, use *estar por* (in the present indicative) followed by a verb in the infinitive.

Estoy por irme para el trabajo.
I'm about to leave for work.

El concierto está por empezar.
The concert is about to begin.

To stress the physical immediacy of an action, use *estar a punto de.* Compare the following sentences:

Estoy por salir.
I'm about to leave. (I'm still getting ready.)

Estoy a punto de salir.
I'm about to leave. (I'm opening the door and walking out.)

3. EL FUTURO CON "IR A" (THE FUTURE WITH IR A)

Ir + a + an infinitive is used to express future events in informal and in semiformal conversation. It is the equivalent of the English future form "to be going to."

Voy a visitar a mis padres mañana.
I'm going to visit my parents tomorrow.

Pedro va a viajar a Méjico el año próximo.
Pedro is going to travel to Mexico next year.

While this form is the one you will probably hear in daily conversation, it is generally avoided in formal situations, where the simple future tense is preferred.

4. *LAS PREPOSICIONES "POR" Y "PARA"* (THE PREPOSITIONS *POR* AND *PARA*)

These prepositions generally give English-speaking students much grief, but they shouldn't. The problem is that they both often translate into English as "for." Here are some helpful guidelines that can make it easier to choose the correct "for."

Para generally indicates an objective. Use it when you have a specific goal in mind. It can be replaced by *a* or *hacia* when introducing a location.

Voy para Buenos Aires.
I'm on my way to Buenos Aires.

No como para adelgazar.
I'm not eating in order to lose weight.

Este regalo es para ti.
This present is for you.

Por is generally used in all other cases, usually to indicate a cause or an exchange. It can be replaced by *de* when used before verbs.

Voy por negocios.
I'm going on business.

Voy a cambiar mi auto por uno nuevo.
I'm going to exchange my car for a new one.

Estoy cansada por/de caminar.
I'm tired from walking.

To understand the difference between *por* and *para* when used with verbs, compare the following sentences:

Me quedo en casa para no tener que trabajar.
I'm staying home in order not to have to work.

Me quedo en casa por no tener que trabajar.
I'm staying home because I don't have to work.

You may want to think of *para* in terms of where an action is headed, and *por* in terms of why or where it began. In addition, note the following idiomatic usage:

Voy por las valijas.
I'm going for the suitcases.

Voy por María.
I'll go get María.

Por can also mean "through, by" or "along" when referring to a place.

¿Vas a pasar por casa?
Are you going to stop by my house?

Están caminando por la playa.
They're walking along the beach.

Pase por esa puerta y doble a la derecha.
Go through that door, and make a right.

Por is also used to express duration of time. In this case it may often be omitted, unless it begins a sentence.

Hemos estado esperando las maletas (por) mucho tiempo.
We've been waiting for our luggage for a long time.

Por quinientos años, los árabes estuvieron en España.
For five hundred years, the Arabs were in Spain.

D. ESTUDIO IDIOMATICO (Word Study)

The basic meaning of the verb *pensar* is "to think."

Pienso, luego existo.
I think, therefore, I am.

Its meaning can change, however, depending on how it is used. When followed by the preposition *en*, it means "to think of someone or something."

Pienso en ti a menudo.
I think of you often.

If *pensar* is directly followed by an infinitive, it takes on the meaning of "to intend" or "to plan" to do something.

Pienso ir al cine mañana.
I intend to go to the movies tomorrow.

Pensar que is used to express a personal opinion[3] based on established fact.

Pienso que Juan va a ser un buen médico.
I think that Juan will be a good doctor. (based on his grades, character, etc.)

If you are less certain about something, use *me parece* (it seems to me) instead.

Me parece que Juan está en casa.
I think Juan is at home. (But I'm not sure.)

Pienso que Juan está en casa.
I think Juan is at home. (I have good reason to believe he is.)

E. HABLEMOS DE NEGOCIOS
(Let's Talk Business)

LOS ENVÍOS (SHIPPING)

To ship goods from the United States to Spain, the standard European Community shipping requirements and procedures should be followed. In Latin America, however, these requirements and procedures vary significantly from country to country. For this reason, private companies have emerged that handle all the paperwork involved with shipments to Latin America. The names and addresses of such companies can be obtained from the Chamber of Commerce of the country to which goods are being shipped.

The following documents, used in Spain, are similar to those used in Latin America and will serve as a good indication of what you will be expected to provide. In general, *el vendedor* (the vendor) must provide the following:

1. *Una factura comercial* (a commercial invoice) or in some cases *una factura consular* (a "consular" invoice, i.e., one that has been endorsed by the Consulate of the recipient country). *Hacer visar* indicates that an invoice requires endorsement by the Consul, and *Visado* indicates that the document has been endorsed.

2. *Un conocimiento de embarque* (a bill of lading) for overseas shipments, or *una carta de porte* (a waybill or note of consignment) for ground, air, or river transportation. The documents that comprise *un conocimiento de embarque* include:

3. The question *¿Qué piensas de Juan?*, which means "What do you think of Juan?" (based on what you know), would be considered somewhat invasive, so if you want to ask someone's opinion about another person, use *¿Qué tal te parece Juan?* (What does Juan seem like to you?).

15

a) *el título de propiedad* (the title, deed, or proof of ownership of the goods)
b) *el contrato de transporte* (the shipping agreement)
c) *el recibo de mercancías por parte de la compañía naviera* (the merchandise receipt on the part of the shipping company)

Una *carta de porte* should contain all but *el recibo de mercancías*.

3. *Certificados de Calidad, Origen, Peso o Sanidad* (various certificates attesting to the quality, origin, weight, or sanitary condition of the goods).

4. *La Póliza de Seguros* (the insurance policy). Note that different types of policies may be required, depending on the method of delivery. The type of policy used is generally indicated using the Incoterm (International Chamber of Commerce) abbreviations that follow the indicated value of the shipment. The following are some international acronyms, and their English and Spanish transcriptions:

CIF (Cost Insurance Freight)	*Coste Seguro Flete*
C&F (Cost and Freight)	*Coste y Flete*
CTP (Carriage and Insurance Paid to . . .)	*Porte pagado hasta punto destino . . .*
DDP (Delivery Duty Paid)	*Entrega de Derechos pagada*
EXW (Ex Works)	*En Fábrica*
FAS (Free Alongside Ship)	*Franco a Costado del Buque*
FOB (Free On Board)	*Franco a Bordo*
FOR (Free on Rail)	*Franco-Vagón*

Finally, the following are some useful shipping terms:

delivery	*entrega*
dispatch	*despacho, expedición*
impoundment (of shipment)	*retención de transferencia*
insurance	*seguro*
list	*lista, relación* (in Spain)
method of delivery	*modalidad de entrega*
origin	*origen*
payment	*pago*
non-	*impago*
policy	*póliza*
request	*pedido*
risk	*riesgo*
shipping	*embarque, envío*
-company	*naviera*
transport	*transporte*
air/land/river/sea	*aéreo/terrestre/fluvial/marítimo*

EXAMEN (QUIZ)

A. *Reformule las oraciones siguientes en el presente del indicativo, haciéndolas informales.* (Rewrite the following sentences in the informal present indicative.)

1. *Voy a ir a su casa mañana.*
2. *¿Va Vd. a viajar al Perú el mes que viene?*
3. *Voy a volver a los EE.UU. después de un mes.*
4. *Mañana vamos a invitar a Juan.*
5. *El mes que viene vamos a volar a España.*

B. *Traduzca las oraciones siguientes al español.* (Translate the following sentences into Spanish.)

1. Mary just entered the terminal.
2. Do you plan to visit your parents in Chile?
3. The plane is about to take off!
4. We just saw that movie on the flight!
5. I'm going to finish reading the book in about three days.
6. We plan to exchange our car for a new one next year.
7. We think of Maria often.

C. *Complete las oraciones siguientes con "por" o "para."* (Complete the following sentences with *por* or *para*.)

1. *Voy _____ Nueva York.*
2. *_____ el frío, me siento mal.*
3. *Quiero cambiar este asiento _____ aquél.*
4. *Voy a traer un regalo _____ ti.*
5. *_____ lo visto, es un muchacho bueno.*
6. *Esta máquina es _____ pesar las maletas.*
7. *Viviana va a hacer el trabajo _____ ti.* (at your place)
8. *Jorge piensa venir _____ terminar unos negocios.*
9. *Pasamos _____ Santiago de Chile.*
10. *¡Vamos _____ las maletas!*

LECCION 2

A. DIALOGO

UNA GRAN CELEBRACIÓN EN EL HOTEL.

La señora Martínez Rosas hace los preparativos para una celebración benéfica en un hotel de La Paz, Bolivia.[1] Viene acompañada de[2] su nieto Darío.

SRA. MARTINEZ ROSAS: **Buenos días, señor. Quisiéramos hablar con el gerente[3] del hotel, por favor.**

RECEPCIONISTA: **¡Cómo no! ¿Con referencia a qué quería Vd. hablarle?**

SRA. MARTINEZ ROSAS: **Queremos organizar una conferencia y una fiesta en el hotel.**

RECEPCIONISTA: **Ya veo. Nuestra gerente[3] es la señorita Vega. Un momentito, por favor.**

SRTA. VEGA: **Buenos días, señora, señor. Tengo entendido[4] que quieren organizar una fiesta en nuestro hotel . . .**

SRA. MARTINEZ ROSAS: **Así es. Soy la presidente[3] de la organización "Lux Paupéribus."[5] Éste es mi nieto y ayudante, el señor Darío Martínez. Este año nuestra organización celebra su vigésimo quinto[6] aniversario y queremos hacer una conferencia seguida de una pequeña fiesta con bufé.**

SRTA. VEGA: **Les aseguro que estamos a su disposición en todo lo que necesiten.[7] ¿Para qué fecha planean la celebración?**

DARIO: **Para el día diecisiete del mes que viene.**

SRTA. VEGA: **Permítanme revisar el libro de reservas . . . sí, el día diez y siete está libre. ¿A cuántas personas esperan para la conferencia?**

DARIO: **A unas ciento cincuenta.**

SRTA. VEGA: **Muy bien. Permítanme mostrarles la sala de conferencias. Está en el ala oeste del hotel.**

Los tres se dirigen al ala oeste . . .

SRTA. VEGA: **Ésta es la sala. Como ven, es bastante amplia.**

SRA. MARTINEZ ROSAS: **¡Nos viene muy bien![8]**

DARIO: **Habrá[9] varios oradores[10] en la conferencia, ¿tienen un podio y micrófonos?**

SRTA. VEGA: **Por supuesto. Hay parlantes incorporados**[11] **en el cielorraso, y tenemos un podio, unas doscientas sillas y una mesa larga en el depósito.**

SRA. MARTINEZ: **¡Excelente! Queremos empezar la conferencia a las diecinueve horas**[12] **y durará**[13] **unas dos horas.**

SRTA. VEGA: **De acuerdo. ¿Qué quieren hacer para el bufé?**

DARIO: **Pienso que será mejor hacerlo al aire libre, habiendo tantas personas . . .**

SRTA. VEGA: **Puedo ofrecerles el jardín a un costo adicional muy bajo. Aquellas puertas dan**[14] **directamente al jardín y ahí hay una hermosa fuente de agua.**

SRA. MARTINEZ ROSAS: **¡Excelente! Podemos servir un bufé, a la americana, y dejar que todos disfruten del aire libre.**

DARIO: **Siempre y cuando el buen tiempo nos acompañe . . .**

SRTA. VEGA: **Tiene razón . . . pero, en todo caso, podemos preparar el bufé adentro.**

DARIO: **¡Bueno! Parece que todo está arreglado, entonces.**

SRA. MARTINEZ ROSAS: **¡Espérate Darío, no olvides a nuestros invitados especiales!**

DARIO: **¡Claro! . . . Srta. Vega, tendremos varios invitados especiales extranjeros que van a quedarse en la ciudad una semana, después de la conferencia. Algunos de ellos viajan con sus cónyuges.**[15] **¿Podemos reservarles las habitaciones por adelantado?**

SRTA. VEGA: **¡Por supuesto! ¿Cuántas van a necesitar?**

DARIO: **Veamos, aquí tengo la lista . . . necesitaremos once habitaciones simples y seis dobles o suites, si las habrá disponibles.**

SRTA. VEGA: **De acuerdo. Puedo ofrecerles las habitaciones y las suites a un descuento del quince por ciento. ¿Qué les parece el ala este? Allí puedo reservárselas en el primer piso.**[16]

SRA. MARTINEZ ROSAS: **¡Muchísimas gracias! ¡Ah! Y . . . una cosita más: uno de nuestros huéspedes**[17] **de los EE.UU., el señor Clark, es un ejecutivo muy importante . . .**

DARIO: **. . . e**[18] **indomable.**

SRA. MARTINEZ ROSAS: **¡Ejém! . . . Como le estaba diciendo, el señor Clark querrá saber sobre qué servicios comerciales ofrece su hotel.**

SRTA. VEGA: Bueno, contamos con[19] líneas de discado directo internacional y también hay en la planta baja una tienda con servicio de telefacsímil. Si necesita algo más en particular, llámenme y veré lo que pueda hacer.

SRA. MARTINEZ: ¡Muy bien! Creo que el telefacsímil le será de ayuda, pero se lo comunicaré. ¿Supongo que hay servicios de lavado y de tintorería en el hotel?

SRTA. VEGA: Así es. Y hay varias tiendas y un salón de belleza en la planta baja.

SRA. MARTINEZ ROSAS: ¡Ahora me quedo más tranquila!

SRTA. VEGA: Me alegro que así sea. En cuanto a lo financiero: ¿prefieren una cuenta global, o cuentas individuales para la conferencia, el bufé y las habitaciones?

DARIO: Ponga los gastos de la conferencia y del bufé en una cuenta, pero las habitaciones se saldarán[20] individualmente.

SRTA. VEGA: De acuerdo. Durante la semana, los llamará el jefe de cocina por lo del bufé. Entretanto, no dejen de llamarme si necesitan cualquier cosa.

SRA. MARTINEZ ROSAS: ¡Muchas gracias, señorita Vega! ¡Ha sido Vd. de muy gran ayuda!

A GRAND CELEBRATION AT THE HOTEL.

Mrs. Martinez Rosas is making arrangements for a benefit at a hotel in La Paz, Bolivia. She is accompanied by her grandson, Dario.

MRS. MARTINEZ ROSAS: Good morning, sir. We would like to speak to the hotel manager, please.

RECEPTIONIST: Of course. May I ask what this is in reference to?

MRS. MARTINEZ ROSAS: We would like to hold a conference and a reception at the hotel.

RECEPTIONIST: I see. Our manager is Miss Vega. Just a moment, please.

MISS VEGA: Good morning, madam, sir. I understand you would like to organize a reception at our hotel . . .

MRS. MARTINEZ ROSAS: That's right. I am president of the "Lux Pauperibus" organization. This is my grandson and assistant, Mr. Dario Martinez. This year, our organization is celebrating its twenty-fifth anniversary, and we'd like to hold a conference followed by a small buffet reception.

MISS VEGA: I assure you that we can provide whatever you may need. When are you planning to have the celebration?

DARIO: On the 17th of next month.

MISS VEGA: Let me check the reservations . . . Yes, the 17th is available. How many people are you expecting at the conference?

DARIO: About one hundred fifty.

MISS VEGA: Very well. Let me show you the conference room. It's in the west wing of the hotel.

All three walk to the west wing. . . .

MISS VEGA: This is the room. As you can see, it's quite large.

MRS. MARTINEZ ROSAS: It'll do fine!

DARIO: We'll have several guest speakers at the conference. Do you have a podium and microphones?

MISS VEGA: Of course. There are speakers built into the ceiling, and we have a podium, about 200 chairs, and a long table in our storage room.

MRS. MARTINEZ ROSAS: Excellent! We'd like the conference to begin at 7 P.M., and it should last about two hours.

MISS VEGA: All right. And what about the buffet?

DARIO: I think it should be outdoors, I mean, with so many people . . .

MISS VEGA: I can offer you the garden at a very low additional cost. Those doors lead directly to it, and it has a beautiful fountain.

MRS. MARTINEZ ROSAS: Excellent! We can serve the buffet American style, and let everyone enjoy the fresh air!

DARIO: As long as the weather is nice . . .

MISS VEGA: You're right . . . but, in any case, we can also set up indoors.

DARIO: Great. So, everything's taken care of!

MRS. MARTINEZ ROSAS: Not yet, Dario. Don't forget our special guests!

DARIO: Of course! . . . Miss Vega, we have several special foreign guests who would like to stay in the city for a week after the conference. Some of them are traveling with their spouses. Can we reserve rooms for them now?

MISS VEGA: Of course! How many rooms will you need?

DARIO: Let's see now, here's the list . . . We'll need eleven singles and six doubles or suites, if they're available.

MISS VEGA: Certainly. I can offer you the rooms and the suites at a 15% discount. How about the east wing? I can reserve them on the second floor.

MRS. MARTINEZ ROSAS: Thank you so much! Oh . . . There's just one more thing. One of our guests from the U.S., Mr. Clark, is an important businessman . . .

DARIO: And he's difficult!

MRS. MARTINEZ ROSAS: Ahem. . . . As I was saying, Mr. Clark will want to know what business facilities your hotel provides.

MISS VEGA: Well, we have direct-dial international phone lines, and there's a fax machine available in a store on the ground floor. If he needs anything else, call me, and I'll see what I can do.

MRS. MARTINEZ ROSAS: Very well. I think the fax will be helpful, but I'll ask him. I assume that you have laundry and dry-cleaning services.

MISS VEGA: Yes. There are also several shops and a beauty salon on the ground floor.

MRS. MARTINEZ ROSAS: That should do.

MISS VEGA: Great! Now, I have a question about the bill. Should I put everything on one bill, or should I prepare separate bills for the conference, the dinner, and the rooms?

MRS. MARTINEZ ROSAS: One bill will do for the conference and the dinner, but the rooms should be billed separately.

MISS VEGA: Very well. Our caterer will get in touch with you during the week to discuss the dinner menu. Meanwhile, if you need anything else, don't hesitate to call me.

MRS. MARTINEZ ROSAS: Thank you very much. You've been very helpful!

B. APUNTES

1. La Paz is the capital of Bolivia, a mountainous country with extensive *altiplanos* (high plains). La Paz is located at approximately 13,000 ft. above sea level and is a remarkable city, whose inhabitants are primarily Native American.

2. Note that the preposition *de* can sometimes replace other prepositions. In this case, it is replacing the passive voice preposition *por*. For more on the uses of *de*, see *Gramática y usos, Lección 15*.

3. Some professions, especially those ending in the letter *-e*, can be used for both men and women. In this case, the article is used to specify the gender of the person. Note that the receptionist tactfully indicates the gender of the *gerente* when he mentions her name.

4. In Old Spanish, the verb *tener* could be used instead of the verb *haber* as the auxiliary verb for the perfect tenses. This rule has left its mark in modern Spanish in phrases such as *tengo entendido* and *tengo visto,* which generally replace *he entendido* and *he visto* in formal situations.

5. *Lux Paupéribus* is a Latin phrase meaning "Light of the Poor." Latin is popular for naming charity and religious organizations. Latin phrases used in Spanish generally maintain their original spelling, but stress marks are added to facilitate pronunciation.

6. The ordinals beyond *décimo* are seldom used, except in formal situations. More casually, the cardinal numbers are used instead. For example, you could also say: *Celebramos nuestro veinticinco aniversario.* (We are celebrating our twenty-fifth anniversary.) See the Appendix for a list of the formally used ordinal numbers.

7. Note the use of the subjunctive when referring to something that is unknown (i.e., Miss Vega does not know exactly what Mrs. Martinez needs). When referring to something you know, use the indicative. For example: *¿Son éstos los artículos que necesitan sus invitados? Les ayudaré a conseguir todo lo que necesitan.* (Are those the articles your guests need? I'll help you obtain everything they need.)

8. The expression *venir(le) bien* means "to be appropriate/good for (someone). For example: *El catorce me viene bien para la cita.* (The 14th is good for me for the meeting.)

9. Remember that *haber* is always singular when it's used to mean "there is/are/was/were/will be," regardless of whether the following noun is singular or plural.

10. *Un parlante* refers to a hi-fi speaker, while *un orador* refers to a person (a speaker) giving a speech.

11. *Incorporado* means "built-in" when used to describe an electronic device, while "built into a wall" is *empotrado.*

12. In Spain and Latin America, the 24-hour clock, known as *hora oficial* or *hora militar,* is used in formal situations and official schedules. At home, or among friends, the 12-hour clock is used.

13. Note the use of the simple future instead of the future with *ir* throughout this dialogue. Remember that the simple future is preferred in formal situations.

14. The expression *dar a* means "to face, to lead to" when used to describe the orientation of a door, window, gate, etc. *La ventana de mi cuarto da a la calle.* (The window in my room faces the street.) *Aquella puerta, ¿adónde da?—Da al jardín.* (Where does that door lead to?—It leads to the garden.)

15. *Cónyuge* (spouse) is often preferred to *esposo* because it is not gender-specific.

16. Keep in mind that floors in Latin America and in Spain are numbered after the ground floor. That is to say, *la planta baja* is the ground floor, i.e., the first floor; *el primer piso* is the second floor, and so on.

17. *Un huésped* is a house guest, whereas *un invitado* is a guest. *¿Cuántos invitados hay para la fiesta?—Hay unos quince.* (How many guests are there for the party?—About fifteen.) *¿Cuántos huéspedes tendrás?* (How many people are staying over at your house?)

18. Remember that *y* changes to *e* when followed by a word beginning with *i-* or *hi-*. Likewise, *o* changes to *u* when followed by a word beginning in *o-* or *ho-*. *María es alta e inteligente.* (Maria is tall and intelligent.) *¿Quieres este libro u otro?* (Do you want this book or another one?)

19. *Contar con* + a noun is a formal expression meaning "to have." It is used only in business situations. *Nuestra empresa cuenta con computadoras de muy alto rendimiento.* (Our company has high performance computers.) *Contar con* can also mean "to count on" someone or something. *¿Podemos contar con su presencia, señor?* (Can we count on your presence, sir?)

20. In business situations, it's *saldar una cuenta* (to settle an account), while colloquially it's *pagar una cuenta* (to pay a bill).

C. GRAMATICA Y USOS

1. *POSESIÓN* (POSSESSION)

a) Possession with *de*
The simplest way to indicate possession in Spanish is with the preposition *de*. Remember that *de* + *el* must be abbreviated to *del*.

La señorita Vega es la gerente del hotel.
  Miss Vega is the manager of the hotel.

Darío es el nieto de la señora Martínez.
  Dario is Mrs. Martinez's grandson.

b) Possessive Adjectives

Possessive adjectives—*mío* (my), *tuyo* (your–informal, singular), *suyo* (his, her, their, your–polite, singular), *nuestro* (our), *vuestro* (informal), *suyo* (your–polite, plural)—must agree in gender and number with the nouns they modify. When they directly precede a noun, *mío, tuyo,* and *suyo(s)* are shortened to *mi, tu,* and *su(s).*[1]

¡Mi casa es su casa!
My home is your home!

Algunos de los invitados de la señora Martínez vienen con sus cónyuges.
Some of Mrs. Martinez's guests are coming with their spouses.

Sr. y Sra. Gómez, vuestra habitación está lista.
Mr. and Mrs. Gomez, your room is ready.

If the exact meaning of *su(s)* is not clear from the context, it may be replaced with *de* + a personal pronoun.

Su equipaje está en su habitación.
El equipaje de él está en la habitación de Vd.
His luggage is in your room.

c) Possessive Pronouns

Possessive pronouns replace possessive adjectives and the nouns they describe and are used to avoid repeating the same noun several times. They consist of the long form of the possessive adjectives and are always preceded by a definite article. They are *el mío* (mine), *el tuyo* (yours–familiar singular), *el suyo* (his, hers, yours–polite, singular), *el nuestro* (ours), *el vuestro* (yours–familiar, plural), and *el suyo* (theirs, yours–polite plural), and *el suyo* (theirs). They agree in gender and number with the noun(s) that they replace.

A menudo mi esposa viaja conmigo cuando tengo viajes de negocios, ¿y la suya?
My wife often travels with me on business, and yours?

Puse mi valija en el ropero, ¿dónde pusiste la tuya?
I put my suitcase in the closet; where did you put yours?

As with possessive adjectives, if the meaning of *lo(s) suyo(s)* and *la(s) suya(s)* is not clear from context, use *de* + a personal pronoun instead.

Esta llave es la vuestra, y esta otra es la suya.
Esta llave es la vuestra, y esta otra es la de ellos.
This key is yours, and this other one is theirs.

---

1. Many adjectives have shortened forms for use before a noun. For more on adjectives, see *Gramática y usos, Lección* 9.

d) Special Uses of the Articles in Possession.

When the possessor of a noun is clear from the context, a definite article is used instead of a possessive adjective.

Pedro tiene la mano en el bolsillo.
Pedro has his hand in his pocket.

Ellas se lavan la cara y las manos.
They are washing their hands and faces.

Note that since each woman is only washing her own face, the singular form, *la cara,* is used.

e) *Ajeno*

Ajeno is an adjective used to indicate "belonging to someone else."

Tengo unos papeles ajenos en el portafolios.
I have someone else's papers in my briefcase.

Las reservas están a nombre ajeno.
The reservations are under somebody else's name.

2. *LOS VERBOS "SER" Y "ESTAR"* (THE VERBS *SER* AND *ESTAR*)

Ser and *estar* both translate into English as "to be," but they are used in different ways. You may want to think of *ser* as describing the essence or inherent characteristics of a person or thing, while *estar* describes its momentary status or its location (whether temporary or permanent).

Juan es alto/simpático/americano/hombre/maestro. [2]
Juan is tall/nice/American/a man/a teacher.

But:

Juan está mal, no está en la oficina hoy.
Juan is not well; he's not in the office today.

¿Dónde está Juan?—Juan está en la oficina.
Where is Juan?—Juan is at the office.

---

2. Note that, unlike in English, no article is required when stating the category of a noun (profession, gender, race, religion, etc.). However, when the category is modified, the article becomes necessary.

> *Darío es abogado, de hecho, es un abogado muy conocido.*
> Dario is a lawyer; in fact, he's a well-known lawyer.

While these rules seem simple, there are cases where the choice between *ser* and *estar* is difficult. This is especially true when describing the state or condition of a person or thing, as the choice rests on whether the state is temporary or permanent.

¡Nunca me di cuenta de lo hermosa que es Viviana, pero hoy en ese vestido está increíble!
I never realized how beautiful Viviana is, but today, in that dress, she's incredible!

Cada vez que lo veo está borracho, ¡debe ser un alcohólico!
Every time I see him he's drunk—he must be an alcoholic!

La Sra. Martínez está nerviosísima con este beneficio, ¡está como loca hoy!
Mrs. Martinez is very nervous about this benefit. It's like she's crazy today!

¿Qué le pasa a Darío? . . . Siempre es tan amable, ¡pero hoy estuvo muy grosero conmigo!
What's wrong with Dario? . . . He's always so nice, but today he was very rude to me!

Este capítulo sobre genética está bien difícil . . . en fin, supongo que el estudiar siempre lo es.
This chapter on genetics is really hard . . . but I suppose studying always is.

3. "A" PERSONAL (PERSONAL A)

In Spanish, if the direct object is a person, it must be introduced by *a*, unless it complements the verb *tener*.

Invitaremos a Luís para la fiesta del 17.
We will invite Luis to the party on the 17th.

¿Qué te parece Darío, conviene tener mozos en el bufé?
What do you think, Dario, sould we have waiters at the buffet?

However, *a personal* can also be used figuratively, with objects, concepts, or animals, to elevate their status, or to personify the noun (usually in poetry).

No se admiten animales en el hotel. Sólo se admiten a perros guía.
Animals are not allowed in the hotel. Only seeing-eye dogs are admitted.

Veo a la Vida, siempre vestida de esperanza.
I see Life, always dressed in hope.

4. *NEGATIVOS* (NEGATIVES)

a) Common Spanish Negatives
The most common negative in Spanish is *no*. It always precedes the verb.

No encuentro el baño para caballeros.
    I can't find the men's room.

No means both "no" and "not," and should be used twice when responding to a question.

¿El hotel está en la calle Bolívar?—No, no está en la calle Bolívar. Está en la calle San Martín.
    Is the hotel on Bolivar Street?—No, it isn't on Bolivar Street. It's on San Martin Street.

Other common negatives include: *nadie* (no one), *nada* (nothing), *nunca/jamás*[3] (never), *ni . . . ni,* (neither . . . nor), *tampoco* (neither), and *ninguno/a* (no, none, not any). When they preceed the verb, these common negatives are used alone, but when they follow the verb, they must be used in conjunction with *no.* Compare:

Voy a llamar mañana. Nadie contesta en la oficina.
Voy a llamar mañana. No contesta nadie en la oficina.
    I'm going to call tomorrow. Nobody is answering the phone at the office.

¡Nunca digas "Nunca, jamás . . ."!
¡No digas nunca "Nunca, jamás . . ."!
    Never say never. (Literally: "I'll never, ever . . . !"—Spanish proverb)

Keep in mind that in Spanish several negative words are often used together in a sentence.

Los grandes empresarios nunca pueden conceder entrevistas a nadie sin cita previa.
    Important businessmen can never give interviews to anyone without an appointment.

b) Other Negative Expressions
Ya no means "no longer."

Ya no nos quedan muchos días de vacaciones.
    We don't have many vacation days left.

---

3. *Nunca* and *jamás* can be used together, to mean "never, ever."

    Nunca, jamás he visto algo semejante.
        (I have never, ever seen anything like this.)

The adjective *alguno* can replace *ninguno*. It must be used following the noun.

No hay ninguna habitación libre en el hotel.
No hay habitación alguna libre en el hotel.
   There are no available rooms in the hotel.

   Sino and *más bien* are used to contradict a negative statement. They can be translated into English as "rather, instead."

Yo no esperaba que la cena fuese/fuera barata, sino cara.
   I didn't expect dinner to be cheap; instead, I expected it to be expensive.

Esta habitación no es grande, es más bien chica.
Esta habitación no es grande, sino chica.
   This room isn't large, it's rather small.

No quiero una habitación, sino dos.
   I don't want one room, but two.

Creí que la conferencia saldría mal, más bien, ¡salió perfecta!
   I thought the conference would go badly, but instead, it turned out perfectly!

D. HABLEMOS DE NEGOCIOS

LOS VIAJES Y EL TURISMO
(TRAVEL AND TOURISM)

Tourism is a very important industry for the Spanish-speaking world, especially in the Caribbean, where it generates a sizeable amount of revenue for the Dominican Republic and Puerto Rico. There are many deluxe hotels, as well as a large number of internationally acclaimed resorts, offering a wide variety of business services to travelers. In Central and South America, tourism is slowly gaining importance, as political conditions stabilize. However, the infrastructure for a large tourist industry does not yet exist, so travelers are well-advised to carefully research the country they wish to visit.

In general terms, the best means of transportation in Spanish-speaking countries is the train. Most countries have a well-developed railroad system, including Spain. The Spanish RENFE *(Red Nacional de Ferrocarriles Españoles)* operates routes between all major cities and towns. In Latin America overall, Argentina, Chile, and Colombia have the best railroad systems.

Highways are another matter altogether. Although highways between major cities are clean and well-kept, only about 25% of roads outside of large cities are paved. Furthermore, the uneven topography of Spain and of most of Latin America compounds the problem.

If you are traveling between different countries in South America, flying is your best choice. There are many local carriers and flights, and prices are comparable to U.S. regional fares. Inquire about special air passes available with local airlines such as AeroPerú.

Within cities, buses and subways are the cheapest and most convenient way to travel. Remember to avoid sitting at the back of old buses, as the noise, vibration, and heat tends to be worse there.

Taxis are also a good bet in Central and South American cities. In Central America, taxis are often not metered, so you must agree on a fare before getting in the taxi. Tipping a cab driver is generally not expected, except in urban areas of Panama.

Business travelers may also consider renting a car, particularly in Mexico and in Central America. International car rental companies have agencies all over Central America and Mexico. In Mexico, renting a car will give a businessperson a certain amount of prestige. Remember that gas prices in Europe and Latin America are much higher than in the U.S.

When traveling to Spain, currency is not a major problem. Banks allow easy transfer of money from accounts in the U.S., and many American credit cards are accepted in Spain. In major cities in Latin America, U.S. dollars are accepted in most downtown stores and boutiques, but not in neighborhood stores. Some Latin American countries have two exchange rates for the dollar, one official rate *(cambio oficial)* and a black market rate *(cambio paralelo)*. It is best to inquire at major hotels for places to exchange money, as doing so on the street can be dangerous. Make sure the bills are not worn, marked, or torn, as they may not be accepted otherwise. In countries with a high rate of inflation, it is best to exchange money once every three days to ensure that you don't end your trip with a large amount of unexchangeable foreign bills.

EXAMEN (QUIZ)

A. *Complete las oraciones siguientes con "ser" o "estar."* (Complete the following sentences with *ser* or *estar*.)

    1. *(Yo)* _____ *perdida, ¿en qué calle* _____?
    2. *En general, las bananas* _____ *dulces.*
    3. *Esta banana* _____ *madura, ésa no.*
    4. *Viviana tiene un bonito vestido. Ella* _____ *muy bonita.*
    5. _____ *o no* _____, *he ahí la cuestión.*
    6. *Hace mucho que no veo a Juan ni a Pedro:* _____ *muy bien.*

B. *Reemplace el posesivo en inglés por el correspondiente en español.* (Replace the English possessive with the appropriate one in Spanish.)

    1. *¡(My) casa es (your) casa!*
    2. (The president's work) *no es muy grato.*
    3. *¿Prefiere Vd.* (our) *hotel, o* (theirs)?
    4. (Our) *fiesta es en* (Juan's) *casa, no en* (mine).
    5. (Their) *auto está al lado del* (yours).

C. *Traduzca al español.* (Translate into Spanish.)

    1. I never drink anything cold.
    2. Nobody likes Mr. Thompson, and neither do I!
    3. They have neither a fax nor businesspeople in their hotel.
    4. We don't see businesspeople often in our hotel.
    5. Nobody's home!
    6. I found someone else's portfolio in my room.
    7. Pedro doesn't have any brothers in Panama.
    8. Juan is a lawyer.
    9. Mrs. Vega is the hotel manager.
   10. Mrs. Martinez is the president of our organization.

LECCION 3

A. DIALOGO

EN LA FERIA DE LIBROS.

Dos amigos visitan la feria "El Libro: Del Autor al Lector" en Buenos Aires, Argentina.[1]

TONY: ¡Qué interesante estuvo! La mesa redonda en sí, fue un poco como los "talk shows" de mi país.

CLAUDIO: ¡Pero en vivo y en directo![2] Al final la discusión se puso un poco acalorada, pero era de esperarse,[3] con tantas opiniones dispares.

TONY: Veo que la gente sigue hablando con los escritores . . .

CLAUDIO: Sí. Los autores están firmando sus libros. A la gente siempre le gusta hablar con los autores en persona: La firma de libros es una de las actividades más populares de la feria.

TONY: A mí me gustó el taller de poesía.[4] ¡Fue la primera vez que escribí poesía en castellano!

CLAUDIO *(fingiendo gran admiración):* ¡Nunca imaginé que fueras tan talentoso!

TONY: ¡En verdad, nunca me sentí más lejos de Cervantes![5]

CLAUDIO: ¡Ni yo tampoco!

TONY: Bueno, cambiando de tema, ¿qué más hay para hacer en la feria?

CLAUDIO: ¡Hay de todo![6] Yo quería ir al concierto de música rock en el salón "Gabriela Mistral," pero todavía tenemos una hora antes de que empiece. Si querés, podemos ver qué libros nuevos salieron este año.

TONY: Yo quisiera ver qué traducciones tienen de libros en inglés.

CLAUDIO: Bueno, vamos a la entrada. Allí hay un catálogo electrónico de todos los libros en la feria.

TONY: Che, Claudio, quiero agradecerte[7] el haberme invitado a la feria. ¡La verdad es que no esperaba divertirme tanto!

CLAUDIO: Te dije que la feria era interesante: es la única de su tipo en Latinoamérica. Yo vengo todos los años, y cada vez la hacen más grande y hay más variedad de actos.

TONY: Así que venís[8] desde que empezó.

CLAUDIO: **No soy tan veterano.[9] Vine por primera vez hace cuatro años y la organizan desde el '74 . . .**

TONY: **Y, decime, ¿quiénes la organizan?**

CLAUDIO: **Lo hace una comisión privada, y la auspician[10] distintas empresas, como por ejemplo, el Diner's Club,[11] bancos, etc.**

TONY: **O sea, que es un esfuerzo internacional.**

CLAUDIO: **¡Sí que lo[12] es! De hecho, cada día hasta el fin de la feria, una nacionalidad diferente celebra su día, casi siempre auspiciado por la embajada. Por ejemplo, ayer fue el día de Polonia y hubo un espectáculo de bailes folklóricos.**

TONY: **Me pregunto cuándo será el día de los EE.UU.**

CLAUDIO: **No sé. Fijémonos en el "Programa General de Actos" . . . a ver . . . ¡ay! fue anteayer.**

TONY: **¡No importa! Vamos a ver lo de los libros.**

Ambos finalmente llegan a la entrada y se acercan a la mesa de información.

RECEPCIONISTA: **¿En qué puedo ayudarles?**

CLAUDIO: **Queremos saber si hay traducciones de autores de lengua[13] inglesa.**

RECEPCIONISTA: **¡Cómo no! ¿Buscan algún género[14] en particular . . . prosa, poesía, literatura infantil . . . ?**

TONY: **¡No esperaba que hubiese tanto para elegir!**

RECEPCIONISTA: **Tenemos de todo. Fíjense[15] en la pantalla. ¿Ven algo que les interese?**

La recepcionista teclea[16] unos instantes y en la pantalla aparece una larga lista de títulos. Tony lee en voz alta. . . .

TONY: **"Género: novela, Autor: Margaret Mitchell, Título: Lo que el viento se llevó."**

CLAUDIO: **Veo que hay muchas obras populares de la literatura americana:** *Un tranvía llamado deseo, Obras completas de Walt Whitman, El viejo y el mar, Mujercitas* . . .

RECEPCIONISTA: **Les voy a preparar un listado parcial de libros. Después, pueden ir a los puestos de las editoriales y allí podrán localizárselos.**

TONY: **Es Vd. muy amable, señorita. Claudio, ¡veo que voy a tener que usar mi tarjeta de crédito!**

CLAUDIO: **¡Por eso mismo no traje la mía! ¡Nunca puedo resistir la tentación de comprar un buen libro!**

AT THE BOOK FAIR.

Two friends visit the fair "Books: From the Authors to the Readers" in Buenos Aires, Argentina.

TONY: That was really interesting! The round table discussion was a little like the talk shows in my country.

CLAUDIO: Yes, but it was live! Near the end, the discussion got a little heated, but that was to be expected, considering the disparity of opinions.

TONY: I see people are still talking to the authors. . . .

CLAUDIO: Yes. Right now, the authors are signing copies of their books. People always like to talk to the authors in person. It's one of the most popular activities at the fair.

TONY: I liked the poetry workshop. It was the first time I ever wrote any poetry in Spanish!

CLAUDIO (pretending to be greatly impressed): I never knew you were so talented!

TONY: Actually, I never felt less like Cervantes!

CLAUDIO: Me, neither!

TONY: Well, to change the subject, what else can we do at the fair?

CLAUDIO: There's a lot to do! I wanted to go to the rock concert in Gabriela Mistral Hall, but we still have an hour before it starts. If you'd like, we can find out what new books came out this year.

TONY: I'd like to see what translations of English books there are.

CLAUDIO: Well, let's go to the entrance hall. There they have a computerized catalog of all the books in the fair.

TONY: Hey, Claudio, I want to thank you for inviting me to the fair. The truth is, I wasn't expecting to have so much fun!

CLAUDIO: I told you the fair was interesting! It's the only one of its kind in Latin America. I come every year, and it gets bigger and more varied each time.

TONY: So, you've been coming since it began.

CLAUDIO: I'm not that much of an expert! I came four years ago for the first time, and it's been going on since '74.

TONY: Tell me, who organizes it?

CLAUDIO: A private commission, and it's also sponsored by different companies, such as Diner's Club, banks, etc.

TONY: So, it's an international effort.

CLAUDIO: It sure is! Actually, every day until the end of the fair, a different nationality celebrates its day, usually sponsored by the local embassy. For example, yesterday was Poland's National Day, and there was a folk dance show.

TONY: I wonder when the U.S. National Day will be.

CLAUDIO: I don't know. We should check in the program . . . Let's see . . . Oh! It was the day before yesterday.

TONY: It doesn't matter! Let's go see about the books.

Finally arriving at the entrance hall, they approach the information desk.

RECEPTIONIST: How may I help you?

CLAUDIO: We'd like to know if there are any translations of English-language authors.

RECEPTIONIST: Sure! Are you looking for any particular genre . . . prose, poetry, children's books?

TONY: I didn't think there'd be so much to choose from!

RECEPTIONIST: We've got a lot! Look at the screen. Do you see anything you're interested in?

The receptionist types for a moment and a long list of titles appears on the screen. Tony reads out loud. . . .

TONY: "Genre: novel; Author: Margaret Mitchell; Title: *Gone with the Wind.*"

CLAUDIO: I can see there is a lot of popular American literature: *A Streetcar Named Desire, The Complete Works of Walt Whitman, The Old Man and the Sea, Little Women.* . . .

RECEPTIONIST: I'll give you a partial printout of books. Then, you can go to the publishers' stands, and they can find them for you.

TONY: You're very kind, miss. Claudio, I see I have to use my credit card!

CLAUDIO: That's exactly why I didn't bring mine! I can never resist the temptation to buy a good book!

B. APUNTES

1. The book fair is located in the *Predio Municipal de Exposiciones* (The Municipal Fair Center), in the park-strewn and very exclusive *barrio* (neighborhood) of Palermo in Buenos Aires. The fair runs for about three weeks a year, usually from mid-March through the first weeks of April.

2. *¡En vivo y en directo!* means "Live!" when referring to a television program. This phrase is sometimes used jokingly in casual conversation to mean "in person."

3. Remember that the preposition *de* + a noun (or an infinitive used as a noun), is used to form derived adjectives and adverbs. For more on the uses of *de,* see *Gramática y usos, Lección 15.*

4. In addition to book-related events, such as *lecturas, presentaciones, firmas de libros, fogones de lectura* (book readings, book presentations, book signings, readings), the book fair features many different cultural events, including *talleres* (workshops), *conferencias* (conferences), and *espectáculos* (shows), such as rock, classical, and folk music concerts, dance shows, and much more.

5. *Nunca me sentí más lejos de* followed by a famous person's name is a standard joke in Spanish. In English, you would say "I tried writing poetry, but I'm no Cervantes!"

6. Notice the reversed word-order in the idiomatic phrase *¡Hay de todo (un poco)!* (literally: There's of everything a little!).

7. *Agradecer* means "to be thankful for." Note that in Spanish, it can be followed by a noun or an infinitive: *Quiero agradecerte el regalo que me mandaste.* (I want to thank you for the present you sent me.) *Quiero agradecerte el haberme mandado un regalo.* (I want to thank you for having sent me a present.) The person you are thanking is the indirect object, usually indicated by an indirect object pronoun.

8. Note the unusual conjugation: *querés, venís, decime.* These second person singular forms are used in a large area of South America, namely Argentina, Uruguay, and parts of Paraguay. For more on this alternate second person form, *vos,* see *Gramática y usos, Lección 16.*

9. In Argentinian slang, *veterano* (veteran) can also be used to describe an experienced, skillful, or older person, i.e., "a pro." For example: *¡Qué bien habla inglés Pedro!—Sí, es veterano.* (Pedro speaks English so well!—Sure, he's a pro!)

10. Another common term for *auspiciar* (to sponsor) is *patrocinar.*

11. Note that names of foreign companies are usually preceded by the masculine article *el. El Diner's Club Internacional también auspicia la feria.* (Diner's Club International also sponsors the fair.)

12. The direct object pronoun *lo* can also be used to replace a noun or an adjective that follows the verbs *ser* or *estar,* even though these verbs are not followed by a direct object. Note that in this case, the pronoun is not changed to reflect gender or number. *Juan, ¿es médico?—Sí, lo es.* (Is Juan a doctor?—Yes, he is.) *María, ¿está bien?—Sí, lo está.* (Is Maria all right?—Yes, she is.)

13. *Lengua* is a more cultured word for *idioma* (language). *Lenguaje* also means "language," but it is used only to refer to an abstract language or code, such as *el lenguaje de los animales, el lenguaje BASIC* (a computer language).

14. *Género* can mean "gender" or "class/type."

15. *Fijarse en* + a noun literally means "to fix your attention on something." It can be translated as "to check" or "to look at." *Fíjate en esos estantes. Allí puede estar el libro que buscas.* (Check those shelves. The books you're looking for could be there.)

16. *Teclear* means "to type," but it cannot be followed by a noun. "To type a report" is *escribir un informe a máquina.*

C. GRAMATICA Y USOS

1. *LOS PRONOMBRES COMPLEMENTOS* (OBJECT PRONOUNS)

In Spanish, the direct, indirect, reflexive, and reciprocal object pronouns have the same form in the first and second persons singular and plural: *me, te, nos,* and *os.* For example, *me* can mean "me, to me," or "myself," depending on its role in the sentence. In the third person, each type of pronoun has a different form.

a) Direct Object Pronouns
The direct object pronoun is used to replace the direct object. (A direct object receives the action of the verb directly, without the help of a preposition.) In Spanish, the direct object pronouns are *me* (me), *te* (you–familiar), *lo* (him), *la* (her),[1] *nos* (us), *os* (you–familiar plural), and *los* and *las* (them/you–formal plural).

Te invito a que vengas a la feria conmigo.
I'm inviting you to come to the fair with me.

---

1. In Spain, *le* sometimes replaces a direct object. This is called *leísmo* and is considered an acceptable regional variant. However, the *Real Academia Española* strongly recommends using only *lo/la.*

¿Viste la exposición de fotografías en la feria ayer?—Sí, la vi.
Did you see the photography exhibit at the fair yesterday?—Yes, I saw it.

Vi a unos amigos en la feria de lejos, pero no los pude saludar.
I saw some friends of mine at the fair from far away, but I wasn't able to greet them.

¿Hay actividades para niños en la feria?—Sí, las hay.
Are there activities for children at the fair?—Yes, there are.

b) Indirect Object Pronouns
Indirect object pronouns replace an indirect object. (An indirect object is the final or indirect recipient of the action in a sentence. It is introduced by the prepositions *a* or *para*.) In Spanish, the indirect object pronouns are *me* (me), *te* (you–familiar), *le* (him/her), *nos* (us), *os* (you–familiar plural), and *les* (them/you–formal plural).

Le pregunté donde estaba el puesto de la editorial "Kapelusz."
I asked him/her where the "Kapelusz" publisher's stand was.

¿Os dieron guías para la feria en la entrada?
Did they give you guides to the fair at the entrance?

A la gente le gustan² las actividades de la feria.
People like the activities at the fair.

When both the direct and indirect object pronouns are used together in a sentence, the indirect object pronouns *le* and *les* are simplified to *se*. The indirect object pronoun then precedes the direct object pronoun.

¿El escritor le firmó el libro a la señorita?—Sí, se lo firmó.
Did the writer sign the young lady's book?—Yes, he signed it for her.

The exact meaning of the pronouns *le, les,* and *se* can be clarified by *a* followed by a prepositional object pronoun.

c) Prepositional Object Pronouns
Prepositional object pronouns are used after prepositions. They are the same as the subject pronouns, except in the first and second persons singular: *mí*³ and *ti*. They are *mí* (me), *ti* (you–familiar singular), *él* (him), *ella* (her), *usted* (you–formal singular), *nosotros* (us), *vosotros* (you–familiar plural), *ellos/ellas* (them), and *ustedes* (you–formal plural).

---

2. Indirect object pronouns are always used with such verbs as *gustar, interesar, parecer,* etc., since these verbs are always followed by an indirect object.

3. Note that *mí* meaning "me" is written with a stress mark to distinguish it from *mi* meaning "my." You can also hear the difference in conversation, since *mí* is generally pronounced with stress or emphasis, while *mi* is not.

No sé si darle los billetes a Juan o a los González. Se los doy a él.
I don't know whether to give the tickets to Juan or to the Gonzalezes. I'll give them to him.

Este libro no es para ti, Juancito. Es para adultos.
This book is not for you, Juancito. It's for grown-ups.

d) Reflexive and Reciprocal Object Pronouns
In Spanish, reflexive and reciprocal pronouns are identical in form. The first and second person forms are the same as for direct and indirect objects, and the third person form is *se*. They are: *me* (myself), *te* (yourself–familiar singular), *se* (himself, herself, itself), *nos* (ourselves; we . . . each other), *os* (yourselves; you . . . each other = familiar plural), and *se* (themselves; yourselves . . . each other . . . = formal plural; they . . . each other).

The distinction in meaning must be made based on context. In reflexive constructions, the subject and the object are the same, i.e., the subject acts upon itself. In a reciprocal construction, the subjects (which are always plural) act upon each other. Note that many verbs that are reflexive in Spanish are not reflexive in English.

Al acercarse al predio, Ramiro y Gonzalo se vieron reflejados en el edificio de vidrio.
On approaching the exhibit center, Ramiro and Gonzalo saw their reflections in the glass building.

Ramiro se pone en la cola para entrar en el predio.
Juan gets in line to enter the exhibit center.

Voy a ir al taller de poesía. Me voy a las siete.
I'm going to go to the poetry workshop. I'm leaving at seven.

Los tres amigos se van a encontrar en la feria a las tres de la tarde.
The three friends are going to meet at the fair at 3 P.M.

If the function of a pronoun is not clear from context, the phrase *a sí mismo* is used to indicate a reflexive action, and the phrase *el uno al otro* is used to indicate a reciprocal action. Both of these phrases must agree in gender and number with the subject to which they refer.

Susanita es coquetísima: ¡se mira a sí misma en el espejo todo el día!
Susanita is very coquettish: she looks at herself in the mirror all day!

Ellos se culpan el uno al otro por el accidente.
They blame each other for the accident.

Gonzalo se compró a sí mismo un regalo de cumpleaños.
Gonzalo bought a birthday present for himself.

Juan y María se vieron de lejos en la feria el uno a la otra.
At the fair, Juan and Maria spotted each other from far away.

A reflexive or reciprocal construction can also be introduced by a preposition plus the invariable pronoun *sí*.

Jorge lee el libro para sí.
    Jorge reads the book to himself.

Ellas hablan entre sí.
    They speak amongst themselves.

e) Placement of Object Pronouns
In Spanish, object pronouns generally precede a conjugated verb. In negative sentences, they are placed between the negative word and the verb.

Viviana se quedó maravillada de la feria y le contó todo a sus amigos.
Viviana was amazed by the fair, and she told her friends about it.

Angel va a ir a la biblioteca mañana. No lo acompañaré.
Angel is going to go to the library tomorrow. I won't accompany him.

Nunca me he ido al Japón.
    I've never been to Japan.

If a verbal expression consists of several words, the pronouns can be attached as suffixes to the last element if it is an infinitive or a gerund, or they can precede the first element.

Voy a entregarle el informe al jefe. Está esperándome en su oficina.
Le voy a entregar el informe al jefe. Me está esperando en su oficina.
    I'm going to turn the report in to my boss. He's waiting for me in his office.

Gloria quiere comprarle una enciclopedia a su hijo. Va a comprársela mañana.
    Gloria wants to buy her son an encyclopedia. She's going to buy it for him tomorrow.

No creo que estén esperándome. Se habrán ido hace mucho.
No creo que me estén esperando. Se habrán ido hace mucho.
    I don't think they're waiting for me. They must have left a long time ago.

Object pronouns are attached as suffixes to an affirmative command, and sandwiched between *no* and the verb in a negative command.

Prepáreme un listado de las editoriales más importantes en la Argentina y déjemelo sobre el escritorio antes de las quince horas.
    Prepare a list of the most important publishers in Argentina for me, and leave it on my desk before three o'clock.

Olvídese de la cuenta Pérez por ahora, pero no la archive.
    Forget the Perez account for now, but don't file it away.

Object pronouns can be attached as suffixes to conjugated verbs in all tenses, but this form is more common in written than in spoken language.

En Latinoamérica, dámosle[4] mucha importancia al estudio de la lengua castellana en la educación primaria.
In Latin America, we place great importance on the study of the Spanish language in elementary school education.

2. *USOS IDIOMATICOS DE LOS PRONOMBRES COMPLEMENTOS* (IDIOMATIC USAGE OF OBJECT PRONOUNS)

Object pronouns are often used together with the objects they are supposed to replace, for added emphasis or politeness.

Viviana lo quiere conocer a su poeta preferido.
Viviana wants to meet her favorite poet.

Juan le va a comprar un libro a su ahijado.
Juan is going to buy his godson a book.

¿Vamos a tomarnos un café en la confitería?
Should we get ourselves a cup of coffee at the café?

A mí me gustan los libros de ciencia ficción, y a Vd, ¿cuáles le gustan?
I like science fiction books, and you, which ones do you like?

Indirect object pronouns can sometimes be used to clarify possession.

Estoy enfadadísimo con Arturo. No quiero verle ni la sombra.
I'm really angry with Arturo. I don't even want to see his shadow.

La gitana quiso leernos las manos, pero rehusamos.
The gypsy wanted to read our palms, but we refused.

---

4. When object pronouns are attached as suffixes, they do not change the stress of the word to which they are attached. A stress mark is then used to maintain stress on the same syllable. Also, when the object pronoun *nos* is attached as a suffix to a third person plural, conjugated verb, the final *-s* of the conjugated verb is dropped to facilitate pronunciation.

> *Encontrémonos a las siete en la puerta del teatro.*
> Let's meet at three o'clock at the entrance to the theater.
> *Vámonos a Italia el año que viene.*
> Let's go to Italy next year.

41

D. HABLEMOS DE NEGOCIOS

LAS FERIAS COMERCIALES (TRADE FAIRS)

Trade fairs, known as *ferias* or *exposiciones,* are an important part of starting or promoting a business, especially in the import/export sector. There are many trade fairs held throughout Latin America and Spain. Agricultural and industrial fairs are generally organized by state entities, although the number of privately-organized consumer fairs is increasing, particularly in Latin America.

Be aware that many Latin American countries permit the import of foreign goods and machinery only through authorized local distributors *(distribui-dores),* so you may participate in fairs only through a joint venture. American banks with international contacts may help you in making contacts with such distributors. Although regulations vary considerably, goods exported for exhibition at a fair are generally free from taxes. For more information, contact the local *Cámara de Comercio* (Chamber of Commerce).

In Spain, there are also many international fairs in fashion, aerospace, tourism, security, electronics, publishing, and many other fields. Most of these fairs take place in Madrid or Barcelona. Keep in mind that there are often changes in the scheduling of these events. The following U.S. government agencies can provide up-to-date information regarding overseas trade fairs:

Trade Information Department
U.S. Department of Commerce
Washington, D.C. 20230
(800) USA-TRADE

U.S. Department of Agriculture
Trade Assistance & Promotion Office
USDA/TAPO
Room 4939 South Building
U.S. Department of Agriculture
Washington, D.C. 20250

Following is a list of local agencies (aside from the *Cámaras de Comercio*) that may also provide valuable information.

Argentina
Dirección Nacional de Promoción Comercial
Depto. de Ferias y Exposiciones
Avda. Julio A. Roca 651
C.P. 1322
Capital Federal, Argentina
Teléfono: 34-3103

Colombia
Corferias
Cra 40, No. 22C-67
Bogotá, Colombia
Teléfono: 571-337-7676
Teléfacsímil: 571-337-7271(2)

Mexico
Exhibimex
Teléfono: 5-264-1155
         5-515-2408

AIC conferencia
Teléfono: 5-203-8004
         5-203-7933

Perú
Confederación de Cámaras de Comercio y Producción del Perú
Avda. Gregorio Escobedo 398
Lima 4, Peru
Teléfono: 633-434

Venezuela
VENEXPO
Comisión Venezolana de Ferias y Exhibiciones
Avenida Guaicaiparo
Qta. Cantoralia
El Rosal
Caracas, Venezuela

EXAMEN (QUIZ)

A. *Complete las oraciones siguientes con los pronombres complemento que corresponda.* (Complete the following sentences with the appropriate object pronouns.)

1. ¿_____ diste el informe al jefe?—Sí, _____ _____ di.
2. ¿Pedro _____ llenó el formulario a María?—No, aún no _____ _____ llenó.
3. A _____ (you–formal, singular), ¿_____ gustan los actos oficiales? —No, no _____ gustan demasiado.
4. ¿ _____ viste a Juan y a María anoche?—No, no _____ vi.
5. ¿Ya _____ entregaron la documentación a Vds.?—Sí, ya _____ _____ entregaron.
6. Vosotros, ¿_____ fuisteis para el teatro ayer?—Sí, _____ fuimos anoche.
7. ¡No _____ _____ voy a hacer! Quiero que Pepito haga los deberes solo.
8. ¡Váyan _____ Vds. solos al cine! A _____ (me) no _____ gustan las películas de terror.
9. ¿_____ vais a encontrar en la puerta del teatro? Juan no _____ sabe. Hay que decir _____ _____.
10. Acabo de comer _____ una porción enorme de torta de chocolate.

B. *Estructure las oraciones siguientes.* (Unscramble the following sentences.)

1. lo/No/dar./voy/a/se
2. los/entrega/Él/a/ellos./se
3. No/dar./quieren/los/nos
4. A/siete,/las/encontramos/para/nos/al/verlo/director.
5. a/no/a/va/hablarte/ti,/Juan/sino/a/Él

C. *Traduzca las frases siguientes al español, usando la cantidad indicada de palabras españolas entre paréntesis.* (Translate the following phrases into Spanish, using the number of Spanish words indicated in parentheses.)

1. I don't like fairs. (5)
2. He gives it to them. (6)
3. They don't want to give them to us. (6)
4. She wants to give it to you (familiar plural). (3)
5. You (familiar, singular) don't like the authors. (5)

LECCION 4

A. DIALOGO

UNA ENTREVISTA DE TRABAJO.

La señorita Roberts tiene cita[1] con el jefe del departamento de compraventas de la compañía Molex, una gran compañía fabricante en Caracas, Venezuela.[2] La entrevista es para el puesto de director de compraventas internacionales.

SR. RAMIREZ: ¡Buenos días señorita Roberts! Tome asiento, por favor.

SRTA. ROBERTS: ¡Muchas gracias!

SR. RAMIREZ: Debo decirle que he estado ansioso de conocerla en persona. No es a diario[3] que entrevistamos a solicitantes del extranjero.

SRTA. ROBERTS: Por mi parte, me alegra que hayan respondido a mi solicitud.

SR. RAMIREZ: He leído su historial de trabajo y estoy muy complacido. Sólo tengo una pregunta para[4] hacerle: ¿qué la motivó a dejar su puesto anterior?

SRTA. ROBERTS: Principalmente, fue la necesidad de cambiar de ambientes.[5] Siempre he querido vivir en el extranjero.[6] He viajado extensamente por Sudamérica y me ha gustado mucho. Fue una decisión que medité[7] profundamente antes de tomar.

SR. RAMIREZ: ¿Cree Vd. realmente que le guste trabajar en Venezuela? El puesto que queremos cubrir[8] requiere una estadía mínima de dos años y temo que, al pasar el tiempo,[9] podría no encontrarse[10] a gusto[11] en nuestro país.[12]

SRTA. ROBERTS: Tenga la seguridad de que mi decisión es firme. Como ya le he dicho, conozco bien Sudamérica, y me he sentido más a gusto aquí en Venezuela que en cualquier otro país. De hecho, tengo muchos amigos y conocidos en el país y ya he iniciado[13] los trámites de inmigración necesarios para quedarme . . .[14]

SR. RAMIREZ: Me place oírlo. Dígame, ¿cuáles eran[15] las responsabilidades de su puesto anterior?

SRTA. ROBERTS: Estaba a cargo de la división de ventas internacionales. Como jefe, supervisaba un equipo de ocho vendedores. Hemos trabajado con clientes de todo el mundo: del Japón, de Europa y de Sudamérica. Juntos logramos un aumento del treinta por ciento en el nivel de ventas.

SR. RAMIREZ: ¡Admirable! Dígame, ¿cómo organizaba e inspiraba Vd. a su equipo de ventas a lograr un tan alto nivel de rendimiento?

SRTA. ROBERTS: Para lograrlo, es necesario crear un ambiente de trabajo positivo, que fomente y desarrolle mucho intercambio de ideas y dedicación a la labor.[16] Creo que eso se logra con el ejemplo. Yo trabajo concienzudamente,[17] inspirando el mismo esfuerzo en el grupo.

SR. RAMIREZ: Y, ¿qué cree Vd. que pueda aportar al funcionamiento de nuestra empresa?

SRTA. ROBERTS: He seguido el mercadeo de los productos de su empresa y creo que con mi experiencia en el comercio internacional, podría aportar al desarrollo y expansión de su sector de exportaciones, sobre todo en el lejano Oriente y en los EE.UU.

SR. RAMIREZ: Estoy de acuerdo. Permítame pasar a un tema más personal . . . Dígame, ¿a qué se dedica Vd. en su tiempo libre? ¿Cuáles son sus intereses extralaborales?[18]

SRTA. ROBERTS: Bueno, me gustan mucho los deportes, sobre todo el tenis. También soy aficionada a la historia de la América precolombina. Me fascinan las antiguas culturas maya, azteca e inca.

SR. RAMIREZ: Se nota que es Vd. una persona de gustos variados. Veo que domina Vd. el español perfectamente, ¿tiene Vd. conocimientos de algún otro idioma?

SRTA ROBERTS: Sí. He estudiado el francés en la escuela secundaria. Lo leo y escribo sin dificultades, pero no lo he tenido que usar cotidianamente. También tengo conocimientos básicos del japonés.

SR. RAMIREZ: ¡Excelente! En base a su historial de trabajo, referencias, y al hablar con Vd. en persona, quiero ofrecerle el puesto de inmediato. ¿Espero que podrá empezar de inmediato?

SRTA. ROBERTS: Por supuesto. Ya he encontrado un departamento aquí en la ciudad . . . Tengo una pregunta, ¿podría Vd. proporcionarme[19] más detalles sobre los recursos que estarían a mi disposición?[20]

SR. RAMIREZ: Con mucho gusto. Como directora de compraventas al exterior, supervisaría un grupo de quince vendedores. Contaría con el apoyo de nuestro secretariado, incluyendo una secretaria personal. También tendría acceso a un fondo de dinero bastante importante. Además, trabajaría con nuestro departamento de mercadeo, desarrollando nuevo material de propaganda para el mercado internacional.

SRTA. ROBERTS: ¡Entiendo! Y, ¿en cuanto a remuneraciones[21] y beneficios?

SR. RAMIREZ: Aquí tiene un legajo con toda esa información. Léalo, considere la oferta y comuníqueme su decisión antes del viernes.[22]

SRTA. ROBERTS: Lo haré. Ha sido un gran placer conocerlo, Sr. Ramírez.

SR. RAMIREZ: El gusto fue todo mío. Esperaré su llamada.

A JOB INTERVIEW.

Miss Roberts has an appointment with the head of the sales division of the Molex company, a large manufacturing firm in Caracas, Venezuela. The interview is for the position of Director of International Trade.

MR. RAMIREZ: Hello, Miss Roberts. Please sit down.

MISS ROBERTS: Thank you very much!

MR. RAMIREZ: I have to tell you that I have been looking forward to meeting you personally. We don't interview candidates from abroad every day.

MISS ROBERTS: I'm very happy that you've responded to my application.

MR. RAMIREZ: I've looked over your résumé, and I am very pleased. I have just one question: What motivated you to leave your former position?

MISS ROBERTS: It was primarily because I felt the need to change environments. I have always wanted to live abroad. I've traveled extensively throughout South America, and I like it a great deal. It was a decision I considered carefully.

MR. RAMIREZ: Do you think you will enjoy working in Venezuela? The position we would like to fill would require a minimum stay of two years, and I'm worried that, as time goes by, you might not feel at home in our country.

MISS ROBERTS: Rest assured that my decision is very firm. As I've told you, I know South America well, and I've felt more comfortable here in Venezuela than in any other country. In fact, I have many friends and acquaintances in this country, and I've already begun the necessary immigration procedures.

MR. RAMIREZ: I'm happy to hear that. Tell me, what were your responsibilities at your previous position?

MISS ROBERTS: I was in charge of the International Sales Division. As director, I supervised a team of eight salespeople. We worked with clients from all over the world: Japan, Europe, and South America. Together, we achieved a 30 percent increase in sales.

MR. RAMIREZ: That's very impressive! Tell me, how did you go about organizing and inspiring your sales team to attain such a high level of performance?

MISS ROBERTS: In order to achieve that, it's necessary to create a positive work environment that promotes and develops the exchange of ideas and dedication to hard work. I believe this is done by example. I work conscientiously, inspiring the same effort in the team.

MR. RAMIREZ: I see. So, what do you think you could contribute to our company?

MISS ROBERTS: I've been following your marketing strategies, and I think that, with my experience in international commerce, I could contribute to the development and expansion of your export section, especially to the Far East and the United States.

MR. RAMIREZ: I agree. Allow me to ask you a more personal question: What do you do in your spare time? What are your interests outside of work?

MISS ROBERTS: Well, I love sports, especially tennis. I am also interested in the history of pre-Columbian America. I'm fascinated by the ancient Mayan, Aztec, and Incan cultures.

MR. RAMIREZ: I can tell you're a person who has a variety of interests. I can see your Spanish is excellent. Do you know any other languages?

MISS ROBERTS: Yes. I studied French in high school. I can read and write without difficulty, but I have seldom had to use it on a daily basis. I also know some basic phrases in Japanese.

MR. RAMIREZ: Excellent! Based on your résumé, references, and after speaking to you in person, I'm ready to offer you the position immediately. I hope you're able to start immediately?

MISS ROBERTS: Of course! I've already found an apartment here in the city . . . I have a question. Could you give me more information about the resources that would be available to me?

MR. RAMIREZ: Of course! As Director of Foreign Trade, you would supervise a group of fifteen salespeople. You would have the help of our secretarial force, including a personal secretary. You would also have a rather large budget available to you. Moreover, you would be working with our marketing department, developing new advertising material for the international market.

MISS ROBERTS: I understand. And with regard to salary and benefits?

MR. RAMIREZ: Here is a folder with all that information. Read it, consider the offer, and get back to me with your decision by Friday.

MISS ROBERTS: I will. It's been a pleasure to meet you, Mr. Ramirez.

MR. RAMIREZ: The pleasure was all mine. I'll be waiting for your call.

B. APUNTES

1. *Tener cita con alguien* means "to have an appointment/date with someone."

2. Caracas is the capital of Venezuela, located in the far north of South America, bordering the Caribbean Sea. Venezuela is actively developing its manufacturing and export industries and is currently one of the more industrialized countries of South America.

3. *A diario* and *cotidianamente* are formal ways of saying *todos los días* (every day).

4. In Spanish, as in English, an infinitive can be used to indicate purpose. For example: *He venido a ver al señor Pérez.* (I've come to meet Mr. Perez.) Note, however, that in Spanish an infinitive that indicates purpose must be introduced by the prepositions *a* or *para*.

5. *Ambiente* has many meanings. *No me gusta el ambiente de este restaurante.* (I don't like the atmosphere in this restaurant.) *Preocupa a todos la contaminación del medio ambiente.* (Everybody is worried about the contamination of the environment.) *Busco un departamento de tres ambientes.* (I'm looking for a three-room apartment.)

6. *El extranjero* means both "foreigner" and "foreign country." This is an example of an adjective used as a noun. For more on adjectives, see *Gramática y usos, Lección 9.*

7. Note that the Spanish verb *meditar* (to meditate), means simply "to think about carefully" when followed by a noun. *Tenemos que meditar el asunto.* (We have to think about the situation carefully.)

8. Note that in English, a position is "filled," but in Spanish it's "covered": *cubrir un puesto de trabajo.*

9. *Al pasar el tiempo* and *con el paso del tiempo* both mean "as time goes by."

10. Note that the reflexive verb *encontrarse* (to find oneself) often replaces the verb *estar* in formal conversation: *¿Cómo se encuentra Vd.?* (How are you?) *El señor Smith se encuentra almorzando en este momento.* (Mr. Smith is having lunch at the moment.) *¿Dónde se encuentra la señorita Vega?* (Where is Miss Vega?)

11. *Sentirse a gusto* (to feel comfortable, content) is used very often in Spanish. *Estoy muy a gusto en vuestra casa.* (I feel very comfortable at your home.) *Estoy muy a gusto con mi televisor nuevo.* (I'm very happy with my new TV set.)

12. Expect to hear questions phrased "indirectly" at a job interview. That is, questions tend to be phrased as hypothetical situations, unrelated to a specific individual.

13. Note the use of the present perfect instead of the preterite and imperfect tenses in this formal conversation.

14. The reflexive verb *quedarse* is a more colloquial way of saying *permanecer* (to remain).

15. Note the use of the imperfect tense here. Had the question been phrased in the preterite, it would have referred to a single incident.

16. Notice that *la labor* is feminine, despite the fact that it ends in a hard consonant.

17. Don't confuse *concienzudamente* (conscientiously) with *conscientemente* (consciously).

18. In most of Latin America, the personal interests and education of an applicant can have great impact on the hiring process.

19. *Proporcionar (algo)* means "to make something available," or simply "to give."

20. *Estar a la disposición de (alguien)* means "to be available to (someone)." Beware of Spanish words that look like English words, but have different meanings.

21. *Remuneraciones, salario,* and *sueldo* all mean "salary" and can be used interchangeably.

22. In Latin America, salary and benefits are seldom discussed during the interview. After being offered a job, candidates are usually given a folder that includes the salary, benefits, rights, and obligations of the applicant. The applicant then considers the details and decides whether to accept, decline, or negotiate at the following appointment.

C. GRAMATICA Y USOS

1. *LOS INTERROGATIVOS* (INTERROGATIVES)

Spanish has many basic question words. They all carry stress marks and are generally placed at the beginning of a question.

a) *¿Qué?* (What?)
¿Qué? or *¿Qué cosa(s)?* both mean "What?"

¿Qué (cosa) trae Vd. en la mano?
What are you carrying in your hand?

¿Qué (cosas) tengo que traer a la entrevista?
What (things) should I bring to the interview?

¿De qué? is used to ask what something is made of or what it contains. Its meaning varies according to the meaning of *de* in the sentence.

¡Qué bonita escultura! ¿De qué es?
What a pretty sculpture! What is it made of?

¿De qué es ese vaso que está sobre la mesa?
What's in that glass on the table?

b) *¿Quién?* (Who?)
¿Quién(es)? agrees in number with the noun to which it refers.

¿Quién es el director de ventas al extranjero?
Who is the director of foreign sales?

¿Quiénes son los nuevos empleados?
Who are the new employees?

¿A quiénes les quieres repartir esos informes?
To whom (to which people) do you want to distribute those reports?

¿A quién[1] va Vd. a llevar al congreso en Caracas?
Who are you taking to the convention in Caracas?

¿A quiénes quiere Vd. presentarme?
What people (whom) do you want me to meet?

---

1. Remember that the *a personal* must be used before a personal direct object. Don't confuse it with the preposition *a*, meaning "to," which is used before an indirect object.

¿De quién es este currículum?[2]
Whose résumé is this?

¿Con quién tengo cita a las quince horas hoy?
With whom is my three o'clock appointment today?

c) *¿Cuál(es)?* (Which one/s?)
¿Cuál(es)? also agrees in number with the noun to which it refers.

¿Cuál de los dos entrevistados tiene más experiencia?
Which of the two interviewees has more experience?

Remember to use *¿Cuál?* instead of *¿Qué?* with the verb *ser,* unless you are asking for a definition.

¿Cuáles eran sus responsabilidades en su trabajo anterior?
What were your responsibilities at your previous position?

Informally, *¿cuál(es)?* can be replaced by *¿qué?* when directly followed by a noun.

¿Cuál idea te gusta más?
¿Qué idea te gusta más?
Which idea do you like best?

d) *¿Cómo?* (How?)

¿Cómo van sus negocios?
How's business?

¿Cómo? is also used in conversation like the English "What?" when you didn't understand or hear something.

¿Cómo? . . . Disculpe, no lo escuché.
What? . . . I'm sorry, I didn't hear you.

e) *¿Cuánto?* (How much? How many?)
¿Cuánto (-a, -os, -as)? agrees in gender and number with the noun it modifies.

¿Cuánto paga Vd. en impuestos por año?
How much do you pay in taxes per year?

¿Cuántas sucursales tiene su banco en la ciudad?
How many branches does your bank have in the city?

---

2. "Whose?" can also be expressed by the interrogatives *¿Cúyo?* or *Cúyos?,* although these are archaic forms that are seldom heard in modern Spanish.

¿Cuánto? has an abbreviated form *¿Cuán?* which is used before adjectives to ask "How tall/short/big/small, etc.?" However, in modern Spanish, you will generally hear *¿Cómo es de . . .?* instead.

¿Cuán difícil les fue entrar en el mercado asiático?
¿Cómo les fue de difícil entrar en el mercado asiático?
How difficult was it for you to break into the Asian market?

Other English questions beginning with "How?" (followed by an adjective or adverb) are generally phrased in Spanish with *¿cuánto?* or *¿qué?* followed by a noun.

¿Cuánta importancia tiene este trabajo para Vd.?
How important is this job for you?
(Literally: How much importance does this job have for you?)

¿Con qué frecuencia viaja Vd. a Europa?
How often do you travel to Europe?
(Literally: With what frequency do you travel to Europe?)

f) *¿Por qué?* (Why?)

¿Por qué ha decidido mudarse Vd. a los EE.UU.?
Why have you decided to move to the U.S.?

Remember that aside from its basic meaning, *¿por qué?* can also mean "what for?" or "through which/what?" depending on the meaning of *por* in the question.

Voy al correo por estampillas. ¿Por qué (cosa) vas tú?
I'm going to the post office to get stamps. What are you going for?

¿Por qué avenida se llega al centro?
By what avenue can I get downtown?

g) *¿Cuándo?* (When?)

¿Cuándo llegaste de tus vacaciones?
When did you get back from your vacation?

¿Desde cuándo trabaja Vd. para la empresa?
When did you begin working for the company?

¿Para cuándo tengo que terminar el informe?
By when do I have to finish the report?

h) ¿Dónde? (Where?)

In Spanish, unlike in English, the distinction must always be made between "where?" (*¿dónde?*) and "where to?" (*¿adónde?*)[3]

¿Dónde está localizada su empresa?
Where is your company located?

¿Adónde piensa ir a almorzar?
Where are you planning to go for lunch?

¿De dónde llegó este paquete para mí?
Where did this package for me come from?

¿Por dónde? is used to ask "through/along where?"

¿Por dónde pasa el tren?
Where does the train pass through?

It can also be used informally to ask for an educated guess on the location of an object or person.

¿Por dónde están mis anteojos?
Where could my glasses be?

2. *EL PRETERITO PERFECTO* (THE PRESENT PERFECT)

All perfect tenses are formed with *haber* followed by the past participle. The past participle of regular verbs is formed by adding *-ado* to the stem of *-ar* verbs and *-ido* to the stem of *-er* and *-ir* verbs (*hablar—hablado, comer—comido, dormir—dormido, ser—sido, estar—estado*). There are a few irregular past participles that must be memorized.[4]

To form the present perfect, the verb *haber* must be conjugated in the present indicative tense. It is equivalent to the English form "to have" + past participle.

	TRABAJAR TO WORK	*OFRECER* TO OFFER	*REUNIR* TO REUNITE
yo he *tú has* *él/ella/Vd. ha* *nosotros hemos* *vosotros habeis* *ellos/ellas/Vds. han*	*trabajado*	*ofrecido*	*reunido*

3. Note that *¿adónde?* is always spelled as one word.

4. For a list of irregular past participles, see Appendix C, p. 319.

The present perfect is used to talk about past actions in a general way, without specifying when they began or were completed. Note that the action may or may not continue in the present.

Durante muchos años como director de ventas, he hecho negocios y trabajado con muchos extranjeros.
During my many years as sales director, I have done business and worked with many foreigners.

The present perfect is also used in formal situations to replace the preterite. Compare the following sentences:

Dicen que Pedro durmió poco anoche y por eso se durmió en la presentación.
Dicen que Pedro ha dormido poco anoche y por eso se durmió en la presentación.
They say Pedro slept little last night, and that's why he fell asleep at the presentation.

He tenido la oportunidad de aprender varias lenguas extranjeras en mi vida.
Tuve la oportunidad de aprender varias lenguas extranjeras en mi vida.
I have had the opportunity to learn many foreign languages in my life.

¿Fuíste alguna vez a España de vacaciones?
¿Ha ido Vd. alguna vez a España de vacaciones?
Did you ever go to Spain on vacation?

D. ESTUDIO IDIOMATICO

Following are some expressions that will help you be more precise about time.

De buenas a primeras, de golpe (All of a sudden)

Juan no decía nada y de buenas a primeras, se levantó y se fue.
Juan wasn't saying anything when, all of a sudden, he got up and left.

A mediados de (Around the middle of)

Voy a viajar a España a mediados de julio.
I'm going to travel to Spain around the middle of July.

A más tardar (At the very latest)

Tengo que terminar el informe a más tardar para el viernes.
I have to finish the report by Friday, at the very latest.

A la larga (In the long run)

A la larga, conviene más vender la casa.
In the long run, it'll be better to sell the house.

Al fin y al cabo (When all is said and done)

Al fin y al cabo, todo salió bien.
When all is said and done, everything turned out fine.

E. HABLEMOS DE NEGOCIOS

BUSCANDO TRABAJO (LOOKING FOR A JOB)

Finding a job in Spain or Latin America usually begins by "asking around" and calling on the help of friends and acquaintances. If you don't know anyone with good connections, the first step is leafing through *los clasificados* (the classifieds). Keep in mind that telephone numbers may not always have seven digits. Also, don't be surprised if the ad includes some personal characteristics, such as gender or age requirements. While discriminatory in the United States, this is considered perfectly acceptable in Spanish-speaking countries. Here are some typical want ads in Spanish:

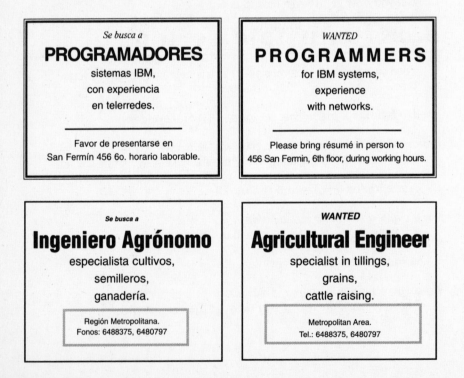

Se busca a

PROGRAMADORES

sistemas IBM,
con experiencia
en telerredes.

Favor de presentarse en
San Fermín 456 6o. horario laborable.

WANTED

PROGRAMMERS

for IBM systems,
experience
with networks.

Please bring résumé in person to
456 San Fermin, 6th floor, during working hours.

Se busca a

Ingeniero Agrónomo

especialista cultivos,
semilleros,
ganadería.

Región Metropolitana.
Fonos: 6488375, 6480797

WANTED

Agricultural Engineer

specialist in tillings,
grains,
cattle raising.

Metropolitan Area.
Tel.: 6488375, 6480797

Importante Empresa Requiere

Encargado Administrativo Contable

con experiencia en balances,
leyes impositivas,
computación.
Edad mínima: 25 años.
Se ofrece remuneración excelente
y amplias posibilidades de ascenso.

Enviar Curriculum Vitae con fotocarnet reciente
a Casilla de Correos No. 2406, Asunción.

Important Enterprise Requires an

Accountant

with experience in balances,
tax laws,
computers.
Minimum Age: 25.
We offer an excellent salary
and great upward mobility.

Send résumé with recent wallet size photograph
to Post Office Box 2406, Asuncion.

Some Latin American countries (notably Venezuela) still prefer *el currículum vitae,* written in essay form, to the chronological/schematic approach of résumés—*un resumé,* or *un historial de trabajo.* Résumés are, however, acceptable everywhere. They should be typed and one or two pages in length. Avoid evaluating your own performance (i.e., "blowing your own horn"). Following is a sample résumé.

Juan José Pérez Fernández
Casilla de Correos No. 457
Buenos Aires, Argentina   8474
Tel: 54 47 34
DNI: 15.684.564

OBJETIVO: Desempeñar la posición de Jefe de Personal

PREPARACIÓN
ACADÉMICA: Licenciatura en Administración Laboral
                         de la Universidad de Buenos Aires, obtenida en 1990.
                         Promedio General: 9,4

EXPERIENCIA
PROFESIONAL: **Jefe de Personal** de Díaz Hnos. S.A.,
                              desde marzo de 1992 hasta el presente.
                         Sus responsabilidades incluían: la selección de
                         empleados, la supervisión de tareas administrativas y
                         el manejo de relaciones con la Unión de Trabajadores.
                         Subdirector de Personal Administrativo
                              para Capilex, S.C.A., 1990–1992
                         Encargado de un equipo de 30 personas, planificó la
                         distribución de tareas y preparó informes mensuales
                         del renidimiento del equipo.

REFERENCIAS
PROFESIONALES:Doctor Luís Ríos
                         Avenida Vergel 7273
                         Azul, Pcia de Bs. As. 1243
                         tel: 75-3423

REFERENCIAS/
PERSONALES: Jorge López Ibáñez
                         Casilla de Correos No. 7454
                         Correo Central, La Plata
                         tel: 74-5534

[firma]   15.1.1996

58

Juan José Pérez Fernández
P.O. Box 457
Buenos Aires, Argentina 8474
Tel: 54 47 34
I.D. # 15,684,564

OBJECTIVE   To perform the duties of Director of Personnel

EDUCATION

B.A. in Human Relations Administration,
University of Buenos Aires, 1990.
Grade Point Average: 9.4

**PROFESSIONAL
EXPERIENCE**

Director of Personnel
DIAZ BROS., INC.   3/92 to present
Responsibilities include: hiring employees,
supervising administrative tasks, acting as liaison
with the Labor Union.

Assistant Director of Personnel
CAPILEX, INC.,   1990–1992
Supervised a team of 30 people, planned the
distribution of tasks and prepared monthly group
performance reports.

**PROFESSIONAL
REFERENCES**

Doctor Luis Rios
Vergel Avenue # 7273
Azul, Province of Buenos Aires. 1243
tel: 75-3423

**PERSONAL
REFERENCES**

Jorge Lopez Ibañez
P.O. Box 7454
Central Post Office, La Plata
tel: 74-5534

Keep in mind that the purpose of a curriculum vitae is to present yourself to your employer personally, as well as professionally. It is important to include both personal and professional references in your résumé. You may also want to include information such as your date of birth, marital status, citizenship, etc., though this is not required.

It is standard practice for some companies to ask that you include a recent wallet size (1″ x 1″) photograph of yourself along with your curriculum vitae. In some countries (e.g., Venezuela), you will also have to present supporting evidence to attest to the accuracy of your résumé. This includes copies of diplomas from any institutions of higher education, as well as letters from previous employers describing your position and the circumstances of your departure from the company.

Résumés should be accompanied by a typed cover letter stating why you are interested in working for the company and offering a concise description of your duties at your former (i.e., current) job. Avoid any self-congratulatory phrases, as this may very well be interpreted as rude. If your work experience is limited, simply state your desire to gain experience in the field in question. The following is a typical cover letter.

Buenos Aires, 15 de enero de 1996

Sr. Ricardo Gómez
Gerente de Personal

Asunto: Envío de Curriculum Vitae

De mi mayor consideración:

Tengo el agrado de dirigirme a Vd., con motivo de presentarle
mi currículum vitae y datos personales, a efectos de ser un
posible colaborador en vuestra empresa.

He leído con sumo interés el anuncio publicado en el periódico La Nación el 10 de enero en el cual expresan el deseo de
cubrir una vacante en vuestro Departamento de Personal. He
desempeñado el cargo de Asistente de Personal en la agencia
de Publicidad Díaz Hnos., durante tres años. Tanto mi experiencia laboral como los estudios formales recibidos, me han
capacitado para manejar un equipo de veinte personas.[5]

Desde ya, estoy a su disposición para ampliar cuando lo considere necesario.

Sin otro particular, aprovecho esta oportunidad para salu-
darlo muy atentamente.

Juan José Pérez Fernández

Anexo: Currículum Vitae

---

5. If you have little or no experience, instead of the preceding paragraph, you may want to say
simply: *Mi premura forma parte de haber finalizado mi carrera y la posibilidad de adquirir experiencia
en el área de personal.* (My haste is due to having finished my career and the possibility of acquiring
experience in the area of personnel.)

Buenos Aires, January 15, 1996

Mr. Ricardo Gomez
Personnel Manager

Re: Resume

Most esteemed Sir:

I am writing to submit my curriculum vitae for consideration
as a possible member of your enterprise.

I have read, with great interest, the advertisement published
in *La Nacion,* in which you express the desire to fill a vacancy
in your personnel department. I held the position of Director
of Personnel in the Diaz Bros. Advertising Agency for three
years. Both my work experience and my formal studies have
provided me with the necessary skills to manage a team of
twenty people.

Of course, I am available to discuss this further at your con-
venience.

Thank you for your attention to this matter.

Juan Jose Perez Fernandez

Juan Jose Perez Fernandez

Enc: Resume

If you get an interview, be cordial and natural, and try to let the interviewer know more about you. Keep in mind that developing a personal relationship is the key to successful business in Spanish-speaking countries. It is not uncommon for companies to request a graphology test during your interview. Because it is more difficult to fire someone in Spain and Latin America than in the United States, employers exercise greater caution when choosing an employee, and a graphologist's evaluation of your personality and character often plays a deciding role in the hiring process.

The initial interview is scheduled more for the benefit of the employer than the prospective employee. This is his or her opportunity to get to know you. Note that interviews tend to be much more formal in Spanish-speaking countries and that questions tend to be phrased indirectly, as if they were hypothetical rather than directly applicable to a specific individual. It is also considered rude to discuss wages or ask very specific questions about the job during this interview.

If you are selected for the position, you will be notified by telegram, letter, or telephone, and will then be asked to attend a second interview, during which you will have the opportunity to discuss the job, salary, and benefits in detail. Some companies may simply give you a folder containing such information for you to review on your own. You will generally be given a week or so to decide whether to accept the job. If you decide to take it, you should notify the employer immediately in writing.

Buenos Aires, 5 de febrero de 1996

Sr. Ricardo Gómez
Gerente de Personal

Estimado Sr. Gómez:

Le agradezco la entrevista que me concedió el 1° de
febrero del corriente, en la que Vd. me dió la posibilidad de
hablarle en persona y de conocer detalles adicionales rela-
tivos a la posición de Director de Personal. Puedo asegurarle que realizaré, a partir del 15 de marzo del corriente,
todas las tareas y responsabilidades inherentes a dicha
posición. Espero con gusto la segunda entrevista que me
ha otorgado el día 10 de febrero, durante la cual podremos
concretar los detalles administrativos correspondientes.
Sin otro particular, reitero mi agradecimiento a su atenta
consideración.

Cordialmente,

Juan José Pérez Fernández

Juan José Pérez Fernández

Buenos Aires, February 5, 1996

Mr. Ricardo Gomez
Personnel Manager

Dear Mr. Gomez:

Thank you for the interview on February 1, at which you
gave me the opportunity to speak to you in person and to
learn more about the position of Director of Personnel.
I can assure you that I will successfuly perform all the
duties and responsibilities for said position, beginning
March 15..

I look forward to the second interview that you have
granted me on February 10, at which time we will discuss
the specific administrative details.

I again thank you for your attention and consideration.

Cordially,

Juan Jose Perez Fernandez

EXAMEN (QUIZ)

A. *Complete las oraciones siguientes con la palabra o frase interrogativa que corresponda.* (Complete the following sentences using the appropriate interrogative word or phrase.)

1. ¿_____ es ese documento?—Es un currículum.
2. ¿_____ va Roberto de vacaciones?
3. Veo muchos autos. ¿_____ es el tuyo?—El verde.
4. ¿_____ es esa escultura?—Es de mármol.
5. ¿_____ pasa el ómnibus?—Por el centro.
6. ¿_____ necesita el informe?—Para el viernes.
7. ¿_____ han hecho la presentación?
8. ¿_____ cuesta el metro de esta tela?
9. ¿_____ vais a invitar al restaurante esta noche?—A Lope y a Teresa.
10. Ese hombre parece extranjero. ¿_____ es?

B. *Traduzca al español.* (Translate into Spanish.)

1. Which people do these coats belong to?
2. By when do you need the client list?
3. In which file cabinet are my documents?
4. How long have you been in the city?
5. Why isn't Gonzalo at the office today?

C. *Traduzca al inglés.* (Translate into English.)

1. ¿Por dónde está Mario?
2. ¿A cuánto están los tomates?
3. ¿Hace cuánto que es Vd. jefe de esta sección?
4. ¿A quiénes les escribes esas cartas?
5. ¿A quién conociste en la fiesta?

D. *Complete las siguientes oraciones con el pretérito perfecto.* (Complete the following sentences using the present perfect.)

1. *(Yo HACER)* muchos viajes por Sudamérica.
2. ¿Dónde *(ESTAR)*? En la oficina te *(ellos ESTAR)* buscando durante varias horas.
3. Su vasta experiencia laboral lo *(CAPACITAR)* para cumplir con todas las obligaciones que el puesto implica.
4. ¿*(PODER)* Vd. comunicarse con el Sr. González?
5. *(Nosotros REVISAR)* su curriculum y *(Nosotros VER)* que Vd. reúne las condiciones necesarias para ser entrevistada.

LECCION 5

A. DIALOGO

Una Navidad en la playa.

José María,[1] un uruguayo, invitó a su primo estadounidense Isaac a pasar las fiestas con su familia en Atlántida, Uruguay.[2] En este momento, toman mate[3] a la sombra de la carpa que alquilaron,[4] mientras la esposa de José María, Lorena, juega en la arena con los niños.

JOSE MARIA: Y, ¿qué tal el almuerzo?

ISAAC: Todo estuvo sabrosísimo, pero me parece que cuando vuelva, nadie me va a reconocer, ¡tan gordito y tan bronceado!

JOSE MARIA: No te preocupes, todos te van a envidiar. Supongo que estarán[5] pasando mucho frío ahora.

ISAAC: Supongo. Cuando salí de Nueva York anteayer, nevaba . . . La verdad es que me resulta difícil creer que sea Navidad y que estemos en la playa.

LORENA *(llega corriendo agitada):* ¡Salud, señores! Veo que la pasan bien[6] acá en la sombrita . . . ¿Me ceban[7] un mate?

JOSE MARIA: ¡Cómo no! Los chicos, ¿se divierten?

LORENA: ¡Claro! Con todos los juguetes nuevos, están re-contentos.[8] Sin embargo, no creo que les duren hasta Reyes.[9]

ISAAC: ¿Reyes? No sé que es eso.

LORENA: El día de los Tres Reyes Magos. El seis de enero, los chicos reciben regalos en los zapatos que dejan la noche anterior al lado de la cama. ¿Vds. no celebran Reyes en el gran país del norte?[10]

ISAAC: No. ¡Qué pena que no conocía la tradición de chico! Siempre recibía regalos sólo en la Navidad y además, teníamos que esperar hasta la mañana, el día de Navidad, para abrirlos.[11] Me acuerdo cómo me costaba[12] dormirme . . .

JOSE MARIA: ¡No me hagas acordar![13] Anoche, ¡los chicos se durmieron a las cuatro!

ISAAC: Y, sí. Además, estaban muy acelerados después de ver el pesebre viviente . . .[14] Anoche fue la primera vez que vi algo parecido. ¿Se hace todos los años?

JOSE MARIA: ¡Claro! Es una tradición que viene de España. Cuando Lorena y yo éramos chicos, siempre nos gustaba participar en él: Era un gran honor. Me acuerdo cómo un par de veces hice de pastor.

LORENA: Sí. Le gustaba tanto que ¡lo tenían que sobornar con promesas de regalazos para Reyes!

ISAAC: La verdad es que es una tradición muy feliz para los niños . . . lo único parecido que tenemos en Nueva York, es el alumbrado del árbol del "Rockefeller Center."

JOSE MARIA: ¡Debe ser muy hermoso! Quizás el año que viene podamos ir a verlo. El año pasado lo vimos por televisión.

ISAAC: ¡Ya saben que los espero cuando puedan!

LORENA: Bueno, vuelvo más tarde. Los chicos me hacen señas para que vuelva . . .

ISAAC: Espérate un momento, que quiero hacer un brindis. José, ¿trajimos la heladerita del auto? Les traje un regalito desde Nueva York . . .

JOSE MARIA *(abriendo la heladerita):* ¡Una botella de champán!

LORENA: ¡Y copas de plástico!

ISAAC: ¡Bárbaro!¹⁵ Chicos, tomemos, salud! ¡Felices fiestas!

TODOS: ¡Felices fiestas!

CHRISTMAS AT THE BEACH.

Jose Maria, a Uruguayan, invited his American cousin Isaac to spend the holiday season with his family in Atlantida, Uruguay. Now, both are drinking *mate* under the shade of the tent they rented, while Lorena, Jose Maria's wife, is playing with their children in the sand.

JOSE MARIA: Well, what did you think of lunch?

ISAAC: Everything was delicious! The only problem is that when I go back home, nobody's going to recognize me. I'll be so tan and chubby!

JOSE MARIA: Don't worry about it! Everybody's going to be jealous. I suppose they must be pretty cold right now.

ISAAC: I guess so. When I left New York the day before yesterday, it was snowing . . . Actually, I find it hard to believe that it's Christmas, and we're at the beach.

LORENA (running up, out of breath): Hello, gentlemen! I see you're enjoying the shade . . . could I have some *mate?*

JOSE MARIA: Sure! Are the kids having fun?

LORENA: They sure are! They're really happy with all their new toys. I get the feeling they won't last until Three Kings Day, though.

ISAAC: Three Kings Day? What's that?

LORENA: The three wise men's visit. On January 6th, children find presents in the shoes they leave out the night before. Don't you celebrate Three Kings Day in the great northern country?

ISAAC: Nope. I'm sorry I didn't know about it when I was a kid. I only got presents for Christmas. And then we had to wait 'til the next day, Christmas Day, to open them. I remember how hard it was to fall asleep . . .

JOSE MARIA: Don't remind me! Last night the kids finally fell asleep at four!

ISAAC: Yeah, I can't believe how excited they were after seeing the "Living Nativity" . . . Last night was the first time I ever saw anything like it. Is it done every year?

JOSE MARIA: Of course! It's a tradition that comes from Spain. When Lorena and I were children, we always loved to participate. It was a great honor! I remember playing a shepherd a few times.

LORENA: Yes. He loved it so much that they had to bribe him with promises of enormous gifts on Three Kings Day!

ISAAC: The truth is that it's a great tradition for children! The closest thing we have to that in New York is the lighting of the tree at Rockefeller Center.

JOSE MARIA: It must be very beautiful! Maybe next year we can go and see it. Last year we saw it on TV.

ISAAC: You know you're welcome anytime you can make it!

LORENA: Well, I'll be back later. The kids are waving for me to come back . . .

ISAAC: Hold on a second, I want to propose a toast. Jose, did we bring the cooler from the car? I brought you all a little present from New York . . .

JOSE MARIA (opening the cooler): A bottle of champagne!

LORENA: And plastic cups!

ISAAC: Great! Guys, let's drink; to your health! Happy Holidays!

EVERYONE: Happy Holidays!

B. APUNTES

1. *José María* is a popular name for men in Spanish. Compare with *María José*, which is a woman's name.

2. *Atlántida* is a seaside city in Uruguay, about 35 miles from Montevideo, the capital. With its white sand beaches surrounded by beautiful eucalyptus and pine forests, as well as its quiet, small-town atmosphere, Atlantida is a popular vacation spot for families from Uruguay and neighboring Argentina. Uruguay is located north of the *Río de la Plata*. Due to its small population, and despite its former rule by military governments, Uruguay is developing a stable and growing economy.

3. *Mate* is a native South American herb prepared like tea. Ground herb leaves are placed into a special holder, also called a *mate*, and hot water is poured over them. The drink is then sipped through a special metal straw. When one person finishes drinking, more hot water is poured into the *mate*, and the next person continues, until the hot water runs out. Drinking *mate* is very popular in Argentina, Paraguay, southern Brazil, and Uruguay, where it represents a ritual of sharing among friends. People usually sip *mate* over the course of a full day. It contains a mild, non-addictive stimulant similar to caffeine, and it also aids digestion.

4. On many South American beaches, a section of the beach far from the seashore is set up with tents that can be rented, usually at a low cost. These tents are very convenient because the weather can be unpredictable, and the sun is dangerous during mid-day hours. South Americans generally spend most of Christmas Day at the beach with their family and friends.

5. The simple future can express doubt when used in place of the present. *¿Dónde podré conseguir más agua para el mate?* (I wonder where I could get more water for the *mate?*) For more on the uses of the simple future, see *Gramática y usos, Lección 7.*

6. *Pasarla bien* (to have a good time) is used very often in Spanish. *¿La pasaron bien en la playa ayer?* (Did you have a good time at the beach yesterday?)

7. *Cebar* (literally: "to feed animals") can also mean "to prepare *mate* for someone" in *mate*-drinking countries.

8. The prefix *re-* is often used with adjectives as an intensifier in South American slang. *Me regalaron un autito de juguete re-bueno para Navidad.* (I got a really good toy car for Christmas.) In proper Spanish, *muy* is used instead.

9. *El día de los reyes magos* (Three Kings Day) is celebrated throughout Latin American and in Spain, and presents (usually toys) are given to children on this day.

10. *El gran país del norte* is a nickname for the U.S.

11. In Spanish-speaking countries, Christmas is actually celebrated on Christmas Eve, with a large dinner party. Presents are opened at midnight on *Nochebuena* (Christmas Eve), not on Christmas morning.

12. When followed by a verb in the infinitive, *costar* means "to be difficult." *Me cuesta mucho levantarme por las mañanas.* (It's difficult for me to get up in the morning.)

13. *¡No me hagas acordar!* (Don't remind me!) is a popular slang expression in Uruguay and Argentina.

14. *El pesebre viviente* (The Living Nativity) is part of a popular religious act where people re-enact the Nativity scene in costumes. It is celebrated throughout Latin America and in Spain and is generally performed in public parks, plazas, or outside of churches.

15. *¡Bárbaro!* (literally: "Barbaric!") is an Argentinian and Uruguayan slang term for "Great!"

C. GRAMATICA Y USOS

1. *EL PRETERITO* (THE PRETERITE)

The preterite tense is formed by adding a series of endings *(-é, -aste, -ó, -amos, -asteis, -aron)* to the stem of *-ar* verbs, and another set of endings *(-í, -iste, -ió, -imos, -isteis, -ieron)* to the stem of *-er* and *-ir* verbs. Some verbs have irregular preterite stems that must be memorized.

	DESCANSAR TO REST	COMER TO EAT	VIVIR TO LIVE
yo	*descansé*	*comí*	*viví*
tú	*descansaste*	*comiste*	*viviste*
él/ella/Vd.	*descansó*	*comió*	*vivió*
nosotros	*descansamos*	*comimos*	*vivimos*
vosotros	*descansasteis*	*comisteis*	*vivisteis*
ellos/ellas/Vds.	*descansaron*	*comieron*	*vivieron*

The preterite tense is used to express actions that were completed at a specified time in the past.

Ayer me levanté, me vestí y me fui al trabajo.
Yesterday I got up, I got dressed, and I left for work.

El año pasado recibí muchos regalos en el día de Reyes.
Last year, I got a lot of presents on Three Kings Day.

2. *EL IMPERFECTO* (THE IMPERFECT)

The imperfect tense is formed by adding the appropriate personal endings to the stem of regular verbs. The endings are: *-aba, -abas, -ábamos, -abais,* and *-aban* for *-ar* verbs, and *-ía, -ías, -ía, -íamos, -íais,* and *-ían* for *-er* and *-ir* verbs. There are only three irregular verbs in the imperfect tense: *ir, ser,* and *ver.*

	NADAR TO SWIM	BEBER TO DRINK	RECIBIR TO RECEIVE
yo	*nadaba*	*bebía*	*recibía*
tú	*nadabas*	*bebías*	*recibías*
él/ella/Vd.	*nadaba*	*bebía*	*recibía*
nosotros	*nadábamos*	*bebíamos*	*recibíamos*
vosotros	*nadabais*	*bebíais*	*recibíais*
ellos/ellas/Vds.	*nadaban*	*bebían*	*recibían*

The imperfect is used to describe continuous or habitual actions in the past. It is equivalent to the English continuous past "was/were" + gerund, or "used to" forms.

Cuando vivíamos cerca de la costa, nos íbamos a la playa casi todos los días.
When we used to live near the coast, we would go to the beach almost every day.

Cuando yo era niño, esperaba ansiosamente las Fiestas.
When I was a child, I used to look forward to the holiday season anxiously.

¿Qué hacías cuando llegaron los reyes, Pablito?—Dormía.
What were you doing when the kings arrived, Pablito?—I was sleeping.

Antes de que construyeran aquel edificio, se veían las montañas desde la ventana de la sala.
Before they erected that building, you could see the mountains from the living room window.

3. *CONTRASTE: EL PRETERITO Y EL IMPERFECTO* (CONTRAST: THE PRETERITE AND THE IMPERFECT)

a) **Emphasis vs. Description**
The preterite and the imperfect tenses can be used to contrast actions in the past. Use the preterite to focus on a specific action, and the imperfect to "set the stage," or to describe simultaneously occurring circumstances. Note the following examples:

Cuando llamaste por teléfono, María miraba televisión, Jorge leía, y yo escribía una carta.
> When you called, Maria was watching TV, Jorge was reading, and I was writing a letter.

Yo dormía y soñaba que la vida era alegría.
Desperté, y ví que la vida era servicio.
Serví, y ví que el servicio era alegría.
> *(Rabindranat Tagore, filósofo y poeta hindú)*

> I was sleeping and dreaming that life was happiness.
> I awoke, and saw that life was service.
> I served, and saw that service was happiness.
> (Rabindranat Tagore, Hindi philosopher and poet)

b) **Verbs That Change Meaning in the Preterite.**
Some verbs have different meanings in the imperfect and in the preterite.

tener (to have; to receive)

De niño, tenía muchos juguetes.
> As a child, I had many toys.

Ayer tuve noticias sobre mi hermano.
> Yesterday I received news of my brother.

querer (to want; to try, when negative: to refuse to)

Quería abrir la puerta, pero no lo hice.
> I wanted to open the door, but I didn't do it.

No quería abrir la puerta.
> I didn't want to open the door.

Quise abrir la puerta, pero no lo logré.
> I tried to open the door, but I didn't manage to.

No quise abrir la puerta.
> I refused to open the door.

poder (to be able to; to succeed in)

No podía comunicarme por teléfono con Caracas.
I wasn't able to get a call through to Caracas.

No pude comunicarme por teléfono con Caracas.
I didn't succeed in getting a call through to Caracas.

conocer (to know; to meet)

De niño, conocía al actual presidente de Uruguay.
As a child, I used to know the current president of Uruguay.

Conocí al presidente de Uruguay anoche.
I met the president of Uruguay last night.

saber (to know; to find out)

Ya sabía acerca de tu problema ayer.
I already knew about your problem yesterday.

Supe acerca de tu problema ayer.
I found out the news yesterday.

4. *EXPRESIONES DE TIEMPO* (EXPRESSIONS OF TIME)

To ask how long an action has been in progress, use *hace cuánto (tiempo que)* + a verb in the present indicative. To express how long an action has been in progress, use *hace* + a period of time + *que* + a verb in the present tense. Note that where English uses a past tense, Spanish uses the present because, although the action began in the past, it continues in the present.

Hace más de veinte años que celebramos la Navidad con mis suegros.
We've been celebrating Christmas with my in-laws for over twenty years.

Hace cinco años que estoy con la empresa y creo que es hora de hacer un cambio.
I've been with the company for five years, and I think it's time for a change.

¿Hace cuánto que me esperan aquí sentados en la playa?—Hace una hora.
How long have you been sitting here at the beach waiting for me?
—For an hour.

When followed by a negative phrase, *hace* expresses how long an action has not occurred.

¿Hace cuánto que no ves a María?—Hace varias semanas.
How long has it been since you last saw Maria?—It's been several weeks.

Hace tres meses que Jorge no llama.
Jorge hasn't called in three months.

When used with a verb in the preterite, *hace* is used to indicate how long ago an action occurred.

Me mudé a los Estados Unidos hace quince años.
I moved to the United States fifteen years ago.

¿Hace cuánto que te fuiste de vacaciones?—Hace seis meses.
How long ago did you go on vacation?—Six months ago.

Another way to express the duration of an action is with *por* and *por cuánto tiempo*. Note, however, that *por* can be used in conjunction with a tense other than the present indicative.

¿Por cuánto tiempo trabajaste en la empresa cuando te despidieron?
How long were you working for the company when you were let go?

Estaré en viaje de negocios por tres semanas.
I will be away on business for three weeks.

D. HABLEMOS DE NEGOCIOS

LOS FERIADOS (HOLIDAYS)

Spanish-speaking people take their holidays very seriously. On national holidays, business usually comes to a halt. Large festivities with *procesiones* (processions) and *actos públicos* (large public acts) are common, even in large cities. Spain and Mexico have many traditional city festivals in small towns, as well. Religious holidays (Spanish-speaking countries are mostly Catholic) are greatly respected and may also reduce or stop business. When calling a Spanish-speaking country on, or the day before a national holiday, it is polite to congratulate people upon finishing the conversation. Following are some phrases you could use to congratulate your business partners on their national holidays:

Lo felicito en el día de . . .
Felicitaciones en el día de . . .
Saludos en vuestro día de . . .
Congratulations on . . . day.

Following is a partial list of national holidays in Latin America and in Spain.

January 1	*Día de Año Nuevo*	New Year's Day	All
January 6	*Reyes Magos*	Three King's Day	Argentina, Colombia, Dominican Republic, Puerto Rico, Spain Uruguay
January 11	*Natalicio de De Hostos*	Birth of De Hostos	Puerto Rico
January 21	*Altagracia*	Day of Altagracia	Dominican Republic
January 26	*Natalicio de Duarte*	Birth of Duarte	Dominican Republic
February 3	*San Blas*	Saint Blas	Paraguay
February 5	*Constitución*	Anniversary of the Constitution	Mexico
February 27	*Día de la Independencia*	Independence Day	Dominican Republic
March 19	*Día de San José*	St. Joseph's Day	Spain (even years), Colombia, Venezuela
March 21	*Natalicio de Benito Juárez*	Birth of Benito Juárez	Mexico
March 22	*Abolición de la Esclavitud*	Abolition of Slavery	Puerto Rico
April 11	*Batalla de Rivas*	Battle of Rivas	Costa Rica
April 16	*Natalicio de De Diego*	Birth of De Diego	Puerto Rico
April 19	*Firma de la Independencia*	Signing of Independence	Venezuela
May 1	*Día del Trabajo*	Labor Day	All except Puerto Rico
May 5	*Batalla de Puebla*	Battle of Puebla	Mexico
May 15	*Día de la Independencia*	Independence Day	Paraguay
May 18	*Batalla de Las Piedras*	Battle of Las Piedras	Uruguay
May 25	*Revolución de Mayo* *Día de la Revolución*	May Revolution Revolution Day	Argentina Chile

June 4	*Día del Ejército*	Army Day	Venezuela
June 10	*Día de la Soberanía*	Sovereignty Day	Chile
June 19	*Natalicio de Artigas*	Birth of Artigas	Uruguay
June 20	*Día de la Bandera*	Flag Day	Argentina
June 24	*Batalla de Carabobo*	Battle of Carabobo	Venezuela
June 29	*Santos Pedro y Pablo*	Sts. Peter and Paul	Chile, Colombia, Peru, Puerto Rico
July 4	*Comicios*	Election Day	Mexico
July 5	*Día de la Independencia*	Independence Day	Venezuela
July 9	*Día de la Independencia*	Independence Day	Argentina
July 17	*Natalicio de Muñoz Rivera*	Birth of Muñoz Rivera	Puerto Rico (half holiday)
July 18	*Primera Constitución*	First Constitution	Uruguay
July 20	*Día de la Independencia*	Independence Day	Uruguay
July 24	*Natalicio de Simón Bolívar*	Birth of Simón Bolívar	Ecuador, Venezuela
July 25	*Día de San Santiago*	St. James's Day	Spain (odd years)
	Día de la Constitución	Constitution Day	Puerto Rico
July 27	*Natalicio de Barbosa*	Birth of Barbosa	Puerto Rico
July 28, 29	*Independencia Nacional*	Independence Day	Peru
August 2	*Virgen de Los Ángeles*	Virgin of Los Angeles	Costa Rica
August 6	*Independencia Nacional*	Independence Day	Bolivia
August 7	*Batalla de Boyacá*	Battle of Boyaca	Colombia
August 15	*Asunción de Nuestro Señor*	Assumption	Colombia, Chile, Spain
	Día de la Madre	Mother's Day	Costa Rica
	Fundación de Caacupé	Founding of Caacupé	Paraguay
August 16	*Día de la Restauración*	Restoration Day	Dominican Republic
	Primer grito de Independencia	First Cry of Independence	Ecuador

77

August 17	*Día del Libertador General San Martín*	Day of General San Martin the Liberator	Argentina
August 25	*Día de la Independencia*	Independence Day	Uruguay
August 30	*Santa Rosa de Lima*	St. Rosa of Lima	Peru
September 1	*Discurso Presidencial*	Presidential Address	Mexico
September 15	*Día de la Independencia*	Independence Day	El Salvador
September 16	*Día de la Independencia*	Independence Day	Mexico
September 24	*Nuestra Señora de las Mercedes*	Our Lady of Mercedes	Dominican Republic
October 12	*Día de la Raza*	Columbus Day	All (except Mexico)
November 1	*Día de todos los Santos*	All Saints' Day	Argentina, Colombia, Dominican Republic, Peru, Spain, Venezuela
November 2	*Día de todas las Almas*	All Souls' Day	Bolivia, Ecuador, Mexico, Uruguay
November 11	*Independencia de Cartagena*	Independence of Cartagena	Venezuela
November 20	*Revolución Libertadora*	Revolution Day	Mexico
November 24	*Día de los Veteranos*	Veterans Day	Puerto Rico
December 8	*Immaculada Concepción*	Immaculate Conception	All
December 25	*Navidad*	Christmas Day	All
December 26	*Día del Boxeo*	Boxing Day	Puerto Rico

The following holidays vary:

February (week of Ash Wednesday)	*Carnaval*	Carnival Week	Argentina, Uruguay, Venezuela
March/April/ May	*Jueves Santo*	Maundy Thursday	All (except Spain)
	Viernes Santo	Good Friday	All
	Corpus Christi	Corpus Christi	All (except Mexico)

EXAMEN

A. *Complete las oraciones siguientes con el pretérito o el imperfecto de los verbos indicados.* (Complete the following sentences with the preterite or the imperfect of the indicated verbs.)

1. *De niño, Yo RECIBIR muchos regalos en las fiestas.*
2. *Cuando yo ENTRAR, el jefe HABLAR por teléfono.*
3. *Yo los OIR mientras ellos DISCUTIR.*
4. *Cuando ellos LLEGAR al aeropuerto, HACER mucho frío.*
5. *Unos hombres CONVERSAR, mientras otros TRABAJAR.*
6. *¿Vosotros RESOLVER el asunto de negocios ayer?*
7. *¿Tú MIRAR la televisión a menudo cuando ESTAR en España el año pasado?*
8. *Anoche, yo no PODER abrir la puerta porque no TENER las llaves.*
9. *A veces, yo no PODER abrir la puerta porque no TENER las llaves.*
10. *Los amigos de Juan QUERER salir ayer a las siete, pero HACER demasiado frío.*

B. *Cambie las oraciones siguientes al pretérito y luego, tradúzcalas.* (Rewrite the following sentences in the preterite, then translate them.)

1. *La compañía no tiene suficientes empleados en la sección de exportaciones.*
2. *¿Por qué no se lo dices al jefe?*
3. *No puedo hacerlo solo. Necesito ayuda.*
4. *Buscáis los informes en el archivero equivocado.*
5. *No tenemos tiempo para ir a la fábrica.*

C. *Traduzca las oraciones siguientes al español.* (Translate the following sentences into Spanish.)

1. We haven't seen Aunt Maria in three months.
2. How long have you *(vosotros)* been in Uruguay?
3. How long ago did Pablo leave for the U.S.?
4. You *(Vds.)* haven't spent Christmas with us in a long time.
5. You *(tú)* played a shepherd in the "Living Nativity" twenty years ago!

LECTURA

La lengua española tiene hoy día una gran difusión[1] en todo el mundo, siendo el idioma nativo de unas trescientas millones de personas. También se conoce con el nombre de lengua castellana, pues este idioma se originó en la región española de castilla, desde la cual se ha extendido hasta los más remotos rincones del planeta. ¿Cuáles son los orígenes de esta lengua? Para conocerlos, debemos familiarizarnos con la historia lingüística de la península ibérica.

Los habitantes más antiguos de la península ibérica eran unos pueblos[2] llamados celtíberos.[3] Estos pueblos nómadas[4] hablaban una lengua sonora y dura. Hoy día, quedan pocas muestras[5] de su sonora lengua en algunos de los vocablos[6] más antiguos del español moderno, tales como perro, zorro y barro.

Otro de los pueblos que habitaron la antigua iberia eran los griegos. La dulce lengua griega influyó en el habla de los antiguos íberos, suavizando la pronunciación de ciertas consonantes, notablemente las interdentales suaves d y c.

Indudablemente, el habla de los íberos fue modificado notablemente con la llegada del latín. La península ibérica fue una de las primeras regiones conquistadas por los romanos, quienes trajeron consigo su lengua. Cabe mencionar que los conquistadores romanos trajeron consigo el sermo vulgaris, *o latín popular, el cual se diferenciaba considerablemente del* sermo nobilis, *o latín noble. De la mezcla del* sermo vulgaris *y de la lengua de los íberos surge el idioma llamado* romance, *denominación[7] que proviene de hablar «a la romana». Esta lengua, esqueleto[8] del español moderno, era hablado por la gente común, mientras que la nobleza de la antigua «Hispania» romana utilizaba el latín. Cabe mencionar que algunos de los escritores de la época de plata de la literatura latina, tales como Séneca y Marcial provenían de esta antigua provincia romana.*

La posterior caída del imperio de Roma y la llegada de los pueblos germánicos aportó[9] aún más vocablos al romance. Muchos de éstos eran de carácter militar, tales como guante, marqués, yelmo y pico alcohol.

La llegada de los árabes a la península en el año 711 de nuestra era influyó considerablemente en la evolución del romance. Al poco tiempo de llegar, la lengua árabe aportó numerosísimos vocablos, tanto de origen comercial (tales como azúcar, aceite y alfombra), *así como militar y financiero (*alguacil y aduana) *al idioma de los españoles.*

Luego de la lenta reconquista del territorio por parte de los cristianos, existían en España varias lenguas neolatinas, algunas de las cuales aún se hablan hoy en día, como por ejemplo el catalán y el gallego. Sin embargo, para la época del

Renacimiento, el idioma castellano fue instaurado por Alfonso X «El Sabio» como lengua oficial de España.

Para esa época, el español se vio enriquecido por aportes de los idiomas indígenas americanos, con palabras de productos y objetos hasta entonces desconocidos, tales como yuca, poncho, piraña, maíz, hamaca, *y* canoa. *Paralelamente, los españoles llevaron su idioma al nuevo mundo, donde tomó raíces en el suelo americano.*

Se puede decir que el idioma español moderno presenta dos variantes principales en su pronunciación. En España, la lengua tiene una pronunciación un tanto más fuerte, mientras que en Latinoamérica ésta es algo más suave. El ceceo, o pronunciación interdental de la z y de la c suave es común sólo en España. En América Latina, por otra parte, el seseo, o pronunciación silbante de la z y de la c suave es de uso común. Algúnos opinan que ello se debe a que la mayoría de los colonos españoles provenían de la región de Andalucía, origen del seseo, mientras que otros opinan que se debe a la influencia de la fonética de los idiomas de los indígenas americanos. Lo cierto es que esta pequeña diferencia de pronunciación no afecta la comprensión en lo absoluto[10] entre españoles y latinoamericanos.

La lengua española presenta una gran homogeneidad en todo el mundo, debido a la acción reguladora de la Real Academia Española, custodia fiel de la evolución de la lengua castellana en todo el mundo. Hoy día, el español se ve enriquecido con aportes de la lengua inglesa, sobre todo en lo comercial y en lo técnico, con palabras tales como finanzas, módem *y* mítin, *sin por ello[11] dejar de mantener su identidad como lengua importantísima en el mundo.*

VOCABULARIO

1. *difusión:* diffusion, spreading
2. *pueblo:* in this context, "people, nation, tribe"
3. *celtíberos: (celtas e íberos):* an ancient people, mixture of Celts and Iberians
4. *nómadas:* nomads, nomadic
5. *muestras:* samples
6. *vocablo:* word
7. *denominación:* name
8. *esqueleto:* skeleton
9. *aportar:* to contribute
10. *en lo absoluto:* absolutely not
11. *por ello:* for that reason/due to it

MARCELO: **Bueno, si compro la computadora y la impresora juntas, ¿me haría³ un precio especial?¹⁴**

VENDEDORA: **En realidad, el precio lo fija la empresa fabricante . . . pero sí. Le puedo hacer un descuento del 10 por ciento, como estudiante. ¿Lo pagaría a crédito o en efectivo?**

MARCELO: **Quiero pagar la mitad en efectivo y el resto a crédito, en cuotas . . . o si no, ¿tienen algún plan de pagos?**

VENDEDORA: **Sí, con nuestro plan, paga menos interés que comprando con tarjeta de crédito. Todo viene con garantía de fábrica, pero también le daremos una nuestra, por 30 días. Si tuviere algún problema, tráiganosla y se la arreglaremos o cambiaremos gratis.¹⁵ Como ve, no tiene nada que perder.**

MARCELO: **Espero no tener que utilizarla, pero me quedo más tranquilo. ¿Tendría algunos folletos que pudiera leer, antes de decidirme?**

VENDEDORA: **¡Cómo no! Aquí los tiene, y también mi tarjeta. Llámeme si tuviere alguna otra pregunta.**

MARCELO: **De hecho, tengo una pregunta más: ¿La computadora viene con algunos programas?**

VENDEDORA: **Sólo los básicos. Temo que tendrá que adquirir lo que necesite por separado.**

MARCELO: **Ya veo. Bueno, hasta luego y muchísimas gracias por su ayuda.**

VENDEDORA: **¡A sus órdenes! ¡Hasta pronto!**

Buying a computer.

Marcelo and his friend, Paula, are walking down *Vía España* in Panama City, when suddenly, Marcelo stops in front of a computer store window.

PAULA: Marcelo, come on, what are you looking at?

MARCELO: Hold on! Take a look at this new computer in the window.

PAULA: Oh! So, you still want to buy a computer for your studies . . .

MARCELO: Yes, I'd like to buy one, but I can't decide which one. For now, I only need it to write papers, and a laptop computer would be ideal. On the other hand who knows what I might need it for later on? Besides, a desktop model is faster and more expandable.

PAULA: Well, why don't we go in? Anyway, it doesn't cost anything to ask, and maybe they can help you decide. What are you waiting for? Let's go already!

Marcelo and Paula go into the store. They are immediately approached by a saleswoman.

SALESWOMAN: Are you being helped?

MARCELO: Not yet. I'd like to see the computer in the window.

SALESWOMAN: Which one are you referring to?

MARCELO: The X-9000.

SALESWOMAN: Oh, yes! It's a relatively new model, and it sells very well. Let me show it to you. We have a demo model on that little table over there.

MARCELO: Of course!

SALESWOMAN: As you know, the X-9000 is a portable model, ideal for people who work outside the office, or those who need a home computer but don't have the room for a desktop.

MARCELO: I'm a university student, and I'd bring it with me to the library.

SALESWOMAN: With the built-in long-life battery, you shouldn't have any problems.

MARCELO: And, what operating system does it run on?

SALESWOMAN: It's a standard graphic operating system. It's compatible with desktop models, so you can run the same programs as on the larger models.

MARCELO: What about the memory?

SALESWOMAN: It has a large memory capacity, both in RAM and on floppy and hard disk. It can also be connected to a CD-ROM drive.

MARCELO: And the display?

SALESWOMAN: As you can see, it's color with very high resolution. See how clear the graphics are?

PAULA: Tell me, can you play any games on it?

SALESWOMAN: Of course. Although it's generally used for word processing and data management, you can also play games, but the audio and the video quality are better with the expansion package. It allows you to connect the computer to a larger monitor, to an audio system, or to stereo headphones.

PAULA: I think I like it much better now. . . .

MARCELO: It's a good thing I came with an expert like you, Paula!

SALESWOMAN: That's okay! Everybody asks about the games. . . . Tell me, what are you most interested in?

MARCELO: Normally, I would use it to write reports and access the university computer network.

SALESWOMAN: This one is just what you need, then. It has a high-speed modem, to save you money on your phone bill.

MARCELO: I'm worried that the keyboard is a little small. I generally write non-stop for several hours, and I'm afraid I might get tired.

SALESWOMAN: Don't worry about that! As I told you, the computer can be expanded easily. You can connect it to a standard size keyboard. You can also add on a monochrome monitor, to rest your eyes more.

MARCELLO: I like the computer a lot. Which printer would you recommend?

SALESWOMAN: I have a laser printer that suits your needs perfectly, and it's also very affordable.

MARCELO: Well, if I buy the computer and the printer together, could I get a special price?

SALESWOMAN: Actually, the price is set by the manufacturer. . . . But, yes, I can offer you a 10% discount, as a student. Would you pay in cash, or credit?

MARCELO: I'd like to pay half in cash and the rest with my credit card, in installments, or . . . Do you have a payment plan?

SALESWOMAN: Yes. Our plan beats the interest rate on all credit cards. Everything comes with a factory guarantee, but we'll also give you a store warranty for 30 days. If you have any problems, bring it to us, and we'll repair or exchange it for free. It's a no-risk deal!

MARCEL: I hope I won't have to use it, but I feel better knowing it's there. Do you have any brochures I can read, before making a final decision?

SALESWOMAN: Of course! Here you go, and here's my card. Call me if you have any questions.

MARCELO: As a matter of fact, I have one more question: Does the computer come with any software?

SALESWOMAN: Only the basics. I'm afraid you'd have to purchase what you need separately.

MARCELO: I see. Well, goodbye, and thank you very much for your help!

SALESWOMAN: At your service. See you soon.

B. APUNTES

1. *Ciudad de Panamá* (Panama City) is the capital of Panama, the country that divides Central America from South America. Thanks to the Panama Canal, Panama is Latin America's largest financial center, with multi-billion dollar banking and commercial activities. *Via España* is a wide, commercial street that turns into *Avenida Central,* Panama City's main avenue.

2. Other words for *vidriera* (store window) are *vitrina, escaparate,* and *parador.*

3. Note the use of the conditional in place of the indicative for politeness.

4. Note the difference between Spanish and English in the usage of prepositions. *Decidirse en/por* (to decide <u>on</u>): *Al final, me decidí por comprar un auto importado.* (In the end, I decided on buying an imported car.) And *depender <u>de</u>* (to depend <u>on</u>): *Todo depende de ti.* (Everything depends on you.).

5. The colloquial expressions *total* (anyway) and *ya que* (since anyway) are used to express a logical alternative. *Ya que vamos al centro, pasemos a saludar a Juan en el trabajo.* (Since we're going downtown anyway, we might as well drop by and visit Juan at work.) The more formal expression is *dado que* (given that). *Dado que es tan tarde, creo que será mejor continuar la reunión mañana.* (Given that it's so late, I think it would be best to continue the meeting tomorrow.)

6. *De una vez (por todas)* means "finally, at last" It is used to express impatience. *¡Ponte el abrigo de una vez, que vamos a llegar tarde!* (Would you finally put on your coat? We're going to be late!) To express joyous expectation or relief, use *¡Por fin!* instead. *¡Por fin vamos a ir a Europa!* (We're finally going to go to Europe!) *¡Por fin llegaste! ¡Estábamos tan preocupados!* (You're here, at last! We were so worried!)

7. Note the use of *se* to indicate an impersonal subject, in this case, the fact that the computer is sold at the store. For more on the uses of "impersonal *se,*" see *Gramática y usos, Lección 8.*

8. Beware of "false friends" (words that look similar but have different meanings in Spanish and English). *Una librería* is a bookstore. A library is *una biblioteca.*

9. *Una batería* is a large battery, whereas *una pila* is a small battery or energy cell used in portable appliances such as radios.

10. Both *estándar* and *norma* mean "standard, norm" but *estándar* is used to refer to commercial product standards, and *norma* is used in all other fields. *Él siempre va en contra de las normas, es un tanto eccéntrico.* (He always goes against the norm; he's a little eccentric.)

11. Aside from its use in comparative sentences, *tanto . . . como* (as much as) is used to replace *y* (and) in a more elegant form. *Me gusta leer tanto como escribir.* (I like to read and write). *Carmen es tanto bonita como inteligente.* (Carmen is both pretty and intelligent.)

12. The adjective *nítido* means "clear, clean, in focus." It is the opposite of *turbio* "unclear, dirty, out of focus." In computer jargon, *nitidez* means "print or display quality."

13. The expression *más que nada* (more than anything) can be used to replace *mayormente* (mostly).

14. Although bargaining *(regatear)* seems somewhat improper to Americans, it is very common in Spanish-speaking countries, especially at flea markets and, to some extent, in specialty stores. It should, however, be avoided in boutiques or expensive shops. *Mónica siempre regatea en el mercado.* (Monica always bargains at the market.)

15. *Gratis* can be used both as an adverb (for free), or as an adjective, replacing *gratuito* (free). Note that *gratis* does not change to reflect gender or number when used as an adjective. *Nuestra tienda ofrece entrega gratuita/gratis.* (Our store offers free delivery.)

C. GRAMATICA Y USOS

1. *EL INFINITIVO* (THE INFINITIVE)

An infinitive is the unconjugated form of a verb: *amar, aprender, bendecir.* As you know, all Spanish infinitives end in *-ar, -er,* or *-ir.*

Ser o no ser, he ahí la cuestión.
To be or not to be, that is the question.

Quiero probar comida japonesa esta noche en el restaurante.
I want to try Japanese food at the restaurant tonight.

Infinitives may be used as nouns, in which case they are considered masculine, singular and are often introduced by the definite article *el.* In a sentence, infinitives can function as the subject or object. Note that the English counterpart to the Spanish infinitive is often the *-ing* form of a verb.

No puedo decidirme, ¿cuál impresora me conviene comprar?
I can't decide which printer to buy.

El hacer ejercicios es bueno para mantener la salud.
Exercising is good for staying healthy.

As in English, infinitives are often used in Spanish to indicate purpose, in which case they must be introduced by the preposition *para*.

El diario envió un corresponsal para entrevistar al Embajador de España.
The newspaper sent a reporter to interview the Spanish ambassador.

Compré la computadora para poder escribir mis informes más fácilmente.
I bought the computer so that I could write my reports more easily.

The preposition *a* may also be used to indicate purpose, usually in conjunction with verbs of motion.

Carlos se fue al centro a buscar la nueva computadora para el hogar que compró ayer.
Carlos went downtown to pick up the new home computer he bought yesterday.

Vine a preguntar el precio de la computadora en la vidriera.
I came to find out the price of the computer in the store window.

To express that an action is easy, difficult, complicated, etc. to perform, use the formula: adjective + *(de)* + infinitive. The agent of the action then becomes the indirect object.

Me es muy difícil (de) comprender las instrucciones que vinieron con la computadora.
It's very hard for me to understand the instructions that came with the computer.

¡A Luisa le resulta imposible (de) encontrar los papeles en tanto desorden!
It's impossible for Luisa to find the papers in such a mess!

The infinitive may also be used with the verbs *ver* and *oír* to indicate seeing or hearing something happen. In this construction, the direct object pronoun is always used in addition to the direct object itself.

Lo vi a Carlos jugar juegos electrónicos con su computadora nueva. ¡Los gráficos son impactantes!
I saw Carlos playing video games on his new computer. The graphics are amazing!

Los escuché a tus colegas hablar mal de ti.
I heard your colleagues speaking poorly of you.

2. LOS ADVERBIOS (ADVERBS)

Spanish adverbs are generally formed by adding the suffix *-mente* to the feminine form of adjectives. Note that the adverb retains the stress pattern of the adjective with the help of an accent.

Nuevamente nos referimos a la nueva línea de ordenadores, que momentáneamente verán.
We are referring again to our new line of computers, which you will see shortly.

Conviene comparar precios cuidadosamente antes de comprar una computadora.
It's better to compare prices carefully before buying a computer.

The only irregular adverbs in Spanish are *bien* (well) and *mal* (wrong, badly, poorly). While the regular forms *buenamente* and *malamente* do exist, they do not mean "well" and "badly." Rather, *buenamente* can mean *fácilmente, cómodamente,* or *voluntariamente,* depending on context, and *malamente* can be used to mean *difícilmente, incómodamente,* or *contravoluntariamente.*

La computadora no funciona bien . . . ¿habré conectado mal los cables?
The computer isn't working well . . . could I have connected the cables incorrectly?

Malamente pudimos caber en el auto.
We barely managed to fit in the car.

Haz las tareas buenamente, o las harás malamente.
You'll do your homework, whether you like it or not!

If two adverbs are used consecutively in the same sentence, the suffix of the first may be omitted.

Esta línea les permitirá manejar datos rápida y eficazmente.
This line will allow you to manage data quickly and efficiently.

Tienes que aprender a bailar más lenta y rítmicamente.
You have to learn to dance more slowly and rhythmically.

For the sake of simplicity and ease of pronunciation, the masculine singular forms of adjectives may be used as adverbs, as long as their meaning in the sentence is clear.

La computadora modelo XR-1 permite hacer cálculos más rápido, porque cuenta con un coprocesador numérico incorporado.
Our computer model XR-1 allows you to crunch numbers more rapidly because it has a built-in numeric co-processor.

Les sugerimos que prueben todos los modelos por sí mismos. Solamente/Sólo[1] al comprobar por sí mismos su calidad, se convencerán.
We just suggest that you try the models yourselves. Only upon verifying their quality on your own, will you be convinced.

Some adverbs of degree have both colloquial and standard forms, such as: *todo/totalmente* (totally), *bastante/lo suficientemente* (enough), *casi todo/mayormente* (mostly), *medio/parcialmente/medianamente* (half, partially, medium, sort of, kind of).

Mayormente, me interesa la programación, pero también la electrónica.
I'm mostly interested in programming, but I also like electronics.

Acabo de comprar este tóner para mi impresora y ya está medio vacío.
I just bought this toner for my new printer, and it's already half-empty.

Estoy medio cansado, ¿podemos descansar un rato?
I'm sort of tired. Can we take a break for a while?

El noticiero pronosticó que hoy estaría parcialmente nublado, y de hecho, ya está medio nublado.
The weatherman predicted that tomorrow would be partly cloudly, and in fact, it's already sort of cloudy.

Other adverbs of degree have a single form that is used both formally and informally: *algo* (somewhat), *un poco/un tanto* (a little), *apenas* (barely), and *nada* (not . . . at all).

Esta impresora parece un tanto cara, ¿qué características especiales tiene?
This printer seems a little expensive. What special features does it have?

Aún estamos algo lejos de casa, y no me siento nada bien. Tomemos un taxi.
We're still somewhat far from home, and I don't feel well at all. Let's take a taxi.

3. *LA FORMACION DE ADVERBIOS Y ADJETIVOS CON "DE"* (THE FORMATION OF ADVERBS AND ADJECTIVES WITH DE)

De followed by a noun can also be used to create derived adjectives and adverbs.

Creo que adquirirá uno de nuestros modelos de buena gana, después de usarlo personalmente.
I think you will gladly buy one of our models after using it personally.

No sé cómo explicártela de la mejor manera. Es una situación de no creer.
I don't know how best to explain it to you. It's an unbelievable situation.

---

1. *Sólo* is the abbreviated form of the adverb *solamente,* which means "just/only." It is written with a stress mark to distinguish it from the adjective *solo,* which means "alone/by oneself."

D. HABLEMOS DE NEGOCIOS

LAS COMPUTADORAS (COMPUTERS AND COMPUTING)

The field of computers is experiencing tremendous growth and expansion in the Spanish-speaking world. In Spain, the computer industry is as developed as in the rest of Europe. In Latin America, the computer revolution hit a little later than in the U.S.: in the early 1980s. Today, some South American countries manufacture and market their own hardware and software. There are many small software firms that produce Spanish-language accounting, bookkeeping, and word-processing programs. The field of consumer electronics is, nevertheless, still dominated by Japanese, German, and U.S. imports to Latin America and Spain. Computer information networks *(telerredes),* especially networks that offer on-line services *(teleservicios de informática)* will continue to experience explosive growth in demand, as Latin America changes politically and economically.

Much of Spanish computer-related vocabulary is derived from English. For example: *bit, byte, cursor, error, hardware* (or *componentes de computación), MÓDEM, mouse* (or *manejacursor* or *selector manual), ROM* (or *memoria de lectura* or *memoria estática), sensor,* and *terminal* are all used in Spanish, as in English. The following diagram introduces the basic computer terms that any *usuario* (user) will need to know.

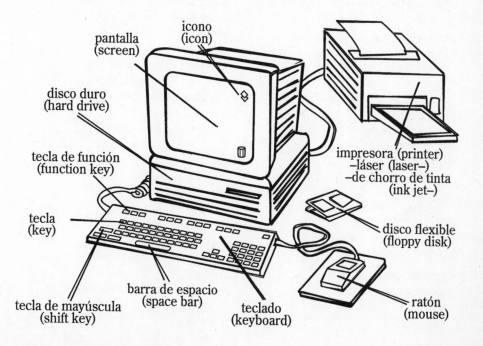

pantalla (screen)
icono (icon)
disco duro (hard drive)
tecla de función (function key)
tecla (key)
tecla de mayúscula (shift key)
barra de espacio (space bar)
teclado (keyboard)
impresora (printer) –láser (laser–) –de chorro de tinta (ink jet–)
disco flexible (floppy disk)
ratón (mouse)

bit (binary digit)	*bit/dígito binario*
bug (logical error in computer code)	*error*
button	*botón*
byte	*byte* (pronounced *báit*)
CAD (Computer-aided Design)	*Diseño electrónico* or *Diseño por Computadora*
CAM (Computer-aided Manufacturing)	*Fabricación con la ayuda de computadoras*
code	*código*
computer	*computador(a), ordenador*
PC (Personal Computer)	*computador personal*
portable computer/laptop	*computador(a) portátil*
-chip	*ficha o chip de computadora*
-language	*lenguaje de Computación*
-science	*informática*
cordless (adj.)	*inalámbrico*
CPU (Central Processing Unit)	*UCP (Unidad Central de Proceso)*
cursor	*curso*
data (computer)	*datos*
-processing	*procesamiento de datos*
debug (verb)	*pulir/limpiar (un programa)*
desktop (adj.)	*de escritorio*
e-mail	*correo electrónico*
error	*error*
file	*archivo*
to backup a -	*hacer una copia de seguridad de un -, salvaguardar un -*
to open a -	*abrir un -*
to close a -	*cerrar un -*
to update a -	*poner al día un -, realmacenar un -*
flowchart	*diagrama de flujo*
font	*(tipo de) letra*
bold	*negrita*
italic	*(en) itálicas*
underline	*subrayada*
graph	*gráfica*
computer	*gráficas de computadora*
graphic (adj.)	*gráfico*
hardware (computer)	*componentes de computación/ "hardware"*
input (to)	*ingresar*

interface	*interfase*
loop	*bucle*
nested-	*-integrado*
microprocessor	*microprocesador*
output (to)	*egresar (datos)*
peripherals	*periféricos*
print (to)	*imprimir*
processor	*procesador*
co-	*coprocesador*
RAM (Random-Access Memory)	*Memoria de Acceso Aleatorio, Memoria principal*
Record (computer information)	*registro*
ROM (Read-Only Memory)	*Memoria de Lectura, ROM, Memoria estática*
save (to)	*almacenar*
select (to)	*seleccionar*
software	*programas de computación*
switch	*interruptor*
word processor	*procesador de textos, textoprocesador*

EXAMEN

A. *Complete las oraciones siguientes con la preposición (a o para) y/o el infinitivo que corresponda.* (Complete the following sentences with the appropriate preposition—*a* or *para*—and/or infinitive.)

1. *Marcelo fue* (to buy) *una computadora a una gran tienda en la Vía España.*
2. *A Marcelo, la computadora le va a servir* (to write) *informes en la biblioteca.*
3. (To save) *dinero, hay que* (to walk around) *mucho* (to compare) *precios.*
4. *Conviene* (to buy) *el paquete de expansión,* (to be able to) (enjoy) *más de los juegos electrónicos.*
5. *Voy a* (to call) *a la vendedora* (to ask her) *el precio de la impresora.*

B. *Complete las oraciones siguientes con el adverbio o frase adverbial que corresponda.* (Complete the following sentences with the appropriate adverb or adverbial phrase.)

1. *Esta impresora imprime más* (fast) *y* (quietly) *que la mía.*
2. *Estoy* (a little) *desilusionado con el rendimiento de esta computadora.*
3. *¿Se ve más* (clearly, in focus) *en los monitores de alta resolución?*
4. *¡Habla más* (loudly) *porque el micrófono no funciona!*
5. *El cielo está* (partly) *nublado hoy.*

C. *Traduzca todas las oraciones del ejercicio B al inglés.* (Translate the sentences in Exercise B into English.)

D. *Traduzca las oraciones siguientes al español.* (Translate the following sentences into Spanish.)

1. I love to play computer games at home.
2. I heard the saleswoman explain how the new program works.
3. Juan heard Maria talk about her problems at the university.
4. We saw a man spend a lot of money on a computer at the store today.
5. Writing a sales report is easy with this new software.

LECCION 7

A. DIALOGO

UNA DIFÍCIL DECISIÓN EDUCATIVA.

Al señor Thompson, le han ofrecido un puesto importante en una empresa fabricante en Quito, Ecuador, por lo cual, habría de mudarse a Quito con su familia. Antes de aceptar, sin embargo, discute el efecto que tendría la mudanza en su familia.

SR. THOMPSON: **Hablando con toda franqueza, Sr. Márquez, el puesto que me ofrecen me interesa muchísimo, pero me preocupa el efecto que tendrá la mudanza en mi familia, en particular en mis hijos, pues ellos tendrán que cursar[1] sus estudios aquí . . . quisiera saber más acerca de la enseñanza en el Ecuador.**

SR. MARQUEZ: **Lo entiendo perfectamente. Yo mismo tengo dos hijos de edad escolar. Permítame asegurarle que la enseñanza en nuestro país es del más alto nivel.**

SR. THOMPSON: **¿Le parece que los niños se adapten con facilidad? ¿Qué tan diferentes son las escuelas aquí?**

SR. MARQUEZ: **Dígame, ¿qué edades tienen sus niños?**

SR. THOMPSON: **Scott tiene trece años y está cursando el octavo grado, y Jeremy, el mayor, tiene diecisiete y está a punto de ingresar[2] a la universidad.**

SR. MARQUEZ: **Bueno, el menor tendrá que elegir una escuela secundaria. Aquí tenemos cuatro tipos de escuelas secundarias: comerciales, bachilleratos, industriales y pedagógicas. Los planes de estudio y las materias son diferentes en cada una.**

SR. THOMPSON: **¿De qué manera?**

SR. MARQUEZ: **Los bachilleratos y las escuelas comerciales duran cinco años y son las más comunes. Los bachilleratos apuntan hacia carreras que tengan que ver con las humanidades: literatura, medicina, arte, etc. Hay énfasis especial en lenguas extranjeras así como en literatura, caligrafía,[3] geografía, e historia. Las comerciales, hacen énfasis en la contabilidad, lengua inglesa, mecanografía, computación, merciología y matemática comercial.**

SR. THOMPSON: **O sea que el niño debe decidirse antes de ingresar en una secundaria, en qué campo general va a realizar sus estudios universitarios.**

SR. MARQUEZ: Claro, pero si cambiara de idea, no sería fatal. Las universidades aceptan a alumnos de cualquier escuela.

SR. THOMPSON: ¿Y en cuánto a las otras escuelas?

SR. MARQUEZ: Las dos restantes son más específicas, ya que duran seis años y no cinco. Las escuelas pedagógicas preparan a los alumnos para ser maestros.[4] Por lo tanto,[5] estudian psicología, latín, pedagogía, etc. Las escuelas industriales suelen ofrecer tres especializaciones: uno se gradúa como técnico electrónico, mecánico o maestro mayor de obras. Si eligiere alguna de éstas y eventualmente decidiere cambiar de carrera, tendrá que convalidar algunas materias.

SR. THOMPSON: Veo que Scott tendrá que pensarlo todo bien, antes de decidirse por una escuela . . . Dígame ¿los niños pasan cuántas horas en clase?

SR. MARQUEZ: En la secundaria, generalmente cinco: desde las siete y media de la mañana hasta las doce y media de la tarde. A veces, tienen horas adicionales de clase para educación física o clases especiales, como computación, etc. Claro que puede elegir entre dos turnos: mañana o tarde.

SR. THOMPSON: ¿O sea que algunos niños van a la escuela por la mañana y otros por la tarde?

SR. MARQUEZ: Así es. Sin embargo, la mayoría va por las mañanas.

SR. THOMPSON: ¿Cómo es el sistema de calificaciones?[6]

SR. MARQUEZ: Los niños son calificados de uno a diez, con un promedio mínimo de aprobación de siete. La mayoría de las tomas de lección[7] y exámenes son orales y la mala conducta del niño puede castigarse con una mala nota. Si el alumno no rinde un promedio de siete en cada materia, debe pasar el examen general para esa materia.

SR. THOMPSON: ¿Son difíciles los exámenes?

SR. MARQUEZ: Bastante. En los exámenes, tres profesores les hacen preguntas orales y escritas a los alumnos sobre el contenido de la materia[8] cursada en el año.

SR. THOMPSON: Parece que a los niños no les va a ser fácil[9] adaptarse a la escuela aquí.

SR. MARQUEZ: Creo que les llevará un tiempito[10] adaptarse.

SR. THOMPSON: Dígame, ¿cómo son las universidades aquí?

SR. MARQUEZ: **Las hay de dos tipos: estatales y privadas. Las estatales son gratis, y las privadas pagadas. Los planes de estudio varían, por supuesto. Todos los diplomas son otorgados por el Estado y valen en toda la república.**

SR. THOMPSON: **Dígame, ¿cómo es el proceso de inscripción universitaria?**

SR. MARQUEZ: **Si decide cursar sus estudios universitarios aquí, tendrá que rendir libres[11] geografía e historia ecuatorianas de nivel secundario. Las demás materias seguramente se le darán[12] por aprobadas.**

SR. THOMPSON: **Quizás sea mejor que Jeremy vaya a la Universidad en los EE.UU., y que nos venga a visitar durante las vacaciones . . . En fin, tendré que discutir todo con mi familia. Muchísimas gracias, señor Márquez, por su tiempo. Lo llamaré antes del viernes con mi decisión.**

A DIFFICULT DECISION ABOUT EDUCATION.

Mr. Thompson has been offered an important job by a manufacturing company in Quito, Ecuador, requiring him to move there with his family. Before accepting, however, he voices some concerns about the effect the move would have on his family.

MR. THOMPSON: To be honest, Mr. Marquez, the job offer is very interesting, but I'm worried about the effect of the move on my family, especially my children. They will have to study here now. I'd like to know more about the educational system in Ecuador.

MR. MARQUEZ: I understand your concern. I have two school-aged children of my own. Rest assured that education in our country is top-notch.

MR. THOMPSON: Do you think the children will adapt easily? How are schools different here?

MR. MARQUEZ: Tell me, how old are your children?

MR. THOMPSON: Scott is thirteen and finishing eighth grade, and Jeremy is seventeen. He's about to start college.

MR. MARQUEZ: Well, the younger one will have to choose a high school. Here we have four types: commercial, "bachelor," industrial, and pedagogical. The subjects and the curricula are different in each.

MR. THOMPSON: In what way?

MR. MARQUEZ: "Bachelor" and commercial high schools offer five-year programs and are the most popular. "Bachelor" schools are geared towards careers in the humanities, literature, medicine, art, etc. There's special emphasis on foreign languages, as well as literature, calligraphy, geography, and history. Commercial high schools emphasize accounting, English, typing, computing, industrial chemistry, and business math.

MR. THOMPSON: So, a child has to decide before entering high school what general field his university studies will be in.

MR. MARQUEZ: That's right, but if he changes his mind, it's not irreversible. Universities accept students from any high school.

MR. THOMPSON: What about the other high schools?

MR. MARQUEZ: The other two are more specialized; they last six years, not five. Pedagogical schools prepare children to become teachers. Therefore, they study psychology, Latin, teaching methodology, etc. Industrial schools generally offer three specialized programs. You can graduate as an electronics or mechanical technician, or as a carpenter. If he chooses one of these and eventually decides to change careers, he will have to pass some equivalency exams.

MR. THOMPSON: I see Scott will have to think carefully before deciding on a school. Tell me, how many hours a day are children in school?

MR. MARQUEZ: In high school, usually five hours, from 7:30 A.M. to 12:30 P.M. Sometimes, they have extra periods in the afternoon for physical education, or special classes, such as computation, etc. Of course, they can choose between two shifts, morning or afternoon.

MR. THOMPSON: So, some children go to school in the mornings, while others go in the afternoon?

MR. MARQUEZ: Yes, but most go in the mornings.

MR. THOMPSON: And what's the grading system like?

MR. MARQUEZ: Children are graded on a scale from one to ten with a minimum passing grade of seven. Most exams are administered orally, and bad behavior in school can be punished with a poor grade. If the student fails to get an average of seven in a subject, he or she must take a final exam in that subject.

MR. THOMPSON: Are the finals difficult?

MR. MARQUEZ: They are. Three teachers ask the student questions about the entire year's content for that subject, and the student must answer orally and in writing.

MR. THOMPSON: It looks like it's going to be hard for the children to adapt to school here.

MR. MARQUEZ: Well, it'll probably take a while.

MR. THOMPSON: And what are universities like?

MR. MARQUEZ: There are two types: state-run and private. The state universities are free, and the private ones aren't. The curricula are different in each, of course. All diplomas are granted by the government, and they are valid throughout the country.

MR. THOMPSON: And what is the application process like?

MR. MARQUEZ: If he decides to study here, he will have to pass equivalency exams in high-school level Ecuadorian history and geography. All his other high school subjects will probably be accepted.

MR. THOMPSON: Maybe Jeremy should go to college in the U.S. and visit us during his vacations . . . Well, I'll have to talk it over with my family. Thank you very much, Mr. Marquez for your time. I'll call you by Friday with my decision.

B. APUNTES

1. The verb *cursar* is used instead of *estudiar* when referring to the general study of a subject. Compare: *Curso Literatura en Montevideo.* (I study Literature in Montevideo.) *Tengo que estudiar para la prueba del lunes.* (I have to study for the test on Monday.)

2. The verbs *ingresar (a)* (to enter) and *egresar (de)* (to exit; to graduate from) are used when referring to schools or universities. *Scott ha egresado de la escuela primaria en noviembre y va a ingresar a la secundaria en marzo.* (Scott finished elementary school in November and is going to start high school in March.)

3. Calligraphy is still taught in Latin American high schools. In school, students are generally not allowed to use *bolígrafos* or *bolis* (ballpoint pens) until they've reached high school. In grade school children write with *plumas fuente* or *lapiceras* (inkwell pens).

4. *Un maestro* is a grade school teacher, while *un profesor* is a teacher of a particular subject at the high school or university level.

5. *Por lo* followed by an adjective is used to indicate a cause. *Por lo lejos que estaban, no pudimos ver quienes eran.* (Because they were so far away, we couldn't see who they were.) *Los impuestos son difíciles de pagar, por lo altos.* (The taxes are hard to pay because they are so high.)

6. *Calificaciones* is the official term for grades used in school. In informal conversation, however, *notas* is preferred. *Por favor traigan sus libretas de calificaciones firmadas mañana.* (Please bring your signed report cards tomorrow.) *Suelo sacar buenas notas en biología, pero no en matemáticas.* (I usually get good grades in biology, but not in math.)

7. *Tomar la lección* refers to administering an oral exam. The student stands in front of the class and recites or talks about the day's lesson. The student is then graded by the teacher.

8. On *un boletín/una libreta de calificaciones* (a report card), the official term for a school subject is *asignatura*.

9. Note the use of the indirect object pronoun to mean "it is easy for them," *les es fácil*.

10. The verb *llevar* (to carry, to take) is often used to express how long an action takes. *Nos lleva mucho tiempo cerrar tratos con el extranjero.* (It takes us a long time to close overseas deals.)

11. *Rendir libre* refers to taking an equivalency exam to make up for missed courses. These exams are often required when transferring to a new school or skipping a grade *(rendir libre un grado)*.

12. In English, you "take," while in Spanish, you "give" something to be true. *Buscaron al alpinista mucho tiempo y lo daban por muerto, pero al final, apareció.* (They looked for the mountain climber for a long time, and they took him for dead, but at last he appeared.) *Gloria dio por perdida su libreta telefónica.* (Gloria took her phone book to be lost.)

C. GRAMATICA Y USOS

1. *EL FUTURO SIMPLE* (THE SIMPLE FUTURE)

The simple future tense of regular verbs is formed by adding the appropriate personal ending *(-é, -ás, -á, -emos, -áis, -án)* to the infinitive. Very few verbs are irregular in the future tense.[1]

	ESTUDIAR TO STUDY	*APRENDER* TO LEARN	*RENDIR* TO RENDER
yo	*estudiaré*	*aprenderé*	*rendiré*
tú	*estudiarás*	*aprenderás*	*rendirás*
él/ella/Vd.	*estudiará*	*aprenderá*	*rendirá*
nosotros	*estudiaremos*	*aprenderemos*	*rendiremos*
vosotros	*estudiaréis*	*aprenderéis*	*rendiréis*
ellos/ellas/Vds.	*estudiarán*	*aprenderán*	*rendirán*

1. For the conjugation of irregular verbs, please refer to the verb charts in the Appendix.

Todo indica que las relaciones comerciales entre nuestras empresas serán muy provechosas.
Everything indicates that business between our companies will be very productive.

Mañana me encontraré con Roberto después del trabajo.
Tomorrow I'll meet Robert after work.

¿Cuando pondréis en orden vuestros cuartos?
When will you clean up your rooms?

The simple future is used primarily in formal situations. Colloquially, the future with *ir* is preferred.

Voy a llamar a nuestro proveedor, parece que hubo un error de facturación.
Llamaré a nuestro proveedor, parece que hubo un error de facturación.
I'm going to call our supplier; it seems there was a billing error.

To express the idea of an obligation to complete an action in the future, use *haber de, deber (de)* and *tener que,* conjugated in the present indicative, followed by an infinitive. *Haber de* denotes a mild obligation, *deber (de)* a stronger one, and *tener que* implies a strong obligation, usually from a source of authority.

Jorge ha de llegar a casa alrededor de las seis esta tarde.
Jorge should be home around six this afternoon.

Debo estar en la escuela a las siete de la mañana.
I have to be at school at 7 A.M.

Tenéis que sacar por lo menos un siete para pasar este examen.
You must get at least a seven to pass this test.

2. *EL POTENCIAL* (THE CONDITIONAL)

The conditional of regular verbs is formed by adding the appropriate personal ending *(-ía, -ías, -ía, -íamos, -íais, -ían)* to the future stem. The same verbs that are irregular in the future are, therefore, irregular in the conditional.

	ESTUDIAR TO STUDY	*APRENDER* TO LEARN	*RENDIR* TO RENDER
yo	*estudiaría*	*aprendería*	*rendiría*
tú	*estudiarías*	*aprenderías*	*rendirías*
él/ella/Vd.	*estudiaría*	*aprendería*	*rendiría*
nosotros	*estudiaríamos*	*aprenderíamos*	*rendiríamos*
vosotros	*estudiaríais*	*aprenderíais*	*rendiríais*
ellos/ellas/Vds.	*estudiarían*	*aprenderían*	*rendirían*

The conditional is used in Spanish much as it is in English: [2]

a) to express a likely or logical consequence.

Sería lógico que fueras copartícipe de su éxito.
It would only be fair for you to share in his success.

Ellos vendrían a casa mañana, pero no van a tener tiempo.
They would come over tomorrow, but they won't have time.

b) to express the intention or desire to do something.

Hace mucho calor, me encantaría tomarme una cerveza ahorita.
It's really hot. I'd love to have a beer right now.

c) to make a statement more polite.

¿Me ayudarías con la tarea? No entiendo nada.
Would you please help me with my homework? I don't understand a thing.

3. *EL POTENCIAL PERFECTO* (THE CONDITIONAL PERFECT)

The conditional perfect is formed with the present conditional of the verb *haber* and the past participle of the main verb. As in English, it is used to express what would have happened, if it had been possible. Note that it is most often used in conjunction with the simple past tenses, i.e., the imperfect and the preterite.

	ESTUDIAR TO STUDY	*APRENDER* TO LEARN	*RENDIR* TO RENDER
yo habría *tú habrías* *él/ella/Vd. habría* *nosotros habríamos* *vosotros habríais* *ellos/ellas/Vds. habrían*	*estudiado*	*aprendido*	*rendido*

Habría estudiado la lección ayer, pero estuve enfermo.
I would have studied the lesson yesterday, but I was sick.

Habríamos partido antes, pero llovía mucho.
We would have left earlier, but it was raining hard.

Habrían terminado el proyecto, pero las computadoras se descompusieron.
They would have finished the project, but the computers broke down.

2. For other uses of the conditional, see *Gramática y usos, Lección 12:* "if clauses."

Le habría terminado de explicar las condiciones del contrato, pero se nos cortó la comunicación.

I would have finished explaining the conditions of the contract to him, but we were disconnected.

4. *USOS IDIOMATICOS DEL FUTURO Y DEL POTENCIAL* (IDIOMATIC USES OF THE FUTURE AND THE CONDITIONAL)

Aside from their basic uses, the future and conditional tenses may be used to express probability in the present and the past, respectively. Note that the expressions *haber de, tener que,* and *deber de,* which imply future obligation, may also be used to indicate probability in the present.

Miguel, ¿dónde se encuentra el Sr. Ramos?—No sé bien. Ha de encontrarse en la fábrica.

Miguel, where is Mr. Ramos?—I don't know for sure. He's probably at the factory.

Laura y Susanita estarán jugando en casa de Karina, ¿no?

Laura and Susanita are probably playing at Karina's place, right?

Supongo que los Castillo la pasarán bien en la playa ahora . . .

I suppose the Castillo's are enjoying the beach right now . . .

Tengo que llamar a mis padres ya mismo, estarán esperando que los llame.

I have to call my parents right away; they must be waiting for me to call.

¿Fuiste a casa ayer y no estábamos? Estaríamos en la plaza a esa hora.

So you came over and we weren't home yesterday? We were probably at the park at the time.

¡Qué raro que Pepe no haya llamado! Ya debería haber llegado a casa.

It's strange that Pepe hasn't called! He must have gotten home by now.

D. ESTUDIO IDIOMATICO

The verb *soler* means "to do something habitually." Use it to talk about your habits, both past and present. This verb is somewhat peculiar because it is never used in the preterite in Spanish.[3] It is used mainly in the present and imperfect tenses where it is always followed by an infinitive.

Suelo ir al parque por las mañanas.

I always go to the park in the mornings.

---

3. There are some verbs that are never conjugated in certain tenses because their meaning inherently contradicts the usage of the tense. These verbs are known as *verbos defectivos* (defective verbs), and *soler* is a prime example.

¿Adónde soléis ir de vacaciones?
Where do you usually go on vacation?

When used in the imperfect, it can be translated as "used to . . .":

Cuando vivía en Asunción, solía bañarme en el río durante el verano.
When I was living in Asuncion, I used to swim in the river during the
summer.

Note that in the above sentence *"solía bañarme"* could be replaced by
simply *"me bañaba,"* although the emphasis on past habit would be lost.

E. HABLEMOS DE NEGOCIOS

LA EDUCACIÓN (EDUCATION)

Elementary education in Spain is, in general, similar to that in the U.S.
Elementary education is known as *Enseñanza General Básica* (often abbreviated to *E.G.B.* in writing). Secondary education, on the other hand,
is very similar to Latin American secondary education. At the time of
publication, the educational system in Spain was undergoing major reform,
but it will probably retain the basic characteristics of its sister systems in
Latin America.

In Latin America, the educational system is somewhat different from the
one in the U.S. There are both public and private schools at the elementary, secondary, and university levels. Due to the difference in climate in
countries south of the equator, classes begin in March and run through
the first part of November. In terms of curriculum and study methods,
education in Latin America is closer to British than to American education.
There is greater emphasis on oral examination and on verbal and memori-
zation skills. Written essay exams and daily oral examinations are the
norm, while multiple choice tests are very rare. Schools generally allow
only 14 days of absenteeism, after which a student must re-register for
school. If a student misses more than 30 days of class a year, he must
take a general exam in all subjects. These exams are very difficult because
a student must be prepared to answer any questions, in written or oral
form, about the entire year's curriculum for each subject.

Preschools are generally known as *preescolares* or *pre-primarias* and are
primarily popular in urban areas. Most parents send their children to
preschools to get accustomed to schooling, not out of necessity. Keep in
mind that many families have grandparents and aunts and uncles that live
together or fairly close to each other.

La escuela primaria (elementary or primary education) is mandatory in Latin America. It generally begins at age six and continues to age twelve, from *jardín de infantes* (kindergarten) to *séptimo grado* (seventh grade).

Secondary schools[4] may take five or six years to complete, from *primer año* to *quinto* or *sexto año*. High schools are variously known as *bachilleratos, liceos,* or *escuelas secundarias*. There are two *turnos* (shifts): *matutino* (morning) and *tarde* or *vespertino* (afternoon or evening). In some countries, the evening shift is reserved for adults wishing to complete their secondary education.

In terms of curriculum, secondary education is more specialized in Latin America than in the U.S. Nevertheless, all high school students study the following basic subjects: *física* (physics), *química* (chemistry), *matemáticas* (mathematics), *historia* (history), *geografía* (geography),[5] *biología* (biology), *lengua castellana* (Spanish), *educación física* (physical education), *formación moral y cívica* (ethics and civic instruction), and *religión* (religion, in religious schools). Although the exact divisions vary, most countries offer different types of high schools designed to prepare students to pursue careers in different general fields.

Pedagógicos, Normales, or *Académicos:* These schools are geared toward students wishing to pursue a career in teaching. *Pedagogía, psicología, latín,* and *lengua y literatura castellana* are common subjects. In order to become an elementary school teacher, an additional two-year course of study in any field at a university is necessary.

Bachilleratos are geared toward the humanities. *Caligrafía, lengua y literatura, música, francés, filosofía,* and *psicología* are common subjects. Physicians, artists, language specialists, and writers are generally graduates of *bachilleratos*.

Comerciales are geared toward careers in business. *Inglés, computación, química inorgánica, mecanografía* (typing), *taquigrafía* (shorthand), *economía,* and *matemática comercial* are common subjects.

Industriales are geared toward providing a more direct entrance to the job market in technical fields. Specializations in electricity, electronics, agriculture, industry, or construction are common. The students graduate

4. Junior high schools are common only in the Caribbean (Puerto Rico and the Dominican Republic) where they are known as *escuelas intermedias* (in Puerto Rico) and as *prebachilleratos* (in the Dominican Republic).

5. Geography and history are generally studied according to area and time throughout high school. For example, in the first year of high school, you would probably study ancient history, astronomy, and world geography. In the second year, you would study medieval history and the geography of Africa and Asia; in the third year, the Renaissance and geography of the American continent, etc.

with the title of technician in their chosen field. These types of schools are generally more popular in rural areas. In addition, there are *liceos militares* (military academies), which are very similar to those in the U.S.

Transfer students in elementary school can generally be incorporated into the school system without major difficulty, provided they can speak Spanish well enough. An alternative is to enroll children in bilingual American schools, which can generally only be found in major cities. Information regarding these schools can be obtained by calling the local American consulate. For transfers at the high school level, students may be required to pass equivalency exams, especially in local geography and history before being granted a high school diploma. Information about transfers at the high school level can be obtained by calling the local embassy.

Public universities, funded by the government, are almost free. Students are expected to pay a nominal yearly fee for studying. They must also buy all the required books and study materials, but these are usually provided at a very low cost by the university itself. Due to the large number of students who want to attend university and the limited number of openings, universities have very difficult entrance exams that may be taken only once a year. Even if they pass, many students are often wait-listed, for lack of openings.

Diplomas are granted by the national government in both public and private universities and are valid throughout the country. Doctors and lawyers, for example, can practice anywhere in the country. They are not required to pass regional qualifying exams.

Transfer students at the university level who wish to complete a course of study in Latin America must pass high-school level history and geography exams before being allowed to receive a government diploma. In most countries there is no "credit" system of study; rather, you must present to the *rector* (dean) a transcript with a certified translation of the content of all subjects studied in college so that it can be compared to the local curriculum. Contact the *rector* of the university for more information regarding the exact procedure for transfers.

EXAMEN

A. *Complete en español las oraciones siguientes.* (Complete the following sentences in Spanish.)

1. *Mi hija aún no sabe en qué tipo de escuela secundaria* (she will enter).
2. *Mi hijo está en una escuela* (pedagogical). *Dentro de dos años se* (will graduate) *de* (school teacher).
3. *Yo* (would transfer myself) *a una universidad en España, pero no sé si* (I will have) *suficiente dinero.*
4. *Me pregunto qúe* (grade) *recibí en* (industrial chemistry) *este trimestre.*
5. *¿Sabes dónde* (they probably are) *los chicos? Llamé a la Universidad y me dijeron que las clases terminaron hace tres horas.*
6. *Jorgito* (would have gone) *de vacaciones con nosotros, pero tuvo que* (take) *un examen de* (chemistry).
7. *Probablemente el* (professor) *nos* (will "take") *la lección oral hoy.*
8. *Pienso que las clases habrán de* (begin) *en la primera semana de marzo.*
9. *Vosotros* (must study) *los tres primeros capítulos del libro de* (history) *para mañana.*
10. *María* (has to take an equivalency exam) *para poder* (transfer) *a la Universidad de Zaragoza en España.*

B. *Traduzca las oraciones precedentes al inglés.* (Translate the preceding sentences into English.)

LECCION 8

A. DIALOGO

TRABAJO NUEVO—VIDA NUEVA.

La Srta. Ríos es la nueva directora de investigaciones químicas para una gran compañía de productos de belleza en Ciudad Guayana,[1] Venezuela. En este momento, la está siendo familiarizando con su nuevo puesto el anterior director de investigaciones, el Sr. Rojas, quien fue ascendido a otro puesto. La señorita Ríos se encuentra en su nueva oficina, cuando entra el señor Rojas.

SR. ROJAS: ¡Buenos días! Ah . . . veo que está ocupada, si quiere vuelvo más tarde . . .

SRTA. RIOS: No, no . . . por favor pase. Estaba desempacando, pero puedo seguir más tarde.

SR. ROJAS: Gracias. Venía para darle una gira[2] de las instalaciones. Acá uno puede perderse muy fácilmente.

SRTA. RIOS: Me lo imagino. Tengo también algunas preguntas que hacerle a la gente de mi sección . . . así que ¿vamos?

SR. ROJAS: Sígame, por favor. Primero quería mostrarle el centro de computación. Como ya sabe, desde las terminales personales se tiene acceso al banco de datos de clientes, productos y demás. Pero si tiene que imprimir algún listado largo, tiene que ir a recogerlo al centro de computación. No queda lejos . . .

Llegan al centro.

SRTA. RIOS: ¡Chuy! Está fresquito aquí . . .

SR. ROJAS: Sí, es por las computadoras. Aquí dentro siempre hace 18°[3] . . . busquemos a Jorge Limón. Es el director del centro. ¡Oh! ¡Ahí está! . . . ¡Limón!

JORGE LIMON: Hola, Rojas. Buenos días, señorita.

SR. ROJAS: Le presento a la Srta. Ríos, está a cargo de investigaciones.

JORGE LIMON: Mucho gusto, jefa.[4]

SRTA. RIOS: Encantada. Así que, parece que tengo que venir a visitarlo para recoger mis informes . . .

JORGE LIMON: La esperamos con los brazos abiertos, siempre y cuando[5] necesite algo con más de cinco años de antigüedad.[6] Todos los datos[7] más recientes se pueden acceder desde las terminales personales. ¿Ya le han dado su clave[8] de acceso?

SRTA. RIOS: **Aún no.**

JORGE LIMON: **Tendrá una en su oficina dentro de un par de horas. Las cambiamos a principios de cada mes, como medida de seguridad.**

SRTA. RIOS: **¿Se teme a la competencia? Me imagino que no se tiene acceso remoto a los datos.**

JORGE LIMON: **Nunca se sabe, con los aficionados fanáticos . . . Discúlpenme, parece que hay otra pequeña emergencia. Nos veremos luego.**

AMBOS: **Hasta luego.**

SR. ROJAS: **Bueno, si no tiene más preguntas, vamos para los laboratorios.**

SRTA. RIOS: **¡Muestre el camino, nomás!** [9]

Ambos llegan a los portones de los laboratorios, en el subsuelo. [10] *El Sr. Rojas saca una tarjeta de seguridad.*

SRTA. RIOS: **¿Esta zona es restringida? Veo que se toman en serio las medidas de seguridad . . .**

SR. ROJAS: **Sí. Aquí no pasa nadie sin tarjeta. A la salida, se le hará una a su nombre.**

Los guardias les permiten pasar. Se encuentran en un largo pasillo con aire acondicionado.

SR. ROJAS: **Aquí están los laboratorios. Como ve, tenemos cinco. A la derecha del pasillo están los de pesquisas. Allí se encuentra la oficina de la jefa de químicos, la Sra. Arminda Bueno. A la izquierda están los laboratorios de producción.**

SRTA. RIOS: **La Sra. Bueno es mi principal contacto con la sección, entonces.**

SR. ROJAS: **Así es. Le advierto que se dice que es un tanto, digamos, inflexible, pero muy capaz. Vayamos a verla.**

Los dos doblan a la derecha y entran en la oficina de la jefe de químicos.

SRA. BUENO: **Buenos días.**

SR. ROJAS: **Buenos días. Le presento a su nueva directora, la señorita Ríos.**

SRA. BUENO: **Encantada de conocerla, señorita. Estoy bien informada de su experiencia y preparación. Estoy segura de que será un gran gusto trabajar con Vd.**

SRTA. RIOS: **Es Vd. muy amable. Debo decirle que estoy dispuesta a mantener los altos niveles de rendimiento que todos han sabido establecer.**

SRA. BUENO: **Estoy a sus órdenes. Por favor llámeme a la extensión 457 a cualquier hora, si me necesita. Es mi número de radiollamada.**[11]

SRTA. RIOS: **Muy bien. La dejamos a su trabajo. La llamaré luego para concertar**[12] **una reunión de sección.**

SRA. BUENO: **Me doy por informada. Hasta pronto.**

SRTA. RIOS: **Hasta pronto.**

SR. ROJAS: **Bueno, qué le parece si, por último, la llevo a conocer la sección preferida de todos. Le aseguro que no hace frío, ni hay tarjetas de seguridad. Allí se puede charlar,**[13] **fumar,**[14] **conocer a los otros empleados y estirar las piernas un poco durante la hora de almuerzo.**

SRTA. RIOS: **¡Me alivia mucho oírlo! ¿Dónde queda ese oasis?**

SR. ROJAS: **¡En la cafetería!**

NEW JOB—NEW LIFE.

Miss Rios is the new director of chemical research for a large beauty products company in Guayana City, Venezuela. At the moment, she is being briefed on her new job by the former director of research, Mr. Rojas, who has been promoted to another position. Miss Rios is in her new office when Mr. Rojas enters.

MR. ROJAS: Good morning! Oh! . . . I see you're busy; I can come back later . . .

MISS RIOS: No, no. . . . Please, come in. I was just unpacking, I can finish later.

MR. ROJAS: Thank you. I've come to give you a tour of the facilities. It's easy to get lost around here.

MISS RIOS: I can imagine. I also have some questions to ask the people in my section. So, I'm ready to go.

MR. ROJAS: Follow me, please. First, I wanted to take you to the computer center. As you know, you can access the client base, product list, and all the other data banks from the office terminals, but if you need to make a long printout, you have to pick it up at the computer center. It's not far . . .

They arrive at the center.

MISS RIOS: Brrr! It's a little chilly in here!

MR. ROJAS: Yes. That's because of the computers. It's always around 68° in here. . . . Let's find Jorge Limon. He's the director of the center. Oh, there he is. Limon!

JORGE LIMON: Hello, Rojas. Good morning, Miss.

MR. ROJAS: This is Miss Rios, she's in charge of research.

JORGE LIMON: Pleased to meet you, boss.

MISS RIOS: Likewise. So, it looks like I'll have to visit you to pick up my printouts.

JORGE LIMON: We welcome you with open arms, if and when you need something over five years old. More recent data can be accessed from the office terminals. Have you been given an access code?

MISS RIOS: Not yet.

JORGE LIMON: You'll have one in your office in a couple of hours. We change them at the beginning of every month, as a security measure.

MISS RIOS: Are we afraid of our competitors? I assume the data can't be accessed from outside.

JORGE LIMON: Well, you never know, with all those hackers out there . . . Excuse me, but that's probably another minor emergency. I'll see you both later.

BOTH: See you later.

MR. ROJAS: Well, if you have no more questions, we can head on over to the labs.

MISS RIOS: Just lead the way!

Both arrive at the lab security gates, underground. Mr. Rojas takes out a security card.

MISS RIOS: Is this a restricted area? Security is pretty tight around here . . .

MR. ROJAS: Yes, it is. No one gets through without a card. You'll be issued one when we leave.

The security guards let them pass through the gates. They enter a long, air-conditioned hallway.

MR. ROJAS: Well, here are the labs! As you can see, there are five. To the right of this hallway are the research labs. There's the office of the chief chemist, Mrs. Arminda Bueno. To the left are the production labs.

MISS RIOS: Mrs. Bueno is my main contact with the section, then.

MR. ROJAS: That's right. I must warn you, they say she's a little, umm, straightlaced, but very capable. Let's go see her.

They turn right and enter the chief chemist's office.

MRS. BUENO: Good morning.

MR. ROJAS: Good morning. This is your new manager, Miss Rios.

MRS. BUENO: Very pleased to meet you, Miss Rios. I am well-informed about your experience and preparation. I'm sure it'll be a great pleasure working with you.

MISS RIOS: You're very kind. I want to let you know that I'm ready to maintain the high performance levels everyone has managed to establish.

MRS. BUENO: I'm at your disposal. Please call me at extension 457 at any time. It's my beeper number.

MISS RIOS: Fine. Well, we'll leave you to your work. I'll call you later to plan a departmental meeting.

MRS. BUENO: I consider myself informed. See you soon.

MISS RIOS: See you soon.

MR. ROJAS: Well, how about if, as a final stop, we visit everyone's favorite section. I assure you it's not cold, and there aren't any security cards there. You can chat, smoke, meet the other employees, and stretch your legs a bit during your lunch break.

MISS RIOS: I'm delighted to hear that! Where is this oasis?

MR. ROJAS: In the cafeteria!

B. APUNTES

1. *Ciudad Guayana* is a large industrial city in eastern Venezuela. It is not far from *Gurí* Dam, the world's second largest hydroelectric power plant.

2. *Una gira* refers to a tour in a business setting or official capacity, as well as to a perfomance tour. A sightseeing/pleasure tour is generally referred to as *un tur*. *La compañía de danza comenzó su gira por Europa.* (The dance company began its tour of Europe.) *Vamos a hacer un tur de la India el año que viene.* (We're going on a tour of India next year.)

3. Note that temperature is measured in Celsius in Spanish-speaking countries. Likewise, for weights and measures, the metric system is used.

4. Spanish-speaking people often refer to their superiors as *jefa* (female) and *jefe* (male).

5. *Siempre y cuando* is a commonly used expression meaning "if and when" or "provided that." Note that it is always followed by a subjunctive clause because it refers to actions that may or may not occur. Similar expressions include *con tal que* and *mientras*. *Jorge debe estar en casa, con tal que haya salido del trabajo a tiempo.* (Jorge must be home by now, provided he left work on time.) *Mientras estés en la ciudad, eres mi huésped.* (As long as you are in the city, you will be my house guest.)

6. *Antigüedad* often refers to the age of documents or to seniority in business meetings. *¿Cuál es su antigüedad en la empresa?* (How long have you been working for the company?) In other settings, *antigüedad* means simply "antiquity."

7. Beware of "false friends." *Dato* means "a datum, a piece of information"; the date of the year is *la fecha*.

8. *Clave* (code, key) appears in many compound words. *No recuerdo mi palabra clave.* (I can't remember my password.) Note that a key that opens a lock is *una llave*. *No encuentro mis llaves del auto.* (I can't find my car keys.)

9. *Nomás* is used often in Spanish. It means "just, only, that's all." It can be used anywhere in a sentence: *Deje nomás las cajas donde sea.* (Just leave the boxes anywhere.) *Nomás mírela, ¿no es simpática mi gatita?* (Just look at her, isn't my kitty cute?)

10. *Un subsuelo* is an underground level in a building. A basement (in a house or an apartment building) is *un sótano*.

11. Note the compound noun *radiollamada* (pager). Another word for pager (used mostly in the U.S.) is *un grillete electrónico* (literally: a small electronic cricket).

12. The verb *concertar* (to organize, set up, or coordinate) is often used in business: *Vamos a concertar los esfuerzos de todas las secciones de la empresa.* (We are going to coordinate the efforts from all sections of the company.) Verbs with similar applications include *coordinar* (to coordinate) and *organizar* (to organize).

13. *Charlar* and *platicar* are two popular terms for chatting. *Platiquemos sobre tus problemas esta tarde.* (Let's talk about your problems this afternoon.)

14. Note that smoking is generally still permitted in offices and public buildings in Latin America.

C. GRAMATICA Y USOS

1. *LAS VOZ PASIVA* (THE PASSIVE VOICE)

Most actions can be expressed in either the active or passive voice. Compare:

Elena preparó los informes.
Elena prepared the reports. (active)

Los informes fueron preparados por Elena.
The reports were prepared by Elena. (passive)

In Spanish, the passive voice is formed with the verb *ser* in the appropriate tense and the past participle of the main verb. Note that the past participle must agree with the subject of the sentence and that the agent of the action is generally introduced by *por*.[1]

La señorita Ríos fue presentada a algunos empleados de la empresa por el Señor Rojas.
Miss Rios was introduced to some of the company employees by Mr. Rojas.

Tres cuartos de la energía eléctrica de Venezuela es generada por la planta hidroeléctrica de Gurí.
Three quarters of Venezuela's electrical energy is generated by the Guri Hydroelectric power plant.

La reunión concertada por la señorita Ríos será atendida por todos los empleados de la sección de investigaciones químicas.
The meeting organized by Miss Rios will be attended by all employees in the chemical research section.

In general, the passive voice is much less common in Spanish than in English. One of its most popular uses is in newspaper headlines and magazine covers where the auxiliary verb *ser* (and the indefinite articles) are generally omitted.

Otro banco robado en la capital.
Another bank robbed in the capital.

Huelga anunciada por ferroviarios.
Strike announced by train worker's union.

---

1. If the verb expresses emotion, the preposition *de* may also be used to indicate the agent of an action in the passive voice.

El jefe es respetado de todos los empleados.
The boss is respected by all the employees.

116

2. "SE" PASIVO E IMPERSONAL (PASSIVE AND IMPERSONAL *SE*)

When the agent of the action is unknown or unimportant, the passive voice can also be expressed with the reflexive pronoun *se*. Note that the verb must be in the third person and must agree in number with the subject of the sentence (i.e., the object of the action).

La computadora se va a arreglar mañana.
The computer is going to be fixed tomorrow.

En el campo, se vive una vida menos frenética que en las grandes ciudades.
In the country, people live less hectic lives than in large cities.

This formula is most commonly used in impersonal expressions to describe general rules or customs. The implied subject in such cases is usually "people," "one," or "they." Note that the verb is always in the third person.

No se puede fumar en las oficinas, sólo en la cafeteria.
Smoking is not allowed in the offices, only in the cafeteria.[2]

No se debe hablar con la boca llena, Luisito.
Luisito, one mustn't speak with one's mouth full.

Note that in written definitions and instructions, the pronoun *se* is often attached to the verb as a suffix.

Dícese "reglamento" al conjuntos de normas y reglas que rigen determinada actividad.
"Regulations" are the norms and rules that govern a specific activity.

Luego de prepararse los ingredientes, mézclense en un recipiénte.
After the ingredients are prepared, they are mixed in a container.

The impersonal *se* is also used to indicate an unexpected or accidental occurrence. In this case, a direct object pronoun indicates who was affected by the action. Note that English often uses an active construction in such cases. In Spanish, however, an impersonal subject is preferred since the action is not voluntary.

Se me perdió el disco donde tenía la lista de clientes de la semana pasada.
I lost the disk on which I put the list of last week's clients.

---

2. Of course, the impersonal pronoun *uno* (one) may also be used. *Uno* is sometimes used to avoid confusion between the impersonal and reciprocal/reflexive uses of *se*.

Se puede relajarse en la cafetería.
Uno puede relajarse en la cafetería.
One can relax in the cafeteria.

¿Dónde está tu otro arete?—No sé, se me habrá caído en la cafetería.
Where is your other earring?—I don't know. I must have dropped it in
the cafeteria.

3. *EL MODO SUBJUNTIVO* (THE SUBJUNCTIVE MOOD)

The subjunctive is the mood of subjectivity. It is used to express wish,
hope, desire, or personal opinion, and to indicate uncertainty as to
whether an action will take place. For example, the indicative mood is
used to give factual information or state conditions that are known to be
true. The subjunctive, on the other hand, is used to give unconfirmed
information or describe hypothetical conditions that are merely possible.

The present subjunctive of regular and irregular verbs is formed using
the first person singular, present indicative stem and the appropriate
personal subjunctive ending. The personal endings for *-ar* verbs are
-e, -es, -e, -emos, -eis, -en; and for *-er* and *-ir* verbs, they are *-a, -as,
-a, -amos, -ais, -an.* For example: *hablar → hablo → habla,
venir → vengo → venga.*

	HABLAR TO SPEAK	*PONER* *TO PUT*	*DECIR* TO SAY
yo	*hable*	*ponga*	*diga*
tú	*hables*	*pongas*	*digas*
él/ella/Vd.	*hable*	*ponga*	*diga*
nosotros	*hablemos*	*pongamos*	*digamos*
vosotros	*habléis*	*pongáis*	*digáis*
ellos/ellas/Vds.	*hablen*	*pongan*	*digan*

The subjunctive must be used in dependent clauses[3] following verbs that
express:

a) a wish, such as *querer* (to want), *desear* (to wish), and *esperar* (to
hope).

El jefe quiere que estén listas las propuestas para el viernes.
The boss wants the proposals to be ready by Friday.

---

3. A dependent clause cannot stand on its own as a sentence; rather, it depends on the main
(or "independent") clause for meaning, and it is generally introduced by *que.*

Main clause:	Dependent Clause:
Quiero	*que me llames mañana.*
I want	you to call me tomorrow.

118

¡Toda la familia les desea que tengan todo lo mejor en su nueva vida en el extranjero!
The whole family wishes you all the best in your new life abroad!

b) a command or request, such as *mandar* (to order), *prohibir* (to forbid), *decir* (to tell, i.e., to order), and *pedir* (to ask for).

Te dijeron que estés en la reunión a las dos.
They told you to be at the meeting at two.

El personal del laboratorio manda que les envíen 30 litros más de alcohol isopropílico.
The laboratory personnel requests that 30 more liters of isopropyl alcohol be sent to them.

c) doubt or denial, such as *dudar* (to doubt), *negar* (to deny).

Dudo que no haya más champú "Súper" en almacén.
I doubt there's any more "Super" shampoo in stock.

d) an opinion, only when negative or interrogative, such as *pensar* (to think, to have an opinion), *creer* (to believe).

¿Cree Vd. que pueda recibir una tarjeta de seguridad hoy mismo?—Creo que pueden preparársela antes de las trece.
Do you think I can get a security card today?—I think they can prepare one for you before 1 P.M.

No pienso que debamos reducir las medidas de seguridad: pienso que son necesarias.
I don't think we should reduce our security measures. I think they are necessary.

Note that an infinitive is often used in English where the subjunctive is used in Spanish. This construction can also be used in Spanish when the subject of the main clause is the same as the subject of the dependent clause. Compare:

Queremos desarrollar una nueva línea de productos totalmente naturales.
We want to develop a new line of all natural products.

Queremos que los laboratorios comiencen a investigar materias primas alternativas que puedan usarse para este propósito.
We want the laboratories to investigate alternative raw material that may be used for this purpose.

D. ESTUDIO IDIOMATICO

Here are some expressions you might find handy on your first day at work:

if you make a mistake . . .

Hay moros en la costa (the coast isn't clear)

No hablen más de Raúl, hay moros en la costa.
Stop talking about Raul, the coast isn't clear!

Meter la pata (to stick your foot in your mouth)

No puedo creer que Roque haya contado un chiste machista a un grupo de feministas: ¡sí que metió la pata!
I can't believe Roque told a sexist joke to a group of feminists—he really stuck his foot in his mouth!

or to describe people . . .

Empinar el codo (to drink; literally: "to tilt one's elbow")

A Carlitos le gusta empinar el codo.
Carlitos likes to drink.

Mirar de reojo (to be suspicious; literally: "to look out of the corner of your eye")

Me parece que el nuevo jefe no gusta de mí, siempre me mira de reojo.
I think the new boss doesn't like me; he's always looking at me distrustfully.

Tomar a pecho (to take it to heart)

No puedo hablar contigo, ¡te tomas todo a pecho!
I can't talk to you—you take everything to heart!

E. HABLEMOS DE NEGOCIOS

LA ETIQUETA EN UN AMBIENTE DE NEGOCIOS (BUSINESS ETIQUETTE)

Business etiquette is much more strict in Spanish-speaking countries than in the U.S. Following are some general guidelines to keep in mind when doing business in the Spanish-speaking world.

Citas (Appointments)

Appointments are necessary and should be made as far in advance as possible—one or two weeks is the norm. First appointments should be scheduled at offices, never at restaurants, and should take place in the morning (usually at 9:30 or 10 A.M.) because business lunches are extremely popular and do not allow time for later appointments. They should be confirmed 24 hours in advance, by phone. Appointments involving travel arrangements should be scheduled several weeks in advance and confirmed one or two weeks in advance, as well. Punctuality is generally not observed among countrymen in business situations, but foreigners are expected to be on time. You mustn't be surprised or annoyed if you are kept waiting for someone for at least ten minutes. This is not considered rude but, rather, gives you an opportunity to relax and gather your thoughts.

El Vestir en un Ambiente Comercial (Business Dress)

Latin Americans and Spaniards are very traditional and conservative when it comes to business dress. Dark-colored (dark grey or navy blue) suits, and conservative ties with white cotton dress shirts are the standard for men, regardless of the climate (and in some Latin American countries temperatures can soar). Avoid bright colors, flamboyant prints, and avant-garde ties, and *never* wear shorts in a business setting. Women can be more creative with their wardrobes. Having a touch of flare (such as a silk scarf or high-heeled shoes) does not detract from a woman's professional appearance. Businesswomen usually wear European cut suits, blouses, or shirts, and skirts just below the knee. Sports suits with pants are also considered acceptable. In the Caribbean, dress is somewhat more casual and punctuality is not taken as seriously as in other Spanish-speaking areas.

Las Tarjetas de Presentacion (Business Cards)

When traveling to a Spanish-speaking country, make sure you have business cards printed in both English and Spanish. Titles are very important, as they convey your degree of authority, and should be printed clearly under your name. Business cards should be distributed to everyone present immediately following introductions. Be sure to use your *right hand*, as using your left is thought to bring bad luck. In Argentina and Uruguay, business cards may be given to a secretary before entering an office.

121

El Estilo Comercial (Business Style)

Latin Americans are very cautious, indirect, and slow-paced when it comes to dealing with new business partners. Keep in mind that forming a positive, personal relationship with business partners is of utmost importance. Negotiations may therefore drag on a bit, but pressure tactics should be avoided at all costs, as they could be disastrously counterproductive! Latin Americans tend to think in the long term. They like to form long-lasting business relationships, and it may take some time to win their trust.

At appointments, introduce yourself with a smile and a firm handshake, and take a seat facing your prospective business partner. The first ten to twenty minutes are generally devoted to "small talk" and getting to know each other. Topics such as internationl news and favorable impressions of the host's country are always good conversation starters. Keep in mind that it will take several meetings at the very least to close a deal, so don't be in a rush. For first appointments, you should be accompanied by an interpreter, unless your Spanish is fluent. Don't assume your business partners speak English, as their second language could very well be French, Italian, or a Native American language. Furthermore, lawyers should not be present in the initial stages of negotiations, as they imply a sense of distrust and may offend your partners. Generally, the person attending the meetings is expected to have the authority to close the deal. Finally, detailed written contracts should be prepared only in the final stages of negotiations.

In Chile, Colombia, and Spain, which have been doing business with the U.S. for many years and have thus adopted some habits from the U.S., negotiations may be opened earlier and may progress at a faster pace. Nevertheless, even here, traditional Latin American procedures are highly respected and valued.

Las Mujeres en Los Negocios (Women in Business)

Although business is still very much a male-dominated world in most of Latin America (not so in Spain), women are participating more and more. Women should follow the same basic guidelines of social behavior as men, although you shouldn't be shocked or offended if you find that doors are being opened for you, or if you are helped out of cars, etc. These basic gallantries are expected and should be accepted with a polite smile. In general, women should avoid giving gifts to male business partners, as this could be interpreted as a personal overture.

EXAMEN

A. *Complete las siguientes oraciones con el subjuntivo o el indicativo del verbo indicado.* (Complete the following sentences with the subjunctive or indicative of the given verb.)

1. *Espero que Vd. (TENER) tiempo hoy para darme una gira por las instalaciones.*
2. *No creo que (RECIBIR nosotros) las claves de acceso nuevas antes del viernes.*
3. *La jefa mandó que (IR nostros) al laboratorio del subsuelo a las once. Creo que ella (QUERER) concertar una reunión de sección.*
4. *Dudo que González todavía (ESTAR) en la cafetería. Ya son las cuatro, y (SOLER) terminar el almuerzo a las tres y media.*
5. *Quiero que tú le (HABLAR) a la directora. Tú (TENER) más antigüedad.*
6. *¡Felicitaciones por tu ascenso! Deseo que te (IR) bien en tu puesto nuevo.*
7. *Mientras (tú SEGUIR) todas las instrucciones al pie de la letra, no creo que este champú te (HACER) daño al pelo.*
8. *Pienso que (nosotros DEBER) reducir las medidas de seguridad. Creo que no (SER) necesario que (ellas SER) tan estrictas.*
9. *¡No (yo RECORDAR) dónde puse el disco con los informes de esta semana! Espero que el disco no se me (HABER) perdido!*
10. *Como sabes, en la cafetería se (PODER) fumar y charlar. ¡Por eso (SER) la sección preferida de todos!*

B. *Traduzca las siguientes oraciones al español.* (Translate the following sentences into Spanish.)

1. Smoking is not allowed in this building.
2. They say our boss is a nice man, but I can't tell you if that's true because I don't speak to him often.
3. I lost my pen when I signed those reports in the elevator.
4. I don't think they'll close the cafeteria tomorrow.
5. How do you say "politically correct" in Spanish?—It isn't said.
6. Liliana forgot her access code.
7. The laboratory is cleaned every morning at seven.
8. Can this terminal be used now?—It was broken yesterday.
9. Provided that you see her, tell Maria to call me.
10. The cover of the magazine says: "Strike Announced by the Computex Office Workers."

LECCION 9

A. DIALOGO

EN BÚSQUEDA DE UN DEPARTAMENTO.

Lorena busca alquilar[1] un departamento nuevo para mudarse, en el Distrito Federal,[2] México. Ya ha hecho varias llamadas, pero hasta ahora, no ha tenido suerte. Ella acaba de marcar otro número.

SR. GOMEZ: ¿Holá?

LORENA: Buenos días, señor. Llamo por el aviso en el diario por un departamento que se alquila.

SR. GOMEZ: Sí. ¿A qué departamento se refiere? Tenemos varios disponibles.

LORENA: Me refiero al de la calle Moreno al 3000. Yo busco uno pequeño, un estudio o uno de una recámara y que no esté[3] muy lejos del centro.

SR. GOMEZ: Lamentablemente, no nos queda ninguno que sea así. Ayer alquilé el último.

LORENA: Ah, bueno. Y, si me permite preguntarle, ¿a cuánto lo alquiló?

SR. GOMEZ: Era uno de una recámara, céntrico, con una pequeña terraza y teléfono.[4] Lo alquilé a $600,[5] con calefacción central.[6]

LORENA: Muchas gracias, y si se le desocupare[7] alguno, por favor llámeme. Mi nombre es Lorena y mi número es el 5/693-4213.

SR. GOMEZ: Así lo haré. ¡Buena suerte!

LORENA *(piensa en voz alta):* Casi, casi . . . Bueno, por lo menos, casi encontré un departamento esta última vez. Probemos este otro número . . .

CONTESTADOR AUTOMATICO: Se ha comunicado Vd. con el 5/678-4524. Por favor deje su mensaje después del tono.

LORENA: Buenos días. Me llamo Lorena y llamo por el aviso del departamento. Por favor, llámenme a cualquier hora al 5/693-4213.

De golpe, suena el timbre. Lorena abre la puerta. Es su mejor amigo, Pablo.

LORENA: ¡Pablito! ¡Qué gusto de verte!

PABLO: Vine para ver cómo andabas . . . pero, ¿qué pasa? Se te ve un poco caritriste . . .

Los dos se sientan en el sofá. Pablo deja el bolso a su lado.

LORENA: Como ya sabes, ando buscando vivienda, pero hasta ahora no tuve mucha suerte.

PABLO: Hmm . . . Mira, quizás pueda ayudarte. Me acuerdo que mi mamá tiene una amiga que trabaja en una inmobiliaria. Quizás ella pueda ayudarte a encontrar algo.

LORENA: ¿Tienes el número a mano?

PABLO: No, pero puedo llamar a casa para que me lo den.

Pablo marca el número de su casa y contesta Maria, la criada.

PABLO: ¿Hola, María? ¿Está mi mamá en casa? . . . Ah, salió . . . Bueno, ¿ves la libreta de teléfonos en la mesita? . . . Busca el número de la señora Arenas . . . Sí, sí, sí, el que dice oficina, ¿cuál es? Gracias, María, eres un amor.[9]

Pablo cuelga el teléfono.

PABLO: Aquí tienes el número. La señora se llama Carmen Arenas. Díle que eres amiga de la señora Salguero.

LORENA: ¡Me salvas la vida, Pablito!

PABLO: Primero, marca, y luego veremos . . .

Lorena marca nuevamente.

RECEPCIONISTA: Inmuebles Centrales, buenos días . . .

LORENA: Con la señora Carmen Arenas, por favor.

RECEPCIONISTA: ¿De parte de quién?

LORENA: De parte de una amiga de la señora Salguero.

RECEPCIONISTA: Ya le paso, un momentito . . .

CARMEN: Habla Carmen . . .

LORENA: Me llamo Lorena Salazar. Soy amiga del hijo de doña Salguero.

CARMEN: Ah! . . . ¿y, cómo andan[10] los Salguero?[11] Hace mucho que no los veo.

LORENA: Bien, bien.

CARMEN: Me alegro mucho. Dime, ¿en qué puedo ayudarte?

LORENA: Mire, estoy buscando un departamento para mudarme, pero hasta ahora no he tenido mucha suerte con los clasificados.

CARMEN: Entiendo. ¿Qué tipo de departamento buscas, querida?

LORENA: Uno que tenga una recámara, que esté en el centro. Preferiría que tuviera una terraza y teléfono.

CARMEN: Y, ¿cuándo quieres mudarte?

LORENA: Ayer, si fuera posible.

CARMEN: Ya veo. Bueno, querida, tengo uno en "El Zócalo," [12] en la calle Guatemala. Tiene unos 50 metros cuadrados y es de una recámara. También tiene un pequeño lavadero. [13] Lo alquilan a $500 y está disponible a principio de mes. El único problema es que tendrías que firmar un contrato de alquiler de un año, como mínimo.

LORENA: No tendría problema alguno. ¿Cuánto es el depósito?

CARMEN: El dueño pide sólo un mes de alquiler como depósito, y un mes por adelantado.

LORENO: Y, ¿cuándo lo podría ver?

CARMEN: Puedo mostrártelo hoy, si te viene bien. ¿Por qué no te vienes a la oficina hoy por la tarde?

LORENA: ¿A qué hora paso?

CARMEN: ¿A las dos?

LORENA: De acuerdo. Muchísimas gracias por su ayuda.

CARMEN: De nada. Mándale muchos saludos a la señora Salguero.

LORENA: Se lo diré. ¡Hasta luego!

CARMEN: Te espero a las dos. ¡Chau!

PABLO: ¿Y, qué tal?

LORENA: Fantástico. Me dijo que fuera a verla a las dos. Si al fin logro mudarme, ¡te hago un monumento!

PABLO: ¡Me bastan [14] unos tamales!

LORENA: ¡Pablito, eres el mejor!

LOOKING FOR AN APARTMENT.

Lorena is looking for an apartment to move into in Mexico City, Mexico. She has already made several calls but hasn't had much luck. She dials another number.

MR. GOMEZ: Hello?

LORENA: Good morning, sir. I'm calling about the ad in the paper for an apartment for rent.

MR. GOMEZ: Which apartment are you referring to? We have several available.

LORENA: I'm talking about the one at 3000 Moreno Street. I'm looking for a small one, a studio or one-bedroom, not too far from downtown.

MR. GOMEZ: Unfortunately, we don't have any like that. I rented the last one yesterday.

LORENA: Oh, I see. If you don't mind my asking, how much did you rent it for?

MR. GOMEZ: Well, it was a small one bedroom, downtown, with a small terrace, and a telephone. I rented it for $600, including central heating.

LORENA: Thank you very much, and if anything comes up, please call me. My name is Lorena, and my number is 5/693-4213.

MR. GOMEZ: Will do. Good luck!

LORENA *(thinking out loud):* Almost, almost! Well, at least I came closer to finding an apartment this last time. Let me try this other number . . .

ANSWERING MACHINE: You've reached 5/678-4524. Please leave your message after the tone.

LORENA: Good morning! My name is Lorena, and I'm calling about the ad for the apartment. Please call me at any time at 5/693-4213.

Suddenly, the doorbell rings. Lorena opens the door. It's her best friend, Pablo.

LORENA: Pablito! How nice to see you!

PABLO: I've come to see how you're doing . . . But, what's wrong? You look a little down . . .

They both sit on the sofa. Pablo sets his bag to the side.

LORENA: Well, you know I'm looking for an apartment, but I haven't had much luck yet.

PABLO: Hmm. Look, maybe I can help. I remember my mom has a friend who works in a real estate agency. Maybe she could help you find something.

LORENA: Do you know her number?

PABLO: No, but I could call home and find out.

Pablo dials his home number, and Maria, the housekeeper, answers.

PABLO: Hello, Maria? Is my mom home? . . . Oh, she went out . . . Well, do you see a phone book on the little table? . . . Look up Mrs. Arena's number . . . Yeah, the one that says "office." What is it? Thanks, Maria, you're great.

Pablo hangs up the phone.

PABLO: Here's the number. Her name is Carmen Arena. Tell her you're a friend of Mrs. Salguero.

LORENA: You've saved my life, Pablito!

PABLO: Just call first, then we'll see . . .

Lorena dials once more.

RECEPTIONIST: Central Real Estate, good morning.

LORENA: Carmen Arenas, please.

RECEPTIONIST: Who shall I say is calling?

LORENA: A friend of Mrs. Salguero.

RECEPTIONIST: Just a moment, please.

CARMEN: Carmen speaking . . .

LORENA: My name is Lorena Salazar. I'm a friend of Mrs. Salguero's son.

CARMEN: Oh! How are the Salgueros? I haven't seen them in a while.

LORENA: Fine, fine.

CARMEN: I'm happy to hear that. Tell me, what can I do for you?

LORENA: Well, I'm looking to move into a new apartment, but I haven't had much luck with the classified ads.

CARMEN: I see. What type of apartment are you looking for, dear?

LORENA: A one bedroom, downtown. I'd prefer one with a balcony and a telephone.

CARMEN: And, when are you planning on moving?

LORENA: Yesterday, if it were possible.

CARMEN: I see. Well, dear, I have one in El Zocalo, on Guatemala Street. It's about 450 square feet, with one bedroom. It also has a small laundry room. They're asking $500, and it's available at the beginning of the month. The only catch is that you have to sign a lease for at least one year.

LORENA: That's no problem at all! How much is the security deposit?

CARMEN: The owner is asking for one month's security deposit and one month's rent in advance.

LORENA: And, when could I see it?

CARMEN: I can show it to you today, if that's okay. Why don't you come over to the office this afternoon?

LORENA: At what time should I come over?

CARMEN: At two o'clock?

LORENA: That's fine. Thank you very much for your help.

CARMEN: Don't mention it. Say hello to Mrs. Salguero for me.

LORENA: I will. Good-bye!

CARMEN: I'll see you at two. Good-bye!

PABLO: So? What's going on?

LORENA: Fantastic! She told me to go see her at two o'clock. If I finally manage to move, I'll build you a monument!

PABLO: Some tamales would be enough!

LORENA: Pablito, you're the greatest!

B. APUNTES

1. Another verb meaning "to rent" is *arrendar*. In Spanish, the verb *rentar* exists, but it means "to earn rent," not "to rent." *El departamento nos renta $4000 por año.* (The apartment earns an annual rent of $4000.)

2. *Ciudad México* and *Distrito Federal* both refer to Mexico City, the capital of Mexico.

3. Note the use of the subjunctive to describe an apartment that Lorena hopes exists, but may not.

4. In many Latin American countries, telephone companies are usually government-run, and the procedure for getting a telephone line is very lengthy. Telephones are registered to a particular address and may not be transferred when a person moves. Therefore, apartments "with telephones" are more expensive than apartments without them.

5. Note that in Latin America and in Spain, the $ sign represents *pesos,* the most common currency in Latin America; U.S. dollars are indicated by US$.

6. Utilities *(luz y gas)* are generally not provided by the landlord *(el dueño)* in Latin America. However, some landlords do provide central heating in the colder months.

7. Note the use of the future subjunctive to talk about remote possibilities in the future. *Si vieres a Juan esta noche, dile que me llame.* (If you see Juan tonight, tell him to call me.) Though grammatically "incorrect," the present indicative often replaces the future subjunctive in conversation. For more on the sequence of tenses in "if" clauses, see *Gramática y usos, Lección 12.*

8. Note the compound adjective *caritriste* (sad-faced). In Spanish, words are often combined in this manner to create new ones. For more on the formation of derived adjectives, see *Gramática y usos,* this lesson.

9. Having *una muchacha* (a housekeeper) is very common in Latin America. Housekeepers often live with their employers and are then considered part of the family.

10. The verb *andar* has many uses in colloquial speech. *Andar* means "to roam" (for people), "to walk" (for animals), "to run" (for machines). It is also used in the sense of "to be doing." *¿Cómo anda Laura? Hace mucho que no la veo.* (How's Laura doing? I haven't seen her in a long time.) *Los trenes andan a tiempo.* (The trains are running on schedule.)

11. Note that *s* is not added to last names when referring to families as a whole; only the definite article is plural. *Los Smith siguen en Europa, visitando a los Hernández.* (The Smiths are still in Europe visiting the Hernandezes.)

12. *El Zócalo* is a beautiful historic district in downtown Mexico City. In this neighborhood, many streets are named after Latin American countries.

13. Although most apartment buildings do not offer laundry facilities to tenants, larger apartments generally have a small balcony-like room called *un lavadero,* with a large sink and a clothesline to wash and dry your clothes. More modern apartments have *un lavarropas* (a washing machine) or *un secarropas* (a dryer) in the *lavadero,* as well.

14. *Bastar* is an indirect object verb meaning "to be sufficient/enough." *Necesito comprar lana, me bastaría con diez metros.* (I need to buy some wool; ten meters would be enough for me.) In formal conversation, *ser suficiente* (to be sufficient) is used instead. *Nos son suficientes tres meses para terminar de construir la casa.* (Three months are enough for us to build the house.)

C. GRAMATICA Y USOS

1. LOS ADJETIVOS (ADJECTIVES)

In Spanish, adjectives generally follow the nouns they modify. However, if an adjective stresses an intrinsic quality of a noun, it must precede it. In either position, adjectives agree in gender and number with the nouns they modify.

Las grandes empresas generalmente están sujetas a un estricto control estatal.
Large companies are generally subject to strict government control.

A few adjectives lose their final -*o* before singular masculine nouns. They are: *primero, tercero, bueno, malo, alguno,* and *ninguno.*

El departamento en alquiler está en el tercer piso, a la derecha del pasillo.
The apartment that's for rent is on the third floor, on the right of the hallway.

The adjective *grande* means "large" when it follows a noun, but "great, famous" when it precedes it. *Grande* may be shortened to *gran* when used before singular nouns.

El General José de San Martín fué un gran prócer sudamericano.
General Jose de San Martin was a great South American patriot.

Los Torreón se compraron una gran casa playera; es grande y muy cómoda.
The Torreons bought themselves a great beach house; it's big and very comfortable.

Señoras y señores, les aseguro que tienen en las manos un gran producto.
Ladies and gentlemen, I assure you that you have a great product in your hands.

Spanish adjectives may also function as nouns, in which case they are preceded by an article.

De las tres propuestas, la segunda me gusta más.
Of the three proposals, I like the second one best.

Ellos se quieren comprar un terreno. —¿Uno grande o uno chico?
They want to buy a plot of land. —A big one or a small one?

¿Cuál de estos departamentos está más cerca de la Universidad?—El de la calle San Antonio.[1]

Which one of these apartments is closest to the university?—The one on San Antonio Street.

Spanish adjectives may be combined with nouns to create compound adjectives. Generally speaking, the ending of the noun is dropped, and the noun is attached to the beginning of the adjective. The letter *i* may be inserted between these elements to facilitate pronunciation. Adjectives of this type generally refer to physical characteristics of people or animals and are often used jokingly or for emphasis.

Ayer la vi a Lorena . . . estaba un poco cabizbaja porque no podía encontrar un departamento.

I saw Lorena yesterday—she was a little droopy-headed because she couldn't find an apartment.

Raúl se compró un gato patilargo, colicorto y barrigón.

Raul bought a long-legged, short-tailed, big-bellied cat.

Spanish adjectives may also be used after verbs like *encontrar* or *parecer(le)*[2] to state an opinion.

Estoy leyendo el libro que me recomendaste y lo encuentro un tanto aburrido.

I'm reading the book you recommended, and I find it somewhat boring.

A los Arena les parecen bastante cansadores el viaje y la estadía.

The Arenas are finding the trip and the stay pretty tiring.

Finally, keep in mind that adjectives may be formed with *de* + a noun or an adverb + an infinitive.

El departamento está en un barrio de mucha categoría.

The apartment is in a very high-class neighborhood.

Los Smith son una familia de muchos amigos.

The Smiths are a family with many friends.

Gustavo es un muchacho de pocas palabras y de buen comer.

Gustavo is a young man of few words and a healthy appetite.

---

1. Remember that the construction *de* + a single word or phrase may function as an adjective. When preceded by an article, this construction functions as a noun and most commonly replaces a relative pronoun in informal conversation.

    ¿Viste a aquel hombre?—¿A cuál?—Al de anteojos.
        (Did you see that man?—Which one?—The one with glasses.)

2. Note that the verb *parecer(le)* is used in conjunction with indirect object pronouns.

2. *EL SUBJUNTIVO EN CLAUSULAS ADJETIVALES Y TEMPORALES* (THE SUBJUNCTIVE IN ADJECTIVAL AND TEMPORAL CLAUSES).

The subjunctive is used in clauses that describe things or people that are imagined but may or may not exist. When referring to something that certainly exists, always use the indicative. When referring to someone or something that certainly does *not* exist, use the subjunctive. Compare:

¿Hay aquí alguien que hable español?
Is there anyone here who speaks Spanish?
(the person may or may not exist)

—Sí, hay una señorita que lo habla, la señorita López.
—Yes. There's a young lady who speaks Spanish, Miss Lopez.
(the person does exist)

—No, aquí no hay nadie que lo hable.
—No. There isn't anyone here who speaks Spanish.
(the person does not exist)

Busco una casa que sea grande y que tenga una piscina.
I'm looking for a house that is large and has a swimming pool.

Me interesa la casa en Providencia al 230 que es grande y que tiene una piscina.
I'm interested in the house at 230 Providence Street, which is large and has a swimming pool.

The subjunctive is also used in clauses that refer to future events, as there is no guarantee that they will actually occur.

Seguramente van a llamarnos de la inmobiliaria en cuanto tengan algo disponible.
They will surely call us from the real estate agency as soon as they have something available.

Cuando reciba el contrato de alquiler, voy a poder instalar el teléfono.
When I receive the lease, I'll be able to install the telephone.

Cuando veas a María mañana, dile que me llame.
When you see Maria tomorrow, tell her to call me.

D. HABLEMOS DE NEGOCIOS

LOS INMUEBLES (REAL ESTATE)

When planning to stay in a country for an extended period of time, it is a good idea to look into the possibility of renting an apartment. Many people advertise *alquileres* or *arriendos* (rents) or *subalquileres* (sublets) of small apartments, and rents are generally 30 to 50% cheaper in Spanish-speaking countries than in the U.S. Be aware that you may get a better deal if you offer to pay in U.S. dollars, particularly in Latin America. Commercial space is also generally cheaper, although large cities can be expensive, even by U.S. standards, especially in Argentina, Venezuela, and Spain. In Latin America, commercial space is often rented in U.S. dollars.

A good opportunity for business with Latin American countries is in the field of export of materials for *casas prefabricadas* (pre-built homes). Due to changing economic conditions, this field will experience considerable expansion, especially in the suburban and seaside areas of Latin America. Many Latin Americans and Spaniards invest in real estate in seaside cities, renting apartments and homes to vacationing families and tourists.

Following is a portion of a typical *contrato de alquiler/locación* (lease) in Spanish:

Contrato de Locación

Entre: ···

(Nombre del locador) _____, con
domicilio legal en (domicilio legal) _____
_____ , en adelante
el LOCADOR, y (nombre del locatario) _____
_____ , quien se identifica con (documento de identificación y número)
_____, en adelante el LOCATARIO

El LOCATARIO se compromete a pagar al LOCADOR un alquiler mensual de
pesos _____ por la vivienda sita en (dirección de la vivienda)
_____
_____ , por el término
de (término del alquiler, en meses) _____ a partir de la fecha
de la firma de este contrato. Ambas partes se comprometen a cumplir con las
obligaciones expuestas en las siguientes cláusulas:···

1. El LOCATARIO se compromete a pagar antes del día diez (10) de cada mes
la suma expuesta en el párrafo anterior en concepto de alquiler. Si no lo hiciere,
se le sumará a aquel monto un recargo de _____ pesos por dia.··········

2. El LOCATARIO se compromete a no realizar adiciones, contrucciones ni
modificaciones permanentes ni semipermanentes a la vivienda sin permiso
expreso escrito del LOCADOR: ··

3. El LOCATARIO se compromete a mantener la vivienda en condiciones
habitables en todo momento. ··

4. El LOCADOR se compromete a realizar reparaciones de la estructura interna
de la vivienda, previo pedido por parte del LOCATARIO. Tales estructuras
internas incluyen cañerías e instalaciones eléctricas. Si el LOCADOR no
respondiere dentro del plazo de siete (7) días a tal pedido por parte del
LOCATARIO, el LOCATARIO podrá realizar las reparaciones por cuenta propia,
notificando luego al LOCADOR del monto total de los gastos incurridos en tales
reparaciones, luego de lo cual el LOCADOR se verá obligado a cubrir tal monto
más un sobrecargo del 25% de total. ··

En caso de violación de cualquiera de los términos de este contrato, ambas
partes se someten al fuero y jurisdicción de los Tribunales de la Provincia,
renunciando expresamente a cualquier otro fuero y jurisdicción. ························

Firmado en común acuerdo este _____ día del mes
de _____ , de_____ , en la ciudad
de _____ .·································

Firma del LOCADOR:_____

Firma del LOCATARIO: _____

1. Another common term for "rent" or "lease" is *arrendamento,* and for "tenant" or "lessee" is *arrendatano.*

Lease Agreement

Between:

(Name of Landlord) _____, with legal
domicile at _____.
_____, heretofore the LANDLORD;
and (Name of Tenant) _____, who verifies
his/her identity with (type and number of legal I.D.) _____,
heretofore the TENANT.

The TENANT agrees to pay the LANDLORD a monthly rent of
_____ pesos for the dwelling located at (address of dwelling)
_____
_____, for the
term of (term in months) _____ , starting from the date of the signing
of this contract. Both parties agree to abide by the obligations expressed in the
following clauses:

1. The TENANT agrees to pay before the tenth (10th) day of each month the
amount stipulated in the preceding paragraph in concept of rent. If he/she were
not to do so, a surcharge of _____ pesos per day will be added to
that sum.

2. The TENANT agrees not to execute permanent or non-permanent additions,
constructions or modifications to the dwelling without express written consent of
the LANDLORD.

3. The TENANT agrees to maintain the dwelling in habitable condition at all
times.

4. The LANDLORD agrees to execute repairs of the internal structures of the
dwelling with prior written request by the TENANT. Such internal structures
include pipes and electrical installations. If the LANDLORD were not to respond
within seven (7) days to such a request by the TENANT, the TENANT may
proceed to execute the repairs by him/herself, notifying the LANDLORD of the
total amount of the repairs, after which the LANDLORD will be obligated to cover
such expenses plus a surcharge of 25% of the total.

In the event that any of the terms of this contract are violated, both parties agree
to submit to the jurisdiction and code of laws of the Provincial Court, renouncing
expressly to any other jurisdiction and code of law.

Signed in mutual agreement on this _____ day of _____ ,
of the year _____ , in the city of _____ .

Signature of LANDLORD: _____

Signature of TENANT: _____

VOCABULARIO

back yard	*fondo (de casa/de propiedad)*
bedroom	*dormitorio/recámara*
cabin (vacation home)	*cabaña*
co-op (apartment)	*(departamentos) cooperativos*
security deposit	*depósito de seguridad*
elevator	*ascensor/elevador*
floor	*piso*
furnished	*amoblado, amueblado*
unfurnished	*sin amoblar, sin muebles*
furniture	*muebles*
interest rate	*tasa de interés*
fixed rate	*tasa fija*
kitchen	*cocina*
land	*tierra/solar/terreno*
lease	*contrato de alquiler*
living room	*sala/"living"*
loan	*préstamo*
lot	*lote*
mortgage	*hipoteca*
owner	*dueño*
parking lot	
(in a building)	*cochera*
(outside)	*playa/plaza de estacionamiento*
property	*propiedad/bien inmueble*
-tax	*impuesto inmobiliario*
real estate	*inmueble(s)/bienes raíces*
-office	*inmobiliaria, oficina de bienes raíces*
rent	*alquiler, arriendo*
rent (to)	*alquilar, arrendar*
room	*cuarto, habitación, ambiente*
service quarters	*dependencias, cuarto de servicios*
superintendent	*encargado*
surface (area of a property)	*superficie*
tenant	*inquilino*
term	*término*

EXAMEN

A. *Complete las oraciones siguientes con el subjuntivo o el indicativo del verbo indicado.* (Complete the following sentences with the subjunctive or the indicative of the verb in parentheses.)

1. *Lorena busca un departamento que (TENER) una recámara.*
2. *¿Hay algún terreno que (PODER) ser convertido en estacionamiento?*
3. *Manuel se mudó a un barrio que (SER) de gran categoría.*
4. *No hay nadie en la oficina que (HABLAR) español.*
5. *Cuando (LLAMAR) a la inmobiliaria, diles que llamas de mí parte.*

B. *Complete las oraciones siguientes en español.* (Complete the following sentences in Spanish.)

1. *Quisiera* (rent) *un* (two-bedroom apartment) *en el* (downtown).
2. (The Gomezes) *tienen una* (great, famous) *empresa* (real estate).
3. *Cuando* (you can), *por favor venga a ver qué pasa con mi salida* (of central heating). *No* (it works) *bien.*
4. *De las tres casas que vimos, me gustó más* (the one on Central Street)
5. *¿En qué piso queda el* (studio)?

C. *Traduzca todas las oraciones precedentes al inglés.* (Translate the sentences in Exercises A and B into English.)

LECCION 10

A. DIALOGO

MIRANDO LA TELE.

Elena ha venido desde Tegucigalpa[1] a visitar a sus parientes[2] en Nueva York. Entre ellos, se encuentra su primo Gerardo quien vive en Nueva York desde que era muy pequeño.

ELENA: ¿Habrá algún buen programa en la tele?[3]

GERARDO: No sé. Enciéndela.[4]

ELENA: ¿Qué veo? ¡Está mi serie favorita desde pequeña: "Viaje a las estrellas!"

GERARDO: ¿Hablas en serio? ¿La pasan[5] en Honduras?

ELENA: ¡Claro! Es una serie clásica de ciencia ficción. De hecho, conozco bien este capítulo: en éste, el capitán Kirk, el doctor McCoy y Spock bajaron para salvar a los habitantes de un planeta que está por explotar, porque el sol está por convertirse en nova. ¿Ves a esos seres cabezones? Se habían llevado a aquella muchacha muda a un laboratorio subterráneo para ver si su especie era digna de ser salvada de la destrucción.

GERARDO: Sí. Y los tripulantes del "Enterprise" también fueron sujetos al experimento.

ELENA *(mirando la pantalla con expresión lastimosa)*: Sí, en cuanto hubieron bajado. ¡Qué pena que esté[6] en inglés! En Honduras la veía doblada[7] al español.

GERARDO: ¿Así que doblan las series estadounidenses por televisión en Honduras? Yo creía que las pasaban con subtítulos.

ELENA: No. Generalmente sólo pasan con subtítulos las películas en el cine, excepto las películas para niños, que también son dobladas.

GERARDO: ¡Qué interesante! Mira, ya termina el episodio. Cambiemos a Telemundo, es un canal en español.

ELENA: Está por empezar "El show de Cristina."[8]

GERARDO: ¿También conoces este programa? ¡No me digas que lo pasan en Honduras!

ELENA: Creo que se ve por toda Latinoamérica. Hay bastantes programas internacionales, sobre todo los documentales, como la revista del "National Geographic."

GERARDO: A mí, los documentales me aburren y los "talk shows" también. Cambio a otro canal en español, Univisión.

ELENA: Dime, ¿cuántos canales hay aquí en total, en Nueva York?

GERARDO: ¡Muchísimos! Hay unas ocho redes en el aire y unos cuarenta más por cable, aunque algunos hay que pagarlos adicionalmente. Hay cinco canales en español.

ELENA: ¡Con razón[9] miran tanta televisión los estadounidenses! En mi país tenemos cuatro redes nacionales y por cable hay una docena más. Yo vivo en Tegucigalpa, y allí hay servicio de televisión por cable, pero en muchas regiones aún no se consigue.

GERARDO: Bueno, aquí tienes otro canal en español. Éste no me gusta mucho, parece que todo el día pasan o telenovelas o programas con música tropical. A mí me gustan las películas.

ELENA: Yo también quisiera ver alguna buena película.

GERARDO: Voy a rastrear los canales. Quizás encontremos algo que nos guste.

Gerardo toca el botón de rastreo, y pasan los canales uno tras otro por la pantalla.

ELENA: ¡Espera! ¡Ah![10] Es "La bella y la bestia" de Cocteau. Me encanta el cine surrealista.

GERARDO: ¿Surrealista? ¡Zás![10] Yo tengo ganas de divertirme, y no de dormirme.[11]

ELENA: Bueno, si te disgusta tanto, cambia. Pero mirarla te haría bien.

GERARDO: Pero, es en francés y no está doblada, sino tiene subtítulos en inglés . . . no me gusta para nada[12] tener que leer. Pongo el canal cinco.

ELENA: Quizás te agrade ésta. Es una americana, de acción, con explosiones, tiroteos y gritos a patadas.[13] No necesita traducción.

GERARDO: Sí, sí, pero ésta, ya la vi.

ELENA: ¡Menos mal! A ver, dame el control remoto, que voy a elegir yo.

GERARDO: ¡Ahí está! Es el canal de videos musicales.

ELENA: No tengo muchas ganas de mirarlo. Yo quería ver alguna película que me hiciera pensar,[14] y no una de cortometraje con mariposas, calaveras y gente estrafalaria.

GERARDO: ¡Y decías que te gustaba el surrealismo!

ELENA: **Yo hablaba de un surrealismo más filosófico.**

GERARDO: **Bueno, ¿por qué no hacemos una cosa? Vamos a la videoteca y elijamos algo que nos guste a los dos: surrealista, filosófico . . . y lleno de acción.**

ELENA: **¿Como qué, por ejemplo?**

GERARDO: **¡Como una película de Schwarzenegger!**

ELENA *(alzando los ojos al cielo):* **¡Paciencia, Señor, dame Paciencia!**

WATCHING TV.

Elena came from Tegucigalpa to visit her relatives in New York. Among them is her cousin Gerardo, who has lived in New York from a very young age.

ELENA: Is there anything good on TV?

GERARDO: I don't know. Turn it on.

ELENA: Wow! It's "Star Trek," my favorite show, ever since I was a kid!

GERARDO: Are you serious? Do they show it in Honduras?

ELENA: Of course! It's a classic science fiction series. In fact, I know this episode: Captain Kirk, Doctor McCoy, and Spock beamed down to save the inhabitants of a planet that is about to explode because its sun is about to turn into a nova. See those big-headed creatures? They had taken that mute girl to an underground laboratory to see if her species was worthy of being saved from destruction.

GERARDO: Yeah. And the crew of the *Enterprise* was also subjected to the experiment.

ELENA (looking at the screen with a pained expression): Yes, as soon as they beamed down. It's too bad that it's in English! In Honduras I saw it dubbed into Spanish.

GERARDO: So they dub American shows into Spanish on Honduran TV? I thought they showed them with subtitles.

ELENA: No. Generally they only use subtitles in the theater, except for children's movies, which are also dubbed.

GERARDO: That's really interesting! Look, the episode is almost over. Let's change to Telemundo, it's a Spanish-language channel.

ELENA: The talk show, "Cristina," is about to begin.

GERARDO: You also know this program? Don't tell me they show it in Honduras, too!

ELENA: I think it's aired throughout Latin America. There are a lot of international programs, especially documentaries, like "National Geographic."

GERARDO: Documentaries bore me, and so do talk shows. Let's change to another Spanish channel. Okay, here's Univision.

ELENA: Tell me, how many channels *do* you have here, anyway?

GERARDO: Lots! There are about eight networks on the air, and another forty or so on cable, although for some you pay extra. There are five Spanish-language channels.

ELENA: No wonder Americans watch so much TV! In Honduras, we have four national networks, and on cable there are a dozen more. I live in Tegucigalpa, and there we have cable, but it's not available in many regions.

GERARDO: Well, here's another cable channel. I don't like this one too much; it seems as though they show either soap operas or programs with tropical music all day. I like movies.

ELENA: I could also go for a good movie.

GERARDO: I'll scan the channels. Maybe we can find something we both like.

Gerardo touches the scan button, and the channels flash by on the screen.

ELENA: Hold it! Oh! It's "Beauty and the Beast" by Cocteau. I love surrealist cinema.

GERARDO: Surrealist! Good grief! I wanted to have a good time, and not go to sleep!

ELENA: If you can't stand it, change it. But, watching it would do you some good.

GERARDO: But, it's in French, and it's not dubbed but subtitled in English! I hate having to read! I'm changing to channel five.

ELENA: Maybe you'll like this one. It's an American one, an action movie with explosions, shoot-outs, and a lot of screaming. It needs no translation.

GERARDO: Yeah, yeah! But I've already seen this one.

ELENA: Thank goodness! Give me the remote. I'm going to choose now!

GERARDO: There we go! It's the music video channel.

ELENA: I don't feel too much like watching it. I wanted to see something that would make me think, not a clip with butterflies, skulls, and tacky people!

GERARDO: And you said you liked surrealism!

ELENA: I was talking about a more philosophical surrealism.

GERARDO: Okay! Why don't we go to the video store, and choose something we both like: surrealistic, philosophical . . . and full of action.

ELENA: Like what, for instance?

GERARDO: Like a Schwarzenegger movie!

ELENA (rolling her eyes): Patience, Lord! Give me patience!

B. APUNTES

1. *Tegucigalpa,* the capital and largest metropolitan area of Honduras, is home to approximately 20% of the country's population. Tegucigalpa enjoys a year-round temperature of 75°–85°F, with cool nights.

   Honduras is a small and peaceful country of relative political stability located in the northern part of Central America. It began a program of diversification of economic products after hurricane Fifi in 1976.

2. Note that the word *parientes* refers to relatives in general. Parents (father and mother) are *los padres.*

3. *La tele* (TV) is short for *la televisión* (television) or *el televisor* (television set). It is mostly used by children or by teenagers. *En la tele, dan películas a eso de las ocho.* (On TV, they show movies at around eight o'clock.) *Se descompuso la tele.* (The TV broke down.)

4. The verbs *encender* (to light; to turn on) and *apagar* (to extinguish; to turn off) are used with all electrical appliances, including lights. *Me olvidé de apagar el ventilador antes de salir.* (I forgot to turn off the fan before leaving). *Dígale a mantenimiento que enciendan las luces en la sala de proyección en cuanto termine la película.* (Tell maintenance to turn on the lights as soon as the film is over.) There are many other regional terms as well, such as *prender* (to catch fire) and *apagar* (to extinguish), which is used in many South American countries, and *abrir* (to open) and *cerrar* (to close), which is used in Spain.

5. Note that, in Spanish, they "pass"—*pasan*—or "give"—*dan*—a movie, while in English they "show" it.

6. Expressions of disapproval or approval, such as *¡qué pena que . . . !* *¡qué lástima que . . . !* (too bad that . . . !), and *¡qué bueno que . . . !* (it's a good thing that . . . !) are always followed by a verb in the subjunctive.

7. Foreign sitcoms, series, and some movies are generally *dobladas* (dubbed) into what is called *español neutro* (nuetral Spanish). Since these films are marketed throughout the Spanish-speaking world, "neutral Spanish" avoids any regional accents or inflections.

8. Note that the English word "show" is also used in Spanish.

9. *¡Con razón (que) . . . !* (no wonder that . . . !) is followed by a verb in the indicative because it refers to an established fact.

10. *¡Zás!* and *¡Uy!* are polite interjections used to express an undesirable surprise. *Ayer caminaba por la calle y, ¡zás!, vi a mi antigua novia.* (Yesterday I was walking down the street and, rats!, I saw my ex-girlfriend!) To indicate a welcome surprise, use *¡Ah!* or *¡Oh!* instead. *Viajaba por Europa y ¡oh, sorpresa! me encontré con un viejo amigo.* (I was traveling in Europe when, surprise!, I ran into an old friend.)

11. *Tener ganas de* followed by a verb in the infinitive is a common expression used to indicate the desire to do something. *Tengo ganas de ir al cine.* (I feel like going to the movies.)

12. The expression *para nada* (not for anything) and *en absoluto* (absolutely not) are used as a very emphatic "no, not!"

13. The expressions *a patadas* (in abundance, plenty) and *a granel* (in bulk) are used after plural nouns to express an indeterminately large amount of something, very much like the English "a whole lot of," "bunches of," and "lots of." *En el depósito hay papeles para fotocopias a granel.* (There is a lot of photocopy paper in the storage room.)

14. Note the use of the subjunctive to describe an imaginary noun, in this case a TV program Elena would like to see. The subjunctive must be used to describe nouns we imagine, but that may not exist or be available.

C. GRAMATICA Y USOS

1. *LOS ADJETIVOS INDEFINIDOS* (INDEFINITE ADJECTIVES)

The principal indefinite adjectives in Spanish are *alguno* (some), *ninguno* (no . . .), *cada* (every, each), *todo* (all), *varios* (several), and *otro* (other). They are used to refer to indefinite quantities of a noun.

Alguno and its negative counterpart *ninguno* generally precede the noun. They are abbreviated to *algún* and *ningún* before masculine singular nouns.

Algunas películas en el cine son dobladas al español, y algunas se pasan con subtítulos.
Some movies are dubbed into Spanish, while others are shown with subtitles.

Algún idiota[1] *desconectó mi sistema de cable.*
Some idiot (male) disconnected my cable system.

Me gustan algunos programas de humor, sobre todo los de México.
I like some comedy programs, especially ones from Mexico.

Note that the plural forms *ningunos* and *ningunas* are seldom used because they refer only to nouns that are inherently plural (i.e., *los anteojos* (eyeglasses), *los pantalones* (pants), etc.

¡No quiero ningunos anteojos naranjas! ¡Parecen de circo!
I don't want any orange glasses! They look like they belong in a circus!

Cada and *todo/a* mean "each, every" when used before a singular noun denoting a category. Note that *cada* does not change to reflect gender.

Tendrás que supervisar cada programa que miren los niños cuando consigas televisión por cable.
You'll have to supervise every program your children watch when you get cable TV.

¡Cada diez minutos hay un bloque de propagandas por televisión!
Every ten minutes there's a block of commercials on TV!

When followed by a noun introduced by an article, *todo* means "all of, the whole" and must agree in gender and number with the noun.

¿Pudiste grabar toda la película, o se te acabó la cinta de video?
Were you able to tape the whole movie, or did you run out of videotape?

No es bueno que los niños miren televisión todo el día.
It's not good for children to watch TV all day.

Mi mujer hizo todas las preparaciones para el cumpleaños de Rosa.
My wife made all the preparations for Rosa's birthday party.

---

1. Some nouns, especially those ending in *-ema* or *-iota,* are neuter and take a masculine article. Most of them are of Greek origin, such as *el problema, el teorema, el tema.* When they refer to people, they do not change endings to reflect gender. Thus we have *el idiota* (the male idiot) and *la idiota* (the female idiot).

Varios means "several" or "various." As in English, it is always followed by plural nouns.

Ya he hecho varias llamadas, pero no he podido encontrar un departamento.
I have already made several calls, but I haven't been able to find an apartment.

Varios de nuestros empleados hablan inglés.
Several of our employees speak English.

2. *EL PRETERITO PLUSCUAMPERFECTO* (THE PAST PERFECT)

The past perfect is formed with the imperfect of the verb *haber* and the past participle of the main verb. It is used to describe an action that was completed prior to another past action.

	MIRAR TO LOOK	*PONER* TO PUT	*IR* TO GO
yo había *tú habías* *él/ella/Vd. había* *nosotros habíamos* *vosotros habíais* *ellos/ellas/Vds. habían*	*mirado*	*puesto*	*ido*

Cuando llegó Enrique a la cena anoche, todos ya habíamos comido.
When Enrique arrived at the dinner last night, we had already eaten.

No quise ir a ver la película con los muchachos porque yo ya la había visto.
I refused to go to the movie with the guys because I had already seen it.

Antes de viajar a España, habían tomado unos cursos de español.
Before traveling to Spain, they had taken some Spanish language courses.

Note that the past perfect is often used with words that imply completion, such as *ya* (already) and *antes* (before). The past perfect is a somewhat formal tense and is often replaced by the preterite in conversation.

Habían estudiado/Estudiaron mucho antes de tomar el exámen.
They had studied a lot before taking the test.

¿Habías leido/Leíste las instrucciones antes de tratar de armar la video-grabadora?
Had you read the instructions before trying to put together the VCR?

146

3. *EL PRETÉRITO ANTERIOR* (THE PRETERITE PERFECT)

To express that an action was completed immediately prior to another action, another past perfect tense, called the *pretérito anterior,* or preterite perfect, is used. It is formed with the preterite of the verb *haber* followed by the past participle. Note that this tense is most often used with phrases such as *en cuanto* (as soon as), and *enseguida después de (que)* (right after).

	LLAMAR TO CALL	COMER TO EAT	IR TO GO
yo hube *tú hubiste* *él/ella/Vd. hubo* *nosotros hubimos* *vosotros hubisteis* *ellos/ellas/Vds. hubieron*	*llamado*	*comido*	*ido*

En cuanto hubo terminado la película, todos salieron del cine.
As soon as the movie had finished, everyone left the movie theater.

Todos dejamos de trabajar en la fábrica enseguida después de que hubo dado la señal de las cinco.
We all stopped working in the factory right after the five o'clock whistle had been blown.

En cuanto se hubo descuidado, se le quemaron los panqueques.
As soon as his attention had strayed, the pancakes burned.

Like the past perfect, the preterite perfect is somewhat formal and is generally replaced by the preterite in conversation.

La Sra. Martínez me llamó en seguida de que hube cortado/corté con Vd.
Mrs. Martinez called me right after I hung up with you.

D. HABLEMOS DE NEGOCIOS

LA PUBLICIDAD (ADVERTISING)

In Spain, the field of advertising is essentially similar to that in the U.S. It may be said, however, that Spanish TV commercials are more liberal and somewhat more risque.

The field of advertising presents many opportunities for American companies in Latin America, although it also offers particular challenges. First, it is necessary to keep in mind the linguistic unity of the region: Spanish is the predominant language, which offers the possibility of developing truly international campaigns in a single language. There is also a high rate of literacy: Latin American countries boast literacy rates of 80% to 95%. Finally, the age distribution is significantly different than in the U.S. Taking Colombia as an example, we find that 50% of the population is under the age of twenty. However, there are also some barriers to advertising. To date, there is a higher degree of government regulation in the public sector, particularly in the higher-income countries of Latin America, which causes processing delays.

Despite the popular image of Latin America as basically agricultural, overall, approximately 60% of the population is urban. In terms of income, we can divide Latin American countries into two groups: higher-income countries, which have a significant degree of regulation, such as Argentina, Mexico, and Venezuela, and middle-income countries, which have a moderate degree of advertising regulation.

Throughout Latin America as well as in Spain the mass media are the most prevalent form of advertising. TV averages 50%, radio ads vary between 10% (in the higher-income group) and 16% (in the middle-income group) of the total, and print absorbed 26% of advertising, the remainder corresponding to miscellaneous or unmeasured forms. Film and outdoor forms are important in Mexico and Argentina. Ads tend to reflect conservative values, such as home and family. References to eroticism in ads are common, and not considered immoral if done in good taste, with no nudity or overt sexuality. Comparative advertising is generally avoided, and even prohibited. In Spain, print ads tend to be the same size as in the U.S. (half- to full-page in magazines), while in Latin America, smaller ads (one-quarter- to half-page formats) are more common.

Consumer protection laws exist in Mexico, Venezuela, Colombia, and Argentina, and will probably be implemented in other countries in the future.

Following is a review of advertising regulations in several countries:

Mexico
Mexico is the most regulated Latin American country in terms of advertising. All ads must be approved by the Department of Industry and Commerce *(Departamento de Industria y Comercio)* and must comply with the following regulations:

a) All advertisements in foreign languages must have an accurate and complete translated Spanish text.
b) Health-related products are under close supervision; for example, food ads must not give the idea that their ingestion will provide heroic qualities.

c) Tobacco products cannot be advertised on television and radio until after 9 P.M., and ads may only refer to the origin and content of the tobacco mixture.
d) Alcohol may not be advertised until 10 P.M.
e) Comparative advertising is prohibited.

Argentina

Advertising is essentially a self-regulatory activity in Argentina, under the supervision of the private organization *CIAP (Comisión Intersocietaria de Autoregulación Publicitaria),* the Inter-company Commission for Advertising Self-regulation. The *CIAP* stipulates rather strict guidelines for the production of ads. For example, advertising costs may not be added to the cost of the finished product, and all commercials must abide by the 1969 code of ethics, which prohibits disrespectful references to public figures, patriotism, religion, customs, and morality. Disloyalty, professional endorsements, comparative advertising, and advertisements promising prizes and targeted at children are prohibited. In addition, foreign films are not allowed, except those that are shot and produced by local residents.

Venezuela

Venezuela has relatively strict foreign investment laws that limit foreign commercial activity. The import of foreign material, except print, is prohibited. There are also duties on "tools of the trade" and many laws that prohibit foreign films, except those shot and produced by local residents, as in Argentina. In addition, laws stipulate the use of local personnel, including actors and musicians.

Middle-income Countries

These countries present another type of challenge to advertising. In general, ad campaigns are executed on a smaller scale, and, due to the wide distribution of the population, sophisticated modern technologies are generally ineffective. Furthermore, the many local languages spoken, (especially in Ecuador, Peru, and Bolivia) preclude a universal campaign. The regulation of advertisements tends to be product-specific in these countries, with special emphasis on the advertisement of health and beauty products, except in professional journals. Ecuador, Nicaragua, and Peru prohibit advertisement of tobacco products on TV or in the press. Furthermore, Peru does not permit ads in a foreign language. In Guatemala, food ads must be approved by the government.

Finally, it is important to note that the *ANCOM* (Andean Common Market), which associates Bolivia, Colombia, Ecuador, Peru, and Venezuela, has laws prohibiting foreign investment in advertising and mass media, though in general these laws have not been enforced as strictly as mandated. These laws stipulate the nationalization of foreign investment by selling shares, 80% of which must belong to nationals.

EXAMEN

A. *Inserte el adjetivo indefinido que corresponda en cada oración.* (Insert the appropriate indefinite adjective in each sentence.)

    1. *No me gusta _____ programa que tenga violencia.*
    2. *_____ propagandas son divertidas, otras no.*
    3. *¿_____ de estos anteojos te gustan? ¡Eres muy difícil!*
    4. *En las películas no aptas* (suitable) *para menores, suelen revisarle los documentos de identificación a _____ persona que parezca demasiado jóven.*
    5. *_____ las semanas me voy al cine con mis amigos, para ver películas europeas.*

B. *Complete las oraciones siguientes con el tiempo verbal que corresponda.* (Complete the following sentences with the appropriate verb form.)

    1. *Te reconocí en cuanto (yo) _____ escuchado tu voz.*
    2. *¿Nunca antes _____ visto una película de Schwarzenegger? ¡No lo puedo creer!*
    3. *Cuando llegaste, la película ya _____ empezado.*
    4. *Ayer quise llamaros por teléfono para avisarlos que no podía ir, pero vosotros ya os _____ ido.*
    5. *Después de que los técnicos _____ instalado el cable, nos sentamos a mirar televisión toda la noche!*

C. *Traduzca las oraciones de los ejercicios A y B al inglés.* (Translate the sentences in Exercises A and B into English.)

PRIMER REPASO (FIRST REVIEW)

A. *Complete las oraciones siguientes.* (Complete the following sentences.)

1. (I've just) *llegar al aeropuerto y* (I'm about to) *tomar un taxi.* (I'm going to be) *en casa en cuarenta minutos.*
2. (I have to reserve for them) *tres* (rooms) *en el hotel "Excelsior".* (They would prefer) *unas que* (were to be) *contiguas.*
3. *¡No he visto* (ever) *un hotel tan hermoso! ¿En* (what) *año* (it) *construyeron?*
4. *¿*(Where) *vas a* (go) *esta noche?—Creo que a la* (book fair). (There will be) *una exposición interesante esta noche.*
5. *¿Qué* (were you doing) *ayer a las cinco?* (You) *llamé y no* (you weren't) *en la oficina.*
6. *Raúl tiene un gato muy cómico: Es* (short-legged) *y* (long-tailed).
7. *La señora Inés quiere ver* (an apartment) *que* (has) *tres* (rooms), *y que no* (is) *demasiado lejos del* (downtown).
8. *No creo que* (there is anything) *que nos guste en el cine, ¡vayamos a la* (fair)!
9. *¿*(Did you manage to) *encontrar a* (your cousins) *cuando* (you traveled) *a Lima?*
10. *A la* (secretary) *no* (her) *gusté mucho, pero al* (personnel director) *sí.*

B. *Traduzca las oraciones siguientes al español.* (Translate the following sentences into Spanish.)

1. Last year, the students traveled through Spain and learned a lot about Spanish culture.
2. While Jorge was living in Caracas, he was working for an important import/export company.
3. This new computer will help us update the client data base quickly and efficiently.
4. It is said that private universities are better than public ones, but I doubt that's true.
5. In all fields of business, computers are used more and more extensively.
6. Julia lost her computer disk and had to type her reports again because she hadn't saved them on the hard drive.
7. As soon as Julian and Marta had seen the house, they knew they would buy it.
8. I wonder if they will show an interesting movie on TV tonight . . .
9. Where did you *(vosotros)* put the forms that we received yesterday?
10. Have you *(tú)* ever seen the lighting of the tree at Rockefeller Center? I haven't seen it.
11. My hotel room faces the mountains, and yours *(vosotros)*?
12. By Monday, Karina has to finish her business here in Panama City and return to New York.

13. Could you lend me your computer for a couple of hours this afternoon?
14. We have promised to finish these author lists, and we have to give them to the boss by Friday.
15. You can prepare a printout of the client addresses from the central data base using this computer, but no one has access to the sales reports without a password.

LECCION 11

A. DIALOGO

LOS CAFETALES DE DON IGNACIO.

El Sr. Troy Gillis, un agricultor estadounidense, ha sido invitado a visitar la finca cafetera de Don[1] Ignacio Esquivel en los ondulantes montes de Colombia cerca de Lérida, en el municipio del Líbano.[2] Troy, el agregado[3] Antonio Jaramillo y cuatro peones viajan en línea[4] por los senderos de la finca.

TROY: Ahora, ¿para dónde vamos?

ANTONIO: Ahorita[5] vamos pal'[6] despulpadero. Ahí se van a bajar los peones y llevar a que se despulpen los granos de café.

TROY: ¿Cómo se despulpan? ¿A mano?

ANTONIO: No, hay una despulpadora automática. Es una máquina eléctrica y bastante simple de hacer funcionar.

TROY: Y después, ¿se los llevan a secar en seguida?

ANTONIO: No, después de despulparlos, se los llevan otra vez al lavadero y se los lavan muy a fondo. El segundo lavado es más importante que el primero. Después se lleva todo al secadero.[7]

TROY: ¡No sabía que el proceso fuese tan complicado!

ANTONIO: No es complicado, pero lleva su tiempo . . .

TROY: . . . y dedicación. Quizás ése sea el secreto del café colombiano . . . algunos dicen que es el mejor del mundo.

ANTONIO: No sabría decirle si es verdad, aunque no me sorprendería que así fuese; aunque, a mí me parece que, de ser como Vd. dice, sería más por la tierra colombiana que por otra cosa: aquí se dan las condiciones ideales para el cafeto.

TROY: ¿Como cuáles?

ANTONIO: Bueno, primero el clima. El cafeto necesita un clima estable, y aquí casi todo el año es igual el tiempo: hace unos 20°. También hay mucha lluvia todo el año.

TROY: ¿Acaso no es difícil cultivar el café en los montes?[8]

ANTONIO: Depende de donde sea: aquí las laderas tienen pendientes muy suaves y eso ayuda a la irrigación natural, porque el agua no se estanca. En las montañas, donde las pendientes son mayores, es más difícil cultivar el café porque el agua de lluvia arrastra las plantas montaña abajo.[9]

TROY: Entiendo . . .

A lo lejos, se ve a un peón solitario abonando el cafetal y a otro recogiendo plátanos.

TROY: ¿Porqué tienen tantos árboles frutales por aquí? ¿No sería mejor dejar que crezcan sólo los cafetos?

ANTONIO: Los platanales están allí a propósito. Sirven para dar sombra a las plantas y también para proveer a la finca. Además, la época de cultivo es sólo una por año y hay que diversificar un poco.

TROY: ¿En qué época del año es la cosecha?

ANTONIO: La cosecha principal es generalmente en octubre y en noviembre, aunque pronto hay una menor, en mayo. A esta cosecha menor le decimos[10] "la traviesa." Claro que, para la cosecha grande llegan muchos recolectores del interior. Don Ignacio es un patrón muy berraco[11] y siempre les da una bodega[12] en donde hospedarse . . . Ahorita vamos pa'[6] la casa del Don, en cuanto descarguen el café.

Luego de que los peones descargan los costales, se despiden[13] de Antonio y de Troy, quienes salen a los senderos nuevamente.

TROY: ¡Qué extensos son los cafetales! No me los imaginaba así antes.

ANTONIO: Y eso que[14] Vd. no ha visto aún los más grandes. Allí, se pierden en el horizonte . . . ¿ve allí aquella casa con tejas? Ésa es la casa del patrón. Ya no queda lejos.

Los dos finalmente llegan a la casa del patrón, situada en la ladera este de la montaña. Es una casa grande y rodeada de platanales y de muchas flores. Doña Lida les sale al encuentro.

ANTONIO: ¡Buenas,[15] doña! Le traigo a su invitado.

DOÑA LIDA: Buenas a Vds., y bienvenido a la finca, Sr. Troy.[16] El Don no está de vuelta del pueblo, pero pasen, pasen, que les tengo unos tintos[17] y muchas ganas de conversar con Vd., Sr. Troy. Mi marido me ha contado mucho acerca de su finca en los Estados Unidos.

TROY: Muchas gracias, señora. Le agradezco su hospitalidad.

DON IGNACIO'S COFFEE FIELDS.

Mr. Troy Gillis, an American farmer, has been invited to visit Don Ignacio Esquivel's coffee plantation in the rolling hills of Colombia near Lerida, in the municipality of Libano. Troy and the foreman, Antonio Jaramillo, along with four workers, are riding on a bus along the plantation roads.

TROY: Where are we headed now?

ANTONIO: Right now we're going to the husker. There, the workers will get off and carry the beans off to be husked.

TROY: And how are they husked, by hand?

ANTONIO: No, there's an automatic husker. It's an electric machine, and it's really simple to operate.

TROY: Is the coffee then dried right away?

ANTONIO: No. After the husking, the beans are taken back to the washer where they're washed once again, very thoroughly. The second wash is more important than the first. After that, everything's taken to be dried.

TROY: I didn't know the process was so complicated!

ANTONIO: It's not complicated, but it takes time!

TROY: . . . and dedication! Maybe that's the secret of Colombian coffee . . . Some say it's the best in the world.

ANTONIO: I couldn't tell you if that's true, but I wouldn't be surprised if it were. I think, if what you say is true, it would be due more to the Colombian soil than anything else. We have ideal conditions for growing coffee plants here.

TROY: Such as?

ANTONIO: First, the climate. The coffee plant needs a stable climate, and here it's around 70°F year-round. There's also abundant rain all year.

TROY: Isn't it hard to grow coffee on the mountains though?

ANTONIO: It depends where. Here the hills have very gentle slopes, and that helps natural irrigation because the water doesn't pool. However, in the mountains with steep slopes, it's harder to grow coffee because the rainwater drags the plants downhill.

TROY: I see . . .

In the distance, a worker can be seen fertilizing the soil, and another one picking plantains.

TROY: Why are there so many fruit trees around here? Wouldn't it be better to plant only coffee?

ANTONIO: The plantains are there for a reason. They provide shade for the coffee and food for the farm. Also, there's only one harvest a year, and we've got to diversify a little.

TROY: When is the harvest?

ANTONIO: The main harvest is generally in October and November, although there will be a small one soon, in May. We call it "the tricky one." Of course, for the main harvest, many workers come from the

157

countryside. Don Ignacio is a very good man—he always provides living quarters for his workers. Now, as soon as the men unload the coffee we're headed for his house.

After the workers unload the bags and say good-bye to Antonio and Troy, they both go back out to the road.

TROY: These plantations are huge! I hadn't imagined them this way!

ANTONIO: And you have yet to see the biggest ones! Those get lost in the horizon . . . Do you see that shingled house? That's the owner's house. It's not far.

They finally arrive at the owner's house, situated on the east slope of a hill. It's a large house surrounded by plantain trees and many flowers. Doña Lida comes out to greet them.

ANTONIO: Mornin', Doña! I've brought your guest!

DOÑA LIDA: Mornin' to you, and welcome to the farm, Mr. Troy. The Don is not back from town yet, but come on in. I have some coffee, and I'd love to speak with you, Mr. Troy. My husband has told me a lot about your farm in the United States.

TROY: Thank you very much, ma'am. I appreciate your hospitality.

B. APUNTES

1. *Don* and *doña* are titles of respect traditionally given to landowners or older people in some Latin American countries. Note that the titles *don* and *doña* are more honorific than *señor* and *señora*.

2. *El Líbano* is a mountainous region in central Colombia where the best coffee is produced.

3. *El agregado* (literally: "the attached or extra one") is a Colombian term for *el capataz* (the plantation chief). *El agregado* and his family usually have a house a little further down the mountain from the *patrones* (landowners).

4. *La línea* (also called *el carro*) is a Colombian term for an open bus, i.e., a bus whose sides have been cut open. It is mainly used to transport *peones* (workers) to and from the coffee fields and to the different coffee-processing buildings.

5. Note that in many Latin American countries, especially near the Caribbean, people have a tendency to use diminutives often. You will often hear *ahorita* (right away), *cerquita* (close, close by), and *lejitos* (somewhat far away).

6. Colloquially, *para* is often shortened to *pa'*, especially in rural areas. Likewise, *para el* (to the) is often shortened to *pal'* before masculine singular nouns.

7. The ending *-adero* can be attached to a verb to indicate the place where the action is performed, such as *despulpadero* (husking-place), *lavadero* (wash room), *secadero* (drying room), *criadero* (place for raising animals, a pen), etc.

8. Although coffee plantations are usually located at great heights in Colombia (the best area is between 1250 and 1750 meters above sea level), coffee is grown on very moderate slopes.

9. Note the use of *abajo* and *arriba* after nouns like *montaña* (mountain), *río* (river), and *arroyo* (creek), to indicate "up-" or "down-": *¡Ahí viene la canoa arroyo abajo!* (Here comes the canoe downstream!)

10. The verb *decir(le)* is often used to state a nickname or a regional term. *Me llamo José, pero me dicen Pepe.* (My name is Jose, but they call me Pepe.) *En Colombia, les dicen "agregados" a los capataces.* (In Colombia, they call the plantation foremen *agregados.)*

11. In Colombia, *un hombre berraco* is *un hombre bueno, tranquilo, y correcto* or "a good, calm, and honest man."

12. Although *una bodega* is technically a wine cellar, it is often used to refer to any kind of large warehouse.

13. The expression *despedirse de* (to take one's leave of) is very common in Spanish. *Bueno, me despido de todos, ¡hasta luego!* (Well, I'm saying good-bye to everyone. So long!)

14. The colloquial conjunction *(y) eso que* is often used instead of the more formal *a pesar de que* (in spite of). *Tengo calor, y eso que llevo pantalones cortos.* (I'm hot, in spite of the fact that I'm wearing shorts.)

15. In rural areas of many Latin American countries *¡Buenos días!*, *¡Buenas tardes!*, and *¡Buenas noches!* are often shortened to just *¡Buenas!*

16. The use of *señor* or *señora* followed by a first name is used to show respect. It is not servile, as it might sound in English.

17. *Un tinto* is *una taza de café* (a cup of coffee) in Colombia. Surprisingly, coffee is not very popular in rural Colombia, where people drink it only on special occasions. The most popular drink is *agua de caña* or *aguapanel* (sugar cane water), a kind of lemonade made from sugar cane.

C. GRAMATICA Y USOS

1. LOS COMPARATIVOS (COMPARATIVES)

a) Comparatives of Inequality
The comparatives of superiority and inferiority are generally formed by placing *más* (more) or *menos* (less) and *que* (that) around the quality being compared. In addition, there are the following irregular comparative forms: *mejor* (better), *peor* (worse), *mayor* (bigger, older), and *menor* (smaller, younger).

Las pendientes menores son más propicias para el cultivo del café que las pendientes mayores.
Gentle slopes are more favorable for growing coffee than steep slopes.

La traviesa es menos rendidora que la cosecha principal.
"The tricky one" is less fruitful than the main harvest.

En Colombia, la "coffea arábica" se suele cultivar más que otras variedades del café.
In Colombia, *Coffea arabica* is grown more than other varieties of coffee.

In affirmative phrases, *de* replaces *que* when followed by a numeral.

En las zonas de cultivo del café, siempre hace más de 20° y menos de 30°.
In coffee-growing areas, the temperature is always higher than 20°C and lower than 30°C.

Rosa no aparenta tener más que treinta años, ¡y tiene más de cuarenta!
Rosa doesn't look a day over thirty, and she's over forty!

b) Comparatives of Equality
Equality is expressed by placing *tan* and *como* around the quality being compared.

El saber descansar es tan importante como el saber trabajar.
Knowing how to rest is as important as knowing how to work.

España es casi tan grande como Colombia.
Spain is almost as big as Colombia.

To indicate equality between measurable quantities, *tanto* and *como* are used. Note that *tanto* must agree in gender and number with the noun to which it refers: *tanto, tanta, tantos, tantas.*

Torres trabaja tantas horas como yo.
Torres works as many hours as I do.

En las fincas cafeteras en Colombia, no se toma tanto café como aguapanel.
On Colombian coffee plantations, they don't drink as much coffee as *aguapanel.*

c) Relative Comparatives
To express a relation of dependency between two nouns, verbs, adverbs, or adjectives, use the comparative formula *cuanto . . . tanto.* Note that in conversation, *tanto* is often omitted.

El hombre es como el oso: cuanto más feo, más hermoso.
Men are like bears: the uglier, the more beautiful. (Spanish saying)

Cuanto más baje la inflación, tanto más aumentará la producción.
The lower the rate of inflation, the higher the rate of production.

Cuanto más estudies español, (tanto) más comprenderás.
The more you study Spanish, the more you'll understand.

2. *LOS SUPERLATIVOS* (SUPERLATIVES)

a) The Relative Superlative
The superlative is used when comparing three or more items. It is formed with the definite article and the comparative form. The Spanish equivalent of "in" (e.g. "the best *in* the world") is *de.* In addition, there are several irregular superlative forms, including *él mejor/óptimo* (best), *el peor/pésimo* (worst), *máximo* (biggest), and *mínimo* (smallest).

El café es el producto de exportación más común entre los países en desarrollo.
Coffee is the most common export product among developing countries.

La casa más grande de la finca, es la de Don Aurelio.
The biggest house on the plantation is Don Aurelio's.

De las tres cataratas más importantes de América—las del Niágara, las del Iguazú, y el Salto del Ángel—la más alta es el Salto del Ángel en Venezuela, con más de 1000 metros de caída.
Of the three most important waterfalls in America—Niagara, Iguazu, and Angel Falls—the highest is Angel Falls in Venezuela, with a drop of more than 1000 meters.

Finally, note that if followed by a relative clause, the superlative usually calls for use of the subjunctive.

Torres y Cía. es la empresa de transporte más confiable que yo conozca.
Torres and Co. is the most reliable shipping company I know.

¡Este es el mejor café que haya probado yo jamás!
This is the best coffee I have ever tasted!

However, if the superlative expresses a verifiable fact, the indicative should be used.

La Secretaría de Agricultura informa que este ha sido el año de más rendimiento de café que Colombia ha tenido en los últimos diez años.
The Department of Agriculture reports that this year Colombia has seen the highest yield of coffee in the last decade.

b) The Absolute Superlative
The absolute superlative expresses an extreme degree or absolute state, without specific comparison. It can be formed with *muy* + an adjective or an adverb, or by adding *-ísimo* to the stem of an adjective, and is commonly translated into English with the adverb "very." In addition, there are irregular absolute superlative forms, including: *celebérrimo* (very famous), *cerquísimo* (very close), *lejísimo* (very far), *misérrimo* (very poor, miserable), and *notabilísimo* (very notable).

La finca de Don Aurelio es grandísima/muy grande.
Don Aurelio's farm is very large.

La situación económica de Europa tiene un fortísimo impacto/un impacto muy fuerte sobre las economías latinoamericanas.
The economic situation in Europe has a very strong impact on Latin American economies.

El general San Martín y Simón Bolívar son dos próceres celebérrimos en Latinoamérica.
General San Martin and Simon Bolivar are very famous national heroes in Latin America.

3. *EL FUTURO PERFECTO* (THE FUTURE PERFECT)

The future perfect is formed with the future of the verb *haber* and the past participle of the main verb.

	DAR TO GIVE	*RECOGER* TO PICK UP	*RENDIR* TO RENDER
yo habré *tú habrás* *él/ella/Vd. habrá* *nosotros habremos* *vosotros habréis* *ellos/ellas/Vds. habrán*	*dado*	*recogido*	*rendido*

The future perfect is used to describe actions that will have been completed prior to a specific time or action in the future.

Para cuando vuelva a visitarnos, ya habrán madurado los plátanos.
By your next visit, the plantains will have ripened.

En Mayo, habremos vivido en la finca exactamente diez años.
In May, we will have lived on the plantation for exactly ten years.

This tense is used primarily in formal situations and in written language. Informally, it is often replaced by the simple future tense, much as in English.

Dolores seguramente llamará/habrá llamado antes de las diez.
Dolores will surely call/have called before ten o'clock.

The most common use of the future perfect in conversation is to question whether a past action actually took place.

¿Habrán recibido ya la carga de café que mandamos hace una semana?
I wonder if they have already received the coffee shipment we sent a week ago?

¿Dónde estarán mis llaves? ¿Las habré dejado en la casa de mi tía?
Where could my keys be? Could I have left them at my aunt's house?

D. HABLEMOS DE NEGOCIOS

LA AGRICULTURA (AGRICULTURE)

Agriculture is the backbone of many Latin American economies, particularly in Central America and the Caribbean. Agriculture accounts for an average of 20% to 25% of the GNP, and employs between 20% and 30% of the population of Spanish-speaking countries. The agricultural products vary according to climate. Most Latin American countries have tropical or subtropical climates and yield mainly coffee, tropical fruit, sugar cane, and flowers. Argentina's, Chile's, and Uruguay's agricultural regions are temperate, which is especially conducive to cultivating grains such as wheat, barley, and corn. Spain's agriculture is, like its climate, Mediterranean, producing mainly olives and grapes. In all Spanish-speaking countries, however, agriculture is in need of modernization and diversification, providing many business opportunities for U.S. companies to export agricultural machinery. At the present time, most agricultural machinery is imported from the U.S. and Europe.

Due to the prevalence of tropical and subtropical climates, as well as the mountainous topography of most of Central and South America (as well as of Spain), cattle-raising for export is significant only in Argentina and

Uruguay. Due to import regulations, South American meat and meat products may only be exported to the U.S. canned, which limits trade. Nevertheless, many European and Asian countries import Argentinian and Uruguayan meat and meat products, and they are considered to be of the highest quality in the international market.

Other types of livestock are also important in Argentina. For example, Argentinian sheep produce wool of excellent quality, for export mainly to Great Britain. More exotic livestock, such as the llama, are raised in Bolivia and Peru, but the international demand for these products is limited.

VOCABULARIO

agricultural	*agrícola*
agriculture	*agricultura*
banana	*banana*
plant	*banano*
plantation	*bananal*
barley	*cebada*
cattle	*ganado*
cedar	*cedro*
climate	*clima*
equatorial	*ecuatorial*
maritime	*marítimo*
Mediterranean	*mediterráneo*
subtropical	*subtropical*
temperate	*templado*
tropical	*tropical*
coffee	*café*
plant	*cafeto*
cow	*vaca*
cattle	*ganado bovino*
crop	*cultivo*
drought	*sequía*
farm	*estancia, hacienda, granja*
farmer	*estanciero, hacendado, granjero, labrador, agricultor*
feed (for animals)	*cebo*
feed (to)	*cebar*
field	*campo (de cultivo)*
fermentation	*fermentación*
fertilize (to)	*abonar, fertilizar*
fertilizer	*abono, fertilizante*
flax	*lino*

164

flood	*inundación*
fodder	*forraje*
grain	*grano*
grape	*uva*
grapevine	*vid/parra de uvas*
harvest	*cosecha*
harvest (to)	*cosechar*
rye	*centeno*
seed	*semilla*
sheep	*oveja*
cattle	*ganado ovino*
sow (to)	*sembrar*
sowing	*siembra*
till (to)	*cultivar, labrar, arar*
tillage	*labranza, cultivo, labor*
plantains	*plátanos*
precipitation	*precipitación*
production	*producción*
wheat	*trigo*
worker	*peón*
yield	*rendimiento*

EXAMEN

A. *Complete las oraciones españolas, usando las palabras entre paréntesis.* (Complete the Spanish sentences using the words in parentheses.)

1. *Bolivia es* (bigger) *que el Uruguay, pero es* (smaller) *que la Argentina.*
2. *Enrique hace* (as many) *negocios con el extranjero* (as) *con empresas nacionales.*
3. *El Perú exporta* (less) *pescado ahora,* (than) *en años anteriores.*
4. *En el Brasil están* (the most) *extensas selvas del mundo.*
5. *El español tiene* (more) *palabras del idioma árabe* (than) *del idioma inglés.*

B. *Traduzca las oraciones siguientes al español.* (Translate the following sentences into Spanish.)

1. Norberto likes aguapanel more than coffee.
2. The plantation chief loaded more than forty bags of coffee beans into the truck.
3. Don Ignacio's farm is one of the largest in the department.
4. That's the most beautiful painting I have ever seen!
5. That's the tallest waterfall in the world.
6. I hope that desk isn't wider than my office door.
7. Miss Lopez doesn't think *(creer)* they sent the faxes before 3 P.M.
8. The boss doesn't wait more than five minutes for someone to arrive *(llegar)*.
9. I paid more than forty pesos for that shirt.
10. The bigger the yield, the more workers we will need.

C. *Complete las oraciones siguientes con los tiempos verbales que correspondan.* (Complete the following sentences with the appropriate verb tenses.)

1. *¿(Haber) terminado Gustavo de secar los granos de café?*
2. *Muéstrenme el catálogo más al día que (tener).*
3. *¡Ésta es la finca más extensa que (yo haber) visitado hasta ahora!*
4. *Antes de la cosecha, (nosotros haber) contratado a más peones.*
5. *Con certeza, (haber) habido por lo menos tres cm. de precipitación antes del fin de mes.*
6. *Me pregunto si alguien me (haber) llamado hoy . . .*
7. *Seguramente vosotros no (haber) visto aún la fábrica. Permitidme mostrárosla.*
8. *¡No (haber) pensado que no quise llamarte! Lo que pasó fue que perdí tu número.*
9. *Dame la bolsa menos pesada que (tener), no puedo levantar nada pesado.*
10. *Les prometo que mañana (haber) recibido la factura antes de las diez. Se la enviaré por telefacsímil.*

LECCION 12

A. DIALOGO

COMPRANDO UN AUTO.

Rosaura, una joven de Asunción,[1] Paraguay, ha ahorrado dinero para dar un depósito para un auto nuevo. Trae a su mejor amiga, María Marta, quien sabe un poco acerca de automóviles, a la concesionaria[2] para ayudarla a elegir. El señor Carlos Laredo las saluda en cuanto entran.

SR. LAREDO: ¡Buenos días! Bienvenidas a automotores[3] Alfa. ¿En qué puedo servirles?

ROSAURA: Me interesa un auto pequeño, de dos puertas, pero con líneas deportivas.

SR. LAREDO: Puedo recomendarle el modelo F-20. Es pequeño, económico, pero tiene un motor bastante potente y caja de cuatro velocidades.[4]

ROSAURA: ¿Es a nafta?[5]

SR. LAREDO: Sí, pero si quiere, se lo podemos cambiar a gas comprimido.[6] Eso lo haría más económico todavía, pero el auto perdería pique.

ROSAURA: Lo que pasa es que quiero poder viajar al Brasil y no sé qué tipo de motor convenga . . . como allá se usa la alconafta.[7]

SR. LAREDO: Tiene razón. En todo caso, si se lleva el motor a nafta, puede usarlo en el Brasil, con sólo cambiarle el filtro de nafta. Permítame mostrarle el auto. Creo que le va a gustar.

El vendedor lleva a las muchachas hasta el pequeño auto. Es muy simpático[8] y su chapa azul oscuro eléctrico parece un espejito pulido.

SR. LAREDO: Aquí lo tiene. Tiene un motor de 1300 cc. con inyección electrónica.

MARÍA MARTA: ¿Cuántos cilindros tiene?

SR. LAREDO: Tiene cuatro cilindros en línea y dieciséis válvulas.

MARÍA MARTA: Ajá. Y, ¿qué opciones tiene disponibles?

SR. LAREDO: Por ejemplo ésta es la configuración más popular, viene con dirección hidráulica, autoestéreo y aire acondicionado. Como[9] va a viajar en autopista, también le aconsejo que elija la opción de caja de quinta.

ROSAURA: Sí, me convenció. Además, quiero alzavidrios[10] automático y techo corredizo. Hablemos de precios y garantía.

SR. LAREDO: **En eso puede ayudarles la señorita Pardo, ella puede explicarles los planes de pagos que tenemos. También pregunte sobre la opción de alarma acústico-óptica . . .**

El señor Laredo llama a la señorita Pardo, y ella dirige al grupo a las oficinas de venta. En eso, justo cuando el señor Laredo se disponía a tomarse un café, entra el señor Rivero, un hombre de negocios con aspecto serio.

SR. LAREDO: **Bienvenido a automotores Alfa, soy Carlos Laredo. ¿Puedo servirle en algo?**

SR. RIVERO: **Vengo para arrendar un vehículo para mi empresa.**

SR. LAREDO: **Bueno, cuénteme[11] ¿qué clase de vehículo tiene en mente: un auto, furgón, camioneta . . . ?**

SR. RIVERO: **Busco una camioneta para repartos en el campo. Necesito algo fuerte, sin lujos pero cómodo, porque voy a hacer largos viajes en carretera con cargas livianas.**

SR. LAREDO: **¿Cuánto peso piensa transportar?**

SR. RIVERO: **No más de una tonelada. Es para reparto de ropa. Llevo telas y ropa hasta el interior y también exporto a Clorinda y a Formosa.[12]**

SR. LAREDO: **Conozco bien la ruta a Formosa . . . puedo recomendarle esta camioneta modelo X 2. Tiene motor diesel para ahorrarle en combustible[13] y tracción a cuatro ruedas, transferible a dos ruedas con simplemente empujar una palanca.**

El señor Rivero echa una ojeada por debajo de la carrocería.

SR RIVERO: **Veo que tiene suspensión de muelles.**

SR. LAREDO: **Sí, en espiral. Esta camioneta es fortísima, y además viene con una garantía por 50.000 km. O dos años de uso.**

SR. RIVERO: **¿Cómo es el plan de arrendamiento?**

SR. LAREDO: **El arrendamiento es a cincuenta cuotas indexables[14] con un depósito del 10% del valor total de la configuración que quiera. Por supuesto, tiene la opción de comprarla al final.**

SR. RIVERO: **Seguramente optaremos por[15] un cambio, pero eso lo veremos con certeza después.**

SR. LAREDO: **Pasemos a mi oficina y hablaremos sobre los detalles.**

SR. RIVERO: **¡Cómo no!**

BUYING A CAR.

Rosaura, a young woman from Asuncion, Paraguay, has saved the money for a down payment on a new car. She brings her best friend, Maria Marta, who knows a little about cars, to the dealership to help her choose. Mr. Carlos Laredo greets them as they enter.

MR. LAREDO: Hello! Welcome to Alpha Motor Vehicles! What can I do for you?

ROSAURA: I'm interested in a small car: a two-door with sporty lines.

MR. LAREDO: I would recommend the F-20. It's small and economical, but it has a pretty powerful engine and four-speed transmission.

ROSAURA: Does it run on gasoline?

MR. LAREDO: Yes, but if you like, we can change it over to bottled gas. That would make it even more economical, but it would have less pick-up.

ROSAURA: The problem is, I want to be able to travel to Brazil, and I don't know what kind of engine I need, since they use gasohol over there.

MR. LAREDO: That's true. Well, if you take the gasoline engine, you can use it in Brazil. All you have to do is change the fuel filter. Let me show you the car. I think you'll like it!

The salesman takes them to a small car. It's very cute, and its dark electric blue bodywork shines like a polished mirror.

MR. LAREDO: Here it is. It has a 1300 cubic centimeter engine, with automatic fuel injection.

MARIA MARTA: How many cylinders does it have?

MR. LAREDO: It has four in-line cylinders, and sixteen valves.

MARIA MARTA: Hmmm. What options are available on it?

MR. LAREDO: This, for example, is the most popular package. It comes with power steering, stereo, and AC. Since you're going to travel on the highway, I suggest you get the five-speed transmission.

ROSAURA: I'm convinced. Also, I want power windows and a sunroof. Let's talk prices and warranty . . .

MR. LAREDO: Well, Ms. Pardo can help you with that. She can explain the payment plans we offer. Also ask about the sound and light alarm option . . .

Mr. Carlos Laredo calls Ms. Pardo, and she leads the young women to the dealership offices. Just then, as he is about to get a cup of coffee, in comes Mr. Rivero, a stern-looking businessman.

MR. LAREDO: Welcome to Alpha Motor Vehicles! I'm Carlos Laredo. How can I help you?

MR. RIVERO: I've come to lease a vehicle for my business.

MR. LAREDO: Tell me, what kind of vehicle did you have in mind: a car, a van, a pick-up truck . . . ?

MR. RIVERO: I'm looking for a pick-up truck for deliveries in the country. I need something strong—no-frills, but comfortable—because I'm going to make long road trips with cargo.

MR. LAREDO: How much weight do you plan to transport?

MR. RIVERO: No more than a metric ton. It's for textile deliveries. I transport materials and clothing out of the city, and I also export to Clorinda and Formosa.

MR. LAREDO: I know the route to Formosa well . . . I recommend this model X 2 truck. It has a diesel engine to save on fuel, and four-wheel drive, which can be changed to two wheels by simply pushing a lever.

Mr. Rivero glances under the truck.

MR. RIVERO: I see it has independent suspension.

MR. LAREDO: Yes, with spiral shocks. This is a very strong truck, and it also comes with a 50,000 kilometer, two-year warranty.

MR. RIVERO: How does your leasing plan work?

MR. LAREDO: The lease is for fifty adjustable payments, with a deposit of 10% of the total value of the package of your choice. Of course, there's an option to buy at the end.

MR. RIVERO: We'll probably decide on an exchange, but we'll see about that later.

MR. LAREDO: Please come into my office, and we'll discuss the details.

MR. RIVERO: Of course!

B. APUNTES

1. Asuncion is a unique city that's both modern and colonial, commercial and rustic, and it's the capital of Paraguay, located in the heart of South America. Paraguay has a relatively small population (4.5 million inhabitants in 1994), but it boasts the world's largest hydroelectric dam: *Itaipú.*

2. *Una concesionaria* can refer to a dealership or a franchise.

3. *Automotores* is a general term meaning "motor vehicles." A "car" is formally *un automóvil,* but informally it can be called *auto, coche,* or *carro.* The term varies from country to country.

4. Cars with automatic transmission are rarely used in Latin America and Spain. Most people prefer manual transmissions, and you cannot get a license without passing a driving test on a stick-shift car.

5. The preposition *a* followed by a noun can be used to indicate a purpose or mode of operation. In this case, it is used to specify the type of fuel a vehicle uses, or to describe its propulsion system. *Hoy en día, casi todos los aviones comerciales son a reacción.* (Nowadays, almost all commercial airplanes have jet engines.)

6. Bottled, natural gas is used in many Latin American countries to fuel automobiles, especially taxis. Bottled gas is more economical, but the car usually accelerates more slowly.

7. In Brazil, gasohol (a mixture of gasoline and alcohol) is used instead of gasoline. Visitors driving into Brazil should keep in mind that engines designed to run on gasoline may be used in Brazil, but the fuel filter and possibly other fuel conduction elements must be changed to avoid alcohol damage to engine parts.

8. In many South American countries, *simpático* (agreeable) may also be used in reference to inanimate nouns in the sense of "cute." Other adjectives used in this way are *monino* (cute, pretty) and *bonito* (pretty).

9. Note the use of *como* (as, like) to introduce the reason for an action. *Como no encontraba las llaves del auto, tuve que llamar al club de automotores.* (As I couldn't find my car key, I had to call the automobile club.) In written Spanish, the phrases *debido a que* (due to the fact that) and *por cuanto* (inasmuch as) are preferred. *Por cuanto Vd. no ha respondido a nuestras cartas anteriores, nos vemos obligados a enviarle esta notificación final.* (Inasmuch as you have not replied to our previous letters, we are forced to send you this final notice.)

10. Note that the gender of the compound noun *alzavidrios* is determined by *vidrio* (glass). For more on the formation of compound nouns, see *Gramática y usos, Lección 14.*

11. The verb *contar* can mean "to count; to tell a story" or "to explain in detail." *Ahora, niños, les voy a contar un cuento . . .* (Now, children, I'm going to tell you a story . . .) *Estoy contando cuántos días faltan para las vacaciones.* (I'm counting how many days are left until vacation.) *Cuénteme lo sucedido.* (Tell me exactly what happened.)

12. Paraguay is landlocked. Its only access to the Atlantic Ocean is via rivers that run through Argentina. Therefore, Paraguayans do a lot of business over highways with their neighbors, especially Argentina and Brazil. Formosa and Clorinda are cities in Argentina that have good business relations with Paraguay.

13. *(El) combustible* is a general term used for any type of "fuel," such as *nafta* (gasoline), *gas* (bottled gas), *alconafta* (gasohol), or *gas-oil* (diesel fuel), etc.

14. Due to the high inflation rate prevalent in many Latin American countries, payments are sometimes adjusted to match the monthly inflation rate. Thanks to more stable conditions in recent years, *cuotas fijas* (fixed-rate payments) are becoming the norm.

15. The expression *optar por* is preferred to *elegir* (to choose) in business settings. Note that *optar por* often implies the notion of a choice made only after careful consideration. *No nos podíamos decidir, pero finalmente optamos por comprar el furgón.* (We couldn't make up our minds, but we finally decided on buying the van.)

C. GRAMATICA Y USOS

1. *EL PRETERITO IMPERFECTO DEL SUBJUNTIVO* (THE IMPERFECT SUBJUNCTIVE)

The imperfect subjunctive is formed by adding the appropriate personal endings to the third personal plural, preterite stem of regular verbs. For first conjugation verbs, the endings are *-ara, -aras, -ara, -áramos, -arais,* and *-aran;* for second and third conjugation verbs, the endings are *-iera, -ieras, -iera, -iéramos, -ierais,* and *-ieran.* In addition to these endings, there is another set of endings used mostly in the spoken language in Spain and in written language in Latin America. For first conjugation verbs, the endings are *-ase, -ases, -ase, -ásemos, -aseis,* and *-asen;* for second and third conjugation verbs, the endings are: *-iese, -ieses, -iese, -iésemos, -ieseis,* and *-iesen.*

	COMPRAR TO BUY	PROPONER TO PROPOSE	DECIDIR TO DECIDE
yo	comprara comprase	propusiera propusiese	decidiera decidiese
tú	compraras comprases	propusieras propusieses	decidieras decidieses
él/ella/Vd.	comprara comprase	propusiera propusiese	decidiera decidiese
nosotros	compráramos comprásemos	propusiéramos propusiésemos	decidiéramos decidiésemos
vosotros	comprarais compraseis	propusierais propusieseis	decidierais decidieseis
ellos/ellas/Vds.	compraran comprasen	propusieran propusieseis	decidieran decidieseis

If a sentence requires the subjunctive, and the verb in the main clause is in a past tense or in the conditional, the verb in the dependent clause should be in the imperfect subjunctive.

Esperaba que viniese a ver el auto más temprano.
I was expecting you to come and see the car earlier.

No creí que tuviéramos/tuviésemos tiempo para terminar el proyecto.
I didn't think we had time to finish the project.

Querría que me enviaran/enviasen un catálogo actualizado de sus productos.
I would like you to send me an updated catalog of your products.

Nunca he visto un auto que fuera/fuese a la vez lujoso y económico.
I've never seen a car that is both luxurious and economical.

2. *EL FUTURO IMPERFECTO DEL SUBJUNTIVO* (THE FUTURE SUBJUNCTIVE)

The future subjunctive is formed by adding the appropriate personal ending to the third person plural preterite stem of regular verbs. For first conjugation verbs, the endings are *-are, -ares, -are, -áremos, -areis,* and *-aren;* for second and third conjugation verbs, the endings are *-iere, -ieres, -iere, -iéremos, -iereis,* and *-ieren.*

	ACELERAR TO SPEED UP	TENER TO HAVE	PARTIR TO LEAVE
yo	acelerare	tuviere	partiere
tú	acelerares	tuvieres	partieres
él/ella/Vd.	acelerare	tuviere	partiere
nosotros	aceleráremos	tuviéremos	partiéremos
vosotros	acelerareis	tuviereis	partiereis
ellos/ellas/Vds.	aceleraren	tuvieren	partieren

The future subjunctive is generally used in subjunctive clauses that refer to a remote possibility in the future. In modern spoken Spanish, this tense is commonly replaced by the present subjunctive or the present indicative (in "if" clauses referring to future events). The future subjunctive can be found, however, in legal documents, and occasionally heard in an elegant style of conversation.

Si llegaren a tener algún problema con la caja de cambios, llámeme.
In case you happen to have a problem with the gearbox, call me.

Ojalá tenga/tuviere tiempo de descansar mañana; pero no creo que así fuere/sea.
Hopefully, I'll have time to rest tomorrow; but I don't think I will.

Si cualquiera de las dos partes no cumpliere con las obligaciones del presente contrato, el mismo quedará nulo.
If either of the two parties were not to comply with the obligations cited in this contract, the same would become null and void.

3. *CLAUSULAS CONDICIONALES* ("IF" CLAUSES)

The subjunctive is commonly used in "if" clauses, as they generally depict hypothetical situations. The tense of the verb in the "if" clause is determined by the tense of the verb in the main clause. Following is the proper sequence of tenses.

VERB IN THE MAIN CLAUSE	VERB IN THE "IF" CLAUSE
the simple future	the present indicative or the future subjunctive
the conditional or any past tense	the imperfect subjunctive
the conditional perfect	the pluperfect subjunctive

Note that in Spanish, the "if" clause generally precedes the main clause.

Si no les aprueban el préstamo en el banco, les prestaré yo mismo el dinero para comprar el auto.
If they don't approve your bank loan, I'll lend you the money myself to buy the car.

Si tuviere alguna noticia de los hijos de Raúl, te llamaré enseguida.
In the off chance that I get any news about Raul's sons, I'll call you right away.

Si fuera rico, estaría manejando una Ferrari en lugar de un Chevrolet.
If I were rich, I'd be driving a Ferrari instead of a Chevrolet.

Si supiera quién me está enviando esas cartas odiosas, llamaría a la policía.
If I knew who was sending me those nasty letters, I'd call the police.

Me habría ido al trabajo, si no hubiese estado enfermo.
I would have gone to work, if I hadn't been sick.

Si me hubieran avisado antes que te quedaste en la ruta, te habría ido a buscar yo misma.
If they had told me earlier that you got stuck on the highway, I would have gone to get you myself.

D. ESTUDIO IDIOMATICO

Buying a car should really give you something to think about, and if you're unlucky, something to be mad about . . .

Aquí hay gato encerrado. (I smell a rat; literally: "There's a hidden cat here.")

Primero, me dijeron que el aire acondicionado estaba incluido en la configuración y ahora me dicen que no lo está . . . aquí hay gato encerrado.
First they said air-conditioning was part of the package, and now they're saying it's not . . . I smell a rat!

Dar en qué pensar (to give food for thought)

Esa película me dio mucho en qué pensar.
That movie really gave me a lot to think about.

Dar en el clavo (to hit the nail on the head)

Cuando Viviana dijo eso, sí que dio en el clavo.
When Viviana said that, she really hit the nail on the head.

Decírselo en la cara (to tell it to one's face)

Llegó la hora de decírselo en la cara.
   It's time to tell it to his face.

Tener que vérselas con uno (to answer to someone)

Si este auto se descompone, ¡tendrás que vértelas conmigo!
   If this car breaks down, you'll have to answer to me!

E. HABLEMOS DE NEGOCIOS

LOS CONTRATOS O LAS CONTRATACIONES (CONTRACTS)

Contracts are an important part of any business transaction. In Spanish-speaking countries, they tend to be prepared only in the final stages of negotiations. Spanish-language contracts are very similar to American contracts in format, and the language tends to be rather formal. The future subjunctive tense is used to refer to unlikely events in the future, so it is commonly found in all types of contracts in Spanish.

In many Latin American countries, there are no "small-claims" courts, and legal actions tend to be very bureaucratic, as the procedures are done entirely through paperwork. Only in the final stages (which may take months or years) do the litigants appear before a judge. Court interpreters are generally not available, so be prepared to bring your own.

Following is a sample contract in Spanish.

Contrato de Trabajo Personal Temporero

Entre Personex, S.R.L., con domicilio legal en la avenida Central, número 3453, cuarto piso, Pachuca Hidalgo CP 42080, México, en adelante el EMPLEADOR, y _____, quien acredita su identidad con _____, con domicilio legal en _____ en adelante, el EMPLEADO. ·······················

Tanto el EMPLEADOR como el EMPLEADO convienen en celebrar el presente contrato de Trabajo de Personal Temporero, conforme a las siguientes cláusulas y condiciones: ···

1) El EMPLEADO se encontrará relacionado con el EMPLEADOR por un contrato de trabajo permanente discontinuo, a efectos de cumplir con servicios a terceras personas de tipo extraordinarios y transitorios, debiendo el EMPLEADO prestar sus servicios en (nombre de empresa) _____, en calidad de (tipo de trabajo) _____, a partir del día _____ hasta el día _____, en el horario de _____ horas a _____ horas, con una remuneración de_____ pesos ·······························

2) La relación laboral contrará con períodos de actividad y de receso. Los períodos de interrupción laboral no podrán superar los sesenta (60) días corridos en el año o los ciento veinte (120) días alternados en un año aniversario. Durante los períodos de inactividad el EMPLEADO no tendrá derecho a recibir remuneración, ni serán computados a efectos de su antigüedad, obligándose a dar cumplimiento a las normas internas que se le comunican por separado en este acto y que firma al pie. ···

3) La actividad laboral del EMPLEADO estará regida por la convención colectiva, representado por el sindicato, y beneficiado por la Obra Social de la actividad en que preste sus servicios. ···

4) El EMPLEADO gozará de todos los derechos y beneficios que le confieren las leyes de contrato de trabajo, teniendo derecho a gozar de condiciones dignas de trabajo y de la remuneración que fije el convenio colectivo aplicable. ···························

5) Agotada la tarea asignada en la empresa usuaria especificada en el artículo 1 de este contrato, el EMPLEADOR podrá designarle nuevo destino laboral dentro del radio de 30 km. del domicilio del EMPLEADO, en cualquier otra actividad, debiendo el EMPLEADO presentarse en dicho nuevo destino dentro de las 48 horas de notificado. Si el EMPLEADO no lo hiciere, se considerará abandono de trabajo. ··········

6) El EMPLEADO se obliga a notificar al EMPLEADOR de todo cambio de domicilio que sufriere dentro del plazo de 48 horas. ···

7) A todos los efectos legales las partes se someten a la jurisdicción y al fuero de los Tribunales Nacionales de Trabajo, renunciando expresamente a cualquier otro Fuero y/o Jurisdicción. ···

En prueba de conformidad se firman dos ejemplares de un mismo tenor y a un solo efecto en la Ciudad de _____ a los _____ días del mes de _____ del año _____. ·······························

Temporary Personnel Work Contract

Between Personex, Inc., with the principal place of business at 3453 Central Avenue, fourth floor, Pachuca Hidalgo CP 42080, Mexico, heretofore the EMPLOYER, and _____, who verifies his/her identity with I.D. _____, and who resides at _____, heretofore the EMPLOYEE.

Both the EMPLOYER and the EMPLOYEE agree to execute the present Temporary Personnel Work Contract, in accordance with the following clauses and conditions.

1) The EMPLOYEE is bound to the EMPLOYER through a permanent discontinuous work contract, in order to provide third parties with services of a non-ordinary and temporary nature. The EMPLOYEE must render his/her services at (company address) _____ _____ in the position of _____, starting from _____ to _____, between the hours of _____ and _____ with a salary of _____ pesos.

2) The working relationship will include periods of inactivity and recess. The periods of interruption of work activities will not surpass sixty (60) consecutive days in the year, or one hundred twenty (120) nonconsecutive days in a year. During the periods of inactivity, the EMPLOYEE will not have the right to receive a salary, nor will the non-working days be added to the computation of his/her seniority, according to the internal regulations specified and signed separately in this contract.

3) The work activity of the EMPLOYEE will be governed by the general conventions represented by the workers' union, and benefited by the workers' union social security plans in which he or she renders his/her services.

4) The EMPLOYEE will enjoy all the rights and benefits conferred on him/her by the labor laws, having the rights to enjoy suitable work conditions and a salary fixed by the appropriate general labor law applicable in each case.

5) When the work assigned at a particular company, specified in Article 1 of this contract, is completed, the EMPLOYER will assign a new work destination to the EMPLOYEE within a 30 km. radius from his/her domicile, in any other activity. The EMPLOYEE must appear at the new place of employment within 48 hours of being notified. If the EMPLOYEE does not do so, he/she will be considered to have abandoned his/her work responsibilities.

6) The EMPLOYEE is obligated to notify the EMPLOYER of any and all domicile changes, within 48 hours of such an occurence.

7) To all legal effects, the parties submit themselves to the jurisdiction and code of laws of the National Labor Court, renouncing expressly to any other code of law and/or jurisdiction.

In proof of the conformity of both parties, two copies of the same type and content and to one effect in the City of _____ on this _____ day of _____ of the year _____.

VOCABULARIO

act of God	*Fuerza Mayor*
annulment	*anulación, rescinsción* (Sp.)
appeal	*apelación, recurso*
appeal to (to)	*apelar, recurrir a*
clause	*cláusula*
contract	*contrato, contratación* (Sp.)
damage	*daño, perjuicio*
delay	*demora*
fulfillment	*cumplimiento*
impoundment (of shipment)	*la retención (de transferencia)*
jurisprudence	*jurisprudencia*
legal	*legal*
list	*lista, relación* (Sp.)
litigant	*litigantes*
litigation	*litigio, pleito*
payment	*pago*
non-	*impago*
rate	*proporción, porcentaje*
of exchange	*tipo de cambio*
of increase	*incremento proporcional*
at the rate of	*a razón de*
rate (to)	*calificar, tasar, valuar*
risk	*riesgo*
sue (to)	*demandar*
sue for (to)	*demandar por*

EXAMEN

A. *Complete con el presente o con el pretérito imperfecto del subjuntivo del verbo indicado y traduzca.* (Complete with the present subjunctive or the imperfect subjunctive of the indicated verb and translate.)

1. *Quiero un auto fuerte, que no (ser) _____ muy lujoso.*
2. *¡No creí que se (pagar) _____ tan poco por mes al comprar en cuotas!*
3. *¿Tratásteis de llamar a alguien que (estar) _____ a cargo?*
4. *¿No te pudieron mostrar ningún auto que (ser) _____ económico?*
5. *No había nadie que (hablar) _____ español en la fiesta de anoche.*
6. *Sabía que no te gustaba el pescado, ¡pero no creí que (hacer) _____ tanto escándalo!*
7. *¿Hay algún vendedor que nos (poder) _____ ayudar?*

B. *Complete las oraciones condicionales siguientes.* (Complete the following "if" sentences).

1. *Si (comprar) _____ un auto más económico, no (tener) _____ tantos gastos de combustible ahora.*
2. *(Ahorrar) _____ dinero, si (optar por) _____ el plan de cuotas fijas.*
3. *Si (decidir) _____ no comprar el auto cuando termine la licitación, nosotros le (dar) _____ crédito para la compra de uno nuevo.*
4. *¿Tú me (hacer) un favor si (poder)?*
5. *¿Vosotros me (dar) una mano, si (tener) tiempo pasado mañana?*

C. *Traduzca las oraciones siguientes al español.* (Translate the following sentences into Spanish.)

1. If I could buy any car I wanted, I would buy myself a Ferrari.
2. I wouldn't have spent so much money on my car, if I had bought a diesel.
3. If we decide to go to Brazil on vacation, I'll have to change the fuel filter.
4. Have you ever seen a car that's both fast and economical?
5. Would you buy a Mercedes if you had the money?

LECCION 13

A. DIALOGO

TAPAS, PAELLA Y ALGO MÁS . . .

El Sr. Thomas Richards va a abrir un restaurante español en los EE.UU. con el Sr. Lope Gómez Rodríguez, el dueño de un bar-restaurante en la calle del Prado[1] en Madrid, España. El Sr. Richards quiere familiarizarse con los platos típicos de España, y habla con el jefe de cocineros, Don Rivero.

SR. RICHARDS: ¡Qué ricas están estas tapas! Y ésta, ¿de qué es?

DON RIVERO: ¿Ésa? Es una orejilla[2] de puerco, con aceitunas.

SR. RICHARDS: Si me lo hubiera dicho antes, no la habría probado, ¡pero es exquisita!

DON RIVERO: ¡No creo que haya probado ni vuelva a probar tapas como estas! Las mías son únicas: y si se me acaban las variedades, pues, invento otras nuevas . . .

SR. RICHARDS: ¡No me diga entonces que Vd. se especializa sólo en estos "canapés"!

DON RIVERO: No. También las sirvo como plato principal. De gustarle alguna tapa en particular, puede pedir una ración.[3] Viene a ser[4] lo mismo, pero en una porción más grande. A los españoles nos gusta mucho picar. Los grupos de personas suelen pedir varias raciones diferentes y luego todos prueban de todo un poco.

SR. RICHARDS: ¡Me gusta mucho esa costumbre! Creo que sería bien recibida en los EE.UU. . . . Dígame, por lo general, ¿qué se acostumbra beber con un plato como este?

DON RIVERO: Con tapas se toma casi siempre jerez, aunque un buen vino tinto nunca cae mal.[5]

SR. RICHARDS: Tengo que decirle que en los EE.UU., cuando uno habla de comida española, lo primero que le viene a uno en mente es la paella de mariscos y el gazpacho. ¿Podría decirme de[6] otras comidas típicas?

DON RIVERO: Bueno, todo depende de la region. Yo mismo soy del norte, de Galicia,[7] donde se comen mucho los mariscos y el pescado: sobre todo la langosta de mar y los cangrejos. Por lo general, la comida gallega es simple y liviana, y no picante. Por otro lado, en el país vasco[8] los platos con pescado son más picantes y complejos. Allí hay mucha variedad de platos con bacalao. El pescado también es popular en el sur, en

Andalucía,[9] pero allí es casi siempre frito. Son exquisitos los chanquetes, las sardinas y las acedías andaluza.

SR. RICHARDS: Veo que el pescado es muy popular en casi toda España. ¿Y aquí, en Castilla?[10]

DON RIVERO: En Castilla se come mucha carne. Quizás el plato más conocido sea[11] el cochinillo[2] de Segovia, ¡es un manjar! También el cordero . . .

SR. RICHARDS: Dígame, ¿se come también pollo? En el sur de los EE.UU., el pollo frito es prácticamente un plato de todos los días.

DON RIVERO: Bueno, en España el pollo frito no es un plato tradicional. Sin embargo, en Cataluña[12] se preparan muchos platos tipo estofado con pollo, aunque combinado con mariscos y también con butifarras. La comida catalana suele ser más picante que la de otras regiones.

SR. RICHARDS: ¿Qué son "butifarras"?

DON RIVERO: Las butifarras son una especie de chorizos picantes.

SR. RICHARDS: ¡Debo confesarle que jamás se me hubiese ocurrido comer pollo con mariscos ni con chorizos! ¿Y el jamón? He oído decir que es muy popular en España.

DON RIVERO: El jamón es sobre todo popular en Burgos y en Granada. Aunque no se come con chorizos, sino con verduras[13] frescas.

SR. RICHARDS: ¡Me alegra oírlo! Dígame Don Rivero, ¿cuál diría Vd. que es la comida más popular en España?

DON RIVERO: Creo que el plato más común es muy poco conocido en el exterior. De hecho, no creo que haya oído hablar de él siquiera.

SR. RICHARDS: ¿De veras? ¿Y cuál es?

DON RIVERO: Tiene distintos nombres según la región, pero se prepara del mismo modo en todas partes, incluso en partes de América Latina. En realidad, es muy simple. Se trata de un plato con carne y verduras. Todo se cuece junto. Primero, se sirve el caldo, y luego la carne y los otros ingredientes, por lo general patatas[14] y otras legumbres.[13] En Madrid lo llamamos "cocido."[15]

En eso, llega una de las meseras.

MESERA: Señor Richards, lo espera el señor Gómez a su mesa.[16]

SR. RICHARDS: Gracias, señorita. Bueno, Don Rivero, ya se me hace agua la boca pensando en todos esos platos . . .

B. APUNTES

1. *La Calle del Prado* is a street near the *Puerta del Sol,* an area with many restaurants in Madrid, the capital of Spain. Madrid is a cosmopolitan city with a unique cultural life, a result of the liveliness of the *madrileños,* natives of Madrid, who never seem to tire!

2. Note that the diminutive ending *-illo* is used mostly in Spain. In many cases, this ending does not convey the notion of "small"; rather, it expresses another noun altogether. Compare: *ventana* (window) and *ventanilla* (car/bank/ticket window), *casa* (house) and *casilla* (storage box).

3. *Una ración* literally means "a ration." *Las raciones del ejército son muy pequeñas.* (The army rations are very small.)

4. The expression *venir a ser* means "to turn out to be" when followed by a noun or an adjective. This expression is also used in the idiomatic expressions *¿Qué viene a ser?* (What exactly is that?/What would that be?) and *Viene a ser . . .* (Actually, it's . . .). *¿Qué viene a ser un "canapé"?—Viene a ser un bocadillo servido sobre una galletita.* (What exactly is a canape?—It's actually a small bit of food served on a cracker.)

5. *Caer mal* is used to express a negative quality about something or someone. It can have several translations in English. *El amigo nuevo de Lope me cayo muy mal.* (Lope's new friend made a bad impression on me.) *La comida me cayó mal.* (The food didn't sit well with me.)

6. Keep in mind that *de* can replace other prepositions for simplicity's sake, as long as the meaning of a sentence is clear. In this case, *de* is replacing the prepositional phrase *acerca de* (about).

7. *Galicia* is a region in the northwest of Spain, best known for its beaches and lovely countryside.

8. *El país vasco* (the Basque region), also known as *Euskadi,* is a mountainous region in northern Spain. It is known for its hardworking people, who are direct descendants of the Celts. The local language, known as *Euskera,* sounds surprisingly different from Spanish.

9. *Andalucía* is the southernmost region of Spain and home of *flamenco* dancing. This region was strongly influenced in its culture by the Arabs, who ruled southern Spain from A.D. 711 to A.D. 1492.

10. *Castilla* is a region in central Spain. This majestic, wind-swept plateau has historically been the region of greatest economic importance, and today it is the political center of Spain. It is home to Spain's capital, Madrid.

11. Remember that sentences introduced by *quizás* (maybe, perhaps) are always in the subjunctive.

12. *Cataluña* is located in the northeast of Spain. Its capital, *Barcelona,* is well known throughout Europe for its beauty. The Catalonians are very proud of their local language, *Catalán,* a distant relative of French *Provençal.*

13. *Verduras, hortalizas,* and *legumbres* all refer to edible vegetables. The general word for a "vegetable" (as opposed to an animal or a mineral) is *un vegetal.*

14. *Patatas* are known as *papas* in many South American countries.

15. Other names for this dish are *potaje* (in Andalusia), *escudella* (in Catalonia), and *puchero* or *cazuela* (in parts of Latin America).

16. Note the use of the preposition *a* (to) instead of *en* (at, in) in the phrase *sentarse a la mesa.*

17. The name *(pil-pil)* of this fried codfish dish comes from the spattering sound produced while frying the codfish in garlic.

C. GRAMATICA Y USOS

1. *EL PRETERITO PERFECTO DEL SUBJUNTIVO* (THE PRESENT PERFECT SUBJUNCTIVE)

The present perfect subjunctive is formed with the present subjunctive of the verb *haber* followed by the past participle of the main verb. It is used in dependent clauses that require the subjunctive, and whose action was to have occurred prior to the action in the main clause. Note that the verb in the main clause is in the present tense.

	PREPARAR TO PREPARE	*COCER* TO COOK	*FREÍR* TO FRY
yo haya *tú hayas* *él/ella/Vd. haya* *nosotros hayamos* *vosotros hayáis* *ellos/Vds. hayan*	*preparado*	*cocido*	*frito*

The present perfect subjunctive is used to express uncertainty, doubt, or hope that an action is finished, or to refer to an action that has yet to be completed.

No creo que se haya terminado aún de cocinar el cochinillo.
I don't think the piglet has finished cooking yet.

En cuanto hayas freído todos los pescados, llámame.
As soon as you've finished frying all this fish, call me.

¿Crees que Juan haya probado alguna vez paella?
Do you think Juan has ever tried paella?

¡Espero que no hayáis sacado la carne del congelador?
I hope you haven't taken the meat out of the freezer!

Necesitamos a un cocinero que haya trabajado en restaurantes por lo menos tres años.
We need a cook who has worked in restaurants for at least three years.

2. *EL PRETERITO PLUSCUAMPERFECTO DEL SUBJUNTIVO* (THE PLUPERFECT SUBJUNCTIVE)

The pluperfect subjunctive is formed with the imperfect subjunctive of the verb *haber* and the past participle of the main verb.

	LAVAR TO WASH	*REVOLVER* TO MIX	*SERVIR* TO SERVE
yo hubiera/hubiese *tú hubieras/hubieses* *él/ella/Vd. hubiera/hubiese* *nosotros hubiéramos/hubiésemos* *vosotros hubiérais/hubiéseis* *ellos/ellas/Vds. hubieran/hubiesen*	*lavado*	*revuelto*	*servido*

The pluperfect subjunctive is used in sentences where the dependent clause requires the subjunctive and refers to completed actions, and the verb in the main clause is in a past tense (preterite, imperfect) or in the conditional. Note that the action in the dependent clause must take place before the action in the main clause.

In other words, the pluperfect subjunctive is used in the same way as the present perfect subjunctive, but in sentences where the main clause is in a past or conditional tense.

Me sorprendería oír que nunca hubiesen probado la paella.
I'd be surprised to hear you had never tried paella.

187

El jefe de cocina habría preparado la comida antes, si hubiese sabido a qué hora vendrían.
The chef would have prepared the food earlier, if he had known when you would arrive.

Él quería que hubiéramos llegado más temprano.
He wished we had arrived earlier.

Yo preferiría que tú hubieras limpiado los platos ya, pero lo haré de todos modos.
I wish you had done the dishes already, but I'll do them anyway.

3. *EL FUTURO PERFECTO DEL SUBJUNTIVO* (THE FUTURE PERFECT SUBJUNCTIVE)

The future perfect subjunctive is formed with the future subjunctive of the verb *haber* (i.e., *hubiere, hubieres, hubiere, hubiéremos, hubiereis, hubiesen*) followed by a past participle. The future perfect subjunctive may be used in dependent clauses when the main clause is in any tense except a past tense. Note that it refers to actions that are unlikely to be completed in the future. The future perfect subjunctive is rarely used in modern Spanish, except in legal documents. In conversation, it is replaced by the present perfect subjunctive.

La parte que no hubiere cumplido con las obligaciones expresadas en este contrato, se considerará en violación de los términos del mismo.
The party who does not fulfill the obligations expressed in this contract will be deemed in violation of the terms of said contract.

Si no hubiéremos recibido noticia por escrito de una reclamación dentro de tres meses de ocurrido un incidente, no nos responsabilizaremos por los daños causados por nuestro producto.
If we were not to have received written notice of a complaint within three months of the occurrence of an incident, we would not be held responsible for any damages caused by our product.

D. HABLEMOS DE NEGOCIOS

LOS ALMUERZOS Y LAS CENAS DE NEGOCIOS (BUSINESS LUNCHES AND DINNERS)

The business lunch is an important part of the businessperson's day throughout the Spanish-speaking world. In fact, it often marks the end of the business day for many Latin Americans. In Latin America and Spain, business lunches tend to be long, leisurely affairs that generally begin at around 1 P.M. and last several hours. During these lunches, the finer points of business may be discussed, albeit more informally than at the office. Do not expect to close a deal or sign a contract over lunch. Business lunches are used to get to know prospective business partners in a more relaxed atmosphere. Most commonly, they begin with cocktails and small talk, generally about the economy or the beauty of the country, and slowly may extend to the business at hand. Generally, the person who extends the invitation is expected to pay for lunch. You should always counter an invitation by extending one of your own on the next occasion.

Business dinners are less common, and are considered to be primarily social events. Take the opportunity to get to know your prospective business partners better. In Spanish-speaking countries, dinner is usually served quite late, at around 9 P.M., although meeting at a restaurant earlier (at around 8 P.M.) for cocktails is common. If spouses are present, the topic of business should be avoided altogether. As with business lunches, prearrange payment with the *maitre d'* to avoid a discussion of who will pay. Latin Americans have a preference for Italian and French cuisine, whereas Spaniards tend to favor their national dishes on such occasions.

Some useful phrases for inviting someone to a business lunch or dinner are: *Por favor, hágame el gusto de cenar/almorzar conmigo esta noche/ tarde.* (Please, allow me the pleasure of dining/having lunch with me this evening/afternoon.) If you wish to invite a couple, you may say: *Háganme, usted y su mujer, el gusto de cenar conmigo esta noche en el restaurante . . .* (Will you and your wife please do me the pleasure of dining with me tonight at . . . restaurant.) You may accept such an invitation with the phrase: *¡Con muchísimo gusto!* (Delighted!) Keep in mind that an invitation to dinner should not be turned down without a legitimate excuse.

Following are some general tips for certain countries:

In Mexico, a cocktail hour at around 7 P.M. is very popular, especially among young businessmen. If you invite your colleagues to dinner, make sure you invite their spouses as well.

In Argentina, your partner will try very hard to pay for dinner. Make sure you insist on paying more than once. You can do so with phrases like: *No, no. Permítame a mí.* (No, no. Please allow me.) *Esta vez invito yo.* (This time it's on me.) *Permítame el gusto de invitarlo(s).* (Allow me the pleasure of inviting you.) If you must give in (after three tries or so), say: *Por favor, permíta(n)me el gusto de invitarlo(s) la próxima vez.* (Please allow me the pleasure of inviting you next time.)

EXAMEN

A. *Complete las oraciones siguientes con el tiempo subjuntivo que corresponda.* (Complete the following sentences with the correct subjunctive tense.)

1. *¡Espero que los Márquez no se _____ perdido entre tanta gente!*
2. *Me sorprendió que no _____ venido ayer, ¿qué te pasó?*
3. *Me cuesta creer que la niña se _____ comido una porción tan grande.*
4. *En cuanto _____ mezclado los ingredientes, ponga la mezcla en el horno veinte minutos.*
5. *No sé por qué no llega, quizás se _____ equivocado de autobús.*
6. *No creí que Vd. se _____ oído hablar del puchero en los EE.UU.*
7. *Dudo que (nosotros) _____ terminado de cenar dentro de media hora.*
8. *Espero que mi mamá _____ hecho cazuela para el almuerzo de hoy, ¡me gusta tanto!*
9. *¡No pensé que vosotros _____ probado alguna vez butifarras!*
10. *¡Nunca pensé que me _____ gustado tanto la comida española!*

B. *Traduzca las oraciones precedentes al inglés.* (Translate the preceding sentences into English.)

190

LECCION 14

A. DIALOGO

Son las diez de la noche en Lima, Perú. Los Martínez acaban de cenar[1] y están mirando la edición nocturna del noticiero nacional en el canal nueve. María Vargas, la locutora preferida de los Martínez, presenta las noticias económicas.

MARIA VARGAS: **Y ahora, el panorama económico. El Ministro de Economía se ha reunido hoy con expertos en el ámbito económico para tratar el estado de la economía nacional. Tenemos en nuestros estudios el Dr. Salazar, el Presidente del Banco de la Nación, quien estuvo presente en la reunión. Muchas gracias, doctor, por su presencia.**

DR. SALAZAR: **El gusto es todo mío.**

MARIA VARGAS: **Usted ha hablado hoy con el Ministro de Economía. Pues, díganos, ¿cómo ve Vd. la economía en lo que va del cuatrimestre?[2]**

DR. SALAZAR: **En lo que va de él, se puede decir que hay un saldo favorable. Los principales indicadores económicos muestran que la situación ha mejorado: la inflación parece estar bajo control. La bolsa ha experimentado un aumento en las transacciones, sobre todo en el sector que más nos interesa, él de la industria nacional. Sin embargo, debemos redoblar los esfuerzos para lograr un mejor control de precios, por medio de la privatización y del fomento a la inversión de capitales en el país, no sólo por parte de extranjeros, sino también de la ciudadanía. Espero hacer que el Banco de la Nación inspire confianza en los inversionistas peruanos.**

MARIA VARGAS: **¿Cómo cree Vd. que pueda lograrse tal[3] control? ¿Acaso[4] no ha dicho Vd. que la dependencia de nuestro país en la exportación de materia prima es el factor que más contribuye a la inflación?**

DR. SALAZAR: **Efectivamente, lo he dicho. Más aún, siempre he dicho que las fluctuaciones de los mercados en Europa y en los EE.UU. provocan trastornos más o menos fuertes en las economías de los países en desarrollo. Aún así, no debemos perder de vista los objetivos de largo plazo. El futuro de nuestra economía depende de nuestra capacidad de integrarnos al mercado mundial, en igualdad de condiciones con los demás países.**

MARIA VARGAS: ¿Cree Vd. realmente que algún día podamos competir económicamente con los gigantes económicos del norte?

DR. SALAZAR: No se trata de competencia,[5] sino de libertad económica.Cuanto menos dependamos de la exportación y más de la producción interna, tanto más se desarrollará un mercado para nuestros productos. Los primeros pasos, creo yo, son la privatización y el fomento a la inversión de capitales.

MARIA VARGAS: Muchos opinan que la privatización hará que extranjeros eventualmente controlen la economía. ¿Como cree Vd. que deba proceder el gobierno para evitar la compra masiva de la industria nacional por parte de inversionistas extranjeros?

DR. SALAZAR: Bueno, de adoptarse un sistema de mercado libre como el que describen algunos, el gobierno no podrá decidir quiénes compren o vendan. Personalmente, no soy partidario de los mercados totalmente libres y abiertos. Los recursos naturales deben permanecer bajo control del gobierno, a fin de que pueda ejercer mayor control impositivo[6] sobre el sector privado y para asegurar la explotación racional de los recursos naturales, protegiendo así no sólo el sistema gubernamental[6] de seguros social y médico,[7] sino también la ecología, sobre todo en las zonas de equilibrio ecológico más precario.

MARIA VARGAS: Supongo que tendrá Vd. sus duros críticos en el norte,[8] por su oposición a un sistema exclusivamente capitalista.

DR. SALAZAR (riendo): Me lo han comunicado, en varias ocasiones en los congresos[9] económicos. Sin embargo, en mi opinión, el camino justo está en el equilibrio y no en los extremos.

MARIA VARGAS: Bueno, gracias por su tiempo, doctor.[10] Esperamos poder entrevistarlo nuevamente pronto.

SR. MARTINEZ: Creo que el doctor ha hablado muy bien. Estoy de acuerdo en que debemos pensar en el futuro y no en el plazo corto . . .

LAURA MARTINEZ: Mi profesor de contabilidad dijo que, en la práctica, los mercados libres y sin control no siempre son estables.

SR. MARTINEZ: Tienes razón. Basta comparar las economías de Europa con la de los EE.UU.

SRA. MARTINEZ: Es difícil tomar a los EE.UU. como ejemplo. Ellos deben su estado económico a otros factores, que poco tienen que ver con el hecho de que tengan[11] un mercado más o menos libre.

LAURA MARTÍNEZ: **Como el hecho de que hayan** [11] **salido de las dos guerras mundiales con la maquinaria económica intacta y con gran prestigio.**

SR. MARTINEZ: **La situación se remonta aún más. Desde el "vamos" los EE.UU. son diferentes del resto del mundo. Desde el principio, la gente iba siempre a quedarse, a radicarse en el país. Los EE.UU. es un país de inmigrantes.**

LAURA MARTINEZ: **Y siempre lo será . . .**

SRA. MARTINEZ: **Bueno, ¿cuál de Vds. doctores en ciencias económicas va a lavar los platos hoy? ¡Aquí voy a implantar un estricto control gubernamental sobre el lavado!**

An interview with the president of the National Bank.

It's 10 P.M. in Lima, Peru. The Martinezes have just finished dinner and are watching the evening news on channel nine. Their favorite reporter, Maria Vargas, presents the evening economic report.

MARIA VARGAS: And now, the economic report. The Minister of Economy called a meeting today with leading business professionals to discuss the state of the national economy. Joining us in our studio is Dr. Salazar, President of the National Bank, who attended the meeting. Thank you very much, Dr. Salazar, for coming in to see us.

DR. SALAZAR: My pleasure.

MARIA VARGAS: You spoke to the Minister of Economy today. Tell us, how do you see the economy thus far into the quarter?

DR. SALAZAR: Thus far, the results are favorable. The chief economic indicators show that the situation has improved: inflation seems to be under control. The stock market has experienced increased activity, especially in the sector that most interests us: national industry. Nevertheless, we must double our efforts to achieve better price control through privatization and promoting the investment of capital in the country, not only by foreign investors, but also by local investors. I hope to make the National Bank more appealing and trustworthy to Peruvian investors.

MARIA VARGAS: How do you think such control can be achieved? Haven't you said that our country's dependence on export of raw materials is what most contributes to inflation?

DR. SALAZAR: That's correct. What's more, I have always maintained that fluctuations in the European and U.S. markets cause more or less significant variations in the economies of developing countries. Even so, we mustn't lose sight of our long-term goals. The future of our economy depends on our ability to integrate ourselves into the world market on an equal basis with other countries.

MARIA VARGAS: Do you really believe that we may, one day, be able to compete with the economic giants of the north?

DR. SALAZAR: It's not about competing; it's about economic freedom. The less we depend on exports, and the more on internal production, the more a market for our goods will develop. The first steps, I believe, are privatization and the promotion of capital investment.

MARIA VARGAS: Many people say that privatization will eventually transfer control of our economy to foreigners. What steps must the government take to avoid massive buy-out of national industry by foreign investors?

DR. SALAZAR: Well, if it decides to adopt a free-market economy like the one some prescribe, the government won't be able to decide who can and cannot buy or sell. Personally, I am not for a completely free and open market. Natural resources should remain under government control, in order to exert greater tax supervision over the private sector and to secure the proper use of natural resources, thus protecting not only the government-sustained medical and social security plans, but also the ecosystem, especially in areas where the ecological balance is most endangered.

MARIA VARGAS: I suppose you have tough critics in the north because of your opposition to an exclusively capitalist system.

DR. SALAZAR (chuckling): They have made this clear, on several occasions in the economic summits. However, it is my opinion that the right road lies in the middle, and not in the extremes.

MARIA VARGAS: Well, thank you for your time, doctor. We hope to be able to interview you again soon.

MR. MARTINEZ: I think the doctor spoke very well. I agree that we should think about the future and not just the short term . . .

LAURA MARTINEZ: My accounting professor said that, in practice, uncontrolled free-market economies are not always stable.

MR. MARTINEZ: You're right. You just have to compare the economies of Europe with the U.S. economy.

MRS. MARTINEZ: It's hard to take the U.S. as an example. It owes its economic status to other factors which have little to do with the fact that it has a more or less free market.

LAURA MARTINEZ: Like the fact that it came out of two world wars with its economic machinery intact, and with great prestige.

MR. MARTINEZ: I think the situation goes back even further. From the "get go" the U.S. is different from the rest of the world. From the very beginning, people went there to stay, to take roots in the country. The U.S. is a country of immigrants.

LAURA MARTINEZ: And it always will be. . . .

MRS. MARTINEZ: Well, which of you two doctors of economics is going to wash the dishes today? I'm going to impose strict governmental control over cleaning!

B. APUNTES

1. Due to the warm climate and long days in most Spanish-speaking countries, dinner is usually served at around 9 P.M., or even later in the summer.

2. The phrase *lo que va de* (thus far) is often used in both formal and informal settings: *En lo que va del proyecto, no hemos podido concretar todos los objectivos.* (Thus far in the project, we haven't been able to reach all our goals.) *Lo que va de la película me gusta.* (So far, I like the movie.)

3. *Tal* is often used instead of *este/ese/aquel tipo de* (this/that type of). *No me gustan tales libros, me gustan los de ciencia ficción.* (I don't like those books, I like science fiction books.) *Tal* is also used for emphasis in exclamations, much like the English "such a . . . !" *¡Tengo tal dolor de cabeza, que no puedo ni pensar!* (I have such a headache that I can't even think!)

4. *Acaso* is used in interrogative sentences to ask for confirmation of a fact. *¿Acaso no fuiste a visitar a Manuela ayer?* (Didn't you visit Manuela yesterday?)

5. *Tratar de* followed by an infinitive means "to try." *Tratamos de caber en el auto, pero no pudimos.* (We tried to fit into the car, but we couldn't.) When followed by a noun, *tratar de* means "to be about, to concern." *No se trata de cuanta gramática sepas, sino de cuanto practiques la conversación.* (It's not about how much grammar you know, it's about how much you practice conversation.) *La película trata de la vida de un gran empresario estadounidense.* (The movie is about the life of a great U.S. businessman.)

6. Note the formal adjectives *impositivo* and *gubernamental* used instead of *de los impuestos* and *del gobierno,* respectively. In formal language, adjectives derived from Latin are preferred to the more Castillian form of *de* + a noun. Compare *Los sueldos mensuales serán entregados el quinto de marzo, según un decreto directorial, anunciado ayer* with *Los sueldos del mes serán entregados el cinco de marzo, según un decreto de los directores, anunciado ayer,* both meaning: The monthly

wages will be distributed on March 5, according to a resolution of the board of directors, announced yesterday.

7. Most Latin American countries have socialized medicine and retirement programs. In general, government-run hospitals offer medical care, from emergency services to surgery, at minimal cost to anyone who requests them. Medication for senior citizens is usually provided virtually free.

8. *El norte* refers to *el norte industrializado,* or the industrialized countries of the northern hemisphere.

9. *Un congreso* refers to any meeting involving authority, such as a summit meeting, or a convention. It's also used to mean *El Congreso de la Nación*—Congress (the House of Representatives and the Senate).

10. As in English, *Doctor* is a title that can refer to anyone with a doctoral degree: *Doctor en Ciencias Económicas* (Doctor of Economic Sciences), *Doctor en Filosofía y Letras* (Doctor of Philosophy and Literature). However, in many countries it can be used to refer to any person of esteem, including someone who holds a high position in a company.

11. Note the use of the subjunctive in a clause that expresses an opinion. With the phrase *el hecho de que* (the fact that) the indicative or the subjunctive may be used, and the speaker's choice of the subjunctive indicates a noncommittal attitude about his opinion.

C. GRAMATICA Y USOS

1. *EL USO DE "DE" EN CLAUSULAS CONDICIONALES* (THE USE OF *DE* IN "IF" CLAUSES)

In sentences with "if" clauses, when the subject of the main clause and the dependent clause is the same, an infinitive may be used instead of the subjunctive, in which case the word *si* must be replaced by *de.* This use of *de* + infinitive instead of *si* + subjunctive is preferred in a more elegant style of speech.

Si decide/decidiere abrir también una cuenta corriente, no tendrá que pagar la tarifa mensual por un año.
De decidir abrir también una cuenta corriente, no tendrá que pagar la tarifa mensual por un año.
If you also decide to open a checking account, you won't have to pay the monthly charges for a year.

Si tengo/tuviere tiempo mañana, iré a visitarlo.
De tener tiempo mañana, iré a visitarlo.
If I have time tomorrow, I will visit him.

Si adoptamos/adoptáremos una política económica nueva, podremos controlar
mejor la inflación.
De adoptar una política económica nueva, podremos controlar mejor la
inflación.
If we adopt a new economic plan, we will be able to control inflation
better.

Si tú fueras rico ahora, ¿dónde vivirías?
De ser rico ahora, ¿dónde vivirías?
If you were rich now, where would you live?

Si no tuviéramos que pagar la deuda externa, ¿cómo sería el presupuesto
nacional?
De no tener que pagar la deuda externa, ¿cómo sería el presupuesto nacional?
If we didn't have to pay the national debt, what would our national budget
be like?

In "if" sentences that refer to the past, instead of the pluperfect
subjunctive, be sure to use the perfect infinitive, which consists of the
verb *haber* followed by a past participle.

Si hubiéramos llamado más temprano ayer, podríamos haber cerrado el trato.
De haber llamado más temprano ayer, podríamos haber cerrado el trato.
If we had called earlier yesterday, we could have closed the deal.

Si no hubieras retirado el dinero de la cuenta, habrías ganado más interés este
año.
De no haber retirado el dinero de la cuenta, habrías ganado más interés este
año.
If you hadn't withdrawn the money from your account, you would've
earned more interest this year.

2. *EL SUBJUNTIVO PRECEDIDO DE CONJUNCIONES* (THE SUBJUNCTIVE AFTER CONJUNCTIONS)

a) Conjunctions That Always Take the Subjunctive.
Conjunctions with an implicit element of doubt always take the
subjunctive. Some of the most common include *mientras* (as long as), *en
caso de que* (in case), *a menos que* (unless), *con tal que* (provided that),
and *sin que* (without).

Mientras el gobierno siga obstaculizando la inversión de capitales extranjeros,
la inflación continuará subiendo.
As long as the government continues to obstruct the investment of
foreign capital, inflation will continue to rise.

Yo no invertiría en aquellos valores, a menos que lo hiciera Vd.
I wouldn't invest in those stocks, unless you do.

Queremos fomentar las actividades del sector industrial privado, con tal que tales actividades no dañen el medio ambiente.
We want to stimulate the activities of the industrial private sector, provided such activities do not damage the environment.

Conjunctions that indicate purpose, such as *para que* and *a fin de que* (in order that) are also always followed by the subjunctive.

Tendremos que establecer relaciones con el sector privado, a fin de que el Banco de la Nación logre inspirar confianza en la ciudadanía.
We will have to establish better relations with the private sector, in order for the National Bank to inspire confidence among the citizens.

The conjunction *antes de que* (before) is always followed by the subjunctive, as it always refers to an action before it occurs.

Es necesario tomar medidas urgentes antes de que se desestabilice aún más la economía.
It is necessary to take urgent measures before the economy destabilizes even more.

¿No os fijásteis si habíais firmado la declaración de rentas antes de que el contador la enviara?
Didn't you check if you had signed the tax return before your accountant mailed it?

b) Conjunctions That Take the Subjunctive or the Indicative.
When the main clause is in a future tense or in the imperative, the subjunctive is used with conjunctions of time as there is no guarantee that the action expressed in the dependent clause will actually occur.

Les giraré el dinero en cuanto se abra el banco.
I will wire you the money to you as soon as the bank opens.

Cuando use su tarjeta bancaria en el exterior, fíjese que el cajero automático lleve la insignia "Telerred."
When you use your bank card abroad, make sure the automatic teller has a sticker that reads "Telerred."

However, when referring to a past action, the indicative is used because it is an established fact that the action occurred.

Carmen llamó al banco en cuanto se le perdió la tarjeta.
Carmen called the bank as soon as she lost her card.

Tuve que hablar con la representante cuando abrí la cuenta en mi nuevo banco.
I had to speak with the representative when I opened the account in my new bank.

The conjunctions *aunque, a pesar de que,* and *aún cuando,* all meaning "even if, even though," can be followed by the indicative or the subjunctive, depending on our certainty about the action expressed in the dependent clause. Compare:

Quiero ir a la playa aunque haga frío hoy.
I want to go to the beach, even if it's cold today.
(But I don't know if it is cold now.—subjunctive)

Quiero ir a la playa aunque hace frío hoy.
I want to go to the beach, even though it's cold today.
(I'm sure it's cold.—indicative)

Aunque no tenga su tarjeta a mano ahora, puede retirar los fondos con la libreta bancaria.
Even if you may not have your card at hand now, you can withdraw the funds with your bank book.

A pesar de que no estás, los chicos se portan bien.
Even though you're not here, the kids are being good.

The conjunction *de modo/manera que* (so that) normally takes the subjunctive. However, it can be followed by the indicative when referring to past actions to indicate that the intended result was realized.

Recibí el listado de transacciones, de manera que pude verificar que cobraron el cheque.
I received my bank statement, so I was able to verify that they cashed the check.

Se me olvidó la tarjeta, de modo que no pude retirar el dinero de la cuenta hoy.
I forgot my card, so I couldn't withdraw the money from my account today.

3. *LA FORMACION DE SUSTANTIVOS COMPUESTOS* (THE FORMATION OF COMPOUND NOUNS)

Compound nouns, as their name suggests, consist of two words (two nouns or a noun and a verb) joined together. While compound nouns are fairly common in Spanish, they must follow very strict rules of formation and require approval by the *Real Academia Española,* which may be a lengthy process.

a) noun + noun

Two nouns can be combined in much the same way as two adjectives: simply place the more important noun first, replace its ending with -*i* (unless the noun ends in -*a* or -*o*), and attach the second noun. The gender of the second noun determines the gender of the compound noun. Like compound adjectives, compound nouns often have humorous or ironic connotations.

La bolsa de valores siempre tiene sus altibajos.
(from *altos* + *bajos*)
  The stock market always has its ups and downs.

¡Estoy cansado de las artimañas de Lorena!
(from *arte* "art" + *maña* "bad habit, trick")
  I'm tired of Lorena's tricks!

La casa de campo siempre está llena de telarañas cuando llegamos.
(from *tela* "cloth" + *araña* "spider")
  The country house is always full of spider webs when we arrive.

b) verb + noun

In noun-verb combinations, the verb precedes the noun. The verb should be in the third person singular, present indicative form, and the noun should, in most cases, be plural. These compound nouns are always considered masculine and singular.

¡Otra vez se descompuso el lavarropas!
(from *lava* "washes" + *ropas* "clothes")
  The washing machine broke down again!

Nunca encuentro el abrecartas cuando lo necesito.
(from *abre* "opens" + *cartas* "letters")
  I can never find the letter opener when I need it.

¿Puedes ayudarme a armar este rompecabezas?
(from *rompe* "breaks" + *cabezas* "heads")
  Can you help me put together this jigsaw puzzle?

Los nuevos rascacielos con sus instalaciones ultramodernas han llamado la atención de muchas empresas e inversionistas nuevos.
(from *rasca* "scratches" + *cielo* "sky")
  The new skyscrapers, with their ultramodern facilities, have attracted many new businesses and investors.

200

D. ESTUDIO IDIOMATICO

Following are some useful expressions for depicting difficult situations.

Costar trabajo (to be very difficult)

Cuesta mucho trabajo convencer a Juan de hacer algo.
It's very hard to convince Juan to do anything.

Dejar plantado (to be stood up)

Tenía una cita con Laura, pero me dejó plantado.
I had a date with Laura, but she stood me up.

Tener más vueltas que un caracol (to be difficult to please)

Nunca sé qué comprarle a María para el cumpleaños, tiene más vueltas que un caracol.
I never know what to buy Maria for her birthday; she's very difficult to please.

Sudar la gota gorda (to go through hell)

Tuve que sudar la gota gorda para pasar el examen.
I had to go through hell to pass the exam.

Estar entre la espada y la pared (to be stuck between a rock and a hard place)

Tengo que confesarte que no sé qué hacer, estoy entre la espada y la pared.
I've got to tell you I don't know what to do; I'm stuck between a rock and a hard place.

E. HABLEMOS DE NEGOCIOS

LA BANCA (BANKING)

Banking services in Spain and the U.S. are very similar. In Latin America, however, despite the current tendency toward deregulation, privatization, and modernization, the banking systems are somewhat different from that in the U.S., especially in the financing and investment sectors. Despite the differences, most services used by American businesses are available in much of Latin America and in Spain.

Accounts

In Spain, nonresidents can open various types of accounts, in any currency valued in Spain. There are various types of deposit accounts available. Foreign currency accounts are tax-exempt, and their balances can be transferred abroad. The foreign currency must be in the form of a check, bank transfer, draft, or money order, to ensure that the money has come from abroad. The most common types of accounts are:

1. *Cuentas a la vista,* which allow withdrawals at any time.

2. *Cuentas a plazo,* similar to certificates of deposit. The interest rates vary according to the length of time of the deposit and the currency.

3. *Cuenta en pesetas convertibles,* which can be converted into any foreign currency.

If you are staying in Spain for a longer period of time, or if you have an apartment there and want the bank to pay your bills you must open a *cuenta en pesetas ordinarias* (account in ordinary pesetas), whose funds are not convertible, or a *cuenta corriente* (checking account).

In Latin America, savings accounts may be opened in the local currency or in dollars, although they generally have a waiting period of three to six months of maturity before withdrawals can be made. Most Latin American countries do not provide checking accounts in foreign currencies. In general, savings accounts are permitted in currencies other than dollars only in foreign-owned national banks. Interest rates also vary according to currency and terms of deposit.

Banking Services

Most banking services available in the U.S. are also available throughout Latin America and Spain. *Cuentas de débito automático* (automatic payment accounts) are available to pay bills automatically, and *cajeros automáticos* (automatic tellers) are commonplace. Following are some sample bank documents.

Opening a Checking Account

Señor Gerente del   No. _____

BANCO DINERAL

Sucursal Buenos Aires   **Lugar y fecha:** _____

SOLICITUD DE APERTURA DE CUENTA CORRIENTE.

Por la presente solicitamos la apertura de una cuenta corriente en este Banco, a cuyo fin indicamos los datos requeridos a continuación.

DENOMINACIÓN: (indicar los apellidos y el nombre completo de la persona física, o la denominación social de la persona jurídica. Si se tratare de un seudónimo, indicar el nombre completo real de la[s] persona[s] física[s])

_____

Persona Física   Seudónimo   Persona Jurídica
                        (Tachar lo que no corresponda)

DOMICILIO REAL O LEGAL:

Calle: _____ No. _____ Piso. _____ Depto. _____

Localidad, Provincia: _____ Código Postal: _____

Tel.: _____

RAMO: (Indicar profesión o actividad comercial a que se dedique principalmente, para determinar el ramo a que deberá pertenecer la cuenta.):

_____

PARA LLENAR EXCLUSIVAMENTE POR PERSONAS JURÍDICAS:

Denominación Social: _____

Número de Inscripción en el Registro Comercial de la Nación: _____

Folio/Tomo: _____ Libro: _____

Número de Identificación Impositiva: _____

Los abajo firmantes declaran bajo juramento que los datos consignados en la presente se ajustan en su totalidad a la verdad y que han tomado nota de la reglamentación relativa al funcionamiento de la cuenta solicitada.

Firma _____

Fecha _____ de _____ de _____

Manager of

DINERAL BANK

Buenos Aires Branch.

No. _____

Location and Date: _____

Request to open a checking account

We hereby request to open a checking account and attest to the following information.

LEGAL NAME: Indicate the first and last names of the physical person or legal entity. If an alias, indicate the complete legal name of the person or persons.)

_____

Physical Person   Alias   Legal Entity

(Cross out those that do not apply)

LEGAL ADDRESS:

Street Number:: _____

Floor: _____ Apartment: _____ City/Province: _____ Zip Code: _____

TYPE OF BUSINESS: (Indicate profession or commercial activity to determine type of account.)

_____

TO BE COMPLETED ONLY BY LEGAL ENTITIES:

Legal Company Name: _____

National Commerce Registry Number: _____

Volume: _____ Book: _____ Tax Identification No.: _____

The undersigned individuals hereby declare under oath that the information contained herewith is true, and that they understand the regulations governing the execution of the requested accout

Signature _____ Date _____ , _____

Please note that in addition to the information on this form, you will be asked to provide personal and professional references, including information on accounts held at other institutions.

Checks

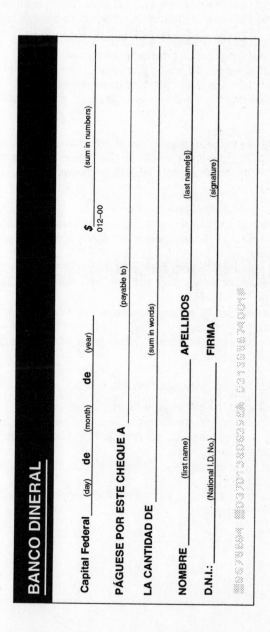

EXAMEN

A. *Reformule las oraciones siguientes, utilizando "de," cuando fuere posible.* (Rewrite the following sentences using *de,* whenever possible.)

1. *Si hubiera sabido lo que sé ahora, nunca habría hecho lo que hice.*
2. *Házme un favor, si tienes/tuvieres tiempo mañana.*
3. *¿Irías al banco por mí hoy, si yo no llego/llegare a tiempo?*
4. *Si tuviere algún problema, no deje de llamarme.*
5. *Podríamos pasar unos días más en la playa, si nos alcanza/alcanzare el dinero.*

B. *Complete las oraciones siguientes con el subjuntivo o el indicativo del verbo entre paréntesis, como fuere necesario.* (Complete the following sentences with the subjunctive or indicative forms of the verbs in parentheses, as necessary.)

1. *Aunque (escuchar) el pronóstico anoche, no traje el paraguas hoy.*
2. *Te divertirás igual, aunque no (conocer) a todos en la fiesta.*
3. *Voy a mandar el cheque, aunque no (saber) si tengo suficientes fondos para cubrirlo.*
4. *Le endorsaré este pagaré, para que (poder) cobrarlo Vd.*
5. *¿No abristeis la cuenta para que se (ahorrar) un poco de dinero? ¿Para qué retirasteis el dinero?*
6. *¡Menos mal que depositamos los cheques de modo que (cubrir) las expensas!*
7. *Gustavo nos envió su número de cuenta, de manera que (poder) depositar el efectivo.*

C. *Traduzca al español.* (Translate into Spanish.)

1. I hope it won't be hot when we leave tomorrow!
2. Elena didn't tell you the secret so that you could tell it to everyone!
3. I won't buy you (singular, informal) that toy, whether (even though) you like it or not!
4. We had some extra time, so (that) we were able to come and visit you all! (informal)
5. Foreign investors always stimulate the economy, even if the Minister says they don't.

LECCION 15

A. DIALOGO

VISITANDO LAS MISIONES EN LA SELVA.

Liliana, una simpática guía de turistas, está explicando las vistas y la historia de las Ruinas de San Ignacio, en la Provincia de Misiones, Argentina.[1]

LILIANA: Estas misiones fueron fundadas por la Compañía de Jesús, un grupo de misioneros jesuíticos en el año 1631. En total, fueron fundadas quince misiones en el territorio de lo que actualmente es la Argentina. En realidad, las primeras reducciones[2] guaraníes[3] fueron fundadas mucho más al norte, en lo que hoy día es el Brasil, en el año 1609.

1ER TURISTA: ¿O sea que hay más ciudades como ésta en la selva?

LILIANA: En total hubo unas treinta ciudades como ésta, dispersas en una región que abarca partes de tres países: Argentina, Brasil y el Paraguay.[4] A su izquierda, pueden ver a lo lejos[5] partes de las ruinas.

1ER TURISTA: ¿Y todas esas piedras fueron talladas por los indígenas?

LILIANA: Sí, claro. Todos esos majestuosos edificios: las viviendas, talleres e iglesias, fueron construídos[6] desde la primera piedra por los guaraníes. Los indígenas[7] desarrollaron unos pueblos únicos, y no sólo tallaban piedras, sino que también fabricaban muebles y hasta[8] instrumentos musicales para exportación a Europa.

1ER TURISTA: ¿Cómo se sustentaban económicamente las misiones?

LILIANA: Bueno, eran tres las actividades económicas principales: la agricultura, la ganadería y las artesanías. Los principales productos eran el algodón, la yerba mate y también el maíz, la mandioca, la batata y las legumbres. En cuanto a las artesanías, entre los indígenas surgieron muchos escultores y excelentes artistas. Todavía podemos ver muestras de su arte en las iglesias de las misiones.

2DA TURISTA: Dígame, ¿alrededor de cuántas personas habitaban la ciudad?

LILIANA: Alrededor de diez mil personas llegaron a habitar esta ciudad. En total llegó a haber, en todas las misiones unas cien mil personas . . . *(El autobús se detiene súbitamente.)* Bueno, señoras y señores, bajémonos ahora y vamos a seguir a pie.

En cuanto se bajan del autobús, todos quedan maravillados por el contraste entre los tonos rojizos[9] de los hermosos edificios de piedra arenisca y los verdes salvajes de la selva circundante. Poco a poco se adentran en el laberinto formado por los muros y ventanas todavía en pie.[10]

LILIANA: Este edificio era una imprenta. Fue en las misiones donde se imprimió el primer libro en esta parte de América. Entre 1704 y 1728, se editaron varios libros en Candelaria, Loreto, Santa María y San Javier.

1ER TURISTA: ¿Entonces los guaraníes hablaban castellano también?

LILIANA: Los monjes enseñaban a todos a hablar el castellano, pero como saben el guaraní es, aún hoy, un idioma importante en esta zona. Incluso hay palabras guaraníes en muchos otros idiomas, como la palabra "piraña," de "pirá" que quiere decir "pez," y "añá" que significa "maldad" o "diablo." De hecho, algunos de los primeros libros editados en esta región de Sudamérica fueron en guaraní.

3ER TURISTA *(indicando al río en el fondo del valle):* Señorita, dígame, ¿cómo se llama aquel río?

LILIANA: Ése es el río Yabebiry. Allí fue donde se fundaron estas misiones. En realidad, los fundadores de estas misiones en particular, llegaron a orillas del río huyendo de los "bandeirantes" o esclavistas provenientes de San Pablo.[11] Se dice que en 1631, partieron unos doce mil indígenas río abajo del Paraná, desde San Ignacio en el Guayrá, en lo que hoy día es el estado de Paraná en el Brasil. En los saltos de Guayrá sufrieron un percance, perdiendo cientos de balsas y canoas. Por fin llegaron a esta zona, y fundaron San Ignacio y Loreto.

2DO TURISTA: ¿Qué hizo que todo esto se destruyera? ¿Qué se hizo de[12] toda la gente?

LILIANA: Bueno, las misiones fueron víctimas de los celos de las comunidades adyacentes. Su prosperidad e independencia económica hizo que todos miraran con envidia el éxito de estas ciudades. Los continuos ataques de los *bandeirantes* también corroyeron el trabajo de los habitantes. Finalmente, el golpe fatal fue dado por Carlos III, quien, bajo presión política, firmó la expulsión de los jesuitas de España y de todos sus dominios, en 1767. Así finalizaron estas ciudades sudamericanas.

3ER TURISTA: Yo soy arquitecto, y quisiera saber, ¿qué nos puede decir acerca de la arquitectura de esta zona? Nunca he visto nada igual.

LILIANA: ¡Tiene Vd. mucha razón, señor! ¡La arquitectura de estas ruinas es en verdad original! Tomemos como ejemplo esta arcada, noten las columnas a ambos lados de la abertura: los fustes son de diseño Dórico, mientras que los ornamentos en los pedestales y en las cornizas, o las partes inferiores y superiores, tienen motivos naturalistas: notarán que están adornados con bellísimas tallas de flores y plantas de esta región. También noten el uso de baldosas, tan típicamente español, [13] en diseños geométricos. En suma, vemos una combinación originalísima de elementos de diseño clásicos, españoles e indígenas. Ahora, vayamos a ver la vieja iglesia. Allí veremos más ejemplos de la arquitectura típica. Síganme . . .

Con esto, el grupo se interna aún más en la misteriosa selva . . .

VISITING THE MISSIONS IN THE JUNGLE.

Liliana, a friendly tour guide, is explaining the sights and history of the ruins of San Ignacio in the Province of Misiones, Argentina.

LILIANA: These missions were founded by the Society of Jesus, a group of Jesuit missionaries, in the year 1631. In all, fifteen missions were founded on the territory of what is now Argentina. Actually, the first Guarani reservations were founded much further north, in present-day Brazil, in 1609.

FIRST TOURIST: You mean to say that there are more cities like this in the jungle?

LILIANA: All in all, there were some thirty cities like this one, spread out in a region that encompasses areas of three countries: Argentina, Brazil, and Paraguay. To your left, you can see parts of the ruins in the distance.

FIRST TOURIST: All those stones were carved by the Native Americans?

LILIANA: That's right. All these majestic buildings—the living quarters, workshops, and churches—were built from the ground up by the Guarani. The Native Americans developed these unique cities, and not only did they carve stones, they also manufactured furniture, and even musical instruments to export to Europe.

FIRST TOURIST: How did the missions support themselves financially?

LILIANA: Well, there were three principal economic activities: farming, cattle-raising, and native artwork. Their principal products were cotton, *mate,* and also corn, manioc, sweet potatoes, and other vegetables. As for the native artwork, among the Indians there were many sculptors and excellent artists. We can still see some examples of their art in the mission churches.

SECOND TOURIST: Tell me, how many people lived in the city?

LILIANA: Up to ten thousand people lived in this city. In total, in all the missions, there were around a hundred thousand people . . . (The bus comes to a sudden halt.) Well, ladies and gentlemen, let's all get off the bus, and we will continue on foot.

As soon as they get off the bus, they are struck by the contrast between the red hues of the beautiful buildings and the untamed green of the surrounding jungle. Slowly, they venture into the labyrinth formed by the walls that are still standing.

LILIANA: This building contained a printing press. The first books in this part of America were printed in the missions. Between 1704 A.D. and 1728 A.D., many books were published in the cities of Candelaria, Loreto, Santa Maria, and San Javier.

FIRST TOURIST: So the Guarani also spoke Spanish?

LILIANA: The monks taught everyone Spanish, but as you know, Guarani is an important language in this region even today. There are Guarani words in many other languages, like the word piranha, from *pirá* meaning "fish" and *añá* meaning "devil" or "evil." Actually, some of the first books published in this part of South America were written in Guarani.

THIRD TOURIST (pointing to the river down in the valley): Miss, what's that river called?

LILIANA: That's the Yabebiry. The founders of this city arrived on the shores of the river while fleeing from the *bandeirantes,* or slave traders, from Sao Paulo. It is said that in 1631 A.D., around twelve thousand Indians left San Ignacio in Guaira, in present-day Parana State, Brazil, and escaped down the Parana River. At Guaira Falls, they met with misfortune and lost hundreds of *balsas* and canoes. Finally, they reached this area, and founded San Ignacio and Loreto.

SECOND TOURIST: How was all this destroyed? What happened to all the people?

LILIANA: Actually, the missions were envied by the surrounding communities. Their prosperity and economic independence made everyone look upon the success of these cities with resentment. The continuous attacks of the *bandeirantes* also undermined the work of the inhabitants. In the end, the fatal blow was given by Carlos III who, under political pressure, signed the expulsion of the Jesuits from Spain and all its dominions in 1767 A.D. Such was the end of these South American cities.

THIRD TOURIST: I'm an architect, and I'd like to know what you can tell us about the architecture of this region. I've never seen anything quite like it!

LILIANA: You're very right, sir! The architecture of these ruins is very original indeed! Let's take this doorway, for instance. Note the columns at both sides. The shafts are basically Doric in design, but the motifs on the pedestals and on the cornices, or bottom and top areas, are naturalistic. You'll notice they're beautifully decorated with carvings of leaves and flowers native to this region. Also note the typically Spanish use of floor tiles in geometric designs. In other words, we see a unique combination of classical Greek, Spanish, and Native American design elements. Now, I'd like to take you to see the old church. There you'll see more examples of this type of architecture. Follow me . . .

And, the group enters deeper into the mysterious jungle . . .

B. APUNTES

1. The ruins of *San Ignacio Miní* are located about 39 miles south of the capital of the province of *Misiones* in Argentina. They are a very popular tourist attraction, despite their remoteness and difficult accessibility.

2. The word *reducción* meant "a bringing together" in Old Spanish.

3. *Los Guaraníes* or *Tupí Guaraní* form one of the largest groups of Native Americans in South America. Their language, known as *el guaraní*, is widely spoken in a large region of South America, including parts of Argentina, Brazil, and Uruguay. It is the second official language of Paraguay, where it is taught in schools and used in mass media. There are other native languages spoken in Latin America, such as *Quechua* (in the central Andes) and *Maya* (in Mexico and parts of Central America), which coexist with Spanish.

4. The names of some countries in Spanish are traditionally preceded by an article. *Visité (el) Paraguay y (la) Argentina el año pasado, pero no Chile.* (I visited Paraguay and Argentina last year, but not Chile.)

5. *A lo lejos* (in the distance) is used when pointing to an object that is actually visible. Equivalent expressions are *en la lejanía* and *allá lejos*. To speak about an unseen object, use *lejos* alone instead. Compare: *¡Mira aquellos palmares allá lejos!* (Look at those palms in the distance!); *Loreto queda lejos de la capital de Misiones.* (Loreto is far away from the capital of Misiones.)

6. Note that the participle *construidos* agrees with the subject of the sentence, *edificios*.

7. Native Americans are traditionally and colloquially called *indios* in Spanish, but the correct terms are *indígenas* or *amerindios*.

8. The preposition *hasta* (until) can be used to mean "even, including." *Ayer estaba enfermo: tosía y ¡hasta tenía fiebre!* (Yesterday I was sick: I was coughing, and I even had a fever!) In formal Spanish, *incluso* is used instead. *Hablé con todos los proveedores, incluso con los del exterior.* (I spoke to all our suppliers, even the foreign ones.)

9. The soil in a small area of South America (in and around the province of Misiones in Argentina, as well as surrounding areas in Paraguay and Brazil) contains ferrous oxide, causing it to have a red tinge, much like Georgia's soil in the U.S.

10. Be sure not to confuse *a pie* (*caminando*, "on foot") with *de pie* (*parado*, "standing"). *Los chicos decidieron volver a casa a pie.* (The children decided to go back home on foot.) *Estuvo de pie durante toda la misa.* (I was standing throughout the entire Mass.)

11. The capture of Native Americans for enslavement was illegal in Spain and in all its dominions, but Portuguese *bandeirantes* (literally "banner-carriers") often raided the forests and captured the natives to be transported and enslaved.

12. *¿Qué se hizo de . . . ?* is a common phrase meaning "What became of . . . ? *¿Qué se habrá hecho de María? Hace mucho que no llama.* (I wonder what became of Maria? She hasn't called in a long while)

13. Note that the adjective *español* refers to *el uso*, and not to *la baldosa*.

C. GRAMATICA Y USOS

1. *EL IMPERATIVO* (THE IMPERATIVE)

The imperative forms of regular verbs are identical to the present subjunctive forms, in all but the second persons singular and plural (i.e., *tú* and *vosotros*) affirmative commands.

	PREGUNTAR TO ASK	APRENDER TO LEARN	ELEGIR TO CHOOSE
tú (affirmative)	*pregunta*	*aprende*	*elige*
tú (negative)	*no preguntes*	*no aprendas*	*no elijas*
él/ella/Vd.	*pregunte*	*aprenda*	*elija*
nosotros	*preguntemos*	*aprendamos*	*elijamos*
vosotros (aff.)	*preguntad*	*aprended*	*elegid*
vosotros (neg.)	*no preguntéis*	*no aprendáis*	*no elijáis*
ellos/Vds.	*pregunten*	*aprendan*	*elijan*

As in English, the imperative is used in Spanish to express a command.

Señores pasajeros, bajen del autobús y llévense todos sus efectos personales.
Passengers, please get off the bus, and take all your personal belongings.

Entre y tome asiento, por favor.
Come in and take a seat, please.

No dejes de llevar un sombrero para el tur, ¡el sol es muy fuerte en la selva!
Don't forget to take a hat on the tour. The sun is very strong in the
jungle!

No os olvidéis de hacerme preguntas durante la visita a las ruinas, ¡para eso estoy!
Don't forget to ask me questions during the visit to the ruins—that's
what I'm here for!

Vamos[1] primero a la iglesia, y luego veamos el resto de las ruinas.
Let's first go to the church, and then let's see the rest of the ruins.

Note that the second person singular *(tú)* affirmative command form of
regular verbs is identical to the third person singular present indicative
form.

Habla con la secretaria y no te olvides de cancelar tu cita de esta tarde.
Talk to your secretary, and don't forget to cancel your afternoon
appointment.

¡Limpia tu habitación antes de que me enoje de veras!
Clean your room before I get angry for real!

The following verbs and their derivatives have irregular affirmative forms
in the second person singular *(tú)*, which can easily be remembered by
memorizing the following sentences.

Ven, ten, ponte la ropa.
Come, take, and put on your clothes.

Sal, haz como digo.
Get out, do as I say.

Ve y sé feliz.
Go and be happy.

1. Note that the form *¡Vamos . . . !* may replace the affirmative command *¡Vayamos . . . !* in
informal situations:

   ¡Vamos a la playa esta tarde, no vayamos al cine!
   Let's go to the beach this afternoon, let's not go to the movies!

For the *vosotros* affirmative command forms, simply replace the final *-r* in all infinitives with a *-d*.[2]

¡No os preocupéis, tirad los abrigos sobre la cama!
Don't worry, just throw your coats on the bed!

¡Venid y celebrad las fiestas con nosotros este año!
Come and celebrate the holidays with us this year!

The imperative is often used together with object pronouns. The pronouns are attached to the verb as a suffix in affirmative commands, and placed before the verb in negative commands.

No me preguntes a mí porqué es rojiza la tierra por aquí, pregúntaselo a la guía.
Don't ask me why the earth is red around here; ask the guide.

Dígame señorita, ¿cuánto tiempo dura la visita a la iglesia?
Tell me, Miss, how long is the visit to the church?

¿Trajísteis la cámara? Prestádmela para sacar una foto de aquel edificio.
Did you bring the camera? Lend it to me to take a picture of that building.

Pidámosle a Jorge que nos preste un rollo de película.
Let's ask Jorge to lend us a roll of film.

When attaching a reflexive pronoun as a suffix to the first and second persons plural *(nosotros* and *vosotros),* the final letter of the verb form *(s* or *d)* is dropped.[3]

Encontrémonos al lado de estas columnas dentro de media hora.
Let's meet next to these columns in half an hour.

Amáos los unos a los otros.
Love one another.

2. *MAS ACERCA DE LAS PREPOSICIONES* (MORE ABOUT PREPOSITIONS)

Prepositions are used to clarify the relationship between two words in a sentence. In Spanish, they can be combined to describe the relationship in more detail, or to add emphasis. In such cases, the prepositions cannot

---

2. Keep in mind that this form is used almost exclusively in Spain. In Latin America, these forms are no longer used, although they may be heard in political speeches, or seen in historical documents dating back to the 19th century.

3. The only exception is the verb *ir* in its second person plural reflexive form *idos (id + os).*

¡Idos ya mismo de aquí!
Get out of here right now!

be translated literally because together the prepositions may express an idea that is quite different from their individual meanings. The principal prepositions in Spanish are: *a* (to), *ante* (before, in front of), *bajo* (under), *con* (with), *contra* (against), *de* (of, from, by), *desde* (from), *en* (in), *entre* (between, among), *hacia* (towards), *hasta* (until), *para, por* (for), *según* (according to), *sin* (without), *sobre* (on top of, over), and *tras* (behind).

De entre todos los edificios que vimos, me gustó más la iglesia.
Of all the buildings we saw, I liked the church best.

¡Se ha enojado hasta con su propio hermano!
He even got angry with his own brother!

The preposition *a* may not be combined with any other. It may, however, be attached as a prefix to other prepositions or words, to create new terms, such as *abajo* (downward), *arriba* (upwards), *adentro* (inward), and *afuera* (outward). Note that the prepositions *para* or *hacia* may be used in conjunction with these words for emphasis.

¿Vamos para afuera a tomar un poco de aire?
Should we go outside and get some fresh air?

No tires, esta puerta abre hacia afuera.
Don't pull; this door opens outward.

The preposition *por* is often used in conjunction with prepositions that indicate location, such as *entre* (between), *al lado de* (next to), and *encima de* (on top of, above) to emphasize the idea of movement.

Las aguas del río Yabebiry se escurren por entre las rocas rojizas.
The waters of the Yabebiry river run between the red rocks.

El avión pasó por encima de las cabezas de los espectadores.
The airplane passed above the spectators' heads.

The preposition *con* changes to *conmigo, contigo,* and *consigo* when followed by the reflexive pronouns *mí, ti,* and *sí,* respectively.

Voy a entrar en las ruinas. ¿Alguien quiere venir conmigo?
I'm going into the ruins. Does anyone what to come with me?

In addition to indicating origin or belonging, the preposition *de* can be used to introduce a phrase describing a noun or a verb.

Ese edificio es de unos 500 años atrás.
That building is about 500 years old.

Raúl hoy tiene cara de pocos amigos.
Raul looks very unfriendly today.

De can also replace other prepositions in informal conversation, especially *con, por,* and *desde,* as long as its meaning within the sentence is clear.

Julia llegó a la fiesta de ayer acompañada por/de su novio.
Julia came to yesterday's party accompanied by her boyfriend.

Spanish also has many prepositional phrases that are used before nouns or verbs in the infinitive. Some of these phrases are used primarily in conversation, while others are found mainly in business correspondence. These include *además de* (besides), *respecto a* (concerning), *tocante a* (relating to), *lejos de* (far from), *a causa de* (due to), *a diferencia de* (unlike), *a excepción de* (except for), *a pesar de* (in spite of), *a través de* (throughout, by means of), *en cuanto a* (regarding, as far as), *en frente de* (across from), *en vez/lugar de* (instead of), *más allá de* (beyond), and *por causa de* (because of).

En cuanto a la arquitectura de las ruinas podemos decir que es originalísima.
As far as the architecture of the ruins goes, we can say it's very original indeed.

A pesar de estar lejos de las grandes ciudades como Asunción y Buenos Aires, las misiones eran importantísimos centros culturales y económicos de la antigua América.
Despite being far from large cities such as Asuncion and Buenos Aires, the missions were very important cultural and economic centers of ancient America.

Lejos de ser olvidado, el guaraní es la segunda lengua oficial del Paraguay.
Far from being forgotten, Guarani is the second official language of Paraguay.

D. HABLEMOS DE NEGOCIOS

UNA SINTESIS DE LAS ECONOMÍAS DE ESPAÑA Y DE AMÉRICA LATINA (GENERAL OVERVIEW OF THE ECONOMIES OF SPAIN AND LATIN AMERICA)

Spain

The economy of Spain has experienced gradual changes since Spain's entrance into the ECM (European Common Market or *MCE Mercado Común Europeo)* in 1986. The banking system stimulates foreign investment, as accounts in foreign currency are not subject to taxation. Spain has experienced much growth in its export of manufactured goods, especially in the transport industry. The major industrial centers of Spain are located near Madrid, and in the northeast, particularly in the Basque region and Catalonia. Fishing has traditionally been one of Spain's major industries, although fish imports are still necessary to meet great internal demands. Mining is important due to Spain's predominantly mountainous topography. Iron, zinc, mercury, copper, and lead are extensively mined. Energy production is a problem, and Spain depends heavily on foreign oil. Good opportunities exist in the development of alternative energy sources, such as hydroelectricity, thermal energy, and natural gas.

Latin America

The economies of Latin American countries are in different stages of development. Drastic changes in political and economic policies have made the region unpredictable and uninviting to foreign investors in the past. The tendency, after democratization, is toward stabilization, deregulation, modernization, and integration of economies, as exemplified by MERCO-SUR *(Mercado Común del Sur),* a common market comprising Argentina, Brazil, Uruguay, and Paraguay, and ANCOM, the Andean Common Market. Perhaps the greatest challenge facing Latin America is attracting sufficient international trade and investors to meet the demands of growing populations and changing economic systems. With this in mind, following is a brief outline of the main imports, exports, and trading partners of Spanish-speaking countries.

COUNTRY	IMPORTS	EXPORTS	TRADE PARTNERS
Argentina	industrial equipment and machinery, petroleum products, automobiles, transport equipment, rubber, industrial chemicals.	beef, animal feed, wheat, grains, cereals, vegetable products, leather.	U.S., E.U. Brazil, China, Japan, Russia, Ukraine.
Bolivia	consumer goods, construction materials, transport and farming equipment, raw materials.	natural gas, tin, petroleum, coffee, sugar, silver, antimony.	Argentina, Brazil, U.S., Mexico, the Netherlands, Japan.
Chile	machinery, consumer and intermediate goods, petroleum.	copper, nickel mining products, fruits, vegetables, fish meal.	U.S., Venezuela, Argentina, Brazil, Germany, Britain, France, Japan.
Colombia	machinery, chemicals, petroleum, base metals, paper, plastics.	coffee, bananas, cotton, flowers, petroleum.	U.S., Venezuela, Peru, Ecuador, E.U., Japan.
Costa Rica	commodities, industrial machinery, communications equipment, paper, iron, steel, chemicals, petroleum.	coffee, bananas, beef, textiles, cocoa, sugar, pharmaceuticals.	U.S., Venezuela, Mexico, Guatemala, El Salvador, Nicaragua, Germany, Japan.
Cuba	machinery and transport equipment, capital goods, fuels, food, raw materials.	citrus fruits, sugar, nickel, seafood, tobacco, computer screens.	Russia, Eastern Europe, France, Spain, U.K., Japan, Germany.

COUNTRY	IMPORTS	EXPORTS	TRADE PARTNERS
Dominican Republic	petroleum, machinery, chemicals, iron, steel, textiles, foodstuffs.	raw sugar, alloys, coffee, cacao, tobacco leaves.	U.S., Canada, Japan, Venezuela, Puerto Rico, the Netherlands, Switzerland.
Ecuador	chemicals, mineral products, technical and construction equipment, foodstuffs, transport equipment.	petroleum, coffee, fish products, bananas.	U.S., Japan, Germany, Italy, Brazil, Panama, Colombia.
El Salvador	basic manufactures, raw materials, chemicals, foodstuffs.	Coffee, industrial goods, cotton, sugar.	U.S., Guatemala, Germany, Costa Rica, Mexico, Venezuela.
Guatemala	chemicals, mineral fuels, lubricants, machinery, transport equipment, food products.	coffee, sugar, bananas, cotton, agricultural products, non-traditional products.	U.S., El Salvador, Germany, Honduras, Costa Rica, Mexico, the Netherlands, Antilles.
Honduras	manufactured products, chemical products, mineral fuels, lubricants, food products, live animals, machinery, transport equipment.	bananas, coffee, wood, seafood, sugar.	U.S., Venezuela, Guatemala, Costa Rica, Trinidad & Tobago, Japan, Germany, Belgium.
Mexico	machinery and transport equipment, grains and oilseeds, chemicals, metals, processed food and drinks.	oil and oil products, autos and auto parts, chemicals.	U.S., E.U., Canada, Japan.

COUNTRY	IMPORTS	EXPORTS	TRADE PARTNERS
Nicaragua	raw materials, intermediate goods, capital goods, fuels and oil.	coffee, meat, cotton, bananas, sugar, shellfish.	Japan, E.U., U.S., Eastern Europe.
Panama	petroleum, machinery, transport equipment, chemical products, food products, beverages, textiles.	bananas, shrimp, sugar, trochus, vegetables.	U.S., Mexico, Ecuador, Japan, Guam.
Paraguay	machines and engines, minerals, fuels and lubricants, food and foodstuffs.	raw cotton, soya, lumber, animal products, tobacco, meat, hides.	U.S., Brazil, Argentina, Algeria, Germany, The Netherlands.
Peru	wheat, processed food, intermediate and consumer goods.	petroleum, copper, marine products, textiles.	U.S., Japan, Brazil, Germany, Belgium, Luxembourg, Great Britain, Italy.
Puerto Rico	chemicals, machinery and transport equipment, petroleum and derivatives, textiles.	chemicals, machinery.	U.S., Virgin Islands.
Spain	chemicals, energy, communications equipment, farming equipment, metal products, machinery.	agricultural products, chemicals, fish, manufactured goods, transport equipment.	U.S., E.U.

COUNTRY	IMPORTS	EXPORTS	TRADE PARTNERS
Uruguay	machinery and electrical equipment, minerals, chemicals, petroleum, transport equipment, paper products.	textiles, meat and meat products, wool, chemicals, agricultural products, electrical energy, ceramics.	Brazil, U.S., Argentina, Germany, Italy.
Venezuela	machinery and transport equipment, intermediate goods, chemicals, food.	petroleum and petroleum products, aluminum, iron and steel, coffee, cocoa.	U.S., Germany, Italy, Japan.

EXAMEN

A. *Inserte la forma imperativa que corresponda en las oraciones siguientes.*
(Insert the correct command forms in the following sentences.)

1. *(vosotros) ¡No (ponerse) nerviosos! La prueba no es tan difícil.*
2. *(Tomar) y (leer) estos informes. Si tuvieren alguna inquietud, (preguntar) me.*
3. *¡(Poner) te el saco, pues hace mucho frío!*
4. *¡(Ir) al cine! Después podemos cenar en un restaurante.*
5. *María, (Vd.) (controlar) al niño. No (dejar) que haga lo que quiera.*
6. *(nosotros) ¡No (levantarse) temprano mañana! (Dormir) hasta más tarde.*
7. *(vosotros) ¡(Irse) al centro mañana! No (irse) hoy.*
8. *¡Por favor, alguien (ayudarme) a encontrar el zapato!*
9. *(tú) (Decir)le al jefe que no puedo venir a la oficina mañana. Tengo que ir al médico.*
10. *(tú) ¡Nunca (decir) nunca jamás!*

B. *Traduzca las oraciones siguientes al inglés.* (Translate the following sentences into English.)

1. *Complete todos los rubros del siguiente formulario, a excepción de los marcados "exclusivamente para uso oficial."*
2. *Prepáreme un informe tocante a las compras hechas por los clientes nuevos, en base al cual proyectaremos los niveles de venta del cuatrimestre que viene.*
3. *A diferencia del inglés, el español se escribe casi fonéticamente.*
4. *A causa de un problema con la computadora central, las aplicaciones se procesarán a mano en lugar de electrónicamente.*
5. *No tengo nada más que decir con respecto a la reunión de directores de ayer.*

C. *Inserte la frase preposicional o la preposicion que corresponda.* (Insert the appropriate preposition or prepositional phrase.)

1. *Quisiera hablar* (with) *Vd.* (about) *el asunto Gómez.*
2. (Unlike) *el año pasado,* (faced with) *el explosivo aumento* (in) *el volumen de ventas, este año nos vemos obligados a modernizar nuestro sistema* (of) *computación.*
3. (Besides) *disminuir los gastos de papeleo, nos permitirá agilizar las transacciones, particularmente en lo* (relating to) *las transacciones de importación y exportación.*
4. *El proyecto entrará en la fase de construcción* (within) *una semana, a más tardar.*
5. (Far from) *ofenderme, me alegra que Vd. no consienta* (with me). (In) *la variedad de opiniones está el progreso.*

LECTURA

La siguiente lectura le dará al alumno una muestra de poesía latinoamericana contemporánea, a través de la obra del reconocido poeta argentino, Atilio Jorge Castelpoggi.

Los Vagabundos

Los vagabundos[1] saben mucho porque nunca descansan
porque conocen los secretos de la noche,
porque en la noche, vienen las muchachas a adivinar[2]
    los sueños.
Inventaré esta historia para cubrir[3] tu ausencia.
Inventaré esta historia como[4] el verano.
Inventaré un murmullo transparente que cubra
    el mundo todo.
Idioma de tu voz, dialecto íntimo apenas pronunciado
    por tu boca.
En soledad,[5] lleno de gentes, adentro del bullicio,
caminando en la noche a veces,
monologando con las formas azules de las puertas.
En Soledad, ciudad de mis sollozos,[6]
me siento solo adentro de mí mismo.
En soledad. En soledad y recordando . . .

Desde que yo te conocí, he comprendido los cantos
    que desnudan[7] la alegría
y el inmenso placer quemándonos los ojos.
Creo que el fin de la vida deberá ser así:
algo como tus pasos cuando llegas
y te estoy esperando.
Seremos vagabundos tomados[8] de la sangre
haciendo amor a grandes rasgos de esperanza
como la noche, que vive enamorada de la sombra
y la persigue[9] por el mundo.

VOCABULARIO

1. *vagabundo:* wanderer (from *vagar* - to wander)
2. *adivinar:* to guess
3. *cubrir:* In this context, *cubrir* (to cover) means "to make up for."
4. The conjunction *como* is often used in poetry to compare two words. Literally: "I will invent *this story* which is like *summer.*"
5. Here, the poet compares his *soledad* (loneliness) to a city, which he calls *Soledad:* "Loneliness."

6. *sollozo(s):* sob(s)
7. *desnudar:* to undress, to lay bare
8. *tomados de la sangre:* "blood in blood" (from: *tomados de la mano:* "hand in hand," "holding hands")
9. *perseguir:* to follow, to persecute

Los sobrevivientes

Desgraciadamente duramos[1] más que la
embriaguez[2]
y apenas nos queda el mito[3] de lo que pudo
ser.

Ahora el adiós ha puesto su sabiduría en el
    hechizo[4] de lo desconocido
mientras rueda un manojo[5] de llaves escaleras
    abajo
y un latido[6] se detiene para siempre.

Las cicatrices[7] emergen de algo que fue nuestro
y luego será olvido y recuerdo socavando[8]
el pasado:
el vano de una puerta tapiada[9] por los días
o una habitación abandonada que arrasa los
    despojos[10] del amor:
objetos, cenizas, ecos,

raíces que crecen como ídolos
o el goce[11] enloquecido aún ardiendo en medio
    de otras sombras.

El sacrilegio está en lo que se ha perdido
nunca en el fruto hermoso del pecado.[12]

VOCABULARIO

1. *durar:* to last; *durar más que:* to outlast
2. *embriaguez:* drunkenness, enebriation
3. *mito:* myth
4. *hechizo:* charm, magical spell
5. *manojo:* handful, bunch
6. *latido:* beat, pulse
7. *cicatriz:* scar
8. *socavar:* to dig into
9. *tapiar:* to wall up, to block up
10. *despojos:* scraps, remains, what's left over
11. *goce:* enjoyment, pleasure (*gozar:* to enjoy, take pleasure in)
12. *pecado:* sin

LECCION 16

A. DIALOGO

UN GRAN ACTO POLÍTICO.

Julio invitó a su amiga estadounidense, Jackie, a un gran acto político en la ciudad de Guatemala. Durante el acto, va a hablar Jorge Juárez, el candidato presidencial del partido político "Unión Cívica Popular."[1] Cuando llegan al parque central,[2] ya hay alrededor de cuarenta mil personas.

JACKIE: ¡Qué mar de gente! ¿Vos ves algo?[3] Apenas alcanzo a ver el podio donde va a hablar Juárez . . .

JULIO: ¡Ésto no es nada! Menos mal que todavía[4] vinimos con el autobús del ateneo.[5] Si no, hubiéramos ido a parar[6] allá lejos, quién sabe dónde . . .

De golpe, se empieza a oír un cantito que surge de un grupo de personas lejano. Jackie no alcanza a distinguir[7] lo que cantan.

JACKIE: ¿Qué están cantando?

JULIO: Es un viejo canto, dice: ¡Se siente, se siente, la UCP está presente! Lo repiten una y otra vez . . . claro que, cada partido reemplaza sus siglas en el canto.

JACKIE: ¿Y qué es ese ruido que los acompaña? Parecen tambores de la selva . . .

JULIO: ¡Son bombos![8] Ahora también los van a sacar los del ateneo. Creo que también trajeron cornetas, ya las van a repartir y te van a dar una a vos también. ¡No puede haber un acto político sin bombos, cornetas y alboroto!

JACKIE: Ni sin carteles, por lo visto. Mirá.

Jackie indica al grupo del ateneo, que empieza a descargar y a desplegar[9] los grandes carteles que han preparado para la ocasión.

JULIO: Tenés razón. Aquél en letras rojas lo ayudé a pintar yo mismo. Lee: ¡Juárez, estamos contigo! UCP.

JACKIE: A mí me gusta aquél otro, el que tiene el retrato de Juárez y del fundador del partido frente a frente.

VOZ DE UNA JOVEN: ¡Eh, Julito! ¡No seás vago y veníte a ayudarnos un poco a repartir los banderines y las cornetas, que ya sale Juárez en un ratito! ¡Traétela a la gringa[10] también!

JULIO: Parece que requieren de nuestra presencia.

225

JACKIE: **Ya me parecía que de alguna manera iba a pagar por el viaje en autobús . . .**

Julio, Jackie y los demás politiqueros[11] *reparten las cornetas y las banderitas a la gente que los rodea. Ya falta poco para que hable Juárez y se siente la expectativa del público como una gran ola que junta sus fuerzas para romper. Nuevamente se sienten*[12] *los bombos y los cantitos llenando el aire . . .*

JULIO: **¿Ya terminastes de repartirlas?**

JACKIE: **A mí ya no me quedan más, me las arrebataron como langostas.**

En el gentío, un hombre que lleva un cartel del partido socialista y otro, quien sostiene el cartel con la imagen de Juárez, empiezan a discutir acaloradamente, a viva voz. La discusión se pone fea, y ambos dejan los carteles y empiezan a empujarse el uno al otro.

JACKIE: **¿Qué está pasando? ¿Qué dicen?**

JULIO: **Parece que no están de acuerdo en cuanto al nuevo plan económico de Juárez. Aquí la gente se toma la política muy en serio.**

La gente que rodea a los hombres empieza a alborotarse y la policía llega corriendo y separa a los dos hombres. De golpe, el ritmo de los bombos crece hasta un frenesí y un rugido, parecido a un ventarrón, pasa por encima de las cabezas de Julio y Jackie.

JACKIE: **¿Apareció? ¿Lo ves?**

JULIO: **¡Sí, sí! Es aquél, vestido de blanco junto a su mujer. Ahora está saludando con la mano.**

JACKIE: **Lo veo. Parece muy carismático. Político nato.**

Un ruido ensordecedor surge del gentío. Los bombos, las cornetas y las voces se funden en un torrente dirigido hacia Juárez. Juárez alza la mano y poco a poco, se apacigua el mar de gente.

JUAREZ *(parsimoniamente):* **¡Compatriotas!**[13] **¡Ciudadanos! Estamos reunidos para celebrar la nueva oportunidad que se nos ofrece para elegir, en un marco democrático y de libertad, a un nuevo Presidente de la República.**

Los bombos agitan y el pueblo ruge otra vez.

JUAREZ: **He venido también para hacer un llamado. Un llamado a que vosotros,**[14] **el pueblo, ejercitéis vuestra libertad cívica, con la convicción y la certeza de que juntos, haremos todo lo posible para llevar adelante a nuestro país . . .**

JACKIE: **Si habla tan lento, vamos a estar aquí un largo rato . . .**

JULIO: **No te preocupés, vale la pena**[15] **escucharlo. Ahora va a describir el plan económico que propone, es muy innovador.**

JACKIE *(con entusiasmo):* **Bueno, escuchémoslo entonces . . .**

A BIG POLITICAL RALLY.

Julio has invited his American friend, Jackie, to a big political rally in Guatemala City. Jorge Juarez, the presidential candidate of the "Popular Civic Union" political party, is going to give a speech. When they arrive at the main square, there are already around forty thousand people there.

JACKIE: Wow, look how many people there are! I can barely see the podium where Juarez is going to speak.

JULIO: This is nothing! It's a good thing we came with the center's bus. Otherwise, we'd have ended up who knows how far away!

Suddenly, they hear a little song coming from a distant group of people. Jackie can't quite make out what they're saying.

JACKIE: What are they singing?

JULIO: It's an old tune. They're saying, "You can feel it, you can feel it, the U-C-P is here!" They just say it over and over again. . . . Of course, every party replaces its initials in the song.

JACKIE: And what's that noise? It sounds like jungle drums . . .

JULIO: They're *bombos!* The people at the center are going to get theirs out, too. I think they also brought some horns, and they're going to give them out, to you, too! Whoever heard of a meeting with no drums, horns, or loud noise?

JACKIE: Or without signs, apparently. Look!

Jackie points to a group of people in the center, who begin to unload and to unfold the large signs they've prepared for the occasion.

JULIO: You're right! I helped paint the one with red letters myself. It says: "Juarez, we love you! PCU."

JACKIE: I like that other one, the one with the picture of Juarez and the founder of the movement face to face.

VOICE OF A YOUNG WOMAN: Hey, Julito! Don't be lazy; come and help us pass out the banners and the horns. Juarez will be here soon. And bring the *gringa* with you!

JULIO: It seems our presence is required.

JACKIE: I knew we'd end up paying for the bus ride somehow!

Julio, Jackie, and the other activists pass out the horns and banners to the people around them. Juarez will begin his speech soon, and the people's expectation is mounting like a large wave gathering strength before it breaks. Once again, the *bombos* and little songs fill the air.

JULIO: Are you done passing them out?

JACKIE I don't have any left; they took them out of my hands like locusts!

In the crowd, a man carrying a sign for the Socialist Party, and another who is holding up the sign with Juarez's image, begin to argue heatedly. The argument turns ugly, and both drop their signs and begin to push one another.

JACKIE: What's going on? What are they saying?

JULIO: It looks like they don't agree on Juarez's new economic plan. People take politics very seriously here.

The people surrounding the men begin to get agitated, and the police arrive running and separate the two men. Suddenly, the rhythm of the *bombos* reaches a hectic pace, and a roar passes over Julio's and Jackie's heads like a great wind.

JACKIE: Is he here? Do you see him?

JULIO: Yeah, yeah! He's that one, dressed in white, next to his wife. Now he's waving!

JACKIE: I see him. He seems very charismatic. A born politician.

A deafening sound comes from the people. The *bombos,* the horns, and the voices merge into a stream rushing toward Juarez. Juarez raises his hand, and slowly the sea of people calms down.

JUAREZ (parsimoniously): Countrymen! Citizens! We have come together to celebrate our newfound opportunity to elect a new President of the Republic in a setting of democracy and freedom.

The *bombos* beat, and the people roar again.

JUAREZ: I have also come to make a call. A call to you, the people, to exercise your civil liberty, with the conviction and certainty that, together, we will do everything possible to bring our country forward.

JACKIE: If he's going to speak so slowly, we're going to be here for a long time!

JULIO: Don't worry; he's worth listening to! He's going to describe his new economic plan. It's very innovative . . .

JACKIE: Oh, let's listen then . . .

B. APUNTES

1. Most Latin American countries have a parliamentary government with three branches—Executive, Legislative, and Judiciary—modeled after the U.S. Unlike in the U.S., however, there is usually a greater variety of political parties in the forefront of elections.

2. *El parque central* is Guatemala City's main square. To the north of the park is *El Palacio Nacional* (The National Palace), which houses the offices of the executive branch of government. To the east and west of the park are the *Catedral Metropolitana* (Metropolitan Cathedral) and the *Archivos Generales de Centroamérica* (General Archives of Central America), respectively.

3. *Vos* is used colloquially in Guatemala instead of *tú*. The *vos* conjugation will be discussed later in this lesson.

4. Note that *todavía* (yet, still) is often used for emphasis, to mean "what's more, actually!" *Después de criticarme, ¡todavía me insultó!* (After criticizing me, he actually insulted me!)

5. *Un ateneo* is a general term for a social club of sorts, such as a philosophical, literary, or political society. The meeting-place for such a group is also called *un ateneo*. In this dialogue, it refers to one of many local political associations, usually a branch of a large political party. Another popular term is simply *club*. *Ateneos* are gathering places for political activists, where they organize drives, collect funds for campaigns, etc. Under military regimes, they were often branded as communist and banned, and were frequently the target of military raids and terrorist attacks.

6. *Ir a parar* (followed by a location) is a popular colloquial expression meaning "to end up at . . ." *Después del acto, todos fuimos a parar en la casa de Julio.* (After the rally, we all wound up at Julio's house.)

7. *Alcanzar* (to reach) followed by *a* and a verb in the infinitive means "to manage to . . ." *No alcanzamos a ver el final de la película porque el bebé se puso a llorar.* (We didn't manage to see the end of the movie because the baby started crying.)

8. *Bombos* are large South American bass drums, originally used for folk music, but also used by young people to liven up large public gatherings, such as rallies and sports events.

9. *Desplegar* (to unfold) is also used in computer terminology to mean "to display."

10. The term *gringo,* which is not used in a derogatory way, doesn't necessarily refer to Americans, but can be used to refer to any foreigner, or foreign language (i.e., not Spanish). The term's etymology is uncertain, but it most likely derives from *griego* (Greek), as in the English expression "It's all Greek to me!"

11. The term *politiquero* is generally used in a derogatory way to mean "politics-monger." It can also be used jokingly to mean *un activista político* (a political activist).

12. The verb *sentir* (to feel) is often used colloquially instead of *oír* (to hear). *¿Qué es ese ruido? ¿Lo sientes?* (What is that noise? Do you hear it?)

13. *Un compatriota* ("a fellow citizen": from the preposition *con* "with" + *patriota* "patriot, citizen") is used not only in political contexts. It is often used informally to refer to people from the same country or region in an endearing way. *Quiero que conozcas a Billy, ¡es compatriota tuyo!* (I'd like you to meet Billy. He's a countryman of yours!)

14. Note that *vosotros* is used in Latin America only in certain settings, such as in political speeches. Even under such formal circumstances, this usage is becoming less and less common.

15. The expression *valer la pena* is very popular in Spanish. *¿Valdrá la pena escuchar todo el discurso?* (Is listening to the whole speech worth the trouble?)

C. GRAMATICA Y USOS

1. *LOS DEMONSTRATIVOS* (DEMONSTRATIVES)

The demonstrative adjectives *este, esta* (this), and *estos, estas* (these) are used to refer to a noun or nouns close to the speaker, whereas *ese, esa* (that), and *esos, esas* (those) are used to refer to a noun or nouns close to the person being addressed. They always precede the noun.

Reparte estos volantes junto con esos botones.
Pass out these flyers with those buttons.

Nunca vi esas fotos, ¿podrías mostrármelas?
I never saw those pictures; could you show them to me?

When the noun or nouns in question are far from both the speaker and the person being addressed, *aquel, aquella, aquellos,* and *aquellas* are used. They can be translated as "that . . . over there; those . . . over there."

¡Aquellos dos hombres están peleándose!
Those two men (over there) are fighting!

Esta carpeta va en ese archivero, y esa carpeta va en aquel archivero más grande.
This folder goes in that file cabinet, and that folder goes in that bigger file cabinet over there.

Demonstrative pronouns are used in place of nouns that have already been introduced. Their forms are virtually identical to that of demonstrative adjectives—they are distinguished only by an accent mark on the pronoun. The demonstrative pronouns are: *éste, ésta, éstas, éstos* (this one, these ones); *ése, ésa, ésos, ésas* (that one, those ones); and *aquél, aquélla, aquéllos, aquéllas* (that one/those ones over there).

La señora de Juárez es la mujer con el vestido azul . . . no aquélla otra!
Mrs. Juarez is the woman with the blue dress . . . no, that other one!

¡Aquél va a todas las manifestaciones!
That guy over there never misses a rally!

¿Cuál trompeta usaste, ésta o ésa?
Which horn did you use, this one or that one?

The neutral demonstrative pronouns *esto* (this), *eso* (that), and *aquello* (that other) are used to refer to abstract ideas that were previously mentioned. They are never used in combination with nouns.

¡Qué calor hace con tanta gente!—Sí, eso es lo peor de las manifestaciones públicas.
It's really hot with all these people here!—Yes, that's the worst thing about rallies.

2. *LOS PRONOMBRES RELATIVOS* (RELATIVE PRONOUNS)

A relative pronoun is used to introduce a clause that modifies a noun.

a) *Que*
The most common relative pronoun in Spanish is *que* (that). It is preceded by a noun introduced by a definite article.

Los carteles que viste fueron pintados por mí.
The signs that you saw were painted by me.

Note that in English, the relative pronoun is often omitted. In colloquial Spanish, the relative pronoun *que* may be dropped only if the verb used in the following clause is *estar,* in which case, *estar* is dropped as well.

El hombre (que está) hablando en el podio es el gobernador.
The man (who is) talking on the podium is the governor.

If the noun to which *que* refers can be inferred from context, it may be omitted, but the article must remain for clarity.

El que llamó, no dijo ni quién era ni qué quería.
The one who called didn't say who he was, nor what he wanted.

Las que vendrán a la manifestacíon más tarde son amigas de la señora Nichols.
The ones who will come to the rally later are friends of Mrs. Nichols.

b) *Quien*
When a clause that refers to a person is introduced by a preposition, *quien* must be used instead of *que.*

Los militantes con quienes estuve en la manifestación fueron arrestados por perturbar la paz.
The activists with whom I attended the rally were arrested for disturbing the peace.

Los clientes, a quienes enviamos las cartas, ¡no saben castellano!
The clients to whom we sent the letters don't know Spanish!

c) *Cual*
The relative pronouns *el cual, la cual, los cuales, las cuales* are used in conjunction with prepositional phrases. These pronouns may also be used instead of *que* and *quienes* in a more elegant style of expression.

A la conferencia, acerca de la cual se ha escrito ya mucho, asistieron enviados de muchos países.
The conference, about which much has already been written, was attended by envoys from many countries.

El juicio, durante el cual seguramente saldrá a luz toda la evidencia, será difundido a las 9 horas.
The trial, during which all the evidence will probably be made known, will be broadcast at 9 A.M.

d) *Cuyo*

The relative pronouns *cuyo, cuya, cuyos, cuyas* (whose) indicate belonging or ownership and must agree in gender and number with the objects possessed.

El ministro Queveda, cuyo plan económico fue duramente criticado, no expresó su opinión acerca del nuevo plan propuesto por el comité especial.
Secretary Queveda, whose economic plan was harshly criticized, didn't comment on the new plan proposed by the special committee.

Las candidatas, cuyos historiales de trabajo está Vd. leyendo, no han sido entrevistadas aún.
The candidates whose résumés you are reading have not been interviewed yet.

e) *Lo que*

Lo que is used to replace an abstract noun. It can be translated into English as "what . . ." or "that which . . ." It is often used for emphasis, as in English.

¡Lo que necesito son unas vacaciones largas!
What I need is a long vacation!

No entendí todo lo que me dijo.
I didn't understand everything he said.

f) Other relative pronouns

All other interrogatives (*dónde, cuándo, cómo,* etc.) may also be used as relative pronouns, with the removal of their stress mark.

Encontrémonos en donde nos encontramos la vez pasada.
Let's meet where we met last time.

Cuando estéis listos, podemos irnos.
We can go whenever you're ready.

Podemos enviarle los paquetes como quiera usted.
We can send you the packages however you like.

3. *EL VOSEO* (CONJUGATION WITH *VOS*)

Vos is an alternative second person singular pronoun used in many Latin American countries[1] instead of *tú*. Although it is historically the singular of *vosotros*, it has not been used in Spain for centuries. It is accepted by the *Real Academia Española* (the official authority of Spanish usage throughout the Spanish-speaking world) as a special form used in several South American countries. Despite its popularity in spoken language, it is almost never seen in print, except in advertising that targets young people, or in works of fiction, where the author attempts to imitate natural conversation. It is never used in official documents.

The *vos* conjugation is very simple in all tenses[2]: simply drop the *i* from all the second person plural *(vosotros)* endings *(vosotros veis > vos ves, vosotros comisteis > vos comistes, que vosotros encontreis > que vos encontrés)*.

¡No me digás que querés ir a la manifestación con este calor!
Don't tell me you want to go to the demonstration in this heat!

¿Podés leerme esta carta? . . . Está en inglés.
Can you help me read this letter? . . . It's in English.

¿Fuistes a lo de Pablito anteayer y le contastes lo que pasó?
Did you go to Pablito's the day before yesterday and tell him what happened?

¿Querés ir al teatro mañana o preferirías ir al cine?
Do you want to go to the theater tomorrow, or would you prefer going to the movies?

Espero que no tengás que volver a hacer el trabajo. ¿Estás seguro de que perdistes el disco?
I hope you won't have to do the work over again. Are you sure you lost the disk?

The direct object, indirect object, and reflexive object pronouns for *vos* are the same as those for *tú*. Only the prepositional object pronoun, *vos*, is different.

¿A vos te gusta más Juárez o el candidato socialista?
Do you like Juarez or the Socialist candidate better?

---

1. *Vos* is used extensively in Argentina, Paraguay, and Guatemala, and also in rural areas of Uruguay, Colombia, Nicaragua, and Costa Rica.

2. Except the simple future, which is very rarely used with *vos*. Only the future with *ir a* is used. Note that the simple future forms of *vos* are identical to the *tú* forms.

> *Vos vas a ir al acto esta tarde, ¿no?*
> *Vos irás al acto esta tarde, ¿no?*
>> You're going to the rally this afternoon, right?

La corneta que queda es para vos.
The horn that's left over is for you.

In the imperative, drop the *-d* ending from affirmative *vosotros* commands, and drop the *-i* from negative commands. Note that the stress of the command form is indicated by a stress mark.

¡Compráte la revista que quieras, no me pidás permiso más!
Buy whatever magazine you want; don't ask me for permission any more!

Contáme qué te pasa, estás un poco caricaído.
Tell me what's wrong; you look a little droopy-faced.

Note that the verb *ir* may not be used in the affirmative imperative. The verb *andar* must be used instead.

¡Andáte a jugar y no volvás tarde!
Go play and don't be back late!

¡No te vayás tan temprano, quedáte un rato más . . . pronto va a hablar el Ministro!
Don't leave so early; stay a little longer! The Minister will speak soon!

D. ESTUDIO IDIOMATICO

We needn't tell you that politicians everywhere love to exaggerate and show off . . .

A las mil maravillas (wonderful)

Julita anda a las mil maravillas.
Julita is doing wonderfully well.

Andar de la Ceca a la Meca (to search high and low)

Tuve que andar de la Ceca a la Meca para encontrar el libro que me pidió Juan.
I had to search high and low to find the book for which Juan asked me.

Estar como la quinta pata de la mesa (to be the fifth wheel)

Ayer en la fiesta, estaba como la quinta pata de la mesa.
I felt like a fifth wheel at yesterday's party.

Codearse con (to be "buddy-buddy" with)

Rosa se codea con los astros del cine internacional.
Rosa is buddy-buddy with international movie stars.

Dárselas de (to claim to be)

Mario se las da de experto en mujeres.
Mario claims to be an expert on women.

E. HABLEMOS DE NEGOCIOS

RESUMEN DE LA HISTORIA DE ESPAÑA Y DE AMÉRICA LATINA (A BRIEF HISTORY OF SPAIN AND LATIN AMERICA)

Spain

Spain has gone through considerable political changes since the founding of the *República* in 1931. A civil war broke out beginning a period of great strife caused by the power struggle between the extreme right (led by General Francisco Franco) and the left (popular) wings. It is estimated that 600,000 people died in this bloody three-year period between 1936 and 1939. Franco won and remained in power until his death in 1975. The first democratic elections in forty years were held in 1977, and a year later a new constitution restored civil liberties and freedom of speech and the press. The entrance of Spain into the European Common Market in 1986 is symbolic of Spain's progress toward democracy, but it is also a challenge for Spain's traditionally agricultural economy.

Latin America

Latin America has encountered considerable political problems throughout its history, leading back to the days of the *Virreinatos* (Viceroyalties). The traditional class division between rich and poor has been a difficult barrier to overcome, particularly due to continual military intervention and economic pressure from foreign countries. The following is a brief outline, by region, of the political history of Latin America.

Central America and the Caribbean

Mexico's independence movement in the early nineteenth century stimulated the rest of Central America to fight for independence. Guatemala, Mexico's neighbor to the south, feared that it might be annexed to Mexico in 1821, so Guatemala declared its independence on September 15 of that year. On July 3, 1823, Central America declared its collective independence, forming the United Provinces of Central America. Immediately, these provinces were divided by two opposing currents: the Liberals, who advocated substantial reform of the political and socioeconomic systems, and the Conservatives, who favored preserving the institutions of the colonial era. This division escalated into a civil war, which caused the slow dismemberment of the federation. By 1842, due to continual and extended civil wars, the individual countries of the federation signed a pact asserting their individuality and independence. The Liberal ideas were ultimately abandoned, and the Conservatives changed their attitudes to embrace a stronger church and a romantic idealization of the Spanish heritage. Many of these attitudes, which lead to an emphasis on nationalism and a strong suspicion of foreign ideas, color the politics of the region even today.

Foreign elements have also strongly influenced the political development of Central America. The region's agricultural wealth attracted the attention of the British Empire, which intended to annex these lands. Constant economic pressures through price control of the region's main products, as well as gunboat diplomacy hindered the development of the region's industries. Furthermore, the idea of the construction of a canal through Central America called forth the intervention of the United States, which also had designs on the region. Ultimately, this led to the consolidation of the Conservatives in power. Eventually, the Great Depression of 1929 marked the beginning of a new era in Central American politics. The crash of '29 was disastrous to the export economy of the region, and a period of military dictatorships and flirtation with communist ideology began and continued through the mid-1980s. This period was marked by much violence and the violation of human rights. Though conditions have stabilized considerably, Central America is still in the process of change.

Mexico and South America

South America's history is similar in many ways to that of Central America. The European powers slowly lost control of the region in the beginning of the nineteenth century, and their empires in the New World crumbled into separate countries. Each new republic had its own national heroes, although two names stand out among them: Simon Bolivar, the Venezuelan-born liberator of Venezuela, Bolivia, Colombia, and Peru; and Jose de San Martin, who liberated his native Argentina, Chile, and Peru. These men had great visions of unity and prosperity for South America, which unfortunately never took shape. The new, fragile republics had little preparation for self-government, and the new constitutions lacked a broad enough popular base to enforce them. Countless *coups d'état*, military regimes, and revolutions have shaken South American soil since the liberation.

Economically, the region experienced a great boom in the 1950s and 1960s, due to massive immigration, the abundance of natural resources, and the fact that Latin America remained unscathed after World War II. The oil boom of 1973–1974 created huge cash surpluses for Mexico and Venezuela. Much of this capital was spent on industrial projects. Eventually, mounting debt led the world into a recession, and the market for the region's products decreased dramatically. Thus, many countries' economies went in the red overnight. In 1982, the situation hit bottom, with Mexico declaring insolvency, followed by the rest of the South American countries. Renegotiations of the region's debt were accompanied by austere measures. The region has since experienced improvement, thanks to political stability and the newfound awareness of the importance of moderate economic policies.

EXAMEN

A. *Complete las oraciones siguientes con los pronombres o adjetivos demostrativos que corresponda.* (Complete the following sentences with the appropriate demonstrative adjective or pronoun.)

1. (That one over there) *es el candidato a presidente.*
2. (This) *modelo es más reciente que* (that one).
3. *¿No son* (those over there) *señoritas unas políticas famosas?*
4. (This) *vaso es de* (that) *hombre, y* (that one) *es de* (that woman over there).
5. *Tu bandera es* (this one) *o* (that one over there)?

B. *Complete las oraciones siguientes con el pronombre relativo que corresponda.* (Complete the following sentences with the appropriate relative pronoun.)

1. *El hombre con* (whom) *hablábamos es el presidente del ateneo.*
2. *¡*(The one who) *no quiere ir al acto es tu hermana, no yo!*
3. *La señorita* (whose) *cartera se cayó al piso es soltera.*
4. *Ayer vi un programa en* (which) *mostraron un día típico en la vida del presidente.*
5. *El asunto al* (which) *nos referiremos hoy es el desarrollo de un nuevo plan económico.*
6. (What) *no entiendo es cómo vamos a mercadear el producto en el exterior.*
7. *Este año, dentro de* (which) *hubo muchos cambios en la política económica, fue más productivo de* (what) *nos habíamos imaginado.*
8. *El ex-presidente,* (whose) *reformas tuvieron gran éxito, reside ahora en una ciudad,* (whose) *nombre se mantendrá confidencial.*
9. (The ones who) *vienen mañana, son amigos de tu primo Ricardo.*
10. *Nuestra clientela extranjera, de* (which) *constantemente recibimos cartas, siempre nos expresa su agrado con los servicios que ofrecemos.*

C. *Traduzca al español.* (Translate into Spanish.)

1. Who were you talking about when I came in?
2. I don't know what to buy my girlfriend; she's angry with me.
3. Whom can I ask how this program works?
4. That guy is a friend of Roberta's, and that girl over there is my best friend.
5. These are my favorite cookies!
6. Let's meet where we met last time.
7. *(Vos)* Don't eat like a pig! Chew!

D. *Complete las oraciones siguientes usando el voseo.* (Complete the following sentences using the *vos* conjugation.)

1. *¿(Ir) al acto ayer por la tarde?*
2. *(Decir)me, ¿hubo mucha gente en la parque central ayer?*
3. *Vos (pertenecer) a la Unión Cívica Popular, ¿no?*
4. *A mí me dieron una corneta roja ¿y a* (you)?
5. *Si (querer), (andar) al ateneo ahorita, y nos encontramos allá a eso de las tres de la tarde.*

LECCION 17

A. DIALOGO

UNA INSPECCIÓN DEL HOSPITAL ROSALES.

Claudia Vizconde, inspectora de Salud Pública,[1] llega al Hospital Nacional Rosales en San Salvador[2] y comienza su inspección en la sala de emergencias. Allí la recibe el jefe de la sección, el doctor Rogelio Cortés, quien resulta ser[3] muy joven, a pesar de su alto puesto.

DOCTOR CORTES: Encantado de recibirla, inspectora.

CLAUDIA VIZCONDE: Espero no sacarlo de su trabajo.

DOCTOR CORTES: En absoluto.[4] Estoy descansando un poco, es mi hora de almuerzo. Dígame, ¿en qué puedo servirle?

CLAUDIA VIZCONDE: Quisiera que me cuente un poco sobre la actividad en esta sección. Ahora parece estar todo bastante tranquilo. Me imagino que más tarde aumenta mucho el volumen de pacientes . . .

DOCTOR CORTES: Así es, en este momento no estamos tratando casos urgentes. Apenas[5] hay un par de personas esperando. Pero los fines de semana, todo cambia. Los sábados por la noche solemos tener por lo menos una treintena[6] de casos más o menos serios y un par de casos graves.

CLAUDIA VIZCONDE: Todo parece limpio en la sala de espera. ¿Podría mostrarme dónde se coloca a los pacientes?

DOCTOR CORTES: Cómo no . . . aquí en estas camillas se trata a los pacientes menos graves. Tratamos de aislar a los pacientes más graves lo más posible, con estas cortinas. Por supuesto, a veces tenemos que derivarlos a[7] cirujía o a otras secciones, como a terapia intensiva.

CLAUDIA VIZCONDE: Muy bien, doctor. Me causó muy buena impresión la sala de emergencias. Todo está muy limpio y en orden.

DOCTOR CORTES: Hacemos todo lo posible para que así sea. Nuestro personal de mantenimiento trabaja incansablemente, en condiciones mucho menos que ideales. No hemos recibido aún algunas provisiones que hemos pedido de Salud Pública, sobre todo las elementales como gasas, algodón y antisépticos.

CLAUDIA VIZCONDE: Ese problema está fuera de mi jurisdicción, pero haré una nota para el departamento de droguería.[8] Este mes ha habido un problema de abastecimiento,[9] tiene que ver con el paro[10] de transportes que hemos tenido.

240

DOCTOR CORTES: Se lo agradecería mucho . . . ¿Puedo serle de ayuda en algo más?

CLAUDIA VIZCONDE: Necesito hablar con alguien en enfermería. ¿Podría indicarme el camino?

DOCTOR CORTES: Si me permite, puedo acompañarla. En este momento, un amigo mío, el doctor Núñez, está por operar a un paciente en el quirófano con observatorio. Queda camino a la enfermería.

Los dos van caminando hacia la enfermería.

DOCTOR CORTES: A ambos lados de este pasillo están las habitaciones privadas. Las semiprivadas quedan en otro piso. Allí al fondo está la enfermería. Bueno, inspectora, la dejo a sus tareas.

CLAUDIA VIZCONDE: Encantada de conocerlo, doctor. Quizá pase por el quirófano más tarde.

DOCTOR CORTES: ¡Cómo no!

La inspectora entra en la enfermería.

CLAUDIA VIZCONDE: Necesito hablar con el jefe de enfermería.

MONICA ARROYOS: Está Vd. hablando con ella. Soy Mónica Arroyos.

CLAUDIA VIZCONDE: Mucho gusto. Soy Claudia Vizconde, inspectora de Salud Pública.

MONICA ARROYOS: Bienvenida al hospital, inspectora. ¿Cómo le puedo ser de ayuda?

CLAUDIA VIZCONDE: Necesitaría visitar a algún paciente en su habitación.

MONICA ARROYOS: A sus órdenes. Elija la habitación que quiera ver.

Las dos caminan por el pasillo, y entran en una habitación al azar. El paciente, un señor mayor,[11] está acabando de almorzar.

MONICA ARROYOS: Con permiso, señor Roble. Si me lo permite, le traigo visita. Esta es la señorita Vizconde, inspectora de Salud Pública.

SEÑOR ROBLE: ¡Pasen, pasen!

CLAUDIA VIZCONDE: Muchas gracias, señor. ¿Me permitiría hacerle unas preguntas?

SEÑOR ROBLE: Por supuesto.

CLAUDIA VIZCONDE: ¿Está Vd. cómodo en su habitación? ¿Cómo lo están tratando?

SEÑOR ROBLE: De maravilla. La señorita enfermera siempre viene cuando la llamo y parece que siempre se la pasan[12] limpiando la habitación.

CLAUDIA VIZCONDE: O sea que higienizan todo a menudo . . .

SEÑOR ROBLE: Así es. Lo único que no me gusta mucho es la comida . . . me gustaría un churrasquito. Aunque supongo que no soy el único que se lo haya dicho.

CLAUDIA VIZCONDE: Debo confesarle que es así. Bueno, no lo molestamos más. Muchas gracias por su ayuda y espero que se recupere del todo pronto.

SEÑOR ROBLE: Gracias. ¡Vuelvan cuando quieran!

MONICA ARROYOS: El señor Roble es muy animado. Le van a dar de alta mañana.

CLAUDIA VIZCONDE: Parece estar muy bien cuidado. La habitación está también limpia. ¿Han tenido problemas de suministración de artículos de limpieza en su sección?

MONICA ARROYOS: Así es, pero hemos podido evitar tener que racionar la limpieza, gracias a donaciones del personal. No han tenido tanta suerte con los artículos médicos . . .

CLAUDIA VIZCONDE: Entiendo. Ya le dije al doctor Cortés que informaré al departamento de droguería que envíen lo necesario lo antes posible. Por favor, firme estos documentos y la dejo a su labor.

MONICA ARROYOS: Por supuesto. ¿Necesita ver algo más?

CLAUDIA VIZCONDE: No en esta sección. ¿Podría dirigirme a los quirófanos, es decir, al quirófano con observatorio?

MONICA ARROYOS: Sí. Siga derecho por este pasillo y tome el ascensor hasta el segundo piso. El quirófano es el número tres, a la izquierda.

La inspectora llega al quirófano y entra. Parece una pequeña habitación con unos grandes ventanales, al lado de los cuales hay unas cuantas sillas simples, de plástico. El doctor Cortés se encuentra sentado al lado de los ventanales, mirando las preparaciones para la intervención desde lo alto.

CLAUDIA VIZCONDE: Con su permiso, doctor.

DOCTOR CORTES: Por favor, pase, inspectora. ¿Viene a observar la intervención?

CLAUDIA VIZCONDE: **En realidad, venía a que me firmara unos papeles . . . necesito la firma de cada jefe de sección que entrevisto.**

DOCTOR CORTES: **¡Cómo no! Aquí tiene.**

CLAUDIA VIZCONDE: **Gracias. Dígame, ¿qué tipo de operación está realizando el doctor?**

DOCTOR CORTES: **Es una apendectomía, pero apenas está empezando. En este momento están preparando al paciente. ¿Ve? El anestesiólogo va adentrándolo poco a poco en la narcosis, vigilándole los signos vitales. Las enfermeras están preparando el instrumental para la operación.**

CLAUDIA VIZCONDE: **¿Cuál es el doctor Núñez?**

DOCTOR CORTES: **Está en el proceso antiséptico. ¿Ve a aquel enfermero que acaba de entrar llevando una caja con instrumentos? Detrás de la puerta por la que entró está el departamento de esterilización. Allí dentro hay un autoclave y unos lavabos donde estará el doctor Núñez. Dentro de muy poco va a entrar en el quirófano.**

CLAUDIA VIZCONDE: **Me gustaría quedarme a ver la intervención, pero no tengo mucho estómago y aún me queda[13] hablar con la administración.**

DOCTOR CORTES: **Puedo acompañarla, si lo desea.**

CLAUDIA VIZCONDE: **¡Es Vd. muy amable, doctor!**

DOCTOR CORTES: **¡El gusto es mío, inspectora!**

AN INSPECTION OF THE ROSALES HOSPITAL.

Claudia Vizconde, a public health inspector, arrives at the Rosales National Hospital in San Salvador and begins her inspection in the emergency ward. She is greeted by the section chief, Doctor Rogelio Cortes, who turns out to be quite young, despite his advanced position.

DOCTOR CORTES: Very pleased to meet you, inspector.

CLAUDIA VIZCONDE: I hope I'm not taking you away from your work.

DOCTOR CORTES: Not at all. I'm just resting now. I'm on my lunch break. Tell me, how can I help you?

CLAUDIA VIZCONDE: I'd like to know about the activities in this section. Things seem pretty quiet now; I imagine there will be more patients later in the day . . .

DOCTOR CORTES: That's right. At the moment, we're not treating any serious cases, and there are only a couple of people waiting. But on weekends, everything changes. On Saturday nights, we usually see at least thirty minor cases, and a couple of serious ones.

CLAUDIA VIZCONDE: Everything seems clean in the waiting room. Could you show me where the patients are placed?

DOCTOR CORTES: Of course. Here, on these beds we treat minor injuries. We try to isolate the serious cases as much as possible, with these curtains. Of course, sometimes we have to send them to surgery or to other sections, such as intensive care.

CLAUDIA VIZCONDE: I'm very impressed with your emergency ward, doctor. Everything is very clean and well-organized.

DOCTOR CORTES: We try our best to keep it this way. Our maintenance personnel work tirelessly, in less than ideal conditions. We still haven't received some supplies we requested from Public Health, especially the basics, like gauze, cotton, and antiseptics.

CLAUDIA VIZCONDE: That problem is out of my jurisdiction, but I'll make a note for the pharmaceutical department. This month there's been a supply problem related to the transportation strike we've had.

DOCTOR CORTES: I greatly appreciate your help. Can I help you in any other way?

CLAUDIA VIZCONDE: I need to speak to someone in the nurses' station. Could you show me the way?

DOCTOR CORTES: If I may, I can take you there. Right now, a friend of mine, Doctor Nuñez, is about to operate on a patient in the observatory O.R., and I'd like to observe. The nurses' station is on the way.

Both head toward the nurses' station.

DOCTOR CORTES: To the sides of this hallway are the private rooms. The semi-private rooms are on another floor. The nurses' station is down the hall. All right, inspector, I'll leave you to your work.

CLAUDIA VIZCONDE: It was a pleasure meeting you, doctor. Perhaps I'll drop by the O.R. later.

DOCTOR CORTES: Please do!

The inspector enters the nurses' office.

CLAUDIA VIZCONDE: I need to speak to the head nurse.

MONICA ARROYOS: That's me! I'm Monica Arroyos.

CLAUDIA VIZCONDE: Pleased to meet you. I'm Claudia Vizconde, the public health inspector.

MONICA ARROYOS: Welcome to the hospital, inspector. How may I help you?

CLAUDIA VIZCONDE: I need to visit one of your patients in his or her room.

MONICA ARROYOS: Of course! Just pick the room you'd like to see.

They walk down the hall, and they enter a room at random. The patient, an older man, is just finishing his lunch.

MONICA ARROYOS: Excuse us, Mr. Roble. If I may, I've brought you some company. This is Ms. Claudia Vizconde, a public health inspector.

MR. ROBLE: Please, come in!

CLAUDIA VIZCONDE: Thank you very much, sir. May I ask you a few questions?

MR. ROBLE: Of course.

CLAUDIA VIZCONDE: Are you comfortable in your room? How are they treating you here?

MR. ROBLE: Wonderfully! The nurse always comes when I call, and it seems like they're always cleaning around here.

CLAUDIA VIZCONDE: So, they clean everything often . . .

MR. ROBLE: That's right. The only thing I don't like is the food . . . I'd love a steak now and then. Although, I suppose I'm not the only one who's told you that.

CLAUDIA VIZCONDE: You're right about that! Well, we won't disturb you any longer. Thanks very much for your help, and I wish you a speedy and complete recovery!

MR. ROBLE: Thank you! Come back whenever you like.

MONICA ARROYOS: Mr. Roble is very lively. He's being released tomorrow.

CLAUDIA VIZCONDE: Well, he certainly seems to be well taken care of! The room is also very clean. Have you had any problems with the cleaning supplies in your section?

MONICA ARROYOS: Yes, we have. But we've managed to avoid rationing the cleaning products thanks to donations from the personnel. They haven't been as lucky with the medical supplies. . . .

CLAUDIA VIZCONDE: I know. I've already told Doctor Cortes that I'll tell the pharmaceutical department to send the necessary supplies as soon as possible. Please sign these documents, and I'll leave you to your work.

MONICA ARROYOS: Sure. Do you need to see anything else?

CLAUDIA VIZCONDE: Not in this section. Could you show me the way to the O.R., I mean, the observatory O.R.?

MONICA ARROYOS: Yes. Walk down this hallway and take the elevator to the third floor. It's O.R. number 3, to the left.

The inspector arrives at the O.R. and goes in. It's a small room with large windows, and several simple plastic chairs. Doctor Cortes is sitting next to the windows, looking down at the preparations for surgery.

CLAUDIA VIZCONDE: Excuse me, doctor.

DOCTOR CORTES: Please come in! Are you here to observe the operation?

CLAUDIA VIZCONDE: Actually, I've come so you can sign some papers for me. I need the signature of every section chief I interview.

DOCTOR CORTES: Of course! Here you are!

CLAUDIA VIZCONDE: Thank you. Tell me, what type of operation is the doctor performing?

DOCTOR CORTES: It's an appendectomy, but it's just beginning. Right now they're preparing the patient. See? The anesthesiologist is putting the patient under slowly, checking his vital signs. The nurses are preparing the instruments for the operation.

CLAUDIA VIZCONDE: Which one is Doctor Nuñez?

DOCTOR CORTES: He's preparing for surgery. Do you see the nurse who just walked in carrying a box with instruments? Behind the door he came through is the scrub room. There's an autoclave and some sinks. Doctor Nuñez is in there, and he'll be in the O.R. very soon.

CLAUDIA VIZCONDE: I'd like to stay and watch the procedure, but I get a little queasy, and I still have to talk to administration.

DOCTOR CORTES: I can take you there, if you like.

CLAUDIA VIZCONDE: You're very kind, doctor.

DOCTOR CORTES: My pleasure, inspector!

B. APUNTES

1. Most Latin American countries have government-run hospitals, which are inspected periodically to ensure that they are clean and well-stocked.

2. San Salvador is the capital of El Salvador, a small, beautiful country on the Pacific coast of Central America. Unfortunately, El Salvador is associated with a history of political instability.

3. The verb *resultar* (to turn out) may be used in conjunction with the verb *ser* or alone, followed by an adjective or a clause. *Los exámenes resultaron (haber sido) innecesarios.* (The exams turned out (to have been) unnecessary.)

4. *En (lo) absoluto* and *de ninguna manera* are polite ways of saying "absolutely not." *No estoy disconforme con su labor en absoluto.* (I'm absolutely not unhappy with your work.)

5. Note that *apenas* (barely) can replace *sólo/solamente* (only) in formal conversation. *Llevo apenas tres semanas en este trabajo.* (I have been working at this job for only three weeks.)

6. The ending *-ena* can be attached to numbers (most often to round numbers, e.g., units of ten) to indicate approximate amounts. Note that the final vowel of the number is dropped. *Aquí tiene una lista de una veintena de elementos que faltan en el hospital.* (Here's a list of approximately twenty elements that are needed in the hospital.)

7. *Derivar(lo) a* is a specific hospital term meaning "to send (a patient) to." *Vamos a derivarla a radiología.* (We're going to send her to radiology.) If you're sending a letter or a package, use *enviar* or *mandar. Voy a enviar esta carta al gerente del banco.* (I'm going to send this letter to the bank manager.)

8. In Latin America, *droguería* refers to a place to store drugs. *La enfermera está en la droguería, buscando unos calmantes.* (The nurse is in the drug supply room, looking for some painkillers.) In Spain, however, *droguería* refers to a pharmacy. The most common word for "pharmacy" in Latin America is *farmacia.*

9. *Abastecimiento, provisión,* and *suministración* are interchangeable terms for "supply." *Provisiones* may be used to mean "supplies." *La suministración de artículos médicos a los hospitales estatales se realiza mensualmente.* (Medical supplies are allocated to government hospitals on a monthly basis.) *Las provisiones llegaron a tiempo.* (The supplies came on time.)

10. Another term for *el paro* (the strike) is *la huelga.*

11. The adjectives *mayor* (greater, larger) and *anciano* (old) are often used to show respect when speaking about older people.

12. The informal verbal expression *pasársela* followed by a gerund means "to pass (time)" or "to do something very often." *Mi amigo se la pasa yendo a la discoteca.* (My friend goes to the disco very often.)

13. When *quedar* is used without an indirect object, it means "to stay" or "to be located." When it's used with an indirect object (like *gustar*, etc.) it indicates an amount that's remaining. *Me quedan tres días antes de las vacaciones.* (I have three days left before my vacation.)

B. GRAMATICA Y USOS

1. *EL GERUNDIO Y EL PARTICIPIO PRESENTE* (THE GERUND AND THE PRESENT PARTICIPLE)

a) The Gerund

The gerund is formed by replacing the *-ar* ending of first conjugation verbs with *-ando,* and the *-er* and *-ir* endings of second and third conjugation verbs with *-iendo.* Some second and third conjugation verbs have irregular gerunds that must be memorized.[1] Gerunds are used to describe actions occurring simultaneously with the main verb, or to modify a verb or noun. Gerunds are also used in the formation of progressive tenses.

Encontré a los cirujanos discutiendo seriamente la condición de un paciente.
I found the surgeons seriously discussing a patient's condition.

¡Por favor, no me hable gritando, estamos en un hospital!
Please don't talk to me in a loud voice!—We're in a hospital!

El mensajero llegó corriendo con el paquete.
The messenger came running with the package.

Gerunds may also be used to replace entire clauses in informal conversation. Note that the subject in such circumstances is determined based on context.

Encontré a unos amigos caminando por la calle.
Encontré a unos amigos (que estaban) caminando por la calle.
Encontré a unos amigos (mientras yo estaba) caminando por la calle.
I met some friends (who were/while I was) walking down the street.

---

1. For a list of irregular gerunds, see Appendix D, p. 320.

b) The Present Participle

The present participle is formed by replacing the infinitive ending with *-ante* for first conjugation verbs and *-iente* for second and third conjugation verbs. For example: *interesante* (interesting), *corriente* (current), and *sobresaliente* (outstanding). The present participle can be used as an adjective or a noun, and therefore changes to reflect gender and number.[2] The present participle is never used in progressive tenses.

El doctor González presentó un proyecto interesante para disminuir los gastos administrativos corrientes.
Doctor Gonzalez presented an interesting project to lower the current administrative expenditures.

2. *LOS TIEMPOS PROGRESIVOS* (THE PROGRESSIVE TENSES)

The progressive tenses are formed with the auxiliary verb *estar* in the appropriate tense (preterite, imperfect, present, or future) followed by the gerund of the main verb. These tenses are used for emphasis, to stress an action in progress. The most commonly used progressive tenses are the present progressive, used to talk about an action occurring as you speak, and the imperfect progressive, used to stress an action that was in progress in the past.

No puedo hablarte ahora, estoy cerrando un negocio importante.
I can't talk to you now; I'm in the process of closing an important business deal.

Carlos está estudiando medicina, de hecho, está haciendo la residencia en el Hospital Rosales.
Carlos is studying medicine; in fact, he's in the process of completing his internship at the Rosales Hospital.

Estábamos operando al paciente cuando, de golpe, empezó a funcionar el generador de emergencia.
We were in the process of operating on the patient when, suddenly, the emergency generator began working.

---

2. For a list of alternative participial forms, see Appendix C, p. 319.

When object pronouns are used in conjunction with the progressive tenses, they may either precede the verb or be attached as suffixes to the gerund. In negative sentences, object pronouns generally precede the verb. In written language, they may also be attached to the auxiliary verb.

El doctor Núñez no está operando aún al paciente, está preparándose para la intervención.
Doctor Nuñez is not operating on the patient yet; he's still getting ready for the operation.

Mire este informe: "El incidente ocurrió cuando el paciente se hallaba caminando por la calle."
Look at this report: "The incident occurred when the patient was walking down the street."

The preterite progressive is used only in special cases, to express what someone has been doing very recently. It is replaced by the present perfect progressive in formal conversation.

¿Que estuvo haciendo Enriqueta la semana pasada?
What was Enriqueta up to last week?

Últimamente estuve/he estado viajando por Europa.
Lately, I've been traveling through Europe.

Other auxiliary verbs, such as *ir, andar,* and *seguir,* can also be used in conjunction with the gerund, to stress different aspects of an action in progress.

Ir, used as an auxiliary, expresses the idea of movement in a certain direction while an action is occurring, or it implies that an action requires a long time to complete.

En el carnaval, la gente va cantando y bailando con la procesión por las calles.
During carnival, people move down the street while singing and dancing with the procession.

Los Gómez ya pagaron el depósito de la casa y van a ir pagando la hipoteca, mes por mes.
The Gomez's already made the down payment on their home, and they will be paying off their mortgage every month, over a long period of time.

Andar expresses the idea of random movement while an action is being completed.

Julia anda buscando un trabajo nuevo, pero todavía no pudo encontrar ninguno.
Julia is going around looking for a new job, but she hasn't been able to find one.

Durante nuestras vacaciones anduvimos pescando, tomando sol y bañándonos en el río.
We went around fishing, sunbathing, and swimming in the river during our vacation.

Seguir can be used to stress the difficulty of an action or to further emphasize the notion that an action has not yet been completed.

A pesar de que sea difícil, sigo tomando clases de inglés.
Even though it's difficult, I'm still taking English lessons.

¿Sigues leyendo el libro que te presté?—Sí, aún no lo terminé.
Are you still reading the book I lent you?—Yes. I haven't finished it yet.

The subjunctive of the auxiliary verb must be used whenever the subjunctive is normally required.

No creo que aún estén operando al paciente, la operación ya debe haber terminado.
I don't think they're still operating on the patient; the operation must have finished by now.

Espero que no sigan arreglando la autopista, ha habido mucho tráfico allí últimamente.
I hope they're still not fixing the highway; there's been a lot of traffic there lately.

Mientras vayamos comprando los regalos, vamos a elegir algo para Karina.
While we're shopping for presents, let's pick something out for Karina.

D. HABLEMOS DE NEGOCIOS

LA MEDICINA (MEDICINE)

All Spanish-speaking countries have public health care systems. In Spain, the government-sponsored insurance plan, INSALUD, covers all employed persons and their families, and provides coverage of up to 60% of the cost of medicine and treatment. This coverage goes up to 100% for retired persons. The plan is primarily financed by contributions *(aportaciones)* made by the workers themselves and by their employers. The government provides 25% of the remaining funds needed to operate the public health care system *(la asistencia sanitaria)*. It is estimated that 96% of Spaniards are covered by INSALUD.

In most of Latin America, the health care system operates somewhat differently. It is divided into Public Health *(Salud Pública)* in the form of government-sustained hospitals *(hospitales públicos)*, and private health services *(servicios médicos privados)* in the form of private hospitals or clinics *(clínicas privadas)* and private doctors' offices, known as *consultorios,* or *oficinas médicas.*

The public health care system is financed by employee contributions to their *obra social* (labor union health plan). These contributions are called *impuestos tributarios, contribuciones,* or *cotizaciones.* In some countries, these contributions go directly to the national government to maintain the public hospitals.

Services at public hospitals are offered free to all citizens and residents of a country. Foreigners may also be seen, although they may be charged a small fee. The patient is generally charged only for medication, or in the case of surgery, for all surgical supplies needed, such as anaesthesia *(anestesia)* and all necessary post-operational drugs. Senior citizens generally receive a 70% discount from the government through various plans, plus additional discounts of up to 25% from the union health plan, financed by their contributions to the union.

In most countries, medical students must complete a certain term (generally from one to three years) of service at a public hospital before graduating and going into private practice. However, many doctors choose to continue working at government hospitals, despite the fact that incomes of doctors in private practice are generally higher.

Many middle-class to upper-class people also choose to buy private health insurance *(seguro médico privado),* which is much like the private health insurance in the U.S. In Latin America, however, health insurance companies tend to be affiliated with certain private clinics and private doctors' offices. As a rule, private clinics tend to have more modern equipment and faster service than public hospitals.

Pharmacies (known as *farmacias* in Latin America and *droguerías* in Spain) are much more important in Latin America than they are in the U.S., as pharmacists *(farmacéuticos* or *boticarios)* often provide basic medical care, such as administering vaccines, suggesting treatment and medication for minor illnesses, and recommending physicians. Pharmacies alternate 24-hour duty, according to a rotating schedule. The on-duty pharmacy is marked by *farmacia de turno.* In Latin America, the commercialization of drugs (for medical use) is far less controlled than in the U.S. Most medications can be bought over-the-counter without a prescription *(una receta médica),* as long as you know the scientific, not the generic or brand name of the drug you want to purchase.

The Spanish word for physician is *el/la médico/a.* Doctors should be addressed with *Doctor/a* followed by their last names. This title is also used in correspondence; there is no Spanish equivalent for English abbreviations, such as M.D., D.C., etc. In Spanish, a physician's name is often followed by his or her specialization, for example: *Doctora López, Oftalmó-*

loga. Note that female physicians often prefer the masculine form preceded by a feminine article (for example: *La doctora Rodríguez es una excelente laringólogo*). Appointments are generally required, and should be made several days in advance. In many countries, the doctor's secretary will call 24 hours in advance to confirm the appointment.

Following is a list of names of some of the common specialists:

allergist	*alergista*
anaesthesia technician	*anestesista*
anaesthesiologist	*anestesiólogo*
chiropractor	*quiropráctico*
dentist	*odontólogo* (commonly: *dentista*)
doctor (general practitioner)	*médico clínico*
ear/nose/throat specialist	*otorinolaringólogo*
gerontologist	*gerontólogo*
gynecologist	*ginecólogo*
opthalmologist	*oftalmólogo*
optician/optometrist	*(técnico) óptico, oculista*
pediatrician	*(médico) pediatra*
plastic surgeon	*cirujano plástico*
proctologist	*proctólogo*
psychiatrist	*psiquíatra*
psychologist	*psicólogo*
surgeon	*cirujano*
veterinarian	*veterinario*

VOCABULARIO

bandage	*venda/vendaje*
Band-Aid	*apósito/"curita"*
CAT (Computer-Aided Tomography) Scan	*tomografía computada*
common cold (rhinitis)	*resfriado, resfrío, rinitis*
counterindications	*contraindicaciones*
cough	*tos*
diagnosis	*la diagnosis, el diagnóstico*
dose	*la dosis*
fever	*fiebre, temperatura, calentura*
I.C.U. (Intensive Care Unit)	*(Unidad de) Terapia Intensiva*
injection	*inyección*
medication	*medicamento*
medicine (science)	*medicina*

MRI (Magnetic Resonance Imaging)	*IRM (Imagén de Resonancia Magnética)*
on an empty stomach	*en ayunas*
operation	*intervención quirúrgica/operación*
prescribe (to)	*recetar*
prescription	*receta (médica)*
prognosis	*pronóstico*
radiology	*radiología*
rheumatism	*reumatismo, reuma*
side effect	*efecto colateral, efecto secundario*
surgical (adj.)	*quirúrgico*
surgery (science)	*cirujía*
syringe	*jeringa, aguja*
three times a day	*tres veces por día*
X-ray (picture)	*radiografía*

EXAMEN

A. *Complete las oraciones siguientes con el verbo auxiliar que corresponda:* "*estar, ir, andar,*" *o* "*seguir*". (Complete the following sentences with the appropriate auxiliary verb: *estar, ir, andar,* or *seguir.*)

1. (I'm still) *tratando de rendir anatomía, pero es muy difícil.*
2. *¿Qué* (has been) *haciendo Felipe últimamente?*
3. *Mi prima hermana* (is) *preparándose para la operación, poco a poco.*
4. *¿Quién sabe qué* (is) *haciendo Ricardo? Es tan menesteroso . . .*
5. *Es mejor* (to be) *tirando lo que no sirva mientras* (we are) *limpiando la habitación del paciente.*
6. (We have been) *preparando el instrumental médico.*
7. *¿Dónde estaban?*—(We were just) *caminando por el jardín del hospital.*
8. *¿Te* (goes on) *llamando por teléfono Raúl? ¡Qué persistencia!*
9. *En este momento, el doctor Cortés* (is) *almorzando. Estará de vuelta en diez minutos.*
10. *¡*(Go on) *practicando el español, que pronto hablaréis con facilidad!*

B. *Coloque los pronombres objeto donde corresponda en las siguientes oraciones.* (Place the object pronouns in the appropriate place in the following sentences.)

1. *El cirujano está lavando las manos. (se)*
2. *¡No estás escuchando! (me)*
3. *¡Estamos buscando, no os inquietéis! (os lo)*
4. *Juan estaba contando, cuando entró Karina. (nos lo)*
5. *Estaba diciendo a los Gómez que vengan a ver al paciente cuando quieran. (les)*

C. *Traduzca las cinco oraciones del ejercicio B al inglés.* (Translate the five sentences in Exercise B into English.)

LECCIÓN 18

A. DIÁLOGO

LA OEA Y HAITÍ. [*]

La Organización de Estados Americanos (OEA)[1] reunida en la ciudad de Belém, decidió ayer endurecer las presiones diplomáticas y comerciales sobre la dictadura militar haitiana para obligarlos a abandonar el poder, pero no sin que[2] antes surgiera una solapada crítica a la República Dominicana por su presunta falta de agresividad en el cumplimiento del embargo impuesto por las Naciones Unidas, así como una airada respuesta por parte del[3] canciller dominicano.

«Si todos los países cumplieran con el embargo, el régimen haitiano caería en cuestión de semanas,» dijo a la prensa el ministro de relaciones exteriores de Jamaica, Benjamín Clare. Sin mencionar a los que violan presuntamente[4] el embargo impuesto desde el 22 de mayo, Clare dijo que todos deberían obedecer la resolución del Consejo de Seguridad, «en particular los países fronterizos,»[5] en obvia referencia a la República Dominicana, que comparte con Haití la isla La Española.

La réplica del canciller dominicano no se hizo esperar. «Es tiempo que se deje de utilizar a la República Dominicana como chivo expiatorio de la manifiesta incapacidad de la comunidad internacional para manejar con idoneidad la crisis haitiana,» dijo el ministro de relaciones exteriores, Juan Arístides Taveras Guzmán, agregando que su país realiza un «esfuerzo extraordinario, titánico» para dar cumplimiento efectivo al embargo, con la movilización[6] de 12.000 soldados en la región fronteriza.

Taveras Guzmán advirtió que la situación ha creado un «alarmante estado de desesperación y angustia» entre la población más humilde y necesitada de Haití, y[7] que será necesaria una «verdadera cruzada continental» para aliviar las «penurias y privaciones del hermano país.»

Sin tener en cuenta el grado de importancia que el gobierno dominicano presidido por Joaquín Balaguer haya dado al embargo hasta ahora, resulta sumamente[8] injusto culpar a la República Dominicana por la prolongación de la tragedia en

---

[*] Reprinted with permission from an editorial that appeared in *El Diario* (June 8, 1994).

256

Haití, cuando harto[8] es reconocido por todos que la solución de la crisis siempre ha estado al alcance de Washington, no de Santo Domingo.

Tapando su impotencia con la hoja de parra de la «no intervención,» la OEA descartó la posibilidad de efectuar una posible intervención armada destinada a restaurar tanto la democracia en Haití como al presidente Jean-Bertrand Aristide al poder.

Para los EE.UU., la opción militar aún no ha sido descartada totalmente, según expresó el subsecretario de estado Strobe Talbott. Su aplicación por parte del presidente Bill Clinton dependerá de la futura evolución de la crisis.

Talbott comunicó el lunes a la prensa que el presidente «se reserva aquella opción» ante la posibilidad de que surjan[9] complicaciones, tal como un incremento descontrolado de la cantidad de refugiados haitianos que llegue a las costas estadounidenses.

Increíblemente, lo que más preocupa al presidente Clinton no es el futuro de la democracia en Haití y en el hemisferio,[10] ni el sufrimiento del pueblo haitiano, sino evitar que una oleada de refugiados llegue a las costas de la Florida.

THE OAS AND HAITI.

The Organization of American States (OAS), meeting in the city of Belem, in Brazil, decided yesterday to toughen its diplomatic and commercial pressure on the Haitian militiary dictatorship to force the generals to leave power, but not without first some veiled criticisms of the Dominican Republic being made over its alleged lack of enthusiasm in enforcing the sanctions imposed by the United Nations, as well as provoking a spirited response from the Dominican foreign minister.

"If all the countries enforced the embargo, the Haitian regime would fall in a matter of weeks," the Jamaican foreign minister, Benjamin Clare, told the press. Without mentioning those who presumably are not enforcing the embargo in force since last May 22, Clare said that the Security Council resolution should be obeyed by all, "in particular the bordering countries," in obvious reference to the Dominican Republic, which shares with Haiti the island of Hispaniola.

The Dominican foreign minister's reply was not long in coming. "It is time to stop using the Dominican Republic as a scapegoat for the international community's manifest incapacity to handle the Haitian crisis properly," said Foreign Minister Juan Aristides Taveras Guzman, adding that his country is making an "extraordinary, titanic effort" to enforce the embargo effectively, mobilizing 12,000 soldiers to the border.

Guzman warned that the situation has created "an alarming state of desperation and anguish in Haiti" among that country's humblest and neediest part of the population, and that it would be necessary to launch a "real continental crusade" to alleviate "the hardships and privations of this sister nation."

Regardless of the degree of importance the government of Dominican president Joaquin Balaguer may or may not have given the embargo to date, it is truly unjust to blame the Dominican Republic for the prolongation of the Haitian tragedy when it is well known by everyone that the solution to the crisis has always been within Washington's reach, not Santo Domingo's.

Covering its impotence with the fig leaf of "non-intervention," the OAS discarded the possibility of effecting an armed intervention aimed at restoring both democracy in Haiti and deposed president Jean-Bertrand Aristide to power.

For the United States, the military option has not been completely discarded yet, according to the Undersecretary of State, Strobe Talbott. Its application by President Bill Clinton, he said, would depend on the future evolution of the crisis.

Talbott said in a press conference on Monday that the president "reserves that option," faced with the possibility of complications arising, such as an uncontrolled increase in the number of Haitian refugees who reach American coasts.

Incredibly, what most worries President Clinton is not the future of democracy in Haiti and in the hemisphere, nor the suffering of the Haitian people, but preventing a wave of refugees from reaching the Florida shores.

B. APUNTES

1. The OEA is an international organization established in the year 1889 in Washington, D.C. with the purpose of promoting understanding and cooperation among the nations of North and South America, as well as to ensure the protection of American countries against outside invasions. The O.A.S. (as it is known in English) still has its headquarters (sede central) in Washington, D.C.

2. Note the use of the subjunctive following the conjunction *sin que* (without).

3. In a more literary style, the prepositional phrase *por parte de* may be used instead of *por* or *de* to indicate the agent of an action in the passive voice.

4. Be sure not to confuse *presuntamente* (presumably) with *presumidamente* (presumptuously).

5. Quotations of only a few words, as opposed to entire phrases or paragraphs, are very common in Spanish journalism.

6. Remember that *móvil* and its derivatives (e.g. *movilidad, movilización, inmovilización*) are spelled with a *v,* and not a *b.*

7. Note how common long sentences composed of many ideas connected by conjunctions such as *y* and *o* are in Spanish. And remember that Spanish conjunctions (*y* and *o*) are generally not preceded by a comma.

8. The adverbs *harto* (completely, overly) and *sumamente* (most highly) are more literary ways of saying *demasiado* (too) and *muy* (very).

9. Note that verbs whose stems end in *g, c,* or *z* undergo spelling changes in the preterite and subjunctive tenses, for example: *surgir* (to surge, to appear) > *surja* (that may appear); *buscar* (to look for) > *busqué* (I looked for). Keep in mind that these verbs, known as spelling-changing verbs, are regular; they merely look irregular due to Spanish orthography rules.

10. Many words that are spelled with *ph* in English are spelled with an *f* in Spanish. For example, *hemisferio* (hemisphere) and *teléfono* (telephone).

Following are other examples of letters you may receive or need to compose. The format should resemble that of the letter of debit.

CARTA DE RECOMENDACION
(LETTER OF RECOMMENDATION)

Durante el período que llevo como asesor principal de la empresa PERIPEX, he conocido y trabajado a diario con el licenciado Hills. He comprobado y puedo constatar fehacientemente la dedicación al trabajo y las aptitudes de mi colega, quien ahora busca emplearse en vuestra empresa como asociado.

Permítame expresar que en PERIPEX nos es difícil aceptar su dimisión, pero que entendemos la necesidad del licenciado Hills de ampliar su experiencia laboral en servicio de vuestra empresa.

Quedo a vuestra disposición en cuanto a cualquier inquietud que tuvieren con respecto a las obligaciones cumplidas por el licenciado con nosotros. Estoy disponible de 8 a 16 horas, los días laborables.

Throughout the time during which I worked as the main consultant for PERIPEX, I have known and worked daily with Esquire Hills. I have witnessed and I can attest to the dedication and the aptitude of my colleague, who is now seeking employment as an associate in your company.

Allow me to express that, at PERIPEX, it is difficult for us to accept his resignation, but we understand Esquire Hills's need to expand his work experience within your company.

I remain at your disposal to answer any questions you may have concerning the duties Mr. Hills fulfilled with us. I am available from 8 a.m. to 4 p.m. on workdays.

CARTA DE RECLAMACION
(LETTER OF COMPLAINT)

El día 20 del mes corriente, he recibido una encomienda enviada por Vds. a nombre de otro cliente. Entiendo que ha habido un error mecánico en la impresión de la orden de envío, puesto que la factura está impresa a mi nombre.

Les agradeceré su colaboración en este asunto, puesto que no quisiera que se afectare mi línea de crédito, hasta ahora impecable. La encomienda se encuentra en mi poder, y pueden retirarla de 9 a 15 horas, los días laborables.

En los años que llevo patrocinando vuestra empresa, jamás he tenido error alguno, muestra cabal de vuestra eficiencia en el procesamiento de las órdenes de compra.

On the 20th of this month, I mistakenly received a package intended for another client. I understand that a technical error occurred in the printing of the delivery order, as the bill is printed in my name.

I would appreciate your help in this matter, as I do not want to jeopardize my credit history, which has been impeccable to date. The package is in my possession, and you may pick it up from 9 a.m. to 3 p.m. on weekdays.

In the many years that I have been a client of your company, I have never experienced any errors whatsoever, which makes me confident of your efficiency in the processing of sales orders.

RESPUESTA A LA CARTA DE RECLAMACIÓN ANTERIOR (RESPONSE TO THE PRECEDING LETTER OF COMPLAINT)

Acusamos recibo de su amable carta del día 21 del corriente. Nuestra más sincera disculpa, señor Torres. Efectivamente, ha habido un error en el procesamiento de la orden de compra de otro de nuestros estimados clientes. Permítanos asegurarle que el día 27 pasaremos a recoger la encomienda que le fue enviada por equivocación.

Como muestra de nuestra disculpa, le envío esta nota de crédito, por valor de $30 redimible en cualquiera de sus órdenes siguientes y permítame asegurarle que su línea de crédito permanece impecable.

Será un placer seguir brindádole nuestros servicios, como hemos hecho ininterrumpidamente durante tanto tiempo.

We acknowledge receipt of your kind letter of the 21st of this month and extend our most sincere apologies, Mr. Torres. There has, in fact, been a technical error in the processing of another of our esteemed client's sales orders. Allow us to assure you that on the 27th we will pick up the package that was sent to you by mistake.

As a token of our apologies, I send you this note of credit in the value of $30, applicable toward any of your future orders, and allow me to assure you that your credit history remains impeccable.

It will be a pleasure to continue providing you our services, as we have done for so long.

EXAMEN

A. *Escoja la palabra que complete cada oración.* (Choose the word that completes each sentence.)

1. *Me pregunto (cómo/como) estará la situación política en el (este/éste). Enciende el televisor.*
2. *A (mi/mí) me parece que (tú/tu) tienes razón. (Él/El) canciller habló muy bien.*
3. *(Ésta/Esta) situación es muy volátil, (ésa/esa) no.*
4. *¿(Dónde/Donde) (está/esta) Haití?— (Esta/Está) en la isla La Española.*
5. *Los países subdesarrollados siempre (sé/se) usan como chivo expiatorio! —No (sé/se) (si/sí) sea verdad lo que dices . . .*

B. *Complete las oraciones siguientes con la palabras entre paréntesis.* (Complete the following sentences with the words in parentheses.)

1. *Muchos* (countries) *han hecho un* (extraordinary effort) *para* (diminish) *la deuda externa.*
2. *La política* (international) *de un país debe ser* (managed properly).
3. *Los* (United States) *y los países* (Latin American) *tienen una larga tradición de aceptar* (political refugees).
4. *La* (U.N.) *a menudo* (mobilizes its army) *para evitar confrontaciones* (military) *en lugares donde existe* (such) *posibilidad.*
5. *Esa* (option) *no está a mi* (reach).
6. (Korea) *es un país del* (far) *oriente.*
7. (French) *es similar al* (Italian).
8. *Los caracteres* (Chinese) *tienen unos cinco mil años de* (antiquity).
9. *Las* (dictatorships) *militares* (impose) *sus mandatos en los* (people).
10. *El* (minister) *de* (foreign affairs) (presumably) *se ha encontrado con algunas* (complications) (during) *la reunión de la* (OAS).

LECCION 19

A. DIALOGO

¡VAMOS PARA EL PRYCA!

La familia Benítez llega a la entrada del estacionamiento de un hipermercado PRYCA en Barberá del Valles[1] en Cataluña, España.

JORGE BENITEZ: Bueno, bajar e ir adentro.[2] Yo voy a aparcar y nos encontramos en la puerta de entrada.

JULIA DE BENITEZ: ¿Escuchásteis niños? ¡Todos afuera! Jorge, por favor trae también un carrito cuando entres . . . ¿tienes cambio?[3]

JORGE BENITEZ: Sí, ¡tengo toda clase de monedas, estáte tranquila! Nos vemos dentro.

Minutos después . . .

JORGE BENITEZ: ¡Aquí estoy! Supongo que los chicos estarán súper-embobados[4] con los juguetes, como de costumbre . . .

JULIA DE BENITEZ: Si no los dejaba ir solos, iban a torturarnos como la semana pasada. Le dije a Carolina que vigile a sus hermanos y que nos vamos a encontrar dentro de una hora en la sección de juguetes. Así tendremos tiempo de[5] hacer todas las compras tranquilos.

JORGE BENITEZ: Estuviste muy bien. Aunque, digas lo que le digas, Carolina se va a llevar a los nenes[6] a ver toda la colección de ropa juvenil, quiéranlo o no. No hubo una sola vez que viniésemos al PRYCA, y que Carolina no se haya llevado algo.[7]

JULIA DE BENITEZ *(riendo):* Hm, hm, tienes razón, menos mal que se le olvidó pedirme dinero, ¡o una tarjeta de crédito! . . . Bueno, dame la lista, a ver, ¿por dónde empezamos? . . . vamos para la sección de lácteos, que[8] tenemos que hacer los canelones para el almuerzo mañana.

JORGE BENITEZ: Vale.[9]

Los dos llegan a la fila de los productos lácteos, y caminan por el pasillo . . .

JORGE BENITEZ: Aquí estamos, a ver, necesitamos leche, queso y nada más, ¿no?

JULIA DE BENITEZ: Estemmm, mejor llevémonos también medio kilo de helado, por si se nos antoja por la tarde. Tráeme aquél, el mixto de chocolate, vainilla y fresas.

JORGE BENITEZ: Aquí lo tienes. Dime, ¿no querías hacer la crema catalana de postre?[10]

JULIA DE BENITEZ: Sí, pero me dijo Elizabet que la iba a traer ella misma.

JORGE BENITEZ: A propósito, ¿a qué hora llegan Josep y Elizabet[11] viniesen?

JULIA DE BENÍTEZ: Les dije que viniesen al mediodía, así que, calculo que llegarán a eso de la una . . . ya los conoces a los Ríus . . .

JORGE BENITEZ: ¡Los conozco a fondo! Los invites a la hora que los invites, ¡siempre llegan una hora tarde! Aquí está el vino . . . ¿cuál te gusta más?

JULIA DE BENITEZ: A mí cualquiera me viene bien . . . Pensándolo bien, llevémonos uno un poco más caro, el vino de mesa de la vez pasada no fue muy bien recibido.

JORGE BENITEZ: Entonces, dos botellas de "El Batch," es un buen tinto de reserva y dos de "Faustino Cuarto." Es un vino de mesa, pero muy bueno.

JULIA DE BENITEZ: Como digas, tú sabrás mejor que yo. Ahora vamos a comprar la carne . . .

JORGE BENITEZ: Bueno, ¿cuánto lomo nos llevamos hoy?

JULIA DE BENITEZ: ¿Lomo? ¡Qué va! ¡Nos llevamos carne pica!

Los dos terminan de hacer las compras.

JULIA DE BENITEZ: Bueno, parece que está todo. Ahora nos faltarían[12] los platos y las servilletas de papel. Yo voy a traerlos y luego a buscar a los niños.

JORGE BENITEZ: Bueno, yo me pongo en la cola para pagar.

JULIA DE BENITEZ: Vale . . . Ah, ¿no dijiste que tenías que comprar aceite o algo así para el coche?

JORGE BENITEZ: ¡Tienes razón! Se me olvidó por completo. En todo caso, puedo volver a buscarlo rapido después de cargar el coche . . .

JULIA DE BENITEZ: No hace falta,[12] lo haré yo ahora mismo. Sólo dime qué es.

JORGE BENITEZ: Amor,[13] ¿qué haría yo sin ti?

JULIA DE BENITEZ: Quemarías el motor, seguro.

JORGE BENITEZ: Tráeme dos latas de aceite multigrado y un embudito de plástico, porque el que tenemos es un poco demasiado grande e incómodo.

JULIA DE BENITEZ: Bueno. Ya voy . . .

JORGE BENITEZ: ¡Ah! Una cosita más, diles a los chicos si quieren alquilar alguna película para ver mañana por la tarde. Podemos pasar a buscarla camino al coche.[14]

JULIA DE BENITEZ: Vale. ¡Nos vemos a la salida, amor!

LET'S GO TO THE PRYCA!

The Benitez family arrives at the entrance to the parking lot of the PRYCA *hypermercado* in Barbera del Valle, in Catalonia, Spain.

JORGE BENITEZ: Okay, everybody out and go inside. I'm going to park the car, and we'll meet at the entrance, next to the food section.

JULIA DE BENITEZ: Did you hear, kids? Everybody out! Jorge, please bring a cart when you come in . . . Do you have any change?

JORGE BENITEZ: Sure, I've got all kinds of coins, don't worry! I'll see you inside.

Minutes later . . .

JORGE BENITEZ: Here's the cart! I guess the kids went crazy over the toys, as usual . . .

JULIA DE BENITEZ: If I hadn't let them go alone, they would've tortured us like last week. I told Carolina to keep an eye on her brother and sister and that we would meet them in an hour in the toy section. That way, we'll have time to shop in peace.

JORGE BENITEZ: That was a great idea. Although, say whatever you may, Carolina is going to drag the kids to see the entire misses department, whether they want to or not. There hasn't been a single time when Carolina has left PRYCA empty-handed.

JULIA DE BENITEZ (chuckling): Ha-ha! You're right! It's a good thing she forgot to ask me for more money, or even worse, my credit card! . . . okay, give me the list; let's see . . . Let's go to the dairy section, we have to make the cannelloni for lunch tomorrow.

JORGE BENITEZ: Okay!

They both walk to the dairy section, and walk down the aisle . . .

JORGE BENITEZ: Here we are. Let's see: we need milk, cheese, and that's it, right?

JULIA DE BENITEZ: Hmmm, we'd better take a gallon of ice cream, in case we feel like having some in the afternoon. Bring me that one over there, the mixed chocolate, vanilla, and strawberry one.

JORGE BENITEZ: Here you are. But, didn't you want to make the Catalan cream for dessert?

270

JULIA DE BENITEZ: Yes, but Elizabet said she'd bring it.

JORGE BENITEZ: By the way, when are Josep and Elizabet coming over?

JULIA DE BENITEZ: I told them to come over at noon, so they should be there at around one . . . you know the Riuses . . .

JORGE BENITEZ: . . . I know them very well. No matter what time you invite them, they always arrive an hour late! Here's the wine—which one do you like best?

JULIA DE BENITEZ: They're all the same to me . . . Actually, let's take a more expensive one this time. The table wine we bought last time didn't go over too well.

JORGE BENITEZ: Let's take two bottles of *El Batch,* then. It's a good reserve red wine. And two of *Faustino Cuarto*—it's a table wine, but it's very good.

JULIA DE BENITEZ: Whatever you say, you know more than I do. Now, let's go get the meat . . .

JORGE BENITEZ: Okay. How much filet mignon are we getting?

JULIA DE BENITEZ: Filet mignon? No way! We're getting ground beef!

The Benitezes finish their shopping.

JULIA DE BENITEZ: Well, I guess that's all. Now we just need the paper plates and napkins. I'll get them, and then I'll go pick up the kids.

JORGE BENITEZ: Fine, and I'll get in line to pay for everything.

JULIA DE BENITEZ: Okay . . . Oh! Didn't you say you had to buy some oil or something for the car?

JORGE BENITEZ: That's right! It completely slipped my mind! In any case, I can run back and get it after loading the car . . .

JULIA DE BENITEZ: You don't have to do that, I'll get it right now. Just tell me what it is.

JORGE BENITEZ: What would I do without you, love?

JULIA DE BENITEZ: You'd burn up your engine, for sure.

JORGE BENITEZ: Bring me two cans of multigrade motor oil and a small plastic funnel. The one we have is a little too big and awkward.

JULIA DE BENITEZ: Okay. I'm on my way . . .

JORGE BENITEZ: Oh! And one more thing—ask the kids if they want to rent a movie for tomorrow afternoon. We can pick up a video on the way to the car.

JULIA DE BENITEZ: Fine. See you at the exit, honey!

B. APUNTES

1. *Barberá del Vallés* is a small, middle-class, industrial town in Catalonia, northeastern Spain.

2. Remember that *vosotros* is used in conversation only in Spain.

3. There are many words for "change" or "coins" in Spanish: *cambio, moneda, vuelto, plata chica.* In *hipermercados,* you pay for the use of shopping carts.

4. The use of *súper* as an intensifier before adjectives is popular among young speakers throughout the Spanish-speaking world. They often say *súper-interesante, súper-grande, súper-bonito,* etc.

5. Note the use of the preposition *de* instead of *para* to indicate purpose. Remember that *de* may replace other prepositions colloquially. For more on the uses of *de*, see *Gramática y usos, Lección 15.*

6. There are many words for "child" in Spanish. The most common term is *niño,* although *nene, chico, pibe,* and *crío* can be heard in different countries.

7. Note the required use of the subjunctive in a dependent clause that describes an imaginary, exaggerated situation. *No ha habido ni una sola cita a la que no hayas llegado tarde.* (There hasn't been a single appointment to which you haven't been late.)

8. In colloquial Spanish, *porque* (because) is often shortened to just *que* in the middle of a sentence. *¡No hables tan fuerte, que no escucho nada!* (Don't talk so loud, 'cause I can't hear a thing!)

9. *¡Vale!* is commonly used in Spain to mean "okay!"; *¡Bueno!* is used in Latin America.

10. *Crema catalana* is a pastry cream made with eggs and milk, very similar to custard. It is generally sprinkled with sugar, browned, and then spread on crackers or bread and served for dessert or as an afternoon snack.

11. *Josep* and *Elizabet* are Catalan, not Spanish names. Catalan is a language spoken in northeastern Spain as well as on the Balearic Islands. Catalonians are a fiercely independent people who are very proud of their local language and culture. In Catalonia's capital, Barcelona, street names are written in Catalan, and Catalan is used in the mass media, as well. Catalan is grammatically very similar to Spanish but sounds like a mixture of Spanish and French.

12. The indirect object verb *hacer falta* (to create a lack) can be translated into English as "to need." The verb *necesitar* (to need) implies a stronger necessity, i.e., a *sine qua non* (something you can't do without). *Me hace falta una revista para leer en el autobús.* (I need a magazine to read on the bus.) *Necesito leche para hacer la crema catalana.* (I need milk in order to make the *crema catalana.*) The indirect object verb *faltar* (to be lacking) is often used to indicate a missing or remaining object. *Me falta un zapato, ¿dónde estará?* (I'm missing a shoe. Where could it be?) *A Roberto le faltan dos capítulos para terminar de leer el libro.* (Roberto has two chapters left to finish reading the book.)

13. *¡Amor! ¡Cariño! ¡Vida mía!* are all romantic terms of endearment in Spanish.

14. Although *hipermercados* carry all kinds of goods (think of them as a cross between A&P and Woolworth's), they do not usually offer video rentals. However, smaller stores, such as video clubs or dry cleaners, are often located in the same building or shopping center.

C. GRAMATICA Y USOS

1. *LOS PREFIJOS* (PREFIXES)

The prefixes used in Spanish and in English are very similar, as they are most often of Greek or Latin origin. Some of the most commonly used prefixes in Spanish are *des-/in-*[1] (meaning "not"), as in *descansar* (to rest) and *imposible* (impossible); *re-* (used to indicate repetition or reversal), as in *rever* (to review) and *reembolsar* (to reimburse); *pre-* (meaning "before, in front of" or "prerequisite for"), as in *prehistórico* (prehistoric), *prever* (to foresee), and *preparar* (to prepare); and *trans-* (meaning "across, beyond," or "through"), as in *transponer* (to transpose), *transatlántico* (transatlantic), and *transcurrir* (to elapse).

Hay un inquietante sentimiento antigubernamental en algunos sectores del país.
There is an unsettling anti-government feeling in some sectors of our country.

The prepositions *en, entre, por, para, de,* and *ante* may also be attached to words as prefixes, thus creating derived words, whose meaning can often be inferred without the help of a dictionary.

Mi supervisor siempre se entremete en mis asuntos.
My supervisor is always butting into my affairs.

1. The prefix *in-* changes to *im-* before *-p* or *-b,* and to *i-* before *-l* and *-r.*

Después de revisar los pormenores de la cuenta de mis tarjetas de crédito, veo que me he endeudado demasiado este mes.
After reviewing the details of my credit accounts, I see that I have gotten myself into too much debt this month.

2. *LOS SUFIJOS* (SUFFIXES)

Suffixes are widely used in Spanish. They are classified, according to their function, into augmentatives and diminutives and must agree in gender and number with the noun to which they are attached. Augmentative and diminutive suffixes may sometimes convey a negative attitude, especially when used with masculine nouns or qualities, and should, therefore, be used with care.

a) Augmentatives indicate larger size or higher degree. The most common Spanish augmentatives are: *-ón, -ote,* and *-azo.*

Cristina se compra un montonazo de ropa cada vez que vamos al PRYCA.
Cristina buys a whole bunch of clothes every time we go to the PRYCA.

Me hace falta una cajota de galletitas para comer con la crema catalana mañana.
I need a big box of crackers to eat with the *crema catalana* tomorrow.

Lamento decirlo, pero el hijo de los Ríus suele portarse como un muchachote maleducado.
I'm sorry to say so, but the Riuses' son tends to act like a rude, overgrown boy!

b) Diminutives are much more common than augmentatives. They are used to convey lesser size, quality, or intensity, or as a term of endearment. The most common diminutives are *-ito, -illo,* and *-ico.* When attached to a word ending in *e, i,* or a consonant, the diminutives change to *-cito, -cillo,* and *-cico.* The choice of diminutive varies greatly from country to country, and they are generally much more popular in Latin America than in Spain. Again, exercise care when attaching diminutives to masculine nouns!

¡Ahorita mismo la atiendo, déme un momentito!
I'll be with you right away; just give me a second!

¿De quién es esta bebita encantadora?
Whose cute little baby girl is this?

No aguanto a los Martínez: Jorgito es un señorito engreído y el padre es un hombrecillo avarísimo.
I can't stand the Martinezes: Jorgito is an overbearing stuck-up boy, and his father is a petty, stingy little man.

3. *LOS PRONOMBRES Y LOS ADVERBIOS INDEFINIDOS* (INDEFINITE PRONOUNS AND ADVERBS)

Many indefinite words (such as the English "whoever, whatever," etc.) are formed by adding the present subjunctive of a verb (generally *ser* or *querer*) to a relative pronoun. In this case, the Spanish subjunctive verb replaces the English endings "-ever" and "-soever."

A quienquiera/quiensea que llame, dile que no estoy en casa.
Whoever is calling, tell him I'm not home.

Vayamos adondesea, quiero dar una vuelta con el auto.
Let's go wherever; I just want to go for a drive.

An alternative form used with verbs other than *ser* or *querer* is:
subjunctive verb + relative pronoun + subjunctive verb.

Llegue cuando llegue, tengo que estar despierto para abrirle la puerta.
Come at whatever time he may, I have to stay up to open the door for him.

Coma lo que coma, este chico siempre tiene hambre.
Whatever he may eat, this kid's always hungry.

Trabajara como trabajara, nunca logré que me ascendieran.
However I may have worked, I never managed to get promoted.

Note that the future subjunctive should be used when referring to future events, though in conversation, the present subjunctive is used instead.

Sea como sea (Fuere como fuere), tendremos que ajustarnos a la situación.
Whatever may be, we will have to adjust to the situation.

D. ESTUDIO IDIOMATICO

Life has its ups. . . .

Andar de juerga (to go on a spree)

¡Vámonos de juerga esta noche!
Let's go on a spree tonight!

Reírse a mandíbula batiente/Matarse de risa (to laugh your head off)

Todos nos reímos a mandíbula batiente cuando Pedro nos contó lo que le pasó.
We all laughed our heads off when Pedro told us what happened to him.

Tomar el pelo (to make fun of/to pull someone's leg)

A Susana le están tomando el pelo: le dijeron que Antonio gusta de ella.
They're pulling Susan's leg; they told her Antonio likes her.

and downs . . .

Andar de mal en peor (to go from bad to worse)

Con tanta inflación, la situación económica anda de mal en peor.
With so much inflation, the economy is going from bad to worse.

Estar en las últimas/Estar con un pie en la tumba (to have one foot in the grave)

Dicen que el abuelo de Julia está en las últimas/con un pie en la tumba.
They say Julia's grandfather has got one foot in the grave.

Estirar la pata (to kick the bucket)

¡Pobre Jorge estiró la pata después del accidente!
Poor Jorge kicked the bucket right after the accident.

E. HABLEMOS DE NEGOCIOS

LAS INVERSIONES Y LAS FINANZAS O RENTAS PÚBLICAS (INVESTMENT AND FINANCES)

Spain

In Spain, the government incentives for capital investment are mainly tax-related. There are two types of state-sponsored incentives available, depending on the needs of the different regions of Spain: the programs for the Zones of Urgent Industrialization (ZUR), and the programs for the Large Areas for Industrial Expansion. Under the ZUR program, which encompasses the regions of Madrid, Andalucia, Asturias, Basque country, Galicia, and Barcelona, companies are eligible for:

a) subsidies of up to 30% on the whole approved investment for specific types of expenditures related to land development
b) priority for official loans; special transportation facilities
c) tax allowances of up to 99% of the General Tax on business turnover.

Under the Large Areas for Industrial Expansion program, which is geared primarily to support investment on new plants in the agricultural, industrial, and service sectors, and which encompasses Andalucia, Cantabria, Castilla-Leon, Castilla-La Mancha, Extremadura, Galicia, La Rioja, and Asturias, eligible companies (i.e., companies that provide new jobs, and that are self-financed to at least 33%) may accrue the following benefits:

a) a subsidy of up to 20% of the investment in fixed assets
b) priority for official loans
c) a deduction of 95% of customs duties to be paid on import of new goods and equipment manufactured outside of Spain
d) an initial deduction of 95% of the Business License Fee
e) a deduction of 95% of the General Business Turnover Tax on new and imported goods and equipment
f) a deduction of 95% of any municipal excise or levy.

In addition to these programs, in specific regions there are other programs that supply greater incentives, such as subsidies on loans and real estate purchases. For more information on the *Programas de Subsidios Industriales* (Industrial Subsidy Programs), contact the local Chamber of Commerce.

Foreign investment in Latin America will gradually be stimulated by stabilizing political conditions and major changes in governmental attitudes toward this area of the economy. In this regard, many Latin American countries show very promising futures in the area of investment, particularly due to the expansion of the private sector, and the massive sell-out of government-controlled companies, particularly in Argentina, Chile, Colombia, Mexico, and Venezuela. Following is a brief outline of the investment regulations in those countries.

Argentina
In Argentina, the financial system is composed of both national and international banks and non-banking entities. Authorization from the BCRA *(Banco Central de la República Argentina)* is needed to operate a financial institution.

Foreign investments are subject to international laws 21382, 23697, and 23763, which guarantee equal rights between foreign and local investors. There are no restrictions on the repatriation of capitals and on the remittance of dividends. There is a 30% tax on profits, applicable to all investors, foreign and local. The Buenos Aires stock exhange, known as *el microcentro,* is attracting many new foreign investors.

Chile
Chile is at the moment Latin America's model economy. Its free-market policies have been extremely successful at stimulating investment. Chile's foreign-investment law is transparent and non-discriminatory. Majority ownership of up to 100% of foreign investments is generally not restricted,

except in the shipping, broadcasting, and hydrocarbons sectors, where Chilean control is required. Foreign investors may fix their tax rate for ten years, or pay the domestic rate. Invested capital must be retained in Chile for twelve months before repatriation, but dividends may be transferred as they are earned.

Colombia
In Colombia, the financial system is divided into credit institutions, which include banks, financing corporations, and savings and loans; and financial services corporations, which handle pensions, trusts, and bonded warehouses. However, the boundaries among these different institutions are not well defined. There has been a slow decrease in regulation of these activities through government decrees. Under the present system, banks are authorized to handle short-term credit as well as foreign trade financing. The FGIF *(Fondo de Garantía de Instituciones Financieras)* has a role similar to that of the FDIC in the U.S. At present, interest rates are between 24% and 35% for deposits, adjustable to inflation.

Venezuela
Venezuela's financial system is currently very similar to Chile's. There is substantial freedom to invest, with the exception of the hydrocarbons sector, which requires congressional approval to allow joint ventures. There are also special limitations on financial and professional services, in which foreign equity participation is capped at 20%.

EXAMEN

A. *Traduzca al español.* (Translate into Spanish.)

1. Whoever it is, tell him I'm not home!
2. Let's go wherever; I just want to go out today.
3. However much they may cost, I want to buy these clothes!
4. Whoever that coat belonged to, now it's no longer where I put it.
5. However much I feed *(dar de comer)* my cat, she's always hungry!
6. However you look at it, it's a shady deal *(un asunto sospechoso).*
7. Whatever you say, I like filet mignon best!
8. Whatever you said to him, he would have done it anyway!
9. Prepare the *crema catalana* whenever you like.
10. We can go to the *hipermercado* whenever you like.

B. *Complete las oraciones siguientes con el diminutivo o aumentativo que ayude a expresar el sentido indicado entre paréntesis.* (Complete the following sentences with the appropriate diminutive or augmentative to convey the idea expressed in parentheses.)

1. *Ahora* (right away) *mismo lo atiendo, señor.*
2. *¡Qué hermosa* (little) *casa!*
3. *¡(Dear) Viviana es una* (young) *muchacha* (very) *hermosa!*
4. *Los Juárez tuvieron un* (cute little boy) *bebé ayer.*
5. *¡Con ese disfraz, Carlos parecía una* (big) *señora muy elegante del siglo dieciocho!*

C. *Elija la palabra que corresponda, en base a sus conocimientos sobre prefijos.* (Choose the correct words, according to your knowledge of prefixes.)

1. *Hoy estoy (desganado/enardecido). No quiero hacer nada.*
2. *Raúl está (encamado/encerrado) en su dormitorio y no puede levantarse.*
3. *Julia es una muchacha (entremetida/encantadora). ¡No la puedo aguantar!*
4. *¡(Endéudate/Despreocúpate)! Te voy a prestar yo el dinero.*
5. *Hablaremos sobre los (pormenores/renombres) del asunto más tarde.*

LECCION 20

A. DIALOGO

Mateo Arias y su mejor amiga, Marta Gómez (ambos hinchas de El América) fueron a ver a un partido de fútbol[1] entre El América y El Cruz Azul, dos equipos popularísimos de México, que se está jugando en el estadio Azteca en la Ciudad de México. En este momento, están en el entretiempo.

MATEO: ¡El primer tiempo estuvo increíble! ¿Viste el golazo[2] de taquito que metió Vergara en los últimos segundos desde la esquina? ¡Y ahorita está reñidísimo el partido![3]

MARTA: A mí me da rabia como lo hicieron caer a López . . . ¡le cometieron una flor de[4] infracción! En realidad, el jugador de El Cruz Azul se merecía una tarjeta roja.[5]

MATEO: ¿Qué esperabas?[6] A los buenos jugadores siempre les tienen rabia, parecería que quisieran desquitarse con ellos.

MARTA: A mí, los empates me ponen nerviosa. ¡Este "uno a uno" me está matando!

MATEO: Quizás desempaten ahorita. Mira, el segundo tiempo va a empezar enseguida, ya están saliendo a la cancha.

Los jugadores toman sus posiciones y con el silbido del árbitro, comienza el segundo tiempo. Se hace el saque inicial y toma control de la pelota Gómez, un jugador de El Cruz Azul. Gómez sobrepasa a dos jugadores, hace un pase largo y López trata de interceptar el balón[7] con un cabezazo, pero se equivoca. Se escucha el silbido del árbitro.

MATEO: ¿Qué pasa? ¿Qué significa ese silbido?

MARTA: ¡El árbitro nos va a cobrar un penal![8]

MATEO *(enojado):* ¡Debe estar mal de la cabeza, la pelota[7] le pasó a medio metro del brazo!

MARTA *(con tono implorante):* ¡Parece mentira! Ese árbitro nos cobra todas, e ignora las infracciones de El Cruz Azul.

MATEO: No me hagas poner nervioso. Ahora están formando la barrera. Voy a escuchar el comentario por la radio,[9] quizás digan quién lo[10] va a patear.

MARTA: ¡Odio los tiros contra el arco!

Mateo intenta escuchar la voz del comentarista por la radio portátil que lleva pegada a la oreja. Sin embargo, se hace difícil por el ruido de las cornetas y el canto de la hinchada.[11]

MATEO: **Apenas escucho . . . va a patear Rodríguez, ahí, ¿lo ves? es el número siete. Está apuntando. Ahora está tomando carrera, ahí va . . .**

Rodríguez hace un tiro fortísimo, pero la pelota rebota contra la barrera y sale volando hacia arriba. Los jugadores se apresuran a tomar control de la pelota, pero finalmente, la atrapa el arquero[12] de El América entre las manos.

MARTA: **¡Qué salvada!**

MATEO: **Bueno, ¿Qué esperabas de nuestro arquerazo?** *(Mateo va repitiendo las jugadas que escucha por la radio)* **controla Juárez, pasa a Pérez . . . lo marca Herrera . . . Pérez pasa a Montes . . . Montes . . .** *(Se escucha un silbido.)* **¡Saque lateral!**

MARTA: **A ver, ¿a quién le pasará Montes la pelota?**

MATEO: **Ahí sacó . . . la atrapó el número cuatro . . . se la pasó al diez . . .**

MARTA: **¡Es Vergara! Mira cómo gambetea,[13] marea a todos los jugadores . . . ¡ahí va!**

El número diez de El América, Vergara, esquiva a dos jugadores que lo marcaban y sale disparado[14] por la cancha, derecho[15] hacia el área del arco. El público ruge y aplaude.

MARTA: **¡Dále[16] Vergara, que ya no te atrapa nadie! ¡a remataaaaar!**

Vergara remata con gran fuerza y el arquero se lanza por el aire. La hinchada de El América se pone de pie y un gran suspiro llena el aire. Por la radio portátil se escucha un largo grito del comentarista . . .

MARTA: **¡Gooooool! ¡Qué golazo! ¿Lo viste, Mateo?**

MATEO: **¡Sí, sí, sí! ¡Cómo juega Vergara!**

MARTA: **No podía nunca atajarla[17] el arquero. No por nada le dicen "el rayo." ¡No lo para[18] nadie!**

El papel picado vuela por el aire, y los gritos del público llenan el estadio. Los jugadores celebran el gol alzando a Vergara y llevándolo en andas[19] por la cancha. Poco a poco, se apacigua la cancha.

MARTA: **El comentarista está anunciando un cambio.[20] ¡Parece que el director técnico de El Cruz Azul está nervioso: va a hacer entrar a Fuentes, el nuevo "as."**

MATEO: **¡Así que, se preparan para el contraataque!**

MARTA: **¡Este partido sí que se va a poner bueno!**

AT A SOCCER MATCH.

Mateo Arias and his best friend, Marta Gómez (both are fans of El America), go to a soccer game between El America and El Cruz Azul, two popular teams in Mexico, that is being played in the Azteca Stadium, in Mexico City. Right now, they're in halftime.

MATEO: The first half was incredible! Did you see the great goal Vergara scored with his heel from the corner in the last few seconds of play? And now the game is really close!

MARTA: It makes me mad how they made Lopez fall, though. They committed a gem of a foul! Actually, the El Cruz Azul player deserved a red card.

MATEO: What did you expect? They always get angry at good players, and they want to get even with them.

MARTA: The thing is, ties make me nervous. This one-to-one is killing me!

MATEO: Maybe they'll break the tie soon. Look! The second half is starting; they're already going out on the field.

The players take their positions, and, with the referee's whistle, the second half begins. The starting kick is given, and Gomez, an El Cruz Azul player, takes control of the ball. Gomez passes two players, makes a long pass, and Lopez tries to intercept with his head, but he makes a mistake. The referee blows his whistle.

MATEO: What's going on now? What does that whistle mean?

MARTA: The referee is going to call a penalty kick!

MATEO: He must be crazy! The ball passed a foot away from Lopez's hand!

MARTA: I can't believe it. That referee calls all our fouls and ignores all of Cruz Azul's.

MATEO: Don't make me nervous. Now they're forming a live wall. I'm going to listen to the commentary on the radio; maybe they'll announce who's going to take the penalty kick.

MARTA: I hate direct kicks against the goal!

Mateo tries to listen to the voice of the commentator over the portable radio he is holding against his ear, but it's difficult to hear because of the noise from the horns and the fans' singing.

MATEO: I can barely hear . . . Rodriguez is going to kick. There, see him? He's number seven. He's aiming; now he's taking a running start. There he goes!

Rodriguez kicks the ball very hard, but it bounces against the goal post and flies upward. The players quickly try to take control of the ball, but, in the end, it's caught by the El America goalie.

MARTA: What a great save that was!

MATEO: Would you expect anything less from our goalie? (Mateo repeats the plays he hears on the radio.) Juarez in control, passes to Perez . . . Herrera stops him . . . Perez passes to Montes . . . Montes. . . . (They hear a whistle.) Out of bounds!

MARTA: I wonder who Montes is gonna pass to . . .

MATEO: There! He threw it . . . number four got it . . . he passed to number ten . . .

MARTA: It's Vergara! Look at his footwork—he's making all the players dizzy! There he goes!

El America's number 10 player, Vergara, avoids two players who were guarding him, and he takes off down the field, straight towards the goal. The crowd roars and cheers!

MARTA: Go, Vergara, go! No one can get you! Kick the baaaaall!

Vergara kicks with great energy and the goalie jumps through the air. El America's fans jump to their feet and a great gasp fills the air. On the portable radio they hear the commentator's long yell . . .

MARTA: Goooooool! What a goal! Did you see it, Mateo?

MATEO: Yeah, yeah! Vergara sure can play!

MARTA: The goalie never had a chance. They don't call Vergara the "lightening bolt" for nothing! Nobody can stop him!

Little bits of paper fly through the air, and the fans' screams fill the stadium. The players celebrate the goal by lifting and carrying Vergara on their shoulders across the field. Slowly, the stadium quiets down.

MARTA: The commentator is announcing a substitution. It looks like El Cruz Azul's technical director is nervous; he's going to put in Fuentes, the new "Ace!"

MATEO: So, they're getting ready for the counterattack!

MARTA: This game is really getting good!

B. APUNTES

1. *Fútbol* (or *balompié* in Spain and the Caribbean) is the favorite national sport throughout Latin America (except in some areas of the Caribbean) and in Spain. There are large soccer stadiums in most cities, and good soccer players are often treated as national heroes. Most countries have many local teams, sometimes even in each neighborhood.

2. The suffix *-azo*, in addition to its role as an augmentative or intensifier, can indicate a blow from an object. *Sin querer, le dí un raquetazo en el brazo a mi amigo.* (I accidentally gave my friend a blow on the arm with my tennis racket.)

3. The adjective *reñido* is often used when speaking about sports, to express that a match or game is close or difficult. *El partido de vóley está reñido.* (The volleyball game is close.) This adjective may also be used in other contexts, such as in business situations. *El asunto Pérez está reñido, no sé cuál propuesta acepten, la nuestra o la de la competencia.* (The Perez deal is close; I don't know if they'll accept our proposal or our competitor's.)

4. The expression *¡flor de . . . !* preceding a noun is used to show surprise, or as an augmentative, much like the English expression "a gem of a . . . !" Note that it is often introduced by an indefinite article. *¡Ayer se jugó un flor de partido, terminó dos a dos!* (They played a gem of a game yesterday; it ended at two all!) *Van a pasar una flor de película esta noche, por el canal 7.* (They're going to show a great movie tonight, on channel 7.)

5. *Una infracción* or *un foul* (a foul) can earn a player a yellow or a red card. After a first serious foul, a player is generally given a yellow card, and a second foul by the same player results in a red card, causing his expulsion *(expulsión)* from the game. A red card can also be issued for a first infraction, if the foul is egregious and deliberate.

6. Note that the verb *esperar* can mean "to hope, to wait for," or "to expect," depending on its context. It takes a direct object or can be immediately followed by an infinitive. *Estoy esperando a mi novia, ya va a llegar.* (I'm waiting for my girlfriend; she'll be here any minute.) *Espero poder cerrar el trato.* (I hope to be able to close the deal.) *Espero recibir la carta mañana por la mañana.* (I expect to receive the letter tomorrow morning.)

7. Both *la pelota* and *el balón* are used to refer to a soccer ball, although *la pelota* is more common in Latin America.

8. *Un penal* (a penalty kick) is called by the referee when any player (except the goalie) touches the ball with any part of his arms or hands. The defensive team is allowed to form a barrier of players, *una barrera* (or "a live wall"), to protect the goal, but, even so, penalty kicks are very difficult for a goalie to intercept.

9. In Spanish, gender is very important, as it often determines the meaning of a word, such as *la radio* (the radio receiver) and *el radio* (the radius of a circle).

10. Note that *lo* refers to *el penal,* and not *el balón.*

11. *La hinchada* or *la porra* are slang soccer terms for the "fans" of a particular team; thus, *la hinchada de El América* (the fans of El América.)

12. A synonym for *el arquero* is *el guardavallas.*

13. *Gambetear* is a verb used in soccer meaning "to do legwork."

14. *Salir disparado* is a colloquial expression meaning "to take off (running)."

15. *Derecho* can function as an adverb meaning "straight": *Siga derecho por esta calle.* (Go straight along this street.); as an adjective meaning "right": *Alce la mano derecha.* (Raise your right hand.); or as a noun, in which case gender determines meaning. *El derecho* means "the (legal) right," while *la derecha* means "the right (side)." *Los jugadores no tienen derecho de disputar un cobro del árbitro.* (The players don't have the right to dispute a referee's call.) *En la esquina, doble a la derecha.* (At the corner, turn to the right.)

16. *¡Dale . . . !* is a colloquial expression used much like the English "Go, . . . go!" *¡Dale campeón!* (Go, champ, go!)

17. *Atajar* (to cut short, interrupt) is a soccer term used to refer to the goalkeeper's action of catching the ball with his hands, or deflecting it away from the goal with any part of his body. *Hubo dos o tres atajadas geniales en el partido.* (There were two or three great saves during the game.)

18. The verb *parar* (to stop, to detain) is often used informally in a reflexive construction to replace *ponerse de pie* (to stand up, to get upright). *La hinchada se paró cuando su equipo metió el gol.* (The fans stood up when their team scored a goal.) *Si sigues yendo tan rápido, te va a parar la policía.* (If you go on speeding, the police will stop you.)

19. *Llevar en andas* literally means "to carry on a hand carriage," but it is used in sports slang to mean "to carry (a player) on the shoulders."

20. *Un cambio* (a change) is used informally to refer to *una sustitución* (a substitution).

C. GRAMATICA Y USOS

1. *EL CAUSATIVO* (THE CAUSATIVE)

The causative expresses the notion of having something done or causing an action to occur. In Spanish, the causative is formed with the verb *hacer* followed by an infinitive or by *que* + a subjunctive clause.

El rocío en la cancha hace que los jugadores se caigan con facilidad.
El rocío en la cancha hace caer a los jugadores con facilidad.
  The dew on the playing field makes the players fall easily.

As with other verbal constructions, object pronouns are used to specify or clarify the causative relationship. The object pronouns have three possible positions. They may precede *hacer,* be attached to it as a suffix, or be attached as a suffix to the infinitive (if one is being used). The object pronouns may also be placed within the subjunctive clause.

No quería mirar el partido anoche, pero mi hermano me hizo mirarlo.
No quería mirar el partido anoche, pero mi hermano me lo hizo mirar.
No quería mirar el partido anoche, pero mi hermano hizo que lo mirase.
  I didn't want to watch the game last night, but my brother made me watch it.

The position of the object pronoun in the subjunctive clause will depend on whether the clause is negative or affirmative.

La inflación hace que bajen la inversión y las compras en todas las áreas de la economía.
  Inflation makes investments and purchases decrease in all areas of the economy.

El jefe me hizo buscar en la computadora a todos los clientes vinculados con la empresa Acme.
  The boss made me research all the clients connected with the Acme company.

¡Practicar deportes hace que te sientas mejor y que mejore tu estado de salud!
  Playing sports makes you feel better and improves your health!

2. *INTERJECCIONES* (INTERJECTIONS)

Interjections (such as "Hey!" "Yikes!" "Eek!" "Yuk!") are used to express emotion. Gramatically they are considered sentences in themselves, as they express a complete idea. In Spanish, interjections vary widely from country to country, but the following few are understood throughout the Spanish-speaking world.

a) The formula—*¡Qué* + noun + *más/tan* + adjective!—is used to express an opinion about an object or person, much like the English construction "What a + adjective + noun!"

¡Qué partido más emocionante!
  What an exciting game!

¡Que estadio tan grande!
  What a large stadium!

b) To express surprise, approval, or disapproval without a more specific description, use *¡Qué* + noun! instead. This is equivalent to the English expression "What a + noun!"

¡Qué golazo! ¡Qué jugadores! ¡Qué partido!
  What a goal! What players! What a game!

c) Some words, such as *¡diablos!* (devils), *¡rayos!* (blazes), and *¡cuernos!* (horns) are used in the middle of the sentences to add emphasis:

¿Qué diablos está diciendo el árbitro?
  What the devil is the referee saying?

¿Cómo cuernos pudo cobrarnos ese penal?
  How in blue blazes could he call that penalty?

d) Following are some more fairly universal Spanish interjections and their English equivalents:

¡Chuy! ¡Qué frío!	Brrrr! It's cold!
¡Uf! ¡Qué calor!	Phew! It's hot!
¡Ay! ¡Qué dolor!	Ouch! That hurts!
¡Ay! ¡Qué pena!	Oh! That's too bad!
¡Olé! ¡Qué cerca estuvo!	Whoa! That was close!
¡Epa/Oye! ¿Qué pasa?	Hey! What's wrong?
¡Ah/Oh! ¡Qué interesante!	Wow! That's interesting!

D. HABLEMOS DE NEGOCIOS

LA "ETIQUETA" O COSTUMBRES SOCIALES (SOCIAL ETIQUETTE)

Greetings *(Saludos)*

Spaniards and Latin Americans are very warm and friendly people. Don't be misled by the formality displayed when making a new acquaintance. If you are liked, you will very shortly be accepted openly and treated as an old friend. This desire for closeness extends to physical proximity: Latin Americans tend to stand very close to each other during conversation, and it is not uncommon for men to hug *(dar un abrazo)* and for women to kiss each other on the cheek after a long absence. While this may seem somewhat inappropriate to Americans, these types of greetings are common in business situations as well. At first, however, a firm handshake suffices, both when meeting someone, and when leaving. When being introduced to someone, say *¡Mucho gusto!* (It's a pleasure to meet you!) to a man, and *¡Encantado!* (I'm enchanted to meet you!) to a woman. The appropriate response is *¡El gusto es mío!* (The pleasure is mine!) or *¡Igualmente!* (Likewise.)

Tú versus *Usted*

When making a new acquaintance, be sure to use *Usted* and the person's last name. Keep in mind that in most Latin American countries and in Spain, people have two last names (the latter being the mother's maiden name) and should be addressed by their father's last name. For example, *el Señor Juan Carlos Rodríguez Gonzále* would be addressed as *Señor Rodríguez*. Do not use *tú* (or *vos* in Paraguay, Uruguay, Argentina, and rural areas) until you are invited to do so with *¡Por favor, no me trates de Usted!* (Please, don't use *usted* with me!), or *Por favor, tutéame!* (Please, use *tú* with me!)

Gifts

Gift-giving is a customary rite among Spanish-speaking people, especially after a friendly relationship has been formed. Always keep in mind that the best gifts are sincere ones that reveal an understanding of a person's needs and tastes, not necessarily lavish or expensive ones. Remember that gifts to colleagues are not given in business, but in social settings. A good time to offer a business gift is the long and leisurely business lunch. Women should avoid giving gifts to male colleagues or clients, as this may be perceived as a personal overture.

Gifts are always given when visiting someone's home, especially for the first time. It is considered in poor taste to arrive empty-handed. If invited for dinner, a good bottle of scotch or fine wine for the host, plus flowers or perfume for the hostess would be in excellent taste. For other occasions, appropriate gifts for men are usually brand name novelties and men's accessories; for women, perfume or flowers. The best flowers are usually the national flowers, which vary from country to country. Gifts for children are always appreciated by parents.

Finally, avoid giving anything black or violet (a symbol of Lent), thirteen of anything (bad luck), any cutting tools, such as knives or scissors (a symbol for cutting off a relationship), or handkerchiefs (a symbol of tears or grief).

A word of caution: avoid admiring your host's possessions too copiously, as you may end up having to take them home with you! General compliments, such as *Tiene Vd. una casa/familia encantadora* (You have an enchanting home/family) are appreciated. However, if you focus on a particular object—*¡Me encanta/gusta mucho esa/ese. . . !)*—it may be offered to you as a gift, and refusing to accept it would be an insult.

Punctuality

In most situations, Spanish-speaking people don't mind tardiness: in fact, it is customary in Latin America to arrive thirty minutes late to a dinner party or an informal gathering, especially if you were invited with the phrase: *Ven(ga) a eso (de)/alrededor de/como las ocho de la noche.* (Come over at around 8 P.M.). In business situations, however, foreigners are expected to be on time, and not to complain if they are kept waiting (see *Hablemos de negocios, Lección 8).*

Conversation

In conversation, avoid making comparisons between countries, particularly comparisons with the U.S. Good topics of conversation include local history and the beauty of the city, culture, fine arts, sports (especially soccer), and travel. Family can be discussed, but only if it is first introduced by your host. Remember not to make negative remarks about bullfighting, particularly in Spain, Colombia, and Mexico. Following are more specific tips for particular countries:

In Spain, avoid giving dahlias and chrysanthemums, as they are associated with death. Appropriate gifts include cakes, pastries, and chocolates. Also avoid discussing politics and religion.

In Argentina, avoid discussing politics, particularly England. Remember that the Falkland Islands are known as *Las islas Malvinas* and belong to Argentina. Gifts to be avoided in Argentina are ties and shirts. Books, lighters, and similar high-quality company mementos are acceptable gifts.

In Bolivia, many people greet each other with a spoken salutation and don't usually shake hands. Gifts are generally not opened until after visitors leave.

In Chile, visitors to a home should wait outside the door until they are invited in.

In Mexico, avoid giving yellow or red flowers, as they are associated with witchcraft.

In Paraguay, you must thank your host for inviting you, and ask permission before entering a home. You may find that many people speak Guarani, and often mix Guarani and Spanish words. The Guarani prefix *che-* (pronounced *sheh*) meaning "my," is often added to Spanish words, to create terms such as *ch-amigo* (my friend).

In Peru, people are somewhat more formal than in other countries, and they are especially proud of their Incan heritage. Dinner invitations are generally for 9 P.M. or later, and it is customary to arrive thirty minutes late.

In Uruguay, avoid comparisons with Argentina. Uruguayans are especially fond of soccer.

In Venezuela, gifts for the office are most appropriate. Venezuelans usually only invite special friends to their homes.

In Puerto Rico, people tend to be more relaxed than in other Latin American countries. Gifts should be unwrapped immediately upon receiving them. Avoid discussing the close ties between Puerto Rico and the U.S.

EXAMEN

A. *Complete las siguientes oraciones causativas.* (Complete the following causative sentences.)

1. *La O.N.U.* (has caused to disappear) *el colonialismo en muchas partes del globo.*
2. *El desarrollo frenético de la industria* (has made) *que* (suffer) *el equilibrio ecológico del planeta.*
3. *La infracción* (made fall) *al jugador y lo* (made lose) control de la (ball).
4. *¡Tantos gritos* (will make you [*vosotros*]) *doler la garganta!*
5. *¿Porqué* (you made me watch) *ese partido de fútbol tan idiota?*
6. *Los embargos* (to make hungry) *a los pueblos, no a los gobiernos.*
7. *¡Mi papá* (made me wear) *la camiseta del club a la cancha!*
8. *Mi abuela* (makes) *que todos* (watch) *el portido de fútbol en silencio, porque le gusta dormir la siesta.*
9. *Hoy mi jefe* (made me) *quedar en la oficina y* (to work) *horas extra.*
10. *La actual situación económica mundial* (makes) *que* (be) *necesario coordinar y organizar los mercados internacionales, para* (distribute) *la riqueza equitativamente.*

B. *Complete las oraciones siguientes con la interjección que corresponda en cada caso.* (Complete the following sentences with the appropriate interjection.)

1. *Cuando me lastimé la pierna, dije "¡_____! ¡Qué dolor!"*
2. *¡_____! ¡Qué frío hace aquí!*
3. *¡_____ estadio _____ grande!*
4. *¡_____ jugador es ese Vergara!*
5. *¡_____! ¡Qué calor hace hoy!*

SEGUNDO REPASO

A. *Traduzca las oraciones siguientes al español.* (Translate the following sentences into Spanish.)

1. That's the funniest commercial I've ever seen!
2. When we have cable TV, we'll be able to see many more channels.
3. If Juana had known how much the car would cost her in the end, she wouldn't have bought it.
4. If you *(ustedes)* happen to have any problem with the van's transmission, call me at 345-4533 anytime.
5. The banana plantations do not allow the rain water to drag the coffee plants down the mountain.
6. Turn on the radio; maybe there's a good classical music program on tonight.
7. Had you told me yesterday that Catalonians eat chicken with seafood, I wouldn't have believed you.
8. I like this dish much more than that one over there.
9. The doctor is now visiting a patient in the emergency room. He'll be with you *(ustedes)* in five minutes.
10. Juan is probably still looking for an apartment in Los Angeles; they say that they're very difficult to find!
11. The Aconcagua is the tallest mountain on the American continent.
12. The Guarani had built beautiful cities in the jungle, helped by the Jesuit missionaries.
13. Let's go to the *hipermercado;* they're advertising a special sale on fruit today.
14. I don't think foreign investors will want to invest in our country until the government takes measures to diminish the restrictions on the repatriation of foreign capital.
15. Is there anyone here who knows the telephone number of a good lawyer?
16. The ball got away from the goalie, whose team I've been a fan of for ten years.
17. Do you see that sign over there that says: "Smoking is not allowed in this building"?
18. I wonder what the Lopezes are doing? Since they're on vacation, they're probably going around sunbathing and swimming in the sea right now!
19. After listening to the Minister of the Economy speak on TV, it makes me want to vote for another candidate in the next election!
20. Go *(vosotros)* on practicing Spanish, 'cause you'll soon be speaking like a native!

LECTURA

LA CORRIDA DE TOROS

Atardece el domingo. Los espectadores ya están en la gran plaza de toros, en espera del matador quien muy pronto hará su entrada, rodeado de su corte de pajes[1] y ayudantes y vestido de su magnífico traje de luces. Se percíbe la gran expectativa del público. ¿Qué estamos por presenciar? ¿Acaso no será éste un espectáculo cruel e impío?[2] ¿O acaso será una lucha de vida o muerte? Ciertamente la corrida de toros provoca en muchas personas toda clase de reacciones e interrogantes.[3] Pero, ¿cuáles son los orígenes de este arte taurino,[4] tan característico de la cultura española?

Las corridas de toros son una tradición antigua de la cultura española y por herencia, también de muchos países latinoamericanos. En España, la corrida de toros se conoce con el nombre de "Fiesta Nacional," aunque existen en este país muchos otros eventos relacionados con toros, como el festival de San Fermín, durante el cual los peligrosos animales son soltados[5] y corren por las calles de la ciudad de Pamplona, en Navarra.

Resulta difícil precisar los orígenes de tales espectáculos, aunque sin duda son remotísimos y han pasado por un largo proceso de evolución.* Desde tiempos remotos en España, existía la tradición del capeo, una especie de lidia de toros popular desorganizada. Ya en el siglo XII de nuestra era, encontramos en las crónicas históricas relatos que describen los torneos de lanzas, en los cuales lanzadores montados a caballo[6] lidiaban[7] con toros durante las grandes "ferias" o festivales públicos. El apogeo[8] de la popularidad de estos torneos ocurrió en el siglo XVI. En aquel tiempo, los torneos llegaron a ser principalmente una actividad de la aristocracia, destinados a homenajear a los caballeros.[9] Nótese que estaba prohibida la matanza de animales a cambio de dinero, por lo cual los caballeros participantes no podían recibir remuneraciones, aunque el prestigio conferido por una buena lucha sería más que suficiente: la plaza pública se vestía de banderines con las insignias de las familias nobles y las multitudes plebeyas[10] participaban indirectamente, rodeando y alentando a los combatientes. El evento más popular de la época era el «rostro a rostro», un enfrentamiento directo con el toro, aunque en ese entonces,[11] el caballero montaba a caballo.

A mediados del siglo XIX, la figura del matador surge como el personaje central de la corrida. Entre los matadores célebres de la época encontramos a Joaquín Rodríguez, llamado "Costillas" y a Antonio Ruíz. Éstos adquieren una fama hasta entonces inaudita, llegando a ser conocidos en toda España. El ascenso

---

* *Algunos investigadores sugieren que las raíces de estas tradiciones se encuentran en los cultos de la antigua Creta, en los cuales el toro era un elemento simbólico poderosísimo, relacionado principalmente con la fuerza y la polaridad masculinas. En esta civilización, jóvenes muchachos practicaban el "salto de toros," ritual destinado sin dudas a demostrar la bravura y la proeza del varón.*

de tales personajes termina por provocar la formalización y reglamentación del arte taurino, adquiriendo las características de su forma actual. En 1852, apareció el primer libro de reglamentos, que legaliza el deporte y estipula la creación de las Plazas de Toros, bajo la supervisión del gobernador local. Finalmente, los reglamentos acerca de la corrida son ampliados en 1930 y en 1962.

Las modernas corridas de toros son similares en todo el mundo, básandose en las normas españolas. Consisten de cuatro secciones o actos. El primer acto, llamado «capeo» es quizás el más conocido por los extranjeros. En él, el matador intenta cansar al toro, incitándolo con su capote a hacer pases a gran velocidad muy cerca de su cuerpo. En los actos siguientes, se desarrolla la ardua lucha entre el hombre y el animal. Durante el segundo acto, participan los picadores[12] a caballo con sus lanzas, en el tercero, el matador inserta sus banderillas de puntas agudas en los músculos del cuello del animal, debilitándolo aún más. Finalmente, en el cuarto acto, el matador demuestra el manejo de la muleta, especie de capa envuelta en un bastón. Ya al final, liquida[13] al animal con su espada.

El público participa también de la lucha, con el tradicional grito de ¡ole!. Por medio de él, expresa su aprobación del arte del torero. A veces, cierto espectador joven e impestuoso logra entrar en la arena, echando en acción a los monosabios, personajes similares a los "payasos de rodeo" estadounidenses, quienes salen al auxilio de quien se encuentre en dificultades en la arena. Por suerte, estos jóvenes impetuosos, llamados espontáneos pocas veces resultan heridos, ¡aunque por cierto no alegran al torero!

VOCABULARIO

1. *pajes:* page, valet, attendant
2. *impío:* impious, merciless
3. *interrogantes:* questions
4. *taurino:* taurean, relating to bulls
5. *soltar:* to let go
6. *a caballo:* on horseback
7. *lidiar:* to fight, to combat, to contend
8. *apogeo:* apogee, highest point (in fame, glory, etc.)
9. *caballeros:* in this context, knights
10. *plebeyo:* plebe, person not of royal or noble descent
11. *en ese entonces:* at that time, in those times
12. *picador:* mounted bullfighter armed with a lance (from *picar:* to prick)
13. *liquidar:* in this context, to kill

RESPUESTAS

LECCION 1

A. 1. *Voy a su casa mañana.* 2. *¿Viaja Vd. al Perú el mes que viene?*
3. *Vuelvo a los EE.UU. después de un mes.* 4. *Mañana invitamos a Juan.*
5. *El mes que viene volamos a España.*
B. 1. *María acaba de entrar en la terminal.* 2. *¿Piensa Vd. visitar a sus*
padres en Chile? 3. *¡El avión está por despegar!* 4. *Acabamos de ver esa*
película durante el vuelo. 5. *Voy a acabar de leer el libro en tres días.*
6. *Pensamos cambiar el auto por uno nuevo el mes que viene.* 7. *Pensamos*
en María a menudo.
C. 1. *para* 2. *por* 3. *por* 4. *para* 5. *por* 6. *para* 7. *por* 8. *para*
9. *por* 10. *por*

LECCION 2

A. 1. *Estoy, estoy* 2. *son* 3. *está* 4. *está* 5. *Ser, ser* 6. *están*
B. 1. *mi, su* 2. *El trabajo del presidente* 3. *nuestro, el de ellos* 4. *nuestra,*
la casa de Juan, la mía 5. *El auto de ellos, tuyo/suyo*
C. 1. *Nunca bebo nada frío.* 2. *A nadie le gusta el Sr. Thompson, ¡ni a mí*
tampoco! 3. *No tienen ni facsímiles ni personas de negocios en su hotel.*
4. *No vemos a personas de negocios a menudo en nuestro hotel.* 5. *No está*
nadie en casa. 6. *Encontré un portafolio ajeno en mi habitación.* 7. *Pedro*
no tiene ningún hermano en Panamá. 8. *Juan es abogado.* 9. *La Srta.*
Vega es la gerente del hotel. 10. *La Sra. Martínez es la presidente de*
nuestra organización.

LECCION 3

A. 1. *Le, se lo* 2. *le, se lo* 3. *Vd., le, me* 4. *Los, los* 5. *les, nos la*
6. *os, nos* 7. *se los* 8. *se, mí, me* 9. *Os, lo, se lo* 10. *me*
B. 1. *No se lo voy a dar.* 2. *Él se los entrega a ellos.* 3. *No nos los quieren dar.*
4. *A las siete, nos encontramos para ver al director.* 5. *Él no va a hablarte a*
ti, sino a Juan.
C. 1. *No me gustan las ferias.* 2. *Él se los da a ellos.* 3. *Ellos no nos los*
quieren dar. 4. *Ella quiere dártelo.* 5. *No te gustan los autores.*

LECCION 4

A. 1. *¿Qué?* 2. *¿Adónde?* 3. *¿Cuál?* 4. *¿De qué?* 5. *¿Por dónde?*
6. *¿Para cuándo?* 7. *¿Quiénes?* 8. *¿Cuánto?* 9. *¿A quiénes?*
10. *¿de dónde?*

B. 1. *¿De quiénes son estos abrigos?* 2. *¿Para cuándo necesita la lista de clientes?* 3. *¿En qué/cuál archivero están mis documentos?* 4. *¿Hace cuánto que está Vd. en la ciudad?* 5. *¿Por qué no está Gonzalo en la oficina hoy?*
C. 1. Where do you think Mario is? 2. How much are the tomatoes? 3. How long have you been head of this section? 4. To whom are you writing those letters? 5. Whom did you meet at the party?
D. 1. *He hecho* 2. *has estado, han estado* 3. *ha capacitado* 4. *Ha podido* 5. *Hemos revisado, hemos visto*

LECCION 5

A. 1. *recibía* 2. *entré, hablaba* 3. *oí, discutían* 4. *llegaron, hacía* 5. *conversaban, trabajaban* 6. *resolvisteis* 7. *miraste, estuviste* 8. *pude, tenía* 9. *podía, tenía* 10. *quisieron, hizo/hacía*
B. 1. *tuvo*—The company didn't have enough employees in its export department. 2. *dijiste*—Why didn't you tell it to the boss? 3. *pude necesité* —I couldn't do it alone. I needed help. 4. *Buscásteis*—You looked for the reports in the wrong file cabinet. 5. *tuvimos*—We didn't have time to go to the factory. (a particular time we tried to go)
C. 1. *Hace tres meses que no vemos a la tía María.* 2. *¿Hace cuánto que estáis en el Uruguay?* 3. *¿Hace cuánto se fue Pablo a los Estados Unidos?* 4. *Hace mucho que Vds. no pasan la Navidad con nosotros.* 5. *¡Hiciste de pastor en el pesebre viviente hace veinte años!*

LECCION 6

A. 1. *a comprar* 2. *para escribir* 3. *Para ahorrar, andar, para comparar* 4. *comprar, para poder, disfrutar* 5. *llamar, para preguntarla*
B. 1. *rápida(mente), silenciosamente* 2. *un poco/un tanto* 3. *nítidamente* 4. *fuerte(mente)* 5. *parcialmente/medio*
C. 1. This printer prints faster and more quietly than mine. 2. I'm a little disappointed with the output of this computer. 3. Do you see clearer on high-resolution monitors? 4. Speak louder because the microphone doesn't work! 5. The sky is partly cloudy today.
D. 1. *Me gusta mucho/encanta jugar juegos electrónicos en casa.* 2. *La oí a la vendedora explicar cómo funciona el nuevo programa.* 3. *Juan la oyó a María hablar acerca de sus problemas en la universidad.* 4. *Lo vimos a un hombre gastar mucho dinero en una computadora en la tienda hoy.* 5. *Escribir un informe de ventas es fácil con este programa nuevo.*

LECCION 7

A. 1. *ingresará* 2. *pedagógica, graduará, maestro* 3. *me transferiría, tendré* 4. *calificación/nota, merciología* 5. *estarán* 6. *habría ido, rendir, química* 7. *profesor, tomará lección* 8. *comenzar* 9. *habéis de estudiar, historia* 10. *tiene que rendir libre, transferir*

B. 1. My daughter doesn't know yet what type of high school she will enter. 2. My son is in a pedagogical high school. In two years he will graduate as a teacher. 3. I would transfer to a university in Spain, but I don't know if I will have encugh money. 4. I wonder what grade I received in Industrial Chemistry this trimester. 5. Do you know where the kids are? I called the university and they told me that the classes finished three hours ago. 6. Jorgito would have gone on vacation with us, but he had to take a chemistry exam. 7. The teacher will probably give the day's oral exam today. 8. I think classes must begin during the first week of March. 9. You must study the first three chapters of the history book for tomorrow. 10. Maria has to take an equivalency exam in order to transfer to the University of Zaragoza, in Spain.

LECCION 8

A. 1. *tenga* 2. *recibamos* 3. *vayamos, quiere* 4. *este, suele* 5. *hables, tienes* 6. *vaya* 7. *sigas, haga* 8. *debemos, es, sean* 9. *recuerdo, haya* 10. *puede, es*

B. 1. *No se permite fumar en este edificio.* 2. *Se dice que nuestro jefe es un hombre simpático, pero no puedo decirte si es verdad, porque no le hablo a menudo.* 3. *Se me perdió la pluma cuando firmé esos informes en el ascensor.* 4. *No creo que cierren la cafetería mañana.* 5. *¿Cómo se dice* "politically correct" *en español?—No se dice.* 6. *A Liliana se le olvidó la clave de acceso.* 7. *El laboratorio se lava todas las mañanas a las siete.* 8. *¿Se puede usar esta terminal ahora? . . . Ayer estaba descompuesta.* 9. *Siempre y cuando la veas, dile a María que me llame.* 10. *La tapa de la revista dice: "Huelga anunciada por los oficinistas de Computex."*

LECCION 9

A. 1. *tenga* 2. *pueda* 3. *es* 4. *hable* 5. *llames*

B. 1. *alquilar/arrendar, departamento de dos recámaras, centro* 2. *Los Gómez, gran, inmobiliaria* 3. *pueda, de calefacción central, anda/ funciona* 4. *la de la calle Central* 5. *estudio*

C. 1. Lorena is looking for a one-bedroom apartment. 2. Is there a lot that could be converted into a parking lot? 3. Manuel moved into a classy neighborhood. 4. There is no one in the office who speaks Spanish. 5. When you call the real estate agency, tell them you're calling on my behalf. 6. I would like to rent a two-bedroom apartment downtown. 7. The Gomezes have a great, famous real estate company. 8. When you can, please come see what's wrong with my central heating vent. It doesn't work well. 9. Of the three houses we saw, I liked the one on Central Street best. 10. What floor is the studio apartment on?

LECCION 10

A. 1. *ningún* 2. *Algunas* 3. *Ningunos* 4. *toda/cada* 5. *todas*
B. 1. *hube* 2. *habías* 3. *había* 4. *habíais* 5. *hubieron*
C. 1. I don't like any violent programs. 2. Some commercials are fun; others aren't. 3. You don't like any of these eyeglasses? You're very difficult! 4. At movies that aren't suitable for minors, they tend to check the I.D.s of everyone who looks too young. 5. Every week I go to the movies with my friends to see European films. 6. I recognized you as soon as I (had) heard your voice. 7. You had never seen a Schwarzenegger movie before? I can't believe it! 8. When you arrived, the movie had already begun. 9. Yesterday I tried to call you on the phone to tell you that I couldn't go, but you had already left. 10. As soon as the technicians had installed the cable, we sat down to watch TV all night!

PRIMER REPASO

A. 1. *Acabo de, estoy por, voy a estar/estaré* 2. *Tengo que, reservarles, habitaciones, Preferirían, fueran* 3. *nunca/jamás, qué, lo* 4. *Adónde, ir, feria del libro, Habrá/Va a haber.* 5. *hacías, Te, estabas* 6. *paticorto, colilargo* 7. *un departamento, tenga, habitaciones, esté, centro* 8. *haya nada, feria* 9. *Pudiste, a tus primos, viajaste* 10. *secretaria, le, jefe de personal*
B. 1. *El año pasado, los estudiantes viajaron por España y aprendieron mucho sobre la cultura española.* 2. *Mientras Jorge vivía en Caracas, trabajaba para una importante empresa de importación y exportación.* 3. *Esta nueva computadora nos ayudará a poner al día la base de datos de clientes rápida y eficientemente.* 4. *Se dice que las universidades privadas son mejores que las públicas, pero dudo que sea verdad.* 5. *En todos los campos de negocios, se usan las computadoras más y más extensamente.* 6. *A Julia se le perdió el disco de computadora, y tuvo que escribir los informes otra vez porque no los había almacenado en el disco rígido.* 7. *En cuanto Julián y Marta hubieron visto la casa, supieron que la comprarían.* 8. *¿Pasarán alguna película interesante en la tele esta noche?* 9. *¿Dónde pusisteis los formularios que recibimos ayer?.* 10. *¿Has visto alguna vez el alumbrado del árbol del "Rockefeller Center"? Yo no lo he visto.* 11. *Mi habitación de hotel da a las montañas, ¿y las vuestras?* 12. *Para el lunes, Karina tiene que terminar sus negocios aquí en Ciudad de Panamá y volver a Nueva York.* 13. *¿Podrías prestarme tu computadora (por) un par de horas esta tarde?* 14. *Hemos prometido terminar estas listas de autores y tenemos que entregárselas al jefe para el viernes.* 15. *Se puede preparar un listado de las direcciones de los clientes de la base de datos central usando esta*

computadora, pero nadie tiene acceso a los informes de ventas sin una palabra clave.

LECCION 11

A. 1. *más grande/mayor, más chica/menor* 2. *tantos, como* 3. *menos, que* 4. *las más.* 5. *más, que*
B. 1. *A Norberto le gusta más el aguapanel que el café.* 2. *El capatáz cargó más de cuarenta bolsas de granos de café en el camión.* 3. *La finca de Don Ignacio es una de las más grandes en el departamento.* 4. *Ésa es la pintura más hermosa que yo jamás haya visto.* 5. *Ésa es la catarata más alta del mundo.* 6. *Espero que este escritorio no sea más ancho que la puerta de mi oficina.* 7. *La señorita López no cree que hayan/hubieren enviado los telefacsímiles antes de las 3 de la tarde.* 8. *El jefe no espera más que cinco minutos a que llegue alguien.* 9. *Pagué más de cuarenta pesos por esa camisa.* 10. *Cuanto mayor el rendimiento, más trabajadores necesitaremos.*
C. 1. *Habrá* 2. *tenga* 3. *hubiera* 4. *habremos* 5. *habrá* 6. *habrá* 7. *habreis* 8. *habrás* 9. *tengas* 10. *habrán*

LECCION 12

A. 1. *sea*—I want to buy a strong car that's not too fancy. 2. *pagara*—I didn't think you would pay so little each month in installments! 3. *estuviera*—Did you try calling someone who was in charge? 4. *fuera*—Couldn't they have shown you any cars that were more economical? 5. *hablara*—There wasn't anyone who could speak Spanish at the party last night. 6. *hicieras*—I knew you didn't like fish, but I didn't think you'd make such a fuss! 7. *pueda*—Is there a salesperson who can help us?
B. 1. *compra/compraré, tendría* 2. *Ahorrará, opta/optara por* 3. *decide/ decidiere, daremos* 4. *harías, tuvieras* 5. *daríais, tuviérias*
C. 1. *Si pudiera comprar cualquier auto que quisiera, me compraría una Ferrari.* 2. *No hubiera gastado tanto dinero en mi auto, si hubiera comprado un diesel.* 3. *Si decidimos/decidiéramos ir al Brasil de vacaciones, tendré que cambiar el filtro de nafta.* 4. *¿Has visto alguna vez un auto que fuera tan rápido como económico?* 5. *¿Comprarías un Mercedes si tuvieras el dinero?*

LECCION 13

A. 1. *hayan* 2. *hubieras* 3. *haya* 4. *haya* 5. *haya* 6. *haya* 7. *hayamos/hubiéremos* 8. *haya* 9. *hubierais* 10. *hubiera*
B. 1. I hope the Martinezes haven't gotten lost among so many people! 2. I was surprised you hadn't come yesterday. What happened? 3. I find

it hard to believe that the girl has eaten such a large portion. 4. As soon as you have mixed the ingredients, put the mixture in the oven for twenty minutes. 5. I don't know why he hasn't arrived; maybe he took the wrong bus. 6. I didn't think you'd heard about *puchero* in the U.S. 7. I doubt we will have finished eating in a half an hour. 8. I hope my mother has made *cazuela* for today's lunch. I like it so much! 9. I didn't think you'd ever tried *butifarras* before! 10. I never thought I'd like Spanish food so much!

LECCION 14

A. 1. *De haber sabido lo que sé ahora, nunca habría hecho lo que hice.*
2. *Házme un favor de tener tiempo mañana.* 3. (not possible) 4. *De tener algún problema, no deje de llamarme.* 5. (not possible)
B. 1. *escuché* 2. *conozcas* 3. *sé* 4. *pueda* 5. *ahorrase*
6. *cubrieron* 7. *pudimos*
C. 1. *¡Espero que no haga calor cuando salgamos mañana!* 2. *¡Elena no te contó el secreto de modo que se lo contaras a todo el mundo!* 3. *¡No te compraré ese juguete, aunque te guste o no (te guste)!* 4. *Tuvimos tiempo extra, de modo que pudimos venir a visitaros!* 5. *Los inversionistas extranjeros siempre estimulan la economía, aún cuando el Ministro diga que no!*

LECCION 15

A. 1. *os pongáis* 2. *Tomen, lean, pregunten* 3. *Pon* 4. *Vamos/Vayamos*
5. *controle, deje* 6. *nos levantemos, dormamos/durmamos* 7. *Idos, os vayáis* 8. *ayúdeme* 9. *Dile* 10. *digas*
B. 1. Complete all the boxes of the following form, except for the ones marked "for official use only." 2. Prepare me a report regarding the purchases made by the new clients, on which we will base the projected sales for the next quarter. 3. Unlike English, Spanish is written almost phonetically. 4. Due to a problem with the central computer system, the applications will be processed by hand instead of electronically. 5. I have nothing more to say about the directors' meeting of yesterday.
C. 1. *con, acerca de/sobre* 2. *A diferencia del, frente a, en, de* 3. *Además de, tocante a* 4. *dentro de/en* 5. *Lejos de, conmigo, en*

LECCION 16

A. 1. *Aquél* 2. *Este, ése* 3. *Aquellas* 4. *Este, ese, aquél, aquella mujer* 5. *ésta, aquélla*
B. 1. *quien* 2. *La que* 3. *cuya* 4. *que/el cual* 5. *cual* 6. *Lo que* 7. *del cual, lo que* 8. *cuyas, cuyo* 9. *Las que* 10. *la cual*
C. 1. *¿(Acerca) De quién hablaban cuando entré?* 2. *No sé lo que comprarle a mi novia, está enojada conmigo.* 3. *¿A quién le puedo preguntar cómo*

funciona este programa? 4. *Ése es un amigo de Roberta, y aquélla es mi mejor amiga.* 5. *¡Éstas son mis galletitas preferidas!* 6. *Encontrémonos donde nos encontramos la vez pasada.* 7. *¡No comás como chancho/puerco! ¡Masticá!*

D. 1. *Fuistes* 2. *Decíme* 3. *pertenecés* 4. *vos* 5. *querés, andá*

LECCION 17

A. 1. *Sigo* 2. *estuvo/ha estado* 3. *va* 4. *anda/andará* 5. *ir/andar, vayamos* 6. *Hemos estado* 7. *Andábamos* 8. *sigue* 9. *está* 10. *Seguid*

B. 1. *El cirujano está lavándose las manos/se está lavando las manos.* 2. *¡No me estás escuchando!* 3. *¡Estamos buscándooslo/Os lo estamos buscando, no os inquietéis!* 4. *Juan estaba contándonoslo/nos lo estaba contando cuando entró Karina.* 5. *¡Estaba diciéndoles/les estaba diciendo a los Gómez que vengan a ver al paciente cuando quieran!*

C. 1. The surgeon is washing his hands. 2. You're not listening to me! 3. We're looking for it for you; don't worry! 4. Juan was telling it to us when Karina came in! 5. I was just telling the Gomezes to come and see the patient whenever they like!

LECCION 18

A. 1. *cómo, este* 2. *mí, tú, El* 3. *Esta, ésa* 4. *Dónde, está, está* 5. *se, sé, si*

B. 1. *países, esfuerzo extraordinario, disminuir* 2. *internacional, manejada con idoneidad.* 3. *Estados Unidos, latinoamericanos, refugiados políticos* 4. *Naciones Unidas, moviliza su ejército, militares, tal* 5. *opción, alcance* 6. *Corea, lejano* 7. *El francés, italiano* 8. *chinos, antigüedad* 9. *dictaduras, imponen, pueblos* 10. *ministro, relaciones exteriores, presuntamente, complicaciones, durante, OEA*

LECCION 19

A. 1. *¡Sea quien sea/Quienquiera que sea dile que no estoy en casa!* 2. *¡Vayamos adónde sea, sólo quiero salir hoy!* 3. *¡Cueste lo que cueste, quiero comprar esta ropa!* 4. *Fuera de quien fuera, el abrigo ya no está donde lo puse.* 5. *¡No importa cuanto le dé de comer, mi gato siempre tiene hambre!* 6. *Lo mires como lo mires, es un asunto sospechoso.* 7. *¡Digas lo que digas, me gusta el lomo más!* 8. *¡Dijeras lo que le dijeras, lo habría hecho de todos modos!* 9. *Prepara la crema catalana cuando quieras.* 10. *Cuando quieras, podemos ir al hipermercado.*

B. 1. *Ahorita* 2. *casita/casica* 3. *Vivianita/Vivianica, muchachita/muchachica, hermosota* 4. *bebito/bebico* 5. *señorona*

C. 1. *desganado* 2. *encamado* 3. *entremetida* 4. *Despreocúpate* 5. *pormenores*

LECCION 20

A. 1. *ha hecho desaparecer* 2. *ha hecho, sufriera/sufriese* 3. *hizo caer, hizo perder, pelota* 4. *os harán doler* 5. *me hiciste mirar* 6. *hacen tener hambre* 7. *me hizo poner(me)* 8. *hace, miremos* 9. *me hizo, trabajar* 10. *hace, sea, distribuir*

B. 1. *Ay* 2. *Chuy* 3. *Qué, más/tan* 4. *Qué* 5. *Uf*

SEGUNDO REPASO

1. *¡Ésa es la propaganda más cómica que haya visto jamás!* 2. *Cuando tengamos televisión por cable, podremos ver muchos más canales.* 3. *Si Juana hubiera/hubiese sabido cuanto le costaría el auto al fin, no lo habría comprado.* 4. *Si tuvieren algún problema con la transmisión del furgón, llámenme al 345-4533 a cualquier hora.* 5. *Los platanales no permiten que el agua de lluvia arrastre los cafetos montaña abajo.* 6. *Enciende/Pon/ Prende la radio, quizás haya algún buen programa de música clásica esta noche.* 7. *De haberme dicho ayer que los catalanes comen pollo con mariscos, no lo habría creído.* 8. *Me gusta este plato muchos más que aquél.* 9. *El doctor está visitando a un paciente en la sala de emergencias, estará con Vds. en cinco minutos.* 10. *Juan probablemente sigue buscando un departamento en Los Ángeles. Se dice que son muy difíciles de encontrar.* 11. *El Aconcagua es la montaña más alta del continente americano.* 12. *Los indígenas guaraníes habían construído hermosas ciudades en la selva, con la ayuda de los misioneros jesuíticos.* 13. *Vamos al hipermercado, se está/están anunciando una venta especial de frutas hoy.* 14. *No creo que los inversionistas extranjeros quieran invertir en nuestro país hasta que el gobierno tome medidas para disminuir las restricciones de repatriación de capitales extranjeros.* 15. *¿Hay alguien aquí que sepa el número de teléfono de un buen abogado?* 16. *La pelota/El balón se le escapó al arquero del equipo del cual soy hincha hace diez años.* 17. *¿Ves aquel cartel que dice: No se permite fumar en este edificio?* 18. *¿Qué estarán haciendo los López? Como están de vacaciones, andarán tomando sol y nadando en el mar ahora mismo.* 19. *¡Escucharlo hablar al Ministro de Economía me hace querer votar por otro candidato en las elecciones próximas!* 20. *¡Seguid practicando el español, que pronto hablaréis como un nativo!*

APPENDIXES

A. PRONUNCIATION CHART

VOWELS

Spanish Sound	Approximate Sound in English	Example
a	(f<u>a</u>ther)	*España*
e	(<u>a</u>ce, but cut off sharply)	*señor*
i	(f<u>ee</u>)	*día*
o	(n<u>o</u>te)	*hotel*
u	(r<u>u</u>le)	*mucho*
y	(f<u>ee</u>t)	*y* (only a vowel when standing alone)

DIPHTHONGS

Spanish Sound	Approximate Sound in English	Example
ai/ay	(<u>ai</u>sle)	*bailar* *hay*
au	(n<u>ow</u>)	*auto*
ei	(m<u>ay</u>)	*peine*
ia	(<u>ya</u>rn)	*gracias*
ie	(<u>ye</u>t)	*siempre*
io	(<u>yo</u>del)	*adiós*
iu	(<u>you</u>)	*ciudad*
oi/oy	(<u>oy</u>)	*oigo* *estoy*
ua	(<u>wa</u>nd)	*cuando*
ue	(<u>we</u>t)	*bueno*
ui/uy	(s<u>wee</u>t)	*cuidado* *muy*

CONSONANTS

The letters *k* and *w* appear in Spanish in foreign words like *kilowatt, kilometer.* In some countries, the *k* is spelled with the Spanish equivalent, *qu: quilómetro.* The *w* in Spanish sounds like an English *v: kilowatt.*

Spanish Sound	Approximate Sound in English	Example
l/m/n/p/s/t	similar to English	
b	at the beginning of a word or after *m,* similar to English	*bueno*
	elsewhere similar to English, but softer, allowing air to pass between lips, like *v*	*cabeza*
c* (be-fore e/i)	s (<u>c</u>ertain)	*cena*
d	similar to English, but softer, allowing air to pass between lips, like th (<u>the</u>)	*verdad*
	after *n,* as in English: d (<u>d</u>o)	*riendo*
c (before a/o/u)	k (<u>c</u>atch)	*como*
cc	cks (a<u>cc</u>ent)	*lección*
ch	ch (<u>ch</u>urch)	*mucho*
g (before a/o/u)	hard g (<u>g</u>o)	*ganar*
g (before e/i)	hard h (<u>h</u>e)	*gente*
h	always silent	*hasta*
j	hard h (<u>h</u>e)	*jefe*
ll	In Latin America: † y (<u>y</u>et) In Spain: lli (mi<u>lli</u>on)	*pollo*
ñ	ny (ca<u>ny</u>on)	*caña*
qu	k (<u>k</u>ite)	*que*
r	[in middle of word; single trill] (th<u>r</u>ow)	*pero*

* In some regions of Latin America: *s* (vi*s*ion).

† In certain Latin American countries, initial *ll* is pronounced with more friction, like *s* in vision, or j in *j*udge.

r	[at beginning of word; double trill]	*rosa*
rr	[double trill]	*carro*
v	v (<u>v</u>ote, but softer, allowing air to pass between lips)	*viernes*
x	cks (ro<u>cks</u>)	*taxi*
y	y (<u>y</u>et)	*yo*
z*	s	*zona*

* In parts of Spain, *z*—and also *c* before *e* or *i*—is pronounced like English *th*. Examples: *zona, cera, cinco.*

B. VERB CHARTS

I. The Forms of Regular Verbs

INDICATIVE

INFINITIVE	PRESENT AND PAST PARTICIPLES	PRESENT INDICATIVE	IMPERFECT	PRETERITE	FUTURE	CONDITIONAL	PRESENT PERFECT	PAST PERFECT	PRETERITE PERFECT
I. -ar ending hablar to speak	hablando hablado	hablo hablas habla hablamos habláis hablan	hablaba hablabas hablaba hablábamos hablabais hablaban	hablé hablaste habló hablamos hablasteis hablaron	hablaré hablarás hablará hablaremos hablaréis hablarán	hablaría hablarías hablaría hablaríamos hablaríais hablarían	he has ha hemos habéis han + hablado	había habías había habíamos habíais habían + hablado	hube hubiste hubo hubimos hubisteis hubieron + hablado
II. -er ending comer to eat	comiendo comido	como comes come comemos coméis comen	comía comías comía comíamos comíais comían	comí comiste comió comimos comisteis comieron	comeré comerás comerá comeremos comeréis comerán	comería comerías comería comeríamos comeríais comerían	he has ha hemos habéis han + comido	había habías había habíamos habíais habían + comido	hube hubiste hubo hubimos hubisteis hubieron + comido
III. -ir ending vivir to live	viviendo vivido	vivo vives vive vivimos vivís viven	vivía vivías vivía vivíamos vivíais vivían	viví viviste vivió vivimos vivisteis vivieron	viviré vivirás vivirá viviremos viviréis vivirán	viviría vivirías viviría viviríamos viviríais vivirían	he has ha hemos habéis han + vivido	había habías había habíamos habíais habían + vivido	hube hubiste hubo hubimos hubisteis hubieron + vivido

INDICATIVE

	FUTURE PERFECT		CONDITIONAL PERFECT	
I.	habré habrás habrá habremos habréis habrán	} hablado	habría habrías habría habríamos habríais habrían	} hablado
II.	habré habrás habrá habremos habréis habrán	} comido	habría habrías habría habríamos habríais habrían	} comido
III.	habré habrás habrá habremos habréis habrán	} vivido	habría habrías habría habríamos habríais habrían	} vivido

SUBJUNCTIVE

	PRESENT SUBJUNCTIVE	IMPERFECT SUBJUNCTIVE (r)	IMPERFECT SUBJUNCTIVE (s)	FUTURE SUBJUNCTIVE	PRESENT PERFECT SUBJUNCTIVE	
I.	hable hables hable hablemos habléis hablen	hablara hablaras hablara habláramos hablarais hablaran	hablase hablases hablase hablásemos hablaseis hablasen	hablare hablares hablare habláremos hablareis hablaren	haya hayas haya hayamos hayáis hayan	} hablado
II.	coma comas coma comamos comáis coman	comiera comieras comiera comiéramos comierais comieran	comiese comieses comiese comiésemos comieseis comiesen	comiere comieres comiere comiéremos comiereis comieren	haya hayas haya hayamos hayáis hayan	} comido
III.	viva vivas viva vivamos viváis vivan	viviera vivieras viviera viviéramos vivierais vivieran	viviese vivieses viviese viviésemos vivieseis viviesen	viviere vivieres viviere viviéremos viviereis vivieren	haya hayas haya hayamos hayáis hayan	} vivido

307

SUBJUNCTIVE

	PAST PERFECT SUBJUNCTIVE (r)	PAST PERFECT SUBJUNCTIVE (s)	FUTURE PERFECT SUBJUNCTIVE	IMPERATIVE	SIMILARLY CONJUGATED VERBS
I.	hubiera hubieras hubiera hubiéramos } hablado hubierais hubieran	hubiese hubieses hubiese hubiésemos } hablado hubieseis hubiesen	hubiere hubieres hubiere hubiéremos } hablado hubiereis hubieren	¡Habla (tú)! ¡Hable (Vd.)! ¡Hablemos (nosotros)! ¡Hablad (vosotros)! ¡Hablen (Vds.)!	amar, armar, bailar, callar, cambiar, caminar, colonizar, contabilizar, contar, charlar, dar, emigrar, enviar, exportar, felicitar, firmar, ganar, hurtar, ilustrar, importar, indagar, ingresar, immigrar, juntar, lavar, liquidar, llevar, mandar, nombrar, operar, pelear, quedar, realizar, rentar, robar, saldar, sondear, teclear, tocar, visualizar
II.	hubiera hubieras hubiera hubiéramos } comido hubierais hubieran	hubiese hubieses hubiese hubiésemos } comido hubieseis hubiesen	hubiere hubieres hubiere hubiéremos } comido hubiereis hubieren	¡Come (tú)! ¡Coma (Vd.)! ¡Comamos (nosotros)! ¡Comed (vosotros)! ¡Coman (Vds.)!	acceder, beber, ceder, deber, defender, depender, emprender, fenecer, haber, pender, prender
III.	hubiera hubieras hubiera hubiéramos } vivido hubierais hubieran	hubiese hubieses hubiese hubiésemos } vivido hubieseis hubiesen	hubiere hubieres hubiere hubiéremos } vivido hubiereis hubieren	¡Vive (tú)! ¡Viva (Vd.)! ¡Vivamos (nosotros)! ¡Vivid (vosotros)! ¡Vivan (Vds.)!	abrir, batir, combatir, cubrir, decidir, empedernir, subir, surtir, planir, unir

II. Stem-changing Verbs

1. FIRST-CLASS STEM-CHANGING VERBS

Only the tenses in which changes occur are given the following tables. First-class stem-changing verbs have changes in their stems, but are otherwise conjugated like regular verbs.

a) e>ie

INFINITIVE	PRESENT INDICATIVE	PRESENT SUBJUNCTIVE	IMPERATIVE	SIMILARLY CONJUGATED VERBS		
pensar to think	*pienso* *piensas* *piensa* *pensamos* *pensáis* *piensan*	*piense* *pienses* *piense* *pensemos* *penséis* *piensen*	*piensa* *pensad*	*acertar* *apretar* *asentar* *calentar* *cerrar* *confesar*	*despertar* *empezar* *gobernar* *negar* *sentarse* *temblar*	*tentar*
perder to lose	*pierdo* *pierdes* *pierde* *perdemos* *perdéis* *pierden*	*pierda* *pierdas* *pierda* *perdamos* *perdáis* *pierdan*	*pierde* *perded*	*ascender* *atender* *defender* *descender* *encender* *entender*	*extender* *querer* *tender*	

b) o>ue

INFINITIVE	PRESENT INDICATIVE	PRESENT SUBJUNCTIVE	IMPERATIVE	SIMILARLY CONJUGATED VERBS
encontrar to find	*encuentro* *encuentras* *encuentra* *encontramos* *encontráis* *encuentran*	*encuentre* *encuentres* *encuentre* *encontremos* *encontréis* *encuentren*	*encuentra* *encontrad*	*acordar* *almorzar* *contar* *costar* *mostrar* *probar* *recordar*
volver to return	*vuelvo* *vuelves* *vuelve* *volvemos* *volvéis* *vuelven*	*vuelva* *vuelvas* *vuelva* *volvamos* *volváis* *vuelvan*	*vuelve* *volved*	*doler* *llover* *mover* *oler* *poder* *soler*

2. SECOND-CLASS STEM-CHANGING VERBS

Second-class stem-changing verbs undergo the same changes in their stems as other stem-changing verbs, but undergo additional changes in the preterite tense. They are few in number and all belong to the third conjugation.

a) e>ie/i

INFINITIVE	PRESENT INDICATIVE	PRETERITE	PRESENT SUBJUNCTIVE	IMPERATIVE	SIMILARLY CONJUGATED VERBS	
sentir to feel	*siento* *sientes* *siente* *sentimos* *sentís* *sienten*	*sentí* *sentiste* *sintió* *sentimos* *sentisteis* *sintieron*	*sienta* *sientas* *sienta* *sintamos* *sintáis* *sientan*	*siente* *sentid*	*arrepentirse* *diferir* *divertir* *herir* *mentir* *preferir*	*referir* *sugerir*

b) o>ue/u

INFINITIVE	PRESENT INDICATIVE	PRETERITE	PRESENT SUBJUNCTIVE	IMPERATIVE	SIMILARLY CONJUGATED VERBS
dormir to sleep	*duermo* *duermes* *duerme* *dormimos* *dormís* *duermen*	*dormí* *dormiste* *durmió* *dormimos* *dormisteis* *durmieron*	*duerma* *duermas* *duerma* *durmamos* *durmáis* *duerman*	*duerme* *dormid*	*morir* (past participle: *muerto*)

311

3. THIRD-CLASS STEM-CHANGING VERBS

Third-class stem-changing verbs undergo a change from *e* to *i* in their stems. They are few in number and all belong to the third conjugation.

a) e>i

INFINITIVE	PRESENT INDICATIVE	PRETERITE	PRESENT SUBJUNCTIVE	IMPERATIVE	SIMILARLY CONJUGATED VERBS	
seguir to follow	*sigo* *sigues* *sigue* *seguimos* *seguís* *siguen*	*seguí* *seguiste* *siguió* *seguimos* *seguisteis* *siguieron*	*siga* *sigas* *siga* *sigamos* *sigáis* *sigan*	*sigue* *seguid*	*competir* *corregir* *despedir* *elegir* *expedir* *pedir*	*reír* *repetir* *servir* *vestir*

III. Irregular Verb Forms

Spanish verbs can have any or all of four basic types of irregularities in the simple tenses:
a) irregularities in the Present Indicative and Present Subjunctive
b) irregularities in the Preterite and the Imperfect Subjunctive
c) irregularities in the Future and Conditional tenses
d) irregularities in the Imperative

The following chart provides only the forms that are irregular.

INFINITIVE	PRESENT INDICATIVE	PRESENT SUBJUNCTIVE	PRETERITE	IMPERFECT SUBJUNCTIVE	FUTURE	CONDITIONAL	IMPERATIVE
adquirir to acquire	*adquiero* *adquieres* *adquiere* *adquirimos* *adquirís* *adquieren*	*adquiera* *adquieras* *adquiera* *adquiramos* *adquiráis* *adquieran*					
andar to go, to roam			*anduve* *anduviste* *anduvo* *anduvimos* *anduvisteis* *anduvieron*	*anduviera* *anduvieras* *anduviera* *anduviéramos* *anduvierais* *anduvieran*			
caber to fit into	*quepo* *cabes* *cabe* *cabemos* *cabéis* *caben*	*quepa* *quepas* *quepa* *quepamos* *quepáis* *quepan*	*cupe* *cupiste* *cupo* *cupimos* *cupisteis* *cupieron*	*cupiera* *cupieras* *cupiera* *cupiéramos* *cupierais* *cupieran*	*cabré* *cabrás* *cabrá* *cabremos* *cabréis* *cabrán*	*cabría* *cabrías* *cabría* *cabríamos* *cabríais* *cabrían*	
caer to fall	*caigo* *caes* *cae* *caemos* *caéis* *caen*	*caiga* *caigas* *caiga* *caigamos* *caigáis* *caigan*					

(continued)

INFINITIVE	PRESENT INDICATIVE	PRESENT SUBJUNCTIVE	PRETERITE	IMPERFECT SUBJUNCTIVE	FUTURE	CONDITIONAL	IMPERATIVE
dar	doy	dé	di	diera			
to give	das	des	diste	dieras			
	da	dé	dió	diera			
	damos	demos	dimos	diéramos			
	dais	deis	disteis	dierais			
	dan	den	dieron	dieran			
decir	digo	diga	dije	dijera	diré	diría	
to say	dices	digas	dijiste	dijeras	dirás	dirías	dí
	dice	diga	dijo	dijera	dirá	diría	
	decimos	digamos	dijimos	dijéramos	diremos	diríamos	
	decís	digáis	dijisteis	dijerais	diréis	diríais	
	dicen	digan	dijeron	dijeran	dirán	dirían	
hacer	hago	haga	hice	hiciera	haré	haría	
to do	haces	hagas	hiciste	hicieras	harás	harías	haz
	hace	haga	hizo	hiciera	hará	haría	
	hacemos	hagamos	hicimos	hiciéramos	haremos	haríamos	haced
	hacéis	hagáis	hicisteis	hicierais	haréis	haríais	
	hacen	hagan	hicieron	hicieran	harán	harían	
oír	oigo	oiga	oí	oyera			
to hear	oyes	oigas	oíste	oyeras			
	oye	oiga	oyó	oyera			
	oímos	oigamos	oímos	oyéramos			
	oís	oigáis	oísteis	oyerais			
	oyen	oigan	oyeron	oyeran			
poder	puedo	pueda	pude	pudiera	podré	podría	
to be able to	puedes	puedas	pudiste	pudieras	podrás	podrías	
	puede	pueda	pudo	pudiera	podrá	podría	
	podemos	podamos	pudimos	pudiéramos	podremos	podríamos	
	podéis	podáis	pudisteis	pudierais	podréis	podríais	
	pueden	puedan	pudieron	pudieran	podrán	podrían	

(continued)

INFINITIVE	PRESENT INDICATIVE	PRESENT SUBJUNCTIVE	PRETERITE	IMPERFECT SUBJUNCTIVE	FUTURE	CONDITIONAL	IMPERATIVE
poner to put to place	*pongo* *pones* *pone* *ponemos* *ponéis* *ponen*	*ponga* *pongas* *ponga* *pongamos* *pongáis* *pongan*	*puse* *pusiste* *puso* *pusimos* *pusisteis* *pusieron*	*pusiera* *pusieras* *pusiera* *pusiéramos* *pusiérais* *pusieran*	*pondré* *pondrás* *pondrá* *pondremos* *pondréis* *pondrán*	*pondría* *pondrías* *pondría* *pondríamos* *pondríais* *pondrían*	*pon* *poned*
querer to like to want to to love (a living being)	*quiero* *quieres* *quiere* *queremos* *queréis* *quieren*	*quiera* *quieras* *quiera* *queramos* *queráis* *quieran*	*quise* *quisiste* *quiso* *quisimos* *quisisteis* *quisieron*	*quisiera* *quisieras* *quisiera* *quisiéramos* *quisiérais* *quisieran*	*querré* *querrás* *querrá* *querremos* *querréis* *querrán*	*querría* *querrías* *querría* *querríamos* *querríais* *querrían*	
reír to laugh	*río* *ríes* *ríe* *reímos* *reís* *ríen*	*ría* *rías* *ría* *riamos* *riáis* *rían*	 *rió* *rieron*	*riera* *rieras* *riera* *riéramos* *rierais* *rieran*			
saber to know (a fact) to know how to	*sé* *sabes* *sabe* *sabemos* *sabéis* *saben*	*sepa* *sepas* *sepa* *sepamos* *sepáis* *sepan*	*supe* *supiste* *supo* *supimos* *supisteis* *supieron*	*supiera* *supieras* *supiera* *supiéramos* *supierais* *supieran*	*sabré* *sabrás* *sabrá* *sabremos* *sabréis* *sabrán*	*sabría* *sabrías* *sabría* *sabríamos* *sabríais* *sabrían*	
salir to go out	*salgo* *sales* *sale* *salimos* *salís* *salen*	*salga* *salgas* *salga* *salgamos* *salgáis* *salgan*			*saldré* *saldrás* *saldrá* *saldremos* *saldréis* *saldrán*	*saldría* *saldrías* *saldría* *saldríamos* *saldríais* *saldría*	*sal*

(continued)

INFINITIVE	PRESENT INDICATIVE	PRESENT SUBJUNCTIVE	PRETERITE	IMPERFECT SUBJUNCTIVE	FUTURE	CONDITIONAL	IMPERATIVE
tener to have to hold	*tengo* *tienes* *tiene* *tenemos* *tenéis* *tienen*	*tenga* *tengas* *tenga* *tengamos* *tengáis* *tengan*	*tuve* *tuviste* *tuvo* *tuvimos* *tuvisteis* *tuvieron*	*tuviera* *tuvieras* *tuviera* *tuviéramos* *tuvierais* *tuvieran*	*tendré* *tendrás* *tendrá* *tendremos* *tendréis* *tendrán*	*tendría* *tendrías* *tendría* *tendríamos* *tendríais* *tendría*	*ten*
traer to bring	*traigo* *traes* *trae* *traemos* *traéis* *traen*	*traiga* *traigas* *traiga* *traigamos* *tragáis* *traigan*	*traje* *trajiste* *trajo* *trajimos* *trajisteis* *trajeron*	*trajera* *trajeras* *trajera* *trajéramos* *trajerais* *trajeran*			
valer to be worth	*valgo* *vales* *vale* *valemos* *valéis* *valen*	*valga* *valgas* *valga* *valgamos* *valgáis* *valgan*			*valdré* *valdrás* *valdrá* *valdremos* *valdréis* *valdrán*	*valdría* *valdrías* *valdría* *valdríamos* *valdríais* *valdrían*	
venir to come	*vengo* *vienes* *viene* *venimos* *venís* *vienen*	*venga* *vengas* *venga* *vengamos* *vengáis* *vengan*	*vine* *viniste* *vino* *vinimos* *vinisteis* *vinieron*	*viniera* *vinieras* *viniera* *viniéramos* *viniérais* *vinieran*	*vendré* *vendrás* *vendrá* *vendremos* *vendréis* *vendrán*	*vendría* *vendrías* *vendría* *vendríamos* *vendríais* *vendría*	*ven*
ver to see	*veo* *ves* *ve* *vemos* *véis* *ven*	*vea* *veas* *vea* *veamos* *veáis* *vean*					

IV. Auxiliary Verbs

The following irregular verbs, *ser*, *ir*, and *haber* are used as auxiliary verbs, and their conjugations must be memorized.

SER
To Be

PRESENT AND PAST PARTICIPLES	PRESENT INDICATIVE	PRETERITE	IMPERFECT	PRESENT SUBJUNCTIVE	IMPERFECT SUBJUNCTIVE	IMPERATIVE
siendo	*soy*	*fui*	*era*	*sea*	*fuera*	
sido	*eres*	*fuiste*	*eras*	*seas*	*fueras*	*sé*
	es	*fue*	*era*	*sea*	*fuera*	
	somos	*fuimos*	*éramos*	*seamos*	*fuéramos*	
	sois	*fuisteis*	*erais*	*seáis*	*fuerais*	
	son	*fueron*	*eran*	*sean*	*fueran*	

IR
To Go

PRESENT AND PAST PARTICIPLES	PRESENT INDICATIVE	PRETERITE	IMPERFECT	FUTURE	PRESENT SUBJUNCTIVE	IMPERATIVE
yendo	voy	fui	iba	iré	vaya	
ido	vas	fuiste	ibas	irás	vayas	ve
	va	fue	iba	irá	vaya	id
	vamos	fuimos	íbamos	iremos	vayamos	vayamos/vamos
	váis	fuisteis	íbais	iréis	vayáis	
	van	fueron	iban	irán	vayan	

HABER
To Have

PRESENT AND PAST PARTICIPLES	PRESENT INDICATIVE	PRETERITE	FUTURE	PRESENT SUBJUNCTIVE	IMPERATIVE
habiendo	he	hube	habré	haya	
habido	has	hubiste	habrás	hayas	hé
	ha	hubo	habrá	haya	habed
	hemos	hubimos	habremos	hayamos	
	habéis	hubisteis	habréis	hayáis	
	han	hubieron	habrán	hayan	

C. IRREGULAR PAST PARTICIPLES

Past participles are used in the formation of all perfect tenses. The participles in the third column are only used as adjectives, and not with the verb *haber*.

INFINITIVE	PAST PARTICIPLE	ADJECTIVE
abrir	*abierto*	
absorber	*absorbido*	*absorto*
bendecir	*bendecido*	*bendito*
componer	*compuesto*	
cubrir	*cubierto*	
decir	*dicho*	
describir	*descrito*	
disolver	*disuelto*	
escribir	*escrito*	
freir	*freído*	*frito*
hacer	*hecho*	
imprimir	*impreso*	
inscribir	*inscrito*	*inscripto*
morir	*muerto*	
poner	*puesto*	
satisfacer	*satisfecho*	
subscribir	*subscrito*	
ver	*visto*	
volver	*vuelto*	

Note that the derivatives of the above listed verbs contain the same irregularities in their past participles. For example:

INFINITIVE	PAST PARTICIPLE
suponer	*supuesto*
deponer	*depuesto*
entrever	*entrevisto*
prever	*previsto*
deshacer	*deshecho*
disponer	*dispuesto*

D. IRREGULAR GERUNDS

Third conjugation stem-changing verbs undergo stem changes in their gerundive forms.

INFINITIVE	GERUND
dormir	*durmiendo*
erguir	*irguiendo*
sentir	*sintiendo*
pedir	*pidiendo*
podrir	*pudriendo*
venir	*viniendo*

Similar verbs are:

INFINITIVE	GERUND
impedir	*impidiendo*
consentir	*consintiendo*
presentir	*presintiendo*
convenir	*conviniendo*

E. DICTIONARY OF GRAMMATICAL TERMS

active voice—*voz activa:* a verb form in which the actor (agent) is expressed as the grammatical subject. The girl ate the orange—*La chica comió la naranja.*

adjective—*adjetivo:* a word that describes a noun; e.g., pretty—*bonita.*

adverb—*adverbio:* a word that describes verbs, adjectives, or other adverbs; e.g., quickly—*rápidamente.*

agreement—*concordancia:* the modification of words to match the words they describe or are related to.

auxiliary verb—*verbo auxiliar:* a helping verb used with another verb to express some facet of tense or mood.

compound tense—*tiempo compuesto:* verb forms composed of two parts, an auxiliary and a main verb.

conditional—*potencial simple:* the mood used for hypothetical (depending on a possible condition or circumstance) statements and questions. I would eat if . . . —*Comería si . . .*

conjugation—*conjugación:* the forms of a verb that reflect person, number, and tense or mood; i.e., the finite forms (vs. nonfinite forms such as the infinitive or participle).

conjunction—*conjunción:* a word that connects other words and phrases; e.g., and—*y.*

definite article—*artículo definido:* a word linked to a noun indicating it is specific; e.g., the —*el* (masculine singular).

demonstrative—*demostrativo:* a word that highlights something the speaker is referring to; e.g., in this book—*este libro,* this—*este* is a demonstrative adjective.

diphthong—*diptongo:* a sequence of two vowels that glide together and act as a single sound.

direct object—*objeto directo:* the person or thing that directly receives the action of a verb (accusative); e.g., in the sentence, The girl ate the orange.— *La chica comió la naranja.,* the orange—*naranja* is the direct object.

ending—*desinencia:* the suffixes added to the stem of a verb that indicate subject, tense, etc.

gender—*género:* grammatical categories for nouns, loosely related to physical gender and/or word ending. Spanish has two genders: masculine and feminine, e.g., *el chico* (m.), *la chica* (f.).

imperative mood—*modo imperativo:* the command form.

imperfect—*imperfecto:* the past tense used for continuous or habitual actions or states; useful for description of past events.

impersonal verb—*verbo impersonal:* a verb in which the person, place, or thing effected is expressed as the indirect object rather than the subject, e.g., to like (to be pleasing to)—*gustar:* I like chicken—*Me gusta el pollo* (literally: The chicken is pleasing to me).

indefinite article—*artículo indefinido:* a word linked to a noun indicating that it is nonspecific, e.g., a/an—*un*—(masculine singular).

indicative mood—*modo indicativo:* the mood used for factual or objective statements and questions.

indirect object—*objeto indirecto:* the person or thing that is the ultimate recipient of an action, usually introduced by a preposition (dative).

infinitive—*infinitivo:* the basic form of a verb that is unspecified for subject (person or number), tense, or mood; e.g., to speak—*hablar.*

mood—*modo:* the attitude toward what is expressed by the verb; the moods in Spanish are: indicative, subjunctive, and imperative.

noun—*sustantivo:* a word referring to a person, place, thing, or abstract concept; e.g., house—*casa.*

number—*número:* the distinction between singular and plural.

participle—*participio:* an unconjugated, unchanging verb form often used with auxiliary verbs to form compound verb forms or to change a verb to another part of speech; e.g., present and past participles: eating/eaten—*comiente/comido.*

passive voice—*voz pasiva:* a verb form in which the recipient of the action is expressed as the grammatical subject. The orange was eaten by the girl—*La naranja fue comida por la chica.*

perfect—*perfecto:* verb forms used for completed actions. I have eaten—*He comido.*

person—*persona:* the grammatical category that distinguishes between the speaker (first person), the person spoken to (second person), and the person and thing spoken about (third person); often applies to pronouns and verbs.

pluperfect—*pluscuamperfecto:* the past perfect formed with the imperfect of *haber*—to have (in either the indicative or the subjunctive) plus the past participle.

possessive—*posesivo:* indicates ownership; e.g., my—*mi* is a possessive pronoun (genitive).

predicate—*predicado:* the part of the sentence containing the verb and expressing the action or state of the subject.

preposition—*preposición:* a word (often as part of a phrase) that expresses spatial, temporal and other relationships; e.g., on—*en.*

preterite—*pretérito:* the past tense used for completed actions or states; useful for narration of events.

progressive—*progresivo:* verb form used for continuous actions. I am eating —*Estoy comiendo.*

pronoun—*pronombre:* a word taking the place of a noun; e.g., personal, relative, or demonstrative; e.g., I—*yo.*

reflexive verb—*verbo reflexivo:* a verb whose action reflects back to the subject; e.g., to wash oneself—*lavarse.*

root—see **stem.**

simple tense—*tiempo simple:* one-word verb forms conjugated by adding endings to a stem.

stem—*raíz:* the basic element from which a word is derived by adding endings, prefixes, suffixes. Often referred to in the conjugation of verbs. The stem of regular verbs is obtained by dropping the infinitive ending: *-ar, -er,* or *-ir;* e.g., *habl-* from *hablar.*

subject—*sujeto:* the person, place, or thing performing the action of the verb or experiencing the state described by it (nominative).

subjunctive mood—*modo subjuntivo:* the mood used for nonfactual or subjective statements or questions.

tense—*tiempo:* the time of an action or state, i.e., past, present, future.

verb—*verbo:* a word expressing an action or state; e.g., (to) walk—*caminar.*

F. GRAMMAR SUMMARY

1. EL ARTÍCULO DEFINIDO (THE DEFINITE ARTICLE)

	SINGULAR	PLURAL
masculine	*el*	*los*
feminine	*la*	*las*

2. EL ARTÍCULO INDEFINIDO (THE INDEFINITE ARTICLE)

	SINGULAR	PLURAL
masculine	*un*	*unos*
feminine	*una*	*unas*

3. GÉNERO (GENDER)

All Spanish nouns are either masculine or feminine. Some words can be grouped by gender, but there are exceptions and it is best to learn the word with its appropriate article.

Masculine words: nouns that end in *-o, -r, -n,* and *-l;* names of items in nature (e.g., mountains); days of the week and months; words of Greek origin ending in *-ma, -pa,* or *-ta;* verbs, adjectives, etc. used as nouns.

Feminine words: nouns that end in *-a, -dad, -tad, -tud, -ción, -sion, -ez, -umbre,* and *-ie;* names of cities, towns, and fruits.

4. NÚMERO (NUMBER)

To form the plural for words ending in a vowel, add *-s.*

For words ending in a consonant or a stressed í or ú, add *-es.*

Nouns ending in *z* change to *c* in the plural; e.g., *niños felices*—happy children.

5. ADJETIVOS Y CONCORDANCIA (ADJECTIVES AND AGREEMENT)

All adjectives must agree in number and gender with the nouns they describe.

For agreement with plural nouns, add *-s* or *-es* (if the adjective ends in a consonant) to the adjective.

When an adjective ends in -o (in its masculine form), its ending changes into -a when it modifies a feminine noun., e.g., *la mujer rica*—the rich woman. For certain adjectives ending in a consonant (or a vowel other than -o) in the masculine form, add -a for the feminine form; for others, simply use the same form for both genders.

6. Pronombres (Pronouns)

Subject Pronouns

I	*yo*
you	*tú*
he	*él*
she	*ella*
you (polite)	*usted (Vd.)**
we	*nosotros, nosotras*
you (familiar)	*vosotros, vosotras*
you (polite)	*ustedes (Vds.)*
they	*ellos, ellas*

Note: Subject pronouns are often omitted since the verbal endings show who or what the subject is.

Other pronouns, listed according to their corresponding subject pronoun, are:

	DIRECT OBJECT	INDIRECT OBJECT	REFLEXIVE/ RECIPROCAL	POSSESSIVE	PREPOSITIONAL OBJECT
yo	*me*	*me*	*me*	*mi/mió*	*mí†*
tú	*te*	*te*	*te*	*ti/tuyo*	*tí†*
él/ella/Vd.	*lo/la*	*le*	*se*	*su/suyo*	*él/ella/Vd.†*
nosotros, -as	*nos*	*nos*	*nos*	*nuestro*	*nosotros, -as*
vosotros, -as	*os*	*os*	*os*	*vuestro*	*vosotros, -as*
ellos, -as, Vds.	*los/las*	*les*	*se*	*suyo*	*ellos, -as, Vds.*

* *Usted* and *ustedes* are treated as if they were third person pronouns, though in meaning, they are second person (addressee) pronouns. *Ustedes* is used as both familiar and polite and *vosotros, -as* is not used in Latin America.

† These pronouns combine with the preposition *con* in the special forms: *conmigo, contigo,* and *consigo.*

7. Adjetivos y pronombres demonstrativos (Demonstrative Adjectives and Pronouns)

The demonstrative adjectives are:

	SINGULAR	PLURAL	
this	*este, -a*	*estos, -as*	these
that	*ese, -a*	*esos, -as*	those
that over there	*aquel, -ella*	*aquellos, -as*	those over there

To form demonstrative pronouns, simply add an accent to the first *e* in the word, as in *No me gusta éste*—I don't like this one. There are also neuter pronouns used for general ideas or situations: *esto, eso, aquello.*

8. Adverbios (Adverbs)

Form adverbs simply by adding *-mente* (which corresponds to -ly in English) to the feminine form of an adjective, as in obviously—*obviamente.*

9. Negación (Negation)

Form negative sentences by adding *no* before the verb and any pronouns, as in *No lo tengo*—I don't have it.

Many other negative constructions involve the use of two negative words; e.g., *No tengo nada*—I don't have anything/I have nothing.

10. Comparación (Comparison)

Form comparative expressions by placing *más*—more or *menos*—less and *que*—than around the quality being compared, e.g., Juan is bigger than Pepe—*Juan es más grande que Pepe;* Juan runs faster than Pepe—*Juan corre más rápidamente que Pepe.* Use *de* instead of *que* before numbers.

To make equal comparisons, use the expressions *tan . . . como* (before adjectives and adverbs) and *tanto . . . como* (before nouns, with which *tanto* must agree). For example, Juan is as big as Pepe—*Juan es tan grande como Pepe;* Juan has as much money as Pepe—*Juan tiene tanto dinero como Pepe.*

Form superlatives by using an article or pronoun *(el* for adjectives, *lo* for adverbs) with the comparative expressions; e.g., Juan is the biggest—*Juan es el más grande;* Pepe is the least big—*Pepe es el menos grande;* Juan runs the fastest—*Juan corre lo más rápidamente.*

Irregular comparative words:

ADJECTIVE	ADVERB	COMPARATIVE
good—*bueno*	well—*bien*	better—*mejor*
bad—*malo*	badly—*mal*	worse—*peor*
much—*mucho*	much—*mucho*	more—*más*
little—*poco*	little—*poco*	less—*menos*
great—*grande*		bigger—*más grande*
		BUT older—*mayor*
		smaller—*más pequeño*
		BUT younger—*menor*

11. PRONOMBRES RELATIVOS (RELATIVE PRONOUNS)

que	that, who which
quien	who(m)
el, la, los, las cuales	who, which
el, la, los, las que	who, which, the one(s) that/who
lo que	what, which (refers to an entire idea)
cuyo, -a, -os, -as	whose (relative adjective)

12. CAMBIOS DE ORTOGRAFÍA (SPELLING CHANGES)

To keep pronunciation consistent and to preserve customary spelling in Spanish, some verbs in certain tenses change their spelling. The rules are:

In verbs ending in *-car, c* changes to *qu* before *e* to keep the sound hard; e.g., *busqué*—I looked *(buscar).*

In verbs ending in *-quir, qu* changes to *c* before *o* and *a;* e.g., *delinco*—I commit a transgression (from *delinquir).*

In verbs ending in *-zar, z* changes to *c* before *e; comencé*—I began (from *comenzar).*

In verbs ending in *-gar, g* changes to *gu* before *e* to keep the *g* hard; e.g., *pagué*—I paid (from *pagar).*

In verbs ending in a consonant + *-cer/-cir, c* changes to *z* before *o,* and *a* to keep the sound soft; e.g., *venzo*—I conquered (from *vencer).*

In verbs ending in *-ger/-gir, g* changes to *j* before *o* and *a* to keep the sound soft; e.g., *cojo*—I catch (from *coger).*

In verbs ending in *-guir, gu* changes to *g* before *o* and *a* to preserve the sound; e.g., *distingo*—I distinguish (from *distinguir).*

In verbs ending in *-guar,* *gu* changes to *gü* before e to keep the "gw" sound; e.g., *averigüé*—I ascertained (from *averiguar*).

In verbs ending in *-eer,* the unstressed *i* between vowels becomes a *y;* e.g., *leyó*—he read (from *leer*).

In stem-changing verbs ending in *-eir,* two consecutive *i*'s become one; e.g., *rio*—he laughed (from *reir*).

In stem-changing verbs beginning with a vowel, an *h* must precede the word-initial diphthong or the initial *i* of the diphthong becomes a *y;* e.g., *huelo*—I smell (sense) (from *oler*).

In verbs with stems ending in *ll* or *ñ,* the *i* of the diphthongs *ie* and *ió* disappears; e.g., *bulló*—it boiled (from *bullir*).

13. CONTRACCIONES (CONTRACTIONS)

de + el = del
a + el = al

G. NUMBERS

The ordinals after "tenth" *(décimo)* are rarely used in conversation, where they are replaced by the cardinal numbers. They may be heard, however, in formal speech or seen in written language. Note that there are various interchangeable forms for the ordinals beyond ten. The third form (cardinal number + *avo)* is a modern variant of the ordinals.

CARDINAL	ORDINAL
uno	*primero*
dos	*segundo*
tres	*tercero*
cuatro	*cuarto*
cinco	*quinto*
seis	*sexto*
siete	*séptimo*
ocho	*octavo*
nueve	*noveno, nono*
diez	*décimo*
once	*undécimo, décimo primero, onceavo*
doce	*duodécimo, décimo segundo, doceavo*
trece	*décimo tercero, treceavo*
catorce	*décimo cuarto, catorceavo*
quince	*décimo quinto, quinceavo*
veinte	*vigésimo, veinteavo*
veintiuno[1]	*vigésimo primero, veintiunavo*
veintidós	*vigésimo segundo, veintidosavo*
veintitrés	*vigésimo tercer(o), veintitresavo*
veinticuatro	*vigésimo cuatro, veinticuatroavo*
veinticinco	*vigésimo quinto, veinticincoavo*
veintiseis	*vigésimo sexto, veintiseisavo*
veintisiete	*vigésimo séptimo, veintisieteavo*
veintiocho	*vigésimo octavo, veintiochoavo*
veintinueve	*vigésimo noveno/nono, veintinonavo*
treinta	*trigésimo, treintavo*
treinta y uno	*trigésimo primer(o), treinta y unavo*
treinta y dos	*trigésimo segundo, treinta y dosavo*
treinta y tres	*trigésimo tercer (o), treinta y tresavo*
cuarenta	*cuadragésimo, cuarentavo*
cincuenta	*quintésimo/quincuagésimo, cincuentavo*

1. When writing checks, the abbreviated forms of the ordinals *veintiuno, veintidós, veintitrés,* etc., are replaced by *veinte y uno, veinte y dos, veinte y tres,* etc. for clarity.

sesenta	sexagésimo, sesentavo
setenta	septuagésimo, setentavo
ochenta	octogésimo, ochentavo
noventa	nonagésimo, noventavo
cien	centésimo, cienavo/centavo
ciento uno	centésimo primero/primo, cientounavo
ciento dos	centésimo segundo, cientodosavo
ciento tres	centésimo tercer(o), cientotresavo
doscientos	ducentésimo, doscientavo
trescientos	tricentésimo, trescientavo
cuatrocientos	cuadringentésimo, cuatrocientavo
quinientos	quingentésimo, quinientavo
seiscientos	hexagésimo, seiscientavo
setecientos	septingentésimo, setecientavo
ochocientos	octingentésimo, ochocientavo
novecientos	noningentésimo, novecientavo
mil	milésimo
cien mil	cienmilésimo
un millón	millonésimo

H. LETTER WRITING

1. *INVITACIONES Y RESPUESTAS FORMALES*
(FORMAL INVITATIONS AND RESPONSES)
INVITACIONES (INVITATIONS)

marzo de 1993

Jorge Fernández y Sra.—Tienen el gusto de participar a Ud. y familia el próximo enlace matrimonial de su hija Carmen con el Sr. Juan García, y de invitarlos a la Ceremonia que se verificará en la Iglesia de Nuestra Señora de la Merced, el día 6 de los corrientes, a las 6 de la tarde. A continuación tendrá lugar una recepción en la casa de los padres de la novia en honor de los contrayentes.

March 1993

Mr. and Mrs. George Fernandez take pleasure in announcing the wedding of their daughter Carmen to Mr. Juan García, and invite you to the ceremony that will take place at the Church of Nuestra Señora de la Merced, on the 6th of this month at 6 in the afternoon. There will be a reception for the newlyweds following the ceremony at the residence of the bride's parents following the ceremony.

Los señores Suárez ofrecen sus respetos a los señores García y les ruegan que les honren viniendo a comer con ellos el lunes próximo, a las ocho.

Mr. and Mrs. Suárez present their respects to Mr. and Mrs. García and would be honored to have their company at dinner next Monday at 8 o'clock.

Los señores Suárez y Navarro saludan afectuosamente a los señores Del Vayo y les ruegan que les honren asistiendo a la recepción que darán en honor de su hija María, el domingo 19 de marzo, a las nueve de la noche.

Mr. and Mrs. Suárez and Navarro cordially greet Mr. and Mrs. Del Vayo and request the honor of their presence at the party given in honor of their daughter María, on Sunday evening, March 19, at nine o'clock.

RESPUESTAS (RESPONSES)

Los señores Del Vayo les agradecen infinito la invitación que se les han hecho y tendrán el honor de asistir a la recepción del domingo 19 de marzo.

Thank you for your kind invitation. We shall be honored to attend the reception on March 19th.

———————

Los señores García tendrán el honor de acudir al convite de los señores Suárez y entretanto les saludan cordialmente.

Mr. and Mrs. García will be honored to have dinner with Mr. and Mrs. Suárez. With kindest regards.

———————

Los señores García ruegan a los señores Suárez se sirvan recibir las gracias por su amable invitación y la expresión de su sentimiento al no poder aceptarla por hallarse comprometidos con anterioridad.

Mr. and Mrs. García thank Mr. and Mrs. Suárez for their kind invitation and regret that they are unable to come due to a previous engagement.

2. *NOTAS DE AGRADECIMIENTO* (THANK-YOU NOTES)

FORMAL

Queridos señor y señora Juárez:

Les enviamos ésta con nuestras más sinceras expresiones de agradecimiento por el hermoso regalo/la hermosa cena/los inolvidables días con el cual nos han Vds. honrado. ¡Gracias por vuestra infinita hospitalidad!

Carmen

Dear Mr. and Mrs. Juarez:

We send this note along with our most sincere expressions of thanks for the beautiful present/the wonderful evening/the unforgettable days with which you have honored us. Thank you for your infinite hospitality!

Carmen

5 de marzo de 1993

Querida Anita,

La presente es con el fin de saludarte y darte las gracias por el precioso florero que me has enviado de regalo. Lo he colocado encima del piano y no te imaginas el lindo efecto que hace.

Espero verte pasado mañana en la fiesta que da Carmen, la cual parece que va a ser muy animada.

Deseo que estés bien en compañía de los tuyos. Nosotros sin novedad. Te saluda cariñosamente, tu amiga.

Laura

March 5, 1993

Dear Anita,

This is just to say hello and also to let you know that I received the beautiful vase you sent me as a gift. I've put it on the piano and you can't imagine the beautiful effect.

I hope to see you at Carmen's party tomorrow. I think it's going to be a very lively affair.

I hope your family is well. Everyone here is fine.

Your friend,
Laura

3. *CARTAS INFORMALES* (INFORMAL LETTERS)

Mi querido Pepe:

Me ha sido sumamente grato recibir tu última carta. Ante todo déjame darte la gran noticia. Pues he decidido por fin hacer un viaje a Madrid, donde pienso pasar todo el mes de mayo.

Isabel se viene conmigo. A ella la encanta la idea de conoceros.

Los negocios marchan bien por ahora y confío que continuará la buena racha. El otro día estuve con Antonio y me preguntó por ti.

Procura mandar a reservarnos una habitación en el Nacional, que te lo agradeceré mucho.

Escríbeme pronto. Dale mis recuerdos a Elena y tú recibe un abrazo de tu amigo,

Juan

Dear Pepe,

I was very happy to get your last letter. First of all, let me give you the big news. I have finally decided to take a trip to Madrid, where I expect to spend all of May.

Isabel is coming with me. She is extremely happy to be able to meet the two of you at last.

Business is good now and I hope it will keep up that way (literally: "that the good wind will continue"). I saw Anthony the other day and he asked me about you.

I'd appreciate your trying to reserve a room for us in the "National."

Write soon. Give my regards to Helen.

Yours,
John

Nueva York, 13 de Febrero de 19

Querido amigo:

Al llegar a casa después de ese viaje tan interesante, me pongo a escribirte estas líneas. Todavía tengo muy presentes todos esos días inolvidables en tu país: las vistas y la gente de tu hermosa ciudad. Quiero agradecerte la hospitalidad que me has demostrado y la amistad que me has ofrecido. Espero que ésta siga creciendo día a día.

Te envío también algunas fotos que nos sacamos juntos, las demás te las mando en cuanto las reciba. Espero que te guste la que saqué desde al avión: ¡salió hermosísima tu ciudad en el atardecer desde el cielo!

De ahora en más, me tengo que dedicar un poco a mi trabajo, puesto que lo he dejado de lado bastante durante todo este mes. En mi ausencia se han desorganizado un poco las cosas, sabes, es cierto lo que se dice: «El ojo del dueño engorda el ganado.» Espero que puedas venir a visitarme en agosto, como me prometiste. ¡Quiero que me des la oportunidad de mostrarte como nos divertimos aquí, en «La Gran Manzana»!

Bueno, Pablito, escríbeme cuanto antes y manténme al tanto de lo que hagas. No te olvides de tu nuevo amigo que te quiere tan bien.

Mil abrazos de tu amigo,

Daniel

P.D.: ¡Mándale saludos a Paula y a los muchachos de la playa!

New York, February 13, 1996

Dear Friend:

Upon getting home after such an interesting trip, I'm sitting down to write you these lines. The unforgettable days I spent in your country are still very much on my mind: the sights and people of your beautiful city. I want to thank you for the hospitality and the friendship you have offered me. I hope the latter continues to grow day by day.

I'm also sending you some pictures we took together; I'll send you the rest as soon as I get them. I hope you like the one I took from the plane: your city sure looks great from above!

From now on, I'm going to have to dedicate myself to my work a little, as I've left it aside for the whole month. While I was away, things got a little disorganized—you know, what they say is true: "The eye of the owner fattens the cattle." I hope you're able to come in August, as you promised. I want to have the chance to show you how we have a good time here, in "The Big Apple!"

OK, Pablito, write me as soon as possible and let me know what you're up to. Don't forget this new friend that is so fond of you.

A thousand hugs from your friend,

Daniel

P.S.: Send my regards to Paula and the gang at the beach!

Queridísimos nuestros:

       Como se imaginarán, la estamos pasando fantásticamente en este país tan bello. Nos la pasamos paseando, comiendo y bañándonos en el mar. El hotel es de primera, sobre todo por lo amable que es la gente. Mañana nos vamos a ver las pirámides, dicen que son de no perderse. Por supuesto, lo único que nos falta es vuestra presencia.

Mil Besos y Abrazos de,

Mónica y Carlos

A:
Familia Hernández
311 East 89th Street
Apt. 3A
New York, NY 10128

Dearest Family:

       As you can well imagine, we're having a fantastic time in such a beautiful country. We're going around sightseeing, eating, and swimming in the sea. Tomorrow, we're going to see the pyramids —they say they're not to be missed! Of course, the only thing we miss is all of you.

Many hugs and kisses from

Monica & Carlos

To:
The Hernandez Family
311 East 89th Street
Apt. 3A
New York, NY 10128

5. FORMS OF SALUTATIONS AND COMPLIMENTARY CLOSINGS

a) Salutations

FORMAL

Señor:	Sir:
Señora:	Madam:
Señorita:	Miss:
Muy señora mía:	Dear Madam:
Muy señores míos:	Gentlemen:
Estimada señora:	Dear Madam:
De mi mayor consideración:	Dear Sir:
Muy distinguido señor:	Dear Sir:
Muy señora nuestra:	Dear Madam:
Muy señores nuestros:	Gentlemen:
Señor profesor:	My dear Professor:
Excelentísimo señor:	Dear Sir: ("Your Excellency:")
Estimadísimo Padre Antonio:	Dearest Reverend Antonio:
Su Excelencia Monseñor Ramírez:	Your excellency Monsignor Ramirez:
Estimado amigo:	Dear Friend:
Querida amiga:	Dear Friend:

INFORMAL

Don Antonio (Aguilera),	My dear Mr. Aguilera,
Doña María (de Suárez),	My dear Mrs. Suárez,
Señorita Laura (Suárez),	My dear Miss Suárez,
Antonio,	Anthony,
Querida Laura,	Dear Laura:
Mi querida Laura,	My dear Laura:
Amada mía,	My beloved,
Querida mía,	My dear,; My beloved,
Amor,	
Cariño,	Dearest (Romantic)
Mi alma,	

b) Complimentary Closings:

Muy atentamente   Very sincerely yours,
Lo/La saluda atte.,   Sincerely yours,

Cariñosamente.   Affectionately yours,
Atentamente.   Sincerely yours,
Sinceramente.   Sincerely yours,
Afectuosamente.   Affectionately yours,
Quien mucho le aprecia.   Affectionately,
De quien te estima.   Affectionately,
De su amigo que le quiere.   Affectionately,
De tu querida hija.   Your loving daughter,
Besos y abrazos.   ⎫
De todo corazón.   ⎬   With love,
De quien te adora.   ⎭

c) Form of the Letter

Estimado Señor:
or *Muy señor mío:*
(Dear Sir:)

_____
_____
_____

                          Sinceramente,
                          (Sincerely yours,)

Querido Juan:
(Dear John,)

_____
_____
_____

Cariñosamente,
(Affectionately,)

d) Common Formulas

Beginning a letter—

1. *Me es grato acusar recibo de su carta del 8 del corriente. Tengo el agrado de . . .*
   This is to acknowledge receipt of your letter of the 8th of this month. I am glad to . . .

2. *Obra en mi poder su apreciable carta de fecha 10 de marzo . . .*
   I have received your letter of March 10th.

3. *En contestación a su carta de ayer . . .*
   In answer to your letter of yesterday . . .

4. *De conformidad con su carta del . . .*
   In accordance with your letter of . . .

5. *Con referencia a su anuncio en "La Nación" de hoy . . .*
   In reference to your ad in today's issue of *The Nation,* . . .

6. *Por la presente me dirijo a Ud. para . . .*
   This letter is to . . .

7. *Nos es grato anunciarle que . . .*
   We are pleased to announce that . . .

8. *Me es grato recomendar a Ud. al Sr. . . .*
   I take pleasure in recommending to you Mr. . . .

9. *La presente tiene por objeto confirmarle nuestra conversación telefónica de esta mañana . . .*
   This is to confirm our telephone conversation of this morning . . .

Ending a letter—
   1. *Anticipándole las gracias, saludo a Vd. atentamente,*
      Thanking you in advance, I am

   Sincerely yours,

   2. *Anticipándoles las más expresivas gracias, quedamos de Uds.*
      Sinceramente,
      Thanking you in advance, we are

   Sincerely yours,

   3. *Quedamos de Ud. atentos y SS.*
      We remain

   Sincerely yours,

   4. *En espera de sus gratas noticias, me repito de Ud.*
      Sinceramente,
      Hoping to hear from you, I am

   Sincerely yours,

   5. *Esperando su grata y pronta contestación, quedo,*
      Sinceramente,
      Hoping to hear from you at your earliest convenience, I am
      Sincerely yours,

The following are often used when beginning a business correspondence:

   6. *Aprovecho esta ocasión para ofrecerme Sinceramente,*
      . . . I am taking advantage of this opportunity to introduce myself.

   Aprovechamos esta ocasión para suscribirnos,
      Sinceramente,
      . . . We are taking this opportunity to introduce ourselves.

6. FORM OF THE ENVELOPE

a.

Félix Valbueña y Cía
Calle de Zurbarán, 6
Madrid

Señor Don
Ricardo Fitó,
Apartado 5042
Barcelona

b.

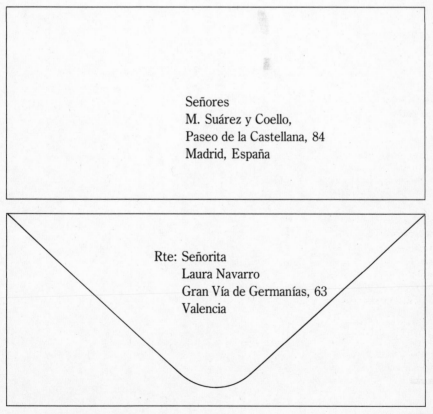

Señores
M. Suárez y Coello,
Paseo de la Castellana, 84
Madrid, España

Rte: Señorita
Laura Navarro
Gran Vía de Germanías, 63
Valencia

GLOSSARY

Abbreviations

adjective	*adj.*	masculine	*m.*
adverb	*adv.*	noun	*n.*
article	*art.*	object	*obj.*
definite	*def.*	plural	*pl.*
direct	*dir.*	possessive	*poss.*
familiar	*fam.*	pronoun	*pron.*
feminine	*f.*	singular	*sg.*
formal	*fml.*	Spain (used in Spain)	*Sp.*
indirect	*ind.*	subjective	*subj.*
literal	*lit.*		

ESPAÑOL-INGLÉS

A

a *to, at, in, on, by, for*
  a bordo *on board*
  a casa *(to) home*
  a causa de *on account of; because of*
  a fondo *completely*
  a menudo *often*
  a pesar de *in spite of*
  a pie *on foot*
  a tiempo *on time*
  a veces *at times*
  al aire libre *in the open air, outdoors*
  al día *up-to-date*
  al fin *finally; at last*
  al (+ infinitive) *on, upon (+ gerund)*
abajo *down*
  río abajo *down the river*
la abertura *opening (physical); gap*

el abogado, -a *lawyer*
el abrigo *overcoat; shelter*
  abril *April*
  abrir *to open*
  abuchear *to boo*
el abuelo,-a *grandfather, grandmother*
  acabar *to finish*
    acabar de *to have just (done something)*
    Acabo de llegar. *I have just arrived.*
el aceite *oil*
  aceptar *to accept*
  aconsejar *to advise*
  acostarse *to go to bed*
  acostumbrarse(a) *to get used/ accustomed (to)*
la actividad *activity*
    actividades diarias *daily activities*
el acto *act*
    acto político *political rally*
el actor *actor*

la actriz *actress*
  actual *contemporary, up-to-date, modern, present-day*
  actualizar *to update, modernize*
    actualizarse sobre las cuestiones *to keep up-to-date on issues*
  actualmente *presently, nowadays (adv.)*
  actuar *to act*
  adiós *good-bye*
  ¿adónde? *where (to)*
  adornar *to decorate*
  adquirir *to acquire*
la aduana *customs*
  llenar la declaración de la aduana *to fill out the customs declaration*
la advertencia *warning*
  advertir *to warn*
  aéreo *air (adj.)*
    transporte aéreo *air transport*
el aeropuerto *airport*
  afeitarse *to shave*
    navaja de afeitar *razor*
la agencia *agency*
    la agencia de cambio *currency exchange office*
    la agencia de viajes *travel agency*
el/la agente *agent*
  agosto *August*
  agotar *to exhaust, to wear out*
    agotarse *to exhaust oneself, wear oneself out*
  agradecer *to be grateful, to thank*
el agricultor *farmer*
el agua *water (f)*
el agujero *hole*
  ahí, allí, allá *there*
  ahora *now*
    ahora mismo *right now*
el aire *air, wind; aspect, look*
    aire acondicionado *air conditioning*
el ala *wing (f.)*
el alcalde/la alcadesa *mayor*
  alegrarse *to be happy*
    alegrarse de *to be happy about*
  algo *something (n.); somewhat (adv.)*
    ¿Algo más? *Something else?*
    El paquete es algo pesado. *The package is somewhat heavy.*
el algodón *cotton*
  alguien *someone*
  algún, alguno,-a *some, any*
el almacén *department store; warehouse*
  almorzar *to eat lunch*

el almuerzo *lunch*
  alquilar *to rent*
    alquilar un coche *to rent a car*
el alquiler *rent; rental; lease*
la altitud *altitude*
  alto,-a *high, tall; loud*
    alta calidad *first-rate; high quality*
    ¡Alto! *Stop!*
  allí, allá (lejos) *there (far away)*
    Están allí. *They're over there.*
  alzar *to lift*
  amarillo, -a *yellow*
el ambiente *environment; room; "ambiance"*
el amigo, -a *friend*
el amor *love*
    amor mío *my darling*
  anaranjado, -a *orange (color)*
el andén *platform*
  animar *to inspire, arouse, excite*
  anoche *last night*
el antiácido *antacid*
  los anteojos *eyeglasses*
  anterior *previous*
  antes *before*
la antigüedad *antiquity; seniority; antique*
    cinco años de antigüedad *five years of seniority*
    tienda de antigüedades *antique shop*
  antipático, -a *unpleasant (person)*
  anunciar *to announce*
    anuncios clasificados *classified ads*
el año *year*
    el año pasado *last year*
    ¡Feliz Año Nuevo! *Happy New Year!*
    por año *yearly, annually*
    todo el año *all year long*
  apagar *to turn off*
    apagar la televisión *to turn off the TV*
el aparato *appliance; equipment*
    aparato de discos compactos *CD player*
    los aparatos electrodomésticos *household appliances*
    los aparatos electrónicos *electronic equipment*
el apartamento/apartamiento *apartment*
el aparto-hotel *apartment hotel*
el apellido *last name, family name*
la apertura *opening (abstract)*
  apetecer *to appeal to*
  aplaudir *to applaud, clap*
  apoyarse *to support oneself (physically)*

aprender *to learn*

aproximarse a *to get close to*

apurado *hurried*

el **apuro** *hurry, rush*

aquel, -lo, -la, -los, -las *that, those (far away) (adj.)*

aquél, -la, -los, -las *that one, those (ones) (pron.)*

aquí *here*
  Está aquí. *It's here.*

archivar *to file*

el **archivo** *file (computer, business) (see legajo)*

la **arena** *sand; arena (sports, bullfighting)*

arrancar *to uproot, pull out; to start up the car*
  arrancar una muela *to pull out a tooth*

el **arranque** *ignition*

arreglar *to fix*
  arreglar las uñas *to do one's nails*

el **arrendamiento** *lease*

arrendar *to lease*
  arrendar un auto *to lease a car*

arriba *on top, above*
  río arriba *up the river*

arribar *to arrive at/in; to reach*

el **arroz** *rice*

el **artículo** *article*

el/la **asaltante** *mugger*

asaltar *to mug, to rob*

el **asalto** *mugging*

ascender *to promote*

el **ascenso** *promotion*
  No había posibilidades de ascenso. *There was no possibility for advancement.*

asegurado *insured*

asegurar *to insure*

el **asesinato** *murder*

así *thus, so*

el **asiento** *seat*
  asiento a la ventanilla *window seat*
  asiento al pasillo *aisle seat*
  asiento delantero *front seat*
  asiento trasero/de atrás *back seat*

asignar *to assign*
  asignar asientos *to assign seats*

la **aspirina** *aspirin*

asustar *to frighten*

atacar *to attack*

atar *to tie, to tie up*

la **atención** *attention*
  prestar atención *to pay attention*

atender *to answer (phone, door), to attend to*

el **ateneo** *political or social club*

el/la **atleta** *athlete*

atrasar *to delay*

el **atún** *tuna*

el **auditorio** *auditorium*

aumentar *to increase*

el **aumento** *increase, growth, raise*

aún *yet (see todavía)*

la **aurora** *dawn, daybreak*

auspiciar *to sponsor (see patrocinar)*

el **auto(móvil)** *car, automobile*

el **autobús** *bus*
  la estación de autobuses *bus station*

el **autocar** *bus (Sp.)*

automático *automatic*

autorizar *to authorize*

el **avance** *advancement, promotion*

el **ave** *bird, fowl (f.)*

la **avenida** *avenue*

el **aviso** *sign*

ayer *yesterday*
  ayer por la tarde *yesterday afternoon*

ayudar *to help*

azul *blue*

B

el **bacalao** *codfish*

bailar *to dance*

bajar *to get off; to go down*
  bajarse del autobús *to get off the bus*
  bajar de peso *to lose weight*

bajo *under, beneath; short*

el **balompié** *soccer (Sp.)*

el **baloncesto** *basketball*

el **banco** *bank*
  en el banco *at the bank*
  ¿Qué servicios ofrece su banco? *What services does your bank offer?*

el **banquero, -a** *banker*

el **bañador** *bathing suit*

bañar *to bathe (someone)*

bañarse *to bathe (oneself)*

el **baño** *bath; bathroom; bathtub*
  baño particular *private bath*

el **bar** *bar*

barato, -a *cheap*

la **barba** *beard*

la **barbería** *barbershop*

el **barbero** *barber*

el barco *boat*
el barquito *a small boat*
el barrio *neighborhood*
   bastante *enough, somewhat, sufficient,*
    rather, fairly
   bastar (le) *to be sufficient, enough*
    me bastan tres días *three days are*
     enough for me
    ¡Basta! *Enough!*
la batata *sweet potato*
la batería *battery*
el batido *milkshake*
el baúl *trunk, chest*
el bautismo *baptism*
   beber *to drink*
la bebida *drink*
    bebida alcohólica *alcoholic drink*
el béisbol *baseball*
   bien *well, right; properly; very; easily;*
    fully; gladly; willingly;
    ¡Bienvenido! *Welcome!*
el bigote *moustache*
el billete *ticket*
    billete de ida y vuelta *round-trip ticket*
la billetería *box office*
   un billón (de) *one billion*
    un billón de pesos *one billion pesos*
   blanco, -a *white*
    en blanco y negro *in black and white*
la blusa *blouse*
la boca *mouth*
el bocadillo *snack; sandwich (Sp.)*
la boda *wedding*
el boleto *ticket*
la bolsa/el bolso *bag, purse*
    la bolsa de valores *stock market*
la bomba *pump; bomb*
    la bomba atómica *atomic bomb*
    la bomba de agua/nafta *water/gas*
    pump
   bonito, -a *pretty, beautiful, graceful*
la botánica *pharmacy (herbs); botany*
el/la botones *bellhop*
el boxeador, -a *boxer*
el boxeo *boxing*
el brazo *arm*
la broma *joke, jest*
   bromear *to joke, to have fun*
   broncearse *to get a tan*
el buceo *scuba diving*
    hacer buceo; bucear *to go scuba diving*
   bueno, -a *good; okay.*
    Buenos días. *Good morning.*

    Buenas noches. *Good evening. Good*
     night.
    Buenas tardes. *Good afternoon.*
el bufé *buffet*
la bujía *spark plug*
   buscar *to look for*
    buscando un departamento *looking for*
    an apartment
    buscando un trabajo *looking for a job*
    ¿Qué tipo de departamento busca
    Vd.? *What kind of apartment are you*
    looking for?
   butifarras *spicy Catalonian sausages*
el buzón *mailbox*
    echar al buzón *to mail*

C

el cabello *hair*
la cabeza *head*
    el dolor de cabeza *headache*
el cable *cable*
   cada *each*
el café *coffee; café*
el cafeto *coffee plant*
la caja *box; case; coffin; chest*
    caja de cambios *gearbox (of a vehicle)*
    caja de valores *safety-deposit box*
el cajero *teller*
    cajero automático *automatic teller*
    machine
la cajita *small box*
los calcetines *socks*
la calidad *quality; condition, capacity*
   caliente *warm, hot*
la calificación *grade, mark*
el calor *heat*
   callarse *to be quiet*
    ¡Cállate! *Be quiet!*
la calle *street*
la cama *bed*
la cámara *room, chamber; camera*
    cámara de comercio *chamber of commerce*
    cámara de video *video camera*
    cámara a lenta *slow motion*
los camarones *shrimps*
   cambiar *to cash; to change*
    cambiar dólares a/en pesos *to change*
    dollars into pesos
    cambiar el canal *to change channels*
    cambiar un cheque de viajero *to cash a*
    traveler's check

el cambio *change, exchange*
>la agencia de cambio *currency exchange office*
>el cambio de marchas *gear shift*

caminar *to walk*

la camisa *shirt, chemise*

el campo *countryside; (sports) field; area (of interest); background*

el canal *channel, station*
>cambiar el canal *to change channels*

la canción *song*

la cancha *playing field; court (sports)*

el candidato *candidate*

la canoa *canoe*

la cantidad *sum, quantity, amount*

la caña de azúcar *sugar cane*

la capacidad *capacity; ability*

la capa *cape*

el capó *hood (car)*

el capote *cape of a bullfighter*

¡Caramba! *Damn!*

¡Caray! *Good heavens! Damn!*

el carbohidrato (el hidrato de carbono) *carbohydrate*

la cárcel *prison*

la carga *charge (of a battery); load*
>Llevaré cargas livianas. *I'll carry light loads.*

cargar *to load, to charge*
>Tengo que recargar la batería. *I have to recharge my battery.*

el cargo *responsibility; work load; job, position*

la caries (de dientes) *cavity (tooth)*

la carne *meat, flesh*
>la carne de res/vaca *beef*

la carnicería *butcher shop*

caro, -a *expensive*
>Es carísimo. *It's very expensive.*

el carrito *shopping cart*

el carro *cart; car, autobmobile (Caribbean)*

la carretera *road*
>servicio de carretera *road service*

la carta *letter; card*
>la carta-llave *card-key*
>cartas de referencia *letters of recommendation*

la cartelera *movie listings*
>consultar la cartelera *to check the movie listings*

el cartero, -a *mailman*

la casa *house; home*
>Jorge está en casa. *Jorge is at home.*

>Julia va a casa. *Julia is going home.*

la casilla *security box, slot*
>la casilla de correo *post office box*

la caspa *dandruff*

catorce *fourteen*

cebar *to serve mate; to feed animals*

la cebolla *onion*

la celebración *celebration*

celebrar *to celebrate*

la cena *supper, dinner*

cenar *to dine, to eat dinner*

el centavo *cent*

centígrado, -a *centigrade, Celsius*

el centro *center, middle, core; club, social; downtown; circle*
>el centro de turismo *tourist office*
>centro comerciale *shopping center*

cepillarse *to brush one's teeth/hair*

el cepillo *brush*
>cepillo de dientes *toothbrush*

cerca (de) *near, nearby*

cero *zero*

la certificación *certification*

certificado, -a *registered (mail)*

certificar *to register*

la cerveza *beer*

el champán *champagne*

la champaña *champagne*

el champú *shampoo*

charlar *to chat*

la chaqueta *jacket, coat*

el cheque *check*
>el cheque de viajero *traveler's check*

la chequera *checkbook*

chico *small*

el chico, -a *boy, girl*

la china *orange (Puerto Rico)*

chiquito, -a *very small*

el chiquito, la chiquita *little child*

los chismes *gossip*
>columna de chismes *gossip column*

chocante *shocking*

el choclo *maiz, corn (Latin America)*

el chorizo *sausage*

la chuleta *cutlet, chop*
>chuleta de cordero *lamb chop*
>chuleta de puerco *pork chop*

el churrasco *steak (Latin America)*

cien(to) *one hundred*
>ciento un, uno, -a *one hundred and one*

cierto, -a *certain; certainly*

el cigarrillo *cigarette*

el cigarro *cigar; cigarette (Mexican)*

cinco *five*
cincuenta *fifty*
el cine *movie, movie theater*
  en el cine *at the movies*
el/la cineasta *moviemaker*
la cinta *cassette tape*
la cintura *waist*
el cinturón *belt*
la cita *appointment, date (romantic)*
  hacer una cita *to make an appointment*
  tener cita con *to have a date/*
    appointment with
  citar *to cite, to quote*
la ciudad *city*
el ciudadano *citizen*
  claro *clear*
  ¡Claro! *Of course! Obviously!*
  claro que sí *of course*
la clase *class; kind, type*
  primera clase *first class*
los clasificados *classified ads*
el/la cliente *customer, client*
la clínica *clinic, hospital*
  cobrar *to collect, receive; to gain, acquire;*
    to charge (a price, fee, or penalty)
  cobrar un cheque *to cash a check*
  cobrar mucho/demasiado *to overcharge*
  cobrar un penal *to call a penalty (soccer)*
la cocina *kitchen*
  cocinar *to cook*
el coche *car*
el coche-cama *sleeping car (train)*
el cognado *cognate*
  colgar *to hang up (telephone); to hang*
  colocar *to put, place*
el color *color; tendency; policy; aspect;*
    pretext
  a colores *in color*
la columna *column; spine (anatomy)*
  la columna Dórica *the Doric column*
  columna de chismes *gossip column*
  la columna vertebral *the spine*
la comedia *comedy*
el comedor *dining room*
  comenzar *to begin, commence*
  comer *to eat*
las cómicas *comics*
  tiras cómicas *comic strips*
la comida *food; meal*
  comidas y bebidas *food and drinks*
  ¿cómo? *what? how?*
  ¿Cómo está Vd.? *How are you?*
  ¡Cómo no! *Of course!*

como si *as if*
la compañía *company* (see *empresa*)
  compararse con *to compare with, be*
    comparable to
el compatriota *fellow citizen, fellow*
    countryman
  competente *competent; able, capable*
  altamente competente *highly qualified*
  completo *full, no vacancies*
  comprar *to buy, shop*
  Lo compré la semana pasada. *I bought*
    it last week.
las compraventas *buying and selling,*
    trade
  comprender *to understand*
el computador/la computadora *computer*
  común *usual; common*
la comunicación *communication*
  comunicar *to be talking on the phone*
  con *with*
  con frecuencia *frequently, often*
  con mucho gusto *gladly; with great*
    pleasure
  conmigo *with me*
  consigo *with him, her, you, them*
  contigo *with you*
  concienzudo *conscientious*
  conciente *conscious*
  concluir *to conclude*
el conductor, -a *driver*
la confusión *confusion, perplexity*
el congelador *freezer*
  conocer *to know, be acquainted with,*
    meet
  conseguir *to get, obtain*
el consejo *advice*
la consonante *consonant*
  construir *to construct, build; to*
    construe
  consultar *to check; to consult*
  consultar la cartelera *to check the movie*
    listings
el consultorio *information bureau;*
    consulting room
  consultorio del médico *doctor's office*
la contaminación *pollution*
  contaminación del medio ambiente
    environmental pollution
  contar *to count*
  contar con *to count on*
  contarle a uno *to tell someone something*
  contento, -a *happy*
  continuar *to continue*

348

contra *against*

la **contratación** *contract* (Sp.)

el **contrato** *contract*

convenir *to agree; to convene, to come together* (used in business)

  convenirle a uno *to be convenient, appropriate*

  convenirse *to come to an agreement*

  convenir en *to agree upon*

el/la **cónyuge** *spouse*

la **cooperación** *cooperation*

la **cooperativa** *cooperative*

la **copia** *copy*

la **corbata** *necktie*

el **cordero** *lamb*

el **corredor (-a) de inmuebles** *real estate agent*

el **correo** *post office*

  en el correo *at the post office*

correr *to run*

el **correr** *running; jogging (n.)*

la **corrida de toros** *bullfight*

cortar *to cut*

  cortar un poco *to trim*

el **corte** *haircut*

el **cortometraje** *short film*

la **cosa** *thing*

coser *to sew*

el **cosmético** *cosmetic, make-up*

el **costado** *side*

costar *to cost*

  ¿Cuánto cuesta? *How much does it cost?*

el **crédito** *credit*

creer *to believe*

  No creo. *I don't think so.*

el **crimen** *crime*

el/la **criminal** *criminal*

el **crítico** *critic*

el **crucigrama** *crossword puzzle*

la **cuadra** *block (street)*

cual *the one that, which, who*

  ¿cuál? *what? which one?*

¿cuán? *how much? to what extent? (used with adjectives)*

cuanto *as much as, as many as*

  Compre cuantas naranjas encuentre. *Buy as many oranges as you can find.*

  cuanto más . . . tanto más . . . *the more . . . the more . . .*

¿cuánto? *how much? how many?*

  ¿Cuánto es el pasaje? *How much is the ticket?*

cuarenta *forty*

la **Cuaresma** *Lent*

cuarto *fourth, quarter*

el **cuarto** *room*

cuatro *four*

cuatrocientos, -as *four hundred*

el **cuello** *neck; collar*

la **cuenta** *bill, account; score (game)*

  cuenta corriente *checking account*

  cuenta de ahorros *savings account*

  el estado de cuenta bancaria *bank statement*

el **cuero** *leather*

el **cuerpo** *body*

el **cuidado** *care, attention*

  ¡Cuidado! *Careful! Watch out!*

cuidadoso *careful*

cuidar *to take care of (someone)*

cuidarse *to take care of oneself*

la **culpa** *blame*

el **cultivo** *culture; cultivation; crop*

  cultivo del cuerpo *cult of the body*

el **cumpleaños** *birthday*

  Feliz cumpleaños. *Happy birthday.*

  festejar el cumpleaños *to celebrate one's birthday*

  quinceañera *girl's fifteenth birthday party*

el **cuñado, -a** *brother-in-law, sister-in-law*

la **cuota** *fee; partial pre-set payment on a payment plan*

D

dar *to give; to deal (cards); to show (a movie)*

  dar a *to face, to lead to*

  dar a la calle *to face the street*

  dar a luz *to give birth*

  dar bien con *to go well with, to get along with*

  dar con alguien/algo *to meet, to come upon*

  dar de comer *to feed*

  darle la mano a alguien *to shake hands with someone*

  darse la mano *to shake hands with each other*

  dar las gracias a *to thank*

  dar los buenos días *to say good morning, to greet*

  dar palmadas *to applaud, clap*

dar recuerdas/memorias a *to give one's regards*

dar un paseo *to take a walk or a ride*

darse cuenta *to realize*

dárselo a *to sell it for (a price)*

¡Dese prisa! *Hurry up!*

de *of; from; for; by; on*

¿De dónde es Vd.? *Where are you from?*

de esta manera/modo *in this way*

De nada. *You're welcome.*

de nuevo *again*

de pie *standing*

de pronto/repente *suddenly*

de vez en cuando *from time to time*

la casa de mi amigo *my friend's house*

deber *to need to, must, ought; to owe*

Debemos irnos. *We have to go.*

No me debe nada. *You don't owe me anything.*

débil *weak*

el **débito** *debit*

décimo, -a *tenth*

decir *to say; to tell; to call, name*

¡Diga! ¿Quién habla? *Hello. Who's speaking?*

¡Dígame! *Tell me.*

el decir *speech; saying*

es decir *that is to say*

¡No me diga! *You don't say! Don't tell me!*

Se lo diré. *I'll tell him/her.*

dedicarse a *to dedicate oneself to*

el **dedo** *finger; toe*

dejar *to sell, yield; to leave; to drop off*

dejar a un precio *to sell at a price*

dejar una posición *to leave a job*

¡Déjeme en paz! *Leave me alone!*

delante de *in front of*

delicado, -a *delicate*

demasiado *too much*

la **democracia** *democracy*

el/la **dentista** *dentist*

el **departamento** *apartment*

el **deporte** *sport*

el/la **deportista** *athlete*

depositar *to deposit*

depositar un cheque *to deposit a check*

el **depósito** *(gas) tank; deposit*

certificado de depósito *certificate of deposit*

libreta de depósitos *bank passbook*

derecho, -a *right; straight; right-hand*

a la derecha *to the right*

Sigues derecho. *Go straight ahead.*

el **derecho** *law, justice; claim, title; right*

derechos de aduana *customs duties*

el **desafío** *challenge*

ofrecer nuevos desafíos *to offer new challenges*

desagradable *unpleasant, disagreeable*

desarrollar *to develop*

desarrollar un programa *to develop a program*

el **desastre** *disaster*

desayunar *to have breakfast*

el **desayuno** *breakfast*

descansar *to rest*

el **descanso** *rest*

el **descuento** *discount*

un descuento del 10% *a 10% discount*

desde *starting from (point of departure or commencement)*

Estaré en la oficina desde el lunes. *I'll be at the office starting Monday.*

desear *to want, desire, wish*

el **deseo** *desire, wish*

el **desfile** *parade*

la **desgracia** *misfortune*

el **desinfectante** *disinfectant*

desinflado, -a *flat (tire, etc.)*

el **desodorante** *deodorant*

despegar *to take off (plane)*

el **despegue** *take-off (plane)*

el **despertador** *alarm clock*

despertar *to wake someone up*

despertarse *to wake up (oneself)*

después *after*

después de que *after*

destruir *to destroy*

el/la **detective** *detective*

detener *to stop, detain; to arrest*

¡Deténganlo! *Stop him!*

detrás de *behind*

devolver *to return (something)*

el **día** *day*

los días laborables *workdays*

el **diálogo** *dialogue*

el **dibujo** *drawing*

los dibujos animados *cartoons*

diciembre *December*

el **dictador, -a** *dictator*

la **dictadura** *dictatorship*

el **diente** *tooth*

cepillo de dientes *toothbrush*

pasta de dientes/dentífrica/
dental *toothpaste*

la dieta *diet*
seguir una dieta *to follow a diet*
diez *ten*
diferente *different*
difícil *difficult*
Diga. *Hello. (on the phone, only)*
Dígame, ¿ . . . ? *Tell me . . . ? (phrase used to introduce a question)*
discutir *to argue*
disminuir *to lessen, diminish*
Los dolores comenzaron a disminuirse. *The pain began to diminish.*

el dinero *money*
¡Dios mío! *My God!*
la dirección *address; direction, management*
dirigir *to direct*
el disco *record; dish antenna*
el disco de computadora *computer disk*
el disco flexible *floppy disk*
disco láser *laser disk*
el disco compacto *compact disc (CD)*
el disco rígido/duro *hard disk*
el aparato de discos compactos *CD player*
Disculpe(n). *Excuse me. I'm sorry.*
Disculpe, sí que me he equivocado. *I'm sorry. I have indeed made a mistake.*
Dispense(n). *Excuse me. I'm sorry.*
Dispense, no pensaba molestarle. *Pardon me. I didn't mean to bother you.*

la disposición *arrangement, layout*
a su disposición *at your service*
distinguir *to distinguish*
la diversión *diversion, amusement, entertainment*
diversiones acuáticas *water sports*
divertirse *to enjoy oneself*
¡Qué se diviertan! *Enjoy yourselves!*
la divisa *currency*
el doblaje *dubbing*
doblar *to bend; to dub*
doce *twelve*
el doctor, -a *doctor*
el dólar *dollar*
el dolor *ache, pain; sorrow*
dolor agudo/constante *sharp/constant pain*
el dolor de cabeza *headache*

el dolor de estómago *stomachache*
tener dolores *to have pains*
el doméstico *household*
dominar *to dominate*
domino el inglés *I speak English fluently*
el domingo *Sunday*
Don/Doña *title of respect (m./f.)*
¿dónde? *where?*
¿Adónde vas? *Where are you going?*
¿De dónde es usted? *Where are you from?*
dormir *to sleep*
el dormitorio *bedroom*
dos *two*
los dos *both*
doscientos, -as *two hundred*
la ducha *shower*
la duda *doubt*
dudar *to doubt*
durante *during*

E

echar *to mail*
echar una carta al buzón *to mail a letter*
el editorial *editorial (newspaper)*
efectivo, -a *effective, certain, actual*
el efectivo *money, cash*
pagar en efectivo *to pay in cash*
eficazmente *effectively*
el ejemplo *example*
por ejemplo *for example*
el ejercicio *exercise*
hacer ejercicios *to exercise*
el *the (def. art.)*
él *he*
la elección *election*
la electricidad *electricity*
elegir *to select, elect*
ella *she*
ello *it (used only for abstract nouns)*
por ello *for that reason*
ellos, ellas *they*
el embrague *clutch*
la emergencia *emergency*
¡Es una emergencia! *It's an emergency!*
la emisión *broadcast, show*
emitir *to broadcast*
emocionante *thrilling*
el empaste *filling*
el empaste de la raíz *root canal*

empezar *to begin*

el empleado, -a *employee*

empotrado *built into a wall* (see *incorporado*)

empotrar *to build into a wall*

la empresa *company, enterprise*

en *in; on; at*

en blanco y negro *in black and white*

en casa de *at the home of*

en cuanto a *as for, as regards*

en julio *in July*

en lugar de *instead of, in place of*

en medio de *in the middle of*

en punto *sharp, on the dot*

en realidad *in reality, actually*

en seguida *at once, immediately*

en verano *in summer*

enamorarse de *to fall in love with*

encantador, -a *charming*

encantar *to love, to like*

Me encanta esta pieza. *I like this play.*

encender *to turn on (lights, TV)*

las encías *gums (mouth)*

encoger *to shrink (material)*

encontrar *to find, meet*

encontrarse (en) *to be (at) (formal synonym of* estar*)*

¿(En) Dónde se encuentra el Sr. López? *Where is Mr. López?*

endosar *to endorse*

enfadarse *to get angry*

enfermo, -a *sick, ill, diseased*

el enfermo, -a *patient; invalid*

enfrente de *in front of; opposite*

enjuagar *to rinse*

el enjuague bucal *mouthwash*

el enlace *linking (pronunciation); wedding (formally)*

la ensalada *salad*

ensalada mixta *tossed salad*

la enseñanza *education, teaching of a subject*

entender *to understand*

No entiendo nada. *I don't understand anything.*

la entrada *entrance; ticket*

Deme dos entradas para la platea. *Give me two tickets in the orchestra.*

entrar (en) *to enter*

entre *between*

la entrega *delivery*

entrega inmediata *special delivery*

entrega nocturna *overnight delivery*

entregar *to give, deliver*

entretener *to entertain*

entretenerse *to entertain oneself, have a good time*

el entretenimiento *entertainment*

la entrevista *interview*

entrevistar *to interview*

entrevistar a alguien *to interview someone*

enviar *to send, mail*

enviar por vía aérea/superficie *to send by air/surface mail*

Quiero enviar una carta. *I want to mail a letter.*

envolver *to wrap*

envolver regalos *to wrap presents*

el equipaje *baggage*

facturar el equipaje *to check baggage*

el equipo *equipment*

equipo de video *video equipment*

equipo estereofónico *stereo equipment*

equipo de música/sonido *music/sound equipment*

equivocarse *to be mistaken*

escalera *staircase*

bajar/subir la escalera *to go down/up the stairs*

escapar *to escape*

intentar escapar *to attempt to escape*

la escena *scene*

escoger *to choose*

escoger asientos *to choose seats*

escribir *to write*

escribir felicitaciones *to write greeting cards*

escuchar *to listen*

ese, esa, esos, esas *that, those (adj.)*

ése, ésa, ésos, ésas *that one, those (ones) (pron.)*

el esmalte *enamel*

el esmalte de uñas *nail polish*

eso *that thing, idea, concept*

especial *special*

la especialidad *specialty*

especialidad de la casa *house specialty*

las especias *spices*

la especie *species; type; kind*

una especie de *a kind of*

el espectáculo *show*

el espectador, -a *spectator*

el espejo *mirror*

esperar *to hope*

el esposo/la esposa *husband/wife*

el esquí acuático *water skiing*
  esquiar *to ski*
la esquina *corner*
  en la esquina *on the corner*
la estación *season; station*
  la estación de servicio *gas station*
  estacionar *to park*
el estadio *stadium*
la estampilla *stamp*
  estar *to be*
    ¿Es usted de . . . ?
      Are you from . . . ?
    Está bien. *It's all right.*
    Están cansados. *They are tired.*
    estar de pie *to be standing*
    estar dispuesto a *to be ready to*
    estar enfermo, -a *to be sick*
    estar listo, -a *to be available*
    estar ocupado, -a *to be busy*
    estar para/a punto de *to be about to*
    estar por *to be about to; to be in favor of*
    estar sano, -a *to be healthy*
    estar seguro, -a *to be sure*
    estar triste *to be sad*
    Estoy bien. *I am well.*
  este, esta, estos, estas *this, these*
    (adj.); this, these
  éste, ésta, éstos, éstas *this thing,*
    idea, concept
el estereofónico *stereo; stereophonic*
  equipo estereofónico *stereo equipment*
  esto *this (pron.)*
el estómago *stomach*
el/la estrella *star (performer); (f.) star (sky)*
  estrenarse *to open (a show)*
el estreno *opening (show)*
el/la estudiante *student*
  estudiar *to study*
la estufa *stove*
la etiqueta *price tag, sales tag*
  evitar *to avoid*
el examen *quiz, test*
  examinar *to examine*
  excelente *excellent*
  excluir *to exclude*
la exhibición *exhibition, showing*
  exhibir *to show, to exhibit*
    ¿Qué exhiben esta noche? *What are*
      they showing tonight?
el éxito *hit, success*
la expresión *expression*
  expresión cortés *polite expression*
la extensión *extension (telephone, etc.)*

extra *extra*
el extranjero, -a *foreigner; a foreign*
  country
  Paula se encuentra en el
    extranjero. *Paula is abroad.*

F

la fábrica *factory*
  fácil *easy*
  fácilmente *easily*
la factura *invoice*
  facturar *to invoice, to check*
    facturar el equipaje *to check baggage*
la falda *skirt*
  faltar *to lack*
    faltarle a uno *to need, to be lacking*
    Me falta el tiempo para descansar.
      I need time to rest.
la familia *family*
el farmacéutico, -a *pharmacist*
la farmacia *pharmacy*
la fatiga *fatigue, weariness*
  fatigar *to tire; to annoy*
  favorito, -a *favorite*
el fax *facsimile, fax*
  febrero *February*
la fecha *date*
  fechar; poner la fecha *to date, write*
    the date
la felicitación *greeting; congratulation*
    ¡Felicitaciones! *Congratulations!*
  felicitar *to greet, congratulate*
  feliz *happy*
    ¡Feliz Navidad! *Merry Christmas!*
    ¡Felices fiestas! *Happy holidays!*
  felizmente *happily, fortunately*
  fenomenal *phenomenal*
el fenómeno *phenomenon*
  feo, -a *ugly*
el feriado *holiday*
    Día de la Acción de
      Gracias *Thanksgiving Day*
    Día de la Raza *Columbus Day*
    Día de los Enamorados *Valentine's Day*
    Día de los Trabajadores *Labor Day*
    el Año Nuevo *New Year*
    la Cuaresma *Lent*
    la Navidad *Christmas*
    la Nochebuena *Christmas Eve*
    la Nochevieja *New Year's Eve*
    Pascuas *Easter*

Reyes *Three Kings*
Víspera de Todos los Santos (Noche de Brujas) *Halloween*
festejar *to celebrate*
festejar el cumpleaños *to celebrate one's birthday*
el festival *festival*
el festival de cine *film festival*
la fiebre *fever; excitement*
tener fiebre *to have a fever*
la fiesta *party*
fijar *to fix in place, set*
fijarse en *to check in*
la fila *row*
la filosofía *philosophy*
el fin *end*
el fin de semana *weekend*
el final *end, final*
al final *finally, at last*
las finanzas *finances, financial pages (newspaper)*
firmar *to sign*
¿Dónde firmo el contrato de arrendamiento? *Where do I sign the leasing agreement?*
firmar un cheque *to sign a check*
la forma *shape, form*
el formulario *(legal) form*
llenar un formulario *to fill out a form*
franco *frank, candid*
el franco *franc*
frecuente *frequent*
frecuentemente *frequently*
los frenos *brakes*
la fresa *strawberry*
fresco, -a *fresh, cool*
los frijoles *kidney beans*
frijoles negros *black beans*
frío, -a *cold*
la fruta *fruit*
la frutería *fruit store*
el fuego *fire*
los fuegos artificiales *fireworks*
fuerte *strong*
fumar *to smoke*
sección de no fumar *non-smoking section*
la función *show (play, film, etc.)*
fundir *to fuse*
el fútbol *soccer*
fútbol (norte)americano/ estadounidense *football*
el/la futbolista *soccer player*

G

la gala *gala affair*
hacer gala de algo *to show something off, put on airs about something*
la galería *balcony*
el ganador, -a *winner*
salir ganador *to win*
ganar *to earn, win*
ganarse la vida *to earn a living*
el garaje *garage*
la garantía *guarantee*
la garganta *throat*
el gas *gas*
la gaseosa *carbonated mineral water*
la gasolina *gasoline*
el súper *super gasoline*
la gasolinera *gas station*
el gasto *expense*
general *general, usual*
el general *general*
el género *class, type, gender, material (clothing)*
la gente *people, crowd*
el/la gerente *manager*
gigante(-sco) *gigantic*
el gigante *giant*
la gira *outing, trip*
el giro *money order*
giro postal *postal money order*
el gobernador, -a *governor*
el gol *goal (in sports)*
el gol de taquito *goal made easily with heel (soccer)*
el golf *golf*
gordo, -a *fat, stout*
el gordo *first prize in lottery (Sp.)*
gozar *to enjoy, to possess*
Goza de buena salud. *She enjoys good health.*
la grabadora *recorder*
grabadora para cintas *tape recorder*
video-grabadora *video recorder; VCR*
gracias *thank you*
las gradas *bleachers*
la gramática *grammar*
gran, grande *great (before noun); big (after noun)*
grasoso, -a *greasy*
gratis *free; free of charge (adv.)*
gratuito, -a *free*
gris *gray*
gritar *to yell*

la guanábana *soursop*
guapo, -a *good-looking, attractive*
el guaraní *Tupi-Guarani*
guardar *to store, keep; to guard, take care of*
la guayaba *guava*
la guerra *war*
la guía telefónica *telephone book*
el guineo *sweet banana*
gustar *to like, be pleasing to*
  Como Vd. guste. *As you please.*
  ¿Le gusta a Vd. . . . ?
  Do you like . . . ?
  Me gusta. *I like (it, him, her).*
  Me gusta mucho este modelo. *I like this model a lot.*
  (Me) gustaría . . . + infinitive *I would like to . . .*
  No me gustan. *I don't like them.*
el gusto *taste; pleasure, liking*
  estar a gusto *to feel at home, comfortable*
  ¡Mucho gusto (en conocerle)! *It's a pleasure to meet you.*

H

haber *to have; to be, exist (see also* hay, *below)*
  haber de + infinitive *to be (supposed) to*
  Han de llegar el sábado. *They are to arrive on Saturday.*
las habichuelas *beans*
la habitación *room*
  habitación doble *double room*
  Quisiera una habitación por una noche. *I'd like a room for one night.*
hablar *to talk, speak*
habrá *there will be*
hacer *to make, do; to be (cold, warm, etc.)*
  Hace buen/mal tiempo. *It's good/bad weather.*
  Hace calor/frío. *It's warm/cold.*
  Hace (+ time expression + preterite) *ago*
  hacer compras *to shop*
  hacer daño a *to harm*
  hacer el favor de (+ infinitive) *please (+ command)*
  hacer falta *to lack*

hacer la maleta *to pack one's suitcase*
hacer las uñas *to do one's nails*
hacer un viaje *to take a trip*
hacer una llamada *to make a call*
hacer una pregunta *to ask a question*
hacer una reserva *to make a reservation*
¿Qué tiempo hace? *What's the weather like?*
hacerse *to become*
hasta *until*
  Hasta luego. *See you later.*
  Hasta mañana. *See you tomorrow.*
  hasta que *until*
hay *there is, there are*
  hay que (+ infinitive) *it is necessary; one must*
  Hay que hacerlo. *It has to be done. One must do it.*
  hay (+ noun + que + infinitive) *there is/are (+ noun + verb)*
  Hay trabajo que hacer. *There is work to do.*
  No hay de qué. *Don't mention it. You're welcome.*
el helado *ice cream*
helar *to freeze*
herir *to wound*
el hermanito *younger brother*
el hermano, -a *brother, sister*
el hijo, -a *son, daughter*
  los hijos *children*
hincharse *to swell*
la hinchazón *swelling*
hispano, -a *hispanic*
¡Hola! *Hello!*
el hombre *man*
el hombro *shoulder*
la hora *clock time*
  ¿Qué hora es? *What time is it?*
el horario *schedule*
el horno *oven*
hospedarse *to stay at a hotel*
  ¿Por cuántos días se hospedará en el hotel? *How many days will you be staying at the hotel?*
el hotel *hotel*
hoy *today*
  hoy día *nowadays*
hubo *there was, there were*
el/la huésped *houseguest*
la humedad *humidity, moisture*
húmedo, -a *humid*

I

la idea *idea; mind*
    Es una buena idea. *It's a good idea.*
el idioma *language* (see *lengua*)
  impedir *to prevent*
el impermeable *raincoat*
  importante *important*
  importar *to import*
  imposible *impossible*
  impresora *printer (computer)*
    -de burbujas *bubble-jet*
    -de chorro (de tinta) *ink-jet*
    -(por) láser *laser printer*
    -de (matriz de) puntos *dot-matrix*
los impresos *printed matter*
el impuesto *tax*
  incluir *to include*
  incorporado *incorporated, built-in*
  indicar *to indicate*
  ineficaz *ineffective*
la información *information; inquiry*
la informática *computer science*
    programa de informática *computer program*
  ingresar *to input (data), to enter (a learning institution)*
  inmediatamente *immediately*
  inmediato, -a *immediate*
    de inmediato *immediately*
  inscribirse en *to enroll (in a learning institution)*
  insistir *to insist*
    insistir en *to insist upon*
    insistir en que *to insist that*
  instalar *to install*
la instrucción *instruction*
el instructor, -a *instructor*
  inteligente *intelligent*
  intentar *to attempt*
el interés *interest*
    tasa de interés *interest rate*
  interesar *to interest*
    interesarse en *to be interested in*
  internacional *international*
la intervención *intervention*
el invierno *winter*
la invitación *invitation*
el invitado *guest, invited person* (see *huésped*)
  invitar *to invite*
el inyección *injection, shot (medicine)*

ir *to go*
el izquierdo, -a *left, left hand/side*
    a la izquierda *to the left*

J

el jabón *soap*
  jamas never
el jamón *ham*
el jarabe *syrup*
el jardín *garden*
el jeans *jeans*
el jefe/la jefa *boss*
el jogging *jogging*
  joven *young*
el/la joven *youngster*
    los jóvenes *young people*
el jueves *Thursday*
  jugar a *to play*
    jugar al tenis *to play tennis*
    jugar al volebol *to play volleyball*
el jugo *juice*
  julio *July*
  junio *June*
  junto, -a *together*
  jurar *to swear, to take an oath*

K

el kilo(gramo) *kilogram*
el kilómetro *kilometer*

L

  la *her, you (fml.); it (f.); the (def. art.)*
el labio *lip*
el lado *side*
    al lado de *next to*
el ladrón/la ladrona *thief*
  lamentar *to regret, lament*
la lana *wool*
  largo, -a *long*
el largometraje *feature-length film*
  las *them (people and things); you (fml. pl. and f.); the (pl. def. art.)*
el lavado *washing, laundry*
la lavandería *laundry room*
el lavandero, -a *launderer*
el lavaplatos *dishwasher*
  lavar *to wash*

lavar a seco *to dry-clean*
lavado y planchado *washing and ironing*
lavarse *to wash oneself*
el lavatorio *bathroom (airplane)*
le *to/for him, her, you (fml. ind. obj. pron.)*
la lección *lesson*
la lechería *dairy store*
el lechón *roast suckling pig*
la lechuga *lettuce*
leer *to read*
el legajo *file, docket, dossier*
la legumbre *vegetable*
lejos (de) *far away (from)*
la lengua *tongue; language*
el lenguaje *language (abstract)*
-de computadora *computer language*
-de los animales *"language" of animals*
les *to/for them (m. f. pl.); to/for you (fml. pl. ind. obj. pron.)*
levantar *to lift, raise*
levantar la voz *to raise one's voice*
levantarse *to get oneself up*
la ley *law; legal standard of quality, weight, or measure*
la libra *pound*
libra esterlina *pound sterling*
el libro *book*
el límite *limit, boundary*
el limpia parabrisas *windshield wiper*
limpiar *to clean*
limpiar la habitación *to clean the room*
la limpieza de los dientes *cleaning (teeth)*
la lista *list*
listo, -a *ready*
estar listo *to be ready*
la llamada *call; marginal note*
llamada a larga distancia *long distance call*
llamada de persona a persona *person to person call*
llamada por cobrar *collect call*
llamar *to call*
llamarse *to be called, to be named*
¿Cómo se llama Vd.? *What is your name?*
Me llamo . . . *My name is . . .*
Se llama . . . *His (her, your) name is . . .*
la llanta *tire*
¿Tiene Vd. una llanta de repuesta? *Do you have a spare tire?*

la llave *key*
la llavetarjeta *keycard*
llegar *to arrive; to come; to reach, succeed*
llegar a ser *to become*
puerta de llegada/salida *arrival/ departure gate*
llenar *to fill, fill out*
llenar un formulario *to fill out a form*
llenar una receta *to fill a prescription*
Llene el depósito/tanque. *Fill the gas tank.*
llevar *to carry, bring; to take (time); to wear clothing*
¿Cuánto tiempo lleva el viaje? *How long does the trip take?*
Lléveselo. *Take it.*
llorar *to cry, lament*
llover *to rain*
Llueve./Está lloviendo. *It's raining.*
lo *him, you (fml.); it (m. dir. obj. pron.)*
lo importante *the important thing*
local *local*
la loción *lotion*
loción bronceadora *suntan lotion*
los *them (people and things, m. pl. and m. + f. pl.); you (fml. pl. dir. obj. pron.)*
lucir *to shine*
¡Cómo vas a lucir! *How beautiful you'll look!*
el luchador *fighter, wrestler*
la luna *moon*
el lunes *Monday*
la luz *light; daylight*

M

la madre *mother*
el madrugador, -a *early riser*
magnético, -a *magnetic*
el maíz *corn*
rosetas de maíz *popcorn*
mal, malo, -a *bad*
la maleta *suitcase*
el maletero *porter*
la mancha *stain*
sacar una mancha *to take out a stain*
manera *manner*
de manera que *so then, so as to*
el mango *mango; handle*
el maní *peanut*

la manicura *manicure*
la mano *hand*
mantener *to maintain, support; to hold, keep*
  mantenerse en forma *to keep in shape*
la manzana *apple*
mañana *tomorrow*
  pasado mañana *the day after tomorrow*
la mañana *morning*
  de la mañana *in the morning; a.m.*
  mañana por la mañana *tomorrow morning*
el mapa *map*
el maquillaje *make-up*
la máquina *machine (in general)*
  la máquina filmadora *video recorder (lit., filming machine)*
  la máquina de lavar/secar *washer/dryer*
el/la mar *sea*
maravilloso, -a *marvelous, wonderful*
la marca *brand name*
marcar *to dial, to mark*
el mareo *dizziness; motion-, sea-, air-, travel-sickness*
los mariscos *seafood*
marrón *brown*
el martes *Tuesday*
marzo *March*
más *more; most; over; besides; plus*
  más grande *bigger*
  más pequeño *smaller*
  Es más, . . . *Moreover, . . .*
matar *to kill*
  el matador *primary bullfighter; the one who kills the bull*
mayo *May*
mayor *older (polite); larger*
  al por mayor *wholesale*
  la mayor parte de *most of, the majority of*
  la mayoría *majority*
me *me; to me; myself*
la medianoche *midnight*
las medias *socks, stockings*
el/la médico *medical doctor, physician*
  en el consultorio del médico *at the doctor's office*
medio, -a *half*
el mediodía *noon*
los medios *means*
  los medios de comunicación *means of communication, media*
meditar *to meditate, ponder, consider*

mejor *better; rather*
  Es mejor. *It is better.*
memoria *memory*
  memoria "buffer" (báfer) *buffer memory*
menor *younger; smaller*
  al por menor *retail*
menos *fewer; minor*
  por lo menos *at least*
el menú *menu*
el mercadeo *marketing*
el mercado *market*
  mercado negro *black market*
  mercado paralelo *parallel market*
el mes *month*
la mesa *table*
el mesero, -a *waiter, waitress*
mi, mis *my (poss. adj.)*
mí *me (prep. obj. pron.)*
mientras *while*
el miércoles *Wednesday*
mil *thousand*
millón *million*
mirar *to look at, watch*
  mirando la televisión *watching television*
mismo, -a *same*
  ahí mismo *right there*
la mitad *half*
  la mitad del precio *half price*
la moda *fashion, style*
el/la modelo *model*
moderno *modern*
la modista *seamstress, dressmaker*
molestar *to bother*
Momentito. *Just a moment. One moment.*
la moneda *money, coin*
el montón *pile*
moreno, -a *brunette*
morir(se) *to die*
el mostrador *store counter*
mostrar *to show*
  mostrar su pasaporte *to show one's passport*
el motor *motor, engine*
mucho, -a *much, many, a great deal; hard*
mudarse *to move (one's residence)*
  Tengo que mudarme. *I have to move.*
la muela *molar tooth*
la mujer *woman*
la multa *penalty, fine*
mundial *worldwide*
el mundo *world*

el músculo *muscle*
musculoso *muscular*
la música *music*
muy *very*

N

la nación *nation*
nacional *national*
la nacionalidad *nationality*
nada *nothing*
De nada. *You're welcome. It's nothing.*
nada más *nothing else, nothing more*
nadar *to swim*
nadie *no one, nobody*
la naranja *orange*
la nariz *nose*
la natación *swimming*
nato *born, from birth*
la naturaleza *nature*
La Navidad *Christmas*
¡Feliz Navidad! *Merry Christmas!*
la neblina *mist, light fog*
necesario, -a *necessary*
Es necesario. *It is necessary.*
necesitar *to need*
Necesito información. *I need (a piece of/ some) information.*
negar *to deny*
los negocios *business*
negro, -a *black*
en blanco y negro *in black and white*
nervioso, -a *nervous*
nevar *to snow*
Nieva. *It's snowing.*
el nieto/la nieta *grandchild*
el nilón *nylon*
ningún, ninguno, ninguna, ningunos, ningunas *none, not any*
no *no, not*
la noche *evening, p.m.*
de/por la noche *in the evening, p.m.*
la Nochebuena *Christmas Eve*
la Nochevieja *New Year's Eve*
el nombre *name; noun*
Mi nombre es . . . *My name is . . .*
nombre de pila *given name*
normal *normal*
normalmente *normally*
nos *us; to us; ourselves (obj. pron.)*
nosotros, nosotras *we; us (subj. and obj. pron.)*

notas *notes; school grades (informally)*
las noticias *news*
el noticiero *news broadcast/program*
la (tele)novela *soap opera*
Esta noche pasan nuestra novela favorita. *Our favorite soap opera is on tonight.*
noveno, -a *ninth*
noventa *ninety*
noviembre *November*
el novio, -a *boyfriend, groom, girlfriend, bride*
nuevamente *once again*
nueve *nine*
nuevo, -a *new*
el número *number*
número equivocado *wrong number*

O

obedecer *to obey*
el objetivo *objective, goal*
la obligación *responsibility; obligation*
la obra *work, labor; play, opus (theater); building; repairs (house); deed, action*
la obturación *filling (tooth)*
ochenta *eighty*
ocho *eight*
octavo, -a *eighth*
octubre *October*
ocupado, -a *busy*
ocuparse *to busy oneself*
ocuparse de *to busy oneself with, to be concerned with*
la oferta *(special) offer*
hacer una oferta *to make an offer*
¡Hágame una oferta! *Make me an offer!*
la oficina *office*
ofrecer *to offer*
ofrecerle una posición *to offer someone a job*
ojalá (que) *if only . . . ; I wish, hope (that) . . .*
el ojo *eye; attention, care; keyhole*
¡Olé! *Bravo! (bullfighting)*
oler *to smell*
ese perfume huele a rosas *that perfume smells like roses*
olvidarse (de) *to forget*
once *eleven*
el operador, -a *operator*
el operario, -a *factory worker*

opinar *to give an opinion*
el orador *speaker (person)*
el ordenador *computer*
la oreja *(outer) ear*
os *you; to you (fam. pl.); yourselves*
    (reflexive, obj. pron.)
ostentoso *ostentatious*
el otoño *autumn*
otro, -a, -os, -as *other(s)*
    otra vez *again*
el otro, -a, -os, -as *the other(s) one(s)*

P

el padre *father*
pagar *to pay*
    pagar en/con efectivo *to pay in cash*
    pager mensualmente/por mes *to pay*
      monthly
    ¿Cuánto paga Vd. por mes? *How much*
      do you pay per month?
el pago *payment*
    pagos mensuales *monthly payments*
el país *country*
la panadería *bakery*
los pantalones *pants*
la pantalla *screen*
el pañuelo *handkerchief*
el papel *paper; role, part*
la papeleta *slip (deposit, etc.)*
el paquete *package*
el par *pair*
    un par de zapatos *a pair of shoes*
para *for, toward, in order to*
el parabrisas *windshield*
el/los paraguas *umbrella*
pararse *to stand up; to stop; to stall*
    El motor se paró. *The engine stopped.*
el parasol *beach umbrella*
parecer *to seem*
el parentesco *family relationship*
el/la pariente *relative, family member*
los (alto)parlantes *hi-fi speakers*
participar *to participate; to share (in)*
la partida *departure*
el partido *match (sports); party (political)*
    el partido Comunista *the Communist*
      party
    el partido de fútbol *the soccer match*
partir *to leave*
    ¿A qué hora parte el tren? *At what time*
      does the train leave?

el pasaje *fare; ticket*
    pasaje de ida y vuelta *round-trip ticket*
el pasajero, -a *traveler, passenger*
el pasaporte *passport*
pasar *to spend (time); to show*
    pasar telenovelas (películas) *to show*
      soap operas (films)
    pasar por *to pass by*
Pascuas/La Pascua Florida *Easter,*
    Passover
    domingo de Pascuas *Easter Sunday*
    Semana Santa *Easter week*
la pastilla *pill, tablet*
patrocinar *to sponsor* (see *auspiciar*)
el pecho *chest; bosom*
pedir *to request, ask for*
    pedir direcciones *to ask for directions*
    pedir un préstamo *to ask for a loan*
pegar *to hit; to stick*
el peinado *hairdo*
peinarse *to comb one's hair*
el peine *comb*
la película *film, movie*
    película sentimental *romantic film*
pelirrojo, -a *redhead*
el pelo *hair*
    pelo teñido *bleached hair*
la peluca *wig*
la peluquería *hairdresser's shop*
el peluquero, -a *hairdresser*
pensar *to think, to believe*
    pensar en *to think of/about; to direct*
      one's thoughts to
    pensar de *to think of; to have an*
      opinion of
peor *worse*
pequeño, -a *small*
perder *to lose*
Perdón./Perdóneme.
    Excuse me; I'm sorry
perfectamente *perfectly; fine, excellent*
el periódico *newspaper*
permanecer *to remain*
la permanente *permanent (hair style)*
Permiso./Con Permiso. *Excuse me;*
    Pardon me (to attract attention or ask
    permission)
permitir *to permit, let, allow*
pero *but*
la persona *person*
el personal *personnel*
    Departamento de Personal *Personnel*
      Department

pesar *to weigh*
la pesca *fishing*
    la pesca marina *deep-sea fishing*
el pescado *fish (caught)*
el pez *fish (live)*
el piano *piano*
la picazón *itching*
el pie *foot, leg; footing, basis*
la piel *skin*
la pierna *leg*
la pieza *piece; play; room*
el pijama *pajamas*
los pimentones *peppers*
la piña *pineapple*
la piscina *swimming pool*
    piscina calentada *heated pool*
el piso *floor (building), storey*
la pista *(running) track; clue*
el plan *plan*
la plana *page*
    primera plana *first page*
  planchar *to iron, press (clothes)*
la planta *sole (foot)*
el platanal *plantain field*
el plátano *plantain*
la platea *orchestra (in a theater)*
    butaca de platea *orchestra seat*
el plato *dish*
    plato del día *daily special*
la playa *beach*
    en la playa *at the beach*
    dar a la playa *to face/be on the beach*
la plaza *plaza; square*
    plaza de toros *bullring*
  poco, -a *few*
    poco a poco *little by little*
    por poco *almost*
  poder *to be able, can*
    ¿Podría Vd. (+ infinitive) *Would*
      you . . . ?
    puede ser *perhaps*
el policía *policeman*
    la mujer policía *policewoman*
    ¡Policía! *Police!*
la policía *police force*
el poliéster *polyester*
la política *politics, policy*
el político, -a *politician*
el pollo *chicken*
  poner *to put, to place*
    poner un botón *to put on a button*
    poner la fecha *to date, to write the date*
    poner la mesa *to set the table*

    poner la televisión *to turn on the TV*
    Quiero que pongas la mesa. *I want you*
      to set the table.
ponerse *to put on (clothing); to become,*
    to get
    ¡No se ponga nervioso! *Don't get*
      nervous.
por *by, through, for*
    al por mayor *wholesale*
    al por menor *retail*
    por aquí *this way*
    por ciento *percent*
    por ejemplo *for example*
    por favor *please*
    por fin *finally, at last*
    por lo general *generally*
    por la mañana/tarde/noche *in the*
      morning/afternoon/evening
    por los menos *at least*
    por poco *almost*
    por supuesto *of course*
    por todas partes *everywhere*
    por vía aérea *by air mail*
    por vía superficie *by surface mail*
¿Por qué? *Why?*
porque *because*
portátil *portable*
el portátil *laptop computer*
posible *possible*
postularse *to become a candidate*
el precio *price*
    la mitad del precio *half price*
    precio fijo *fixed price*
    precio máximo *top price*
    último precio *final price*
precioso, -a *handsome, beautiful;*
    precious
preferible *preferable*
preguntar *to ask, inquire*
    ¿Puedo preguntarle algo? *May I ask*
    you something?
el premio *prize*
prender *to seize; to pin; to arrest, to*
    capture
la prensa *press*
preocuparse (por/de) *to worry (about)*
    ¡No os preocupéis! *Don't worry!*
presentar *to present, to introduce, to*
    show
    Le presento a Juan. *I'd like you to meet*
    Juan.
presentarse *to put in an appearance, to*
    show up; to present oneself

el **presidente/la presidenta** *president*
el **preso** *prisoner*
el **préstamo** *loan*
  prestar *to lend*
    prestar atención *to pay attention*
  primavera *spring*
  primer, primero, -a *first*
el **primo, -a** *cousin*
el **problema** *problem*
el **procesador de palabras** *word processor*
la **producción** *production*
  producir *to produce*
el **producto** *product*
el **programa** *program*
  desarrollar un programa *to develop a program*
  prometer *to promise*
  pronto *prompt; quick*
    lo más pronto posible *as soon as possible*
la **pronunciación** *pronunciation*
  propio, -a *own self; fit, suitable*
  proporcionar *to give, to make available, to contribute*
el/la **protagonista** *star (performer)*
  proteger *to protect*
la **proteína** *protein*
  proveer *to provide*
la **publicación** *publication*
el **público** *audience*
el **pueblo** *village, town; people, nation*
el **puerco** *pork*
la **puerta** *door, gate*
  puerta de embarque *departure gate*
  puerta de llegada *arrival gate*
  pues . . . *well, well then . . .*
el **puñal** *knife, dagger*
el **puntaje** *score (game)*
la **puntación** *score (game)*

Q

  que *that, which, who, whom; than*
  ¿Qué? *What? How?*
    ¡Qué bueno! *How wonderful!*
    ¿Qué hacemos? *What do we do?*
    ¿Qué hay de nuevo? *What's new?*
    ¿Qué pasa? *What's going on?*
    ¡Qué ruido! *What a noise!*
    ¿Qué tal? *How's it going? How are things?*

    ¡Qué va! *What nonsense!*
  quedar(se) *to remain; to have left; to fit; to be located*
    ¿Cuántos dólares le quedan? *How many dollars does he (do you) have left?*
    Este traje le queda bien. *This suit fits you well.*
    Esto queda entre los dos. *This is just between the two of us.*
    Le queda un dólar. *He has one dollar left.*
    No me quedan entradas. *I don't have any tickets left.*
    Quédese sentado. *Remain seated.*
  querer *to wish, to want, to desire; to like; to love*
    querer decir *to mean*
    Quiero a mis padres. *I love my parents.*
    Quisiera (+ infinitive) *I would like to . . .*
  querido, -a *beloved, dear*
  quien, -es *who, whom*
    ¿A quién . . . ? *Whom; To whom . . . ?*
    ¿Con quién . . . ? *With whom . . . ?*
    ¿De quién . . . ? *Whose . . . ?*
    ¿Para quién . . . ? *For whom . . . ?*
  quieto, -a *quiet, still*
la **quijada** *jaw*
el **quilómetro** *kilometer*
  quince *fifteen*
la **quinceañera** *girl's fifteenth birthday party*
  quinientos, -as *five hundred*
  quinto, -a *fifth*
  quitar *to take (from someone)*
    ¿Qué se les quitó? *What was taken from you?*
    quitar la llanta *to take off the tire*
    quitarse (+ article of clothing) *to take off*
  quizá(s) *perhaps*

R

el **radio** *radius*
la **radio** *radio*
  el radiograbador *radio/cassette player*
la **radiografía** *x-ray*
  sacar una radiografía *to take an x-ray*
la **raíz** *root*
  rápidamente *rapidly*

rápido, -a *rapid*

el rato *a short while*
   Nos vemos en un rato. *We'll see each other shortly.*

la raya *part (hair)*

la razón *reason; right (see* **tener***)*

reaccionar *to react*

la realidad *reality; truth*

realizar *to accomplish, perform, realize*

la rebaja *discount*
   rebaja de veinticinco por ciento *a 25% discount*

el recado *errand*
   recados domésticos *household errands*

la recepción *lobby, reception desk*

el/la recepcionista *receptionist*

la receta *prescription*

recetar *to prescribe*

recibir *to receive, accept*

el recibo *receipt*

recoger *to pick up*

recomendar *to recommend*

la red *network*

reemplazar *to replace*

el refresco *soft drink, refreshment*

el refrigerador *refrigerator*

regalar *to give a gift*

el regalo *gift, present*
   envolver regalos *to wrap gifts*

regatear *to bargain*

el régimen *program; diet; regime*

reírse *to laugh*
   reírse de *to laugh at, laugh about*

el reloj *watch, clock*

el remedio *remedy, cure; help*
   No me queda otro remedio. *I have no other choice.*

el rendimiento *performance (of a product, person, etc.)*

la renta *earnings, rent*

rentar *to earn rent*

las rentas públicas *finances*

la renuncia *resignation, waiver*

renunciar (a) *to give up, to resign, to surrender, to waive*
   presentar la renuncia *to present a letter of resignation*
   renunciar a pagar *to give up payment*
   renunciar una cuota *to waive a fee*

reparar *to repair*

el reparto *cast (theater)*

el repaso *review*

repente, de repente *suddenly*

repetir *to repeat*
   Repita eso, por favor. *Please repeat that.*

la representación *representation; performance (theater)*

el/la representante *representative, congressperson*

representar *to represent; to express; to perform*
   representar un papel *to play a role*

el repuesto *spare part, extra*

la reseña *review (book, film, theater)*

la reserva *reservation*
   hacer una reserva *to make a reservation*
   Tengo una reserva. *I have a reservation.*

la reservación *reservation*

el resfriado *cold (illness)*

la respuesta *answer*

el restaurante *restaurant*

los resultados *results*

resultar *to turn out to be, to result*

el resumen *résumé*

retirar *to withdraw; to pull back; to conceal*
   retirar dinero *to withdraw money*

el retiro *withdrawal*
   hacer un retiro *to make a withdrawal*

reunirse *to meet, get together*

revisar *to check; to review*
   Revise el aceite. *Check the oil.*
   Revise la batería. *Check the battery.*

el revólver *gun, revolver*

Reyes *Three Kings Day*

el riesgo *risk*

rico, -a *rich*

el río *river*

el rizo *curl*

robar *to rob*

el robo *robbery*

el rock *rock music*

rodar *to film*

rojo, -a *red*

la ropa *clothing*

la rosa *rose*

la roseta: rosetas de maíz *popcorn*

rubio, -a *blond*

el ruido *noise*

S

el sábado *Saturday*
saber *to know, to know how to*
  sabe(s) . . . *you know* . . .
sacar *to draw; to take out, to pull out*
  sacar dinero *to withdraw money*
  sacar una mancha *to take out a stain*
  sacar una muela *to pull out a tooth*
  sacar una radiografía *to take an x-ray*
la sala *living room*
el salario *salary*
el saldo *balance*
la salida *exit*
salir *to leave, to go out*
  ¿De qué andén sale el tren? *From which platform does the train leave?*
  salir bien/mal *to come out well/poorly*
  salir de *to leave (a place); to go out of*
  salir ganador, -a *to win*
el salmón *salmon*
el salón *salon*
  el salón de belleza *beauty parlor*
la salsa *sauce*
la salud *health*
  ¡Salud! *Cheers!*
los saludos *greetings*
el/la salvavidas *lifeguard*
la santería *Afro-Caribbean spiritist religion*
el santo *saint, saint's (birth)day*
  Día de Todos los Santos *All Saint's Day*
el sastre *tailor*
la sastrería *tailor's shop*
el satélite *satellite*
  vía/por satélite *by satellite*
se *to him, her, it, you: oneself, himself, herself, itself; impersonal one, you, they (used to form passive obj. pron.)*
el secador *dryer*
secar *to dry*
la sección *section*
  sección de no fumar *non-smoking section*
la seda *silk*
seguir *to follow; to pursue; to continue*
  Seguí sus instrucciones. *I followed your instructions.*
según *according to*
segundo, -a *second*
seguramente *surely*
la seguridad *security*
seguro, -a *sure*
el seguro *insurance; safety*

  Es seguro. *It is certain.*
  seguro social *social security*
seis *six*
el sello *stamp*
la semana *week*
  el fin de semana *weekend*
  la semana pasada *last week*
  Semana Santa *Easter week*
el senador, -a *senator*
el sendero *country road, path*
sentar *to sit*
  ¡Siéntese! *Sit down! (fml.)*
  ¡Siéntate! *Sit down! (fam.)*
sentir *to feel; to percieve; to regret*
  ¿Sientes? *Do you hear that?*
  ¡Siento mucho calor! *It's hot (weather)!*
el sentir *feeling, opinion, perception*
sentirse *to feel*
  No me siento bien. *I don't feel good*
la señal *signal*
el señor *Mr., sir, gentleman*
la señora *Mrs., madam, Ms.*
la señorita *Miss, Ms.*
septiembre *September*
séptimo, -a *seventh*
la sequía *drought*
ser *to be*
  Fue muy desagradable. *It was very unpleasant.*
  Soy de . . . *I am from . . .*
el servicio *service*
  servicio de carretera *road service*
  servicio de cuarto *room service*
servir *to serve; to do a favor; to be used for*
  ¿En qué puedo servirle? *How can I help you?*
  No sirve para nada. *It's no good./It's good for nothing.*
  ¿Para qué sirve esta máquina? *What's this machine for?*
servirse de *to use, to make use of*
sesenta *sixty*
setenta *seventy*
sexto, -a *sixth*
si *if*
sí *yes, indeed (emphatic)*
  Yo sí sé una cosa. *I do know one thing.*
siempre *always; ever*
siete *seven*
similar *similar*
simpático, -a *pleasant, friendly*
simple *simple*

sin *without*
  sin duda *without doubt*
  sin embargo o *still, however*
sintonizar *to tune in*
el **sobrino, -a** *nephew, niece*
¡Socorro! *Help!*
la **soda** *soda*
  el refresco *soft drink*
sol *sun*
soleado *sunny*
la **solicitud** *application; petition*
la **sombra** *shade*
el **sombrero** *hat*
sonar *to ring*
soñar *to dream*
  soñar con *to dream about*
la **sopa** *soup*
  sopa del día *soup of the day*
subir *to go up; to lift (something) up*
  subir a *to get on (the bus, train, etc.)*
la **sucursal** *branch (agency) of a bank or company*
el **sueldo** *salary*
la **suerte** *luck*
  ¡Buena suerte! *Good luck!*
el **suéter** *sweater*
sufrir *to suffer*
sugerir *to suggest*
  sugerir tácticas de venta *to suggest sales tactics*
el **super** *super (gasoline)*
el **supermercado** *supermarket*
el **surfe** *surfing*
  hacer surfe *to go surfing*

T

el **tacón** *heel (shoe)*
la **táctica** *tactic*
tal vez *maybe, perhaps*
tal(es) *that kind of, such*
  de tal manera *in that way*
  tal(es) como *such as*
también *too, also*
tan *so, so much; as, as much*
la **taquilla** *box office*
  la taquilla del teatro *theater box office*
tarde *late*
  más tarde *later*
la **tarde** *afternoon*
  por/de la tarde *in the afternoon, p.m.*
la **tarifa** *fee*

la **tarjeta** *card*
  la tarjeta de crédito *credit card*
  la tarjeta postal *postcard*
  ¿Cuántos sellos necesito para una tarjeta postal? *How many stamps do I need for a postcard?*
la **tasa** *rate, price; appraisement, measure*
  tasa de cambio *exchange rate*
  tasa de interés *interest rate*
el **taxi** *taxi, cab*
el **taxímetro** *meter (of a taxi)*
la **taza** *cup (of coffee)*
  te *you; to you (fam.); yourself (fam. obj. pron.)*
el **té** *tea*
el **teatro** *theater, playhouse*
la **tecla** *key (of an instrument or computer)*
el **teclado** *keyboard*
teclear *to type*
la **tela** *cloth, material*
telefonear *to telephone*
el **teléfono** *telephone*
  por teléfono *by phone*
  la guía telefónica *telephone book*
la **tele(visión)** *television*
el **televisor** *television set*
  televisor de/a colores *color TV set*
el **telón** *curtain (theater)*
  El telón sube a las ocho. *The curtain goes up at eight.*
el **tema** *theme, subject of a conversation*
temer *to fear*
temprano *early*
tener *to have, to possess; to hold; to take; to be (hungry, warm, etc.)*
  tener acceso a *to have access to*
  tener . . . años *to be . . . years old*
  tener calor/frío *to be warm/cold*
  tener cuidado *to be careful*
  tener en exhibición *to be showing*
  tener éxito *to be successful*
  tener ganas de *to feel like (doing something)*
  tener hambre/sed *to be hungry/thirsty*
  tener la bondad de + infinitive *to be so good as + infinitive*
  tener lugar *to take place*
  tener (mala) suerte *to be (un)lucky*
  tener miedo de *to be afraid of*
  tener planes *to have plans*
  tener prisa *to be in a hurry*
  tener que *to have to*
  tener sueño *to be sleepy*

(no) tener razón *to be right (wrong)*
tener tiempo *to have time*
tener una cita *to have an appointment/
    date*
¿Qué tiene Vd.? *What's the matter with
    you?*
el tenis *tennis*
    jugar al tenis *to play tennis*
    la cancha de tenis *tennis court*
el/la tenista *tennis player*
    teñir *to bleach*
    tercer, tercero, -a *third*
    terrible *terrible*
el testigo *witness*
    ti *you (fam. prep. obj. pron.)*
el tiempo *time; weather*
la tienda *store*
las tijeras *scissors*
la tilde *mark (˜) over the n (ñ)*
el tinte *color (of a dye)*
la tintorería *dry cleaner's*
el tintorero, -a *dry cleaner*
el tío, -a *uncle, aunt*
    los tíos *aunts and uncles*
    tirar *to shoot*
el titular *headline*
la toalla *towel*
el tocadiscos *record player*
    tocar *to touch; to play (an instrument); to
        ring; to concern, to interest*
    ¿A quién le toca? *Whose turn is it?*
    Me tocó un aumento. *I got a raise.*
    ¡No tocar! *Don't touch!*
    Toca el piano. *She plays the piano.*
    tocarle a uno *to be one's turn; to fall to
        one's share*
    todavía *yet; still; what's more*
    todo, -a, -os, -as *all, every*
    todo el mundo *everybody*
    el todo *everything*
    tomar *to take; to eat; to drink*
    tomar el almuerzo *to have lunch*
    tomar el autobús *to take the bus*
    tomar a bien/mal *to take it well, the
        right way/ the wrong way*
    tomar a broma *to take as a joke*
    tomar en cuenta *to take into account*
    tomar el desayuno *to have breakfast*
    tomar interés en *to take an interest in*
    tomar parte en *to take part in*
    tomar el pelo *to make fun of, to tease*
    tomar un trago *to have a drink*
el tomate *tomato*

el torero *bullfighter*
la tormenta *storm*
el toro *bull*
la tortilla *corn flour pancake (Mexico,
    Central America); omelette (Spain)*
la tos *cough*
    el jarabe para la tos *cough syrup*
    la pastilla para la tos *cough drop*
la tostada *(a piece of) toast*
    trabajar *to work*
el trabajo *work, job*
    traducir *to translate*
    traer *to bring*
    ¿Puedo traerlo conmigo? *Can I bring it
        with me?*
la tragedia *tragedy*
el trago *drink (alcoholic)*
el traje *suit; costume*
    traje a medida *a custom-made suit
        (dress)*
el trámite *procedure*
la transacción *transaction*
el transbordador *shuttle*
    el transbordador espacial *space shuttle*
el transbordo *transfer (travel)*
el transporte *transportation*
    tratar(se) *to treat; to deal; to try; to
        discuss*
    ¿De qué se trata? *What's it all about?*
    tratar de *to try to*
    trece *thirteen*
    treinta *thirty*
el tren *train*
    la estación ferroviaria/de trenes *train
        station*
    tres *three*
    tres veces al día *three times a day*
    triste *sad*
    trocar *to exchange; to barter*
    tu *your (sg. fam. poss. adj.)*
    tú *you (sg. fam. subj. pron.)*
    tumbarse *to lie down*

U

    un, uno, -a *one*
la uña *nail*
    el esmalte de uñas *nail polish*
    usar *to use, to be accustomed to; to wear*
    usted (Vd., Vd.) *you (sg. fml.)*
    ustedes (Vds., Vds.) *you (pl. fml. and
        fam. in Latin America; fml. in Spain)*

usual *usual*
usualmente *usually*
las uvas *grapes*

V

las vacaciones *vacation*
    estar de vacaciones *to be on vacation*
    Estoy de vacaciones. *I'm on vacation.*
la vacuna *vaccine*
el vagón *car (of a train)*
    el vagón-restaurante *dining car*
valer *to be worth*
    No vale tanto. *It's not worth that much.*
    Vale. *Okay. (Sp.)*
el valor *value, worth, merit, bravery*
varios, -as *several*
la vecindad *neighborhood*
veinte *twenty*
el velero *sailboat*
la venda *bandage*
    vendar *to bandage, dress (a wound)*
el vendedor, -a *salesperson*
    vender *to sell*
    venir *to come*
    venir a ser *to turn out to be*
la venta *sale*
    venta especial *special sale*
    campaña de ventas *sales campaign*
    tácticas de venta *sales tactics*
la ventanilla *(sales) window*
    ver *to see*
el verano *summer*
las veras *truth; earnestness*
    ¿De veras? *Really?*
la verdad *truth*
    ¿No es verdad? *Isn't it true? Right?*
    ¿Verdad? *Is that so?*
    verde *green*
la verdura *vegetable, greens*
el vértigo *dizziness, vertigo*
    sentir vértigo *to feel dizzy*
el vestido *dress*
la vez *time; turn*
    a la vez *at the same time; while*
    a veces *at times; occasionally*
    algunas/unas veces *sometimes*
    de vez en cuando *from time to time*
    muchas veces *many times*
    otra vez *again*
    tal vez *perhaps*
    una vez, dos veces *once, twice*

viajar *to travel*
el viaje *trip*
    ¡Buen viaje! *Have a good trip!*
    Estoy aquí en viaje de negocios. *I'm here on a business trip.*
    hacer un viaje *to take a trip*
el/la víctima *victim*
el video/vídeo *video*
    equipo de video *video equipment*
la videograbadora *VCR, video recorder*
el viento *wind*
    Hace viento. *It's windy.*
el viernes *Friday*
el vino *wine*
    vino blanco *white wine*
    vino tinto *red wine*
la violación *rape*
la visa *visa*
    visa de negociante *business visa*
    visa de turista *tourist visa*
la visita *visit, call*
    visitar *to visit*
la víspera *eve (before a holiday)*
    Víspera de Todos Los Santos *Halloween*
la vista *view*
    vista a la calle *a view of the street*
    vista al mar *a view of the ocean*
    vivir *to live*
el vocabulario *vocabulary*
el voleibol *volleyball*
    volver *to return*
    volver a (+ infinitive) *to do something again*
    Vuelvo en seguida. *I'll be right back.*
    volverse *to become*
    vos *you (sg. sub. and prep. obj. pronoun)*
    vosotros/vosotras *you (pl. sub. pron., Sp.)*
el/la votante *voter*
    votar *to vote*
    votar por/en un candidato *to vote for a candidate*
el voto *voting, vote*
el vuelo *flight*
    El vuelo está atrasado. *The flight is delayed.*

X

la xenofobia *xenophobia*
    xerocopiar *to photocopy*

Y

y *and*
ya *already; now; finally*
ya no *no longer*
yo *I*
la yuca *yucca, cassava*

Z

la zapatería *shoe repair shop*
el zapatero *shoemaker*
el zapato *shoe*
la zona *zone, area; belt*

ENGLISH-SPANISH

A

able (to be) *poder*
accept (to) *aceptar*
accomplish (to) *realizar*
according to *según*
account *la cuenta*
  checking account *cuenta corriente*
  savings account *cuenta de ahorros*
  statement of account (bank) *el estado de cuenta bancaria*
accustom (to) *acostumbrarse a*
ache *el dolor*
acquire (to) *adquirir*
act *el acto*
act (to) *actuar*
activity *la actividad*
actor *el actor*
actress *la actriz*
actual *real, verdadero*
address *la dirección*
advancement *el avance*
advice *el consejo*
advise (to) *aconsejar*
after *después*
afternoon *la tarde*
  in the afternoon, *por/de la tarde*
again *de nuevo, otra vez, nuevamente*
against *contra*
agency *la agencia*
agent *el/la agente*
agree (to) *acordar (law)*
agricultural *agrícola*
agriculture *agricultura*
aid (to) *ayudar, prestar*
air *el aire*
  air conditioning *aire acondicionado*
  air sickness *el mareo*

airport *el aeropuerto*
aisle *el pasillo*
all *todo, -a, -os, -as*
allergist *alergista*
allergy *alergia*
allow (to) *permitir*
almost *casi; por poco*
already *ya*
also *también*
altitude *la altitud*
always *siempre*
amount *la cantidad*
amplifier *amplificador*
amusement *la diversión, entretención*
anaesthesia *anestesia*
anaesthetician *anestesista*
anaesthesiologist *anestesiólogo*
and *y, e*
angry (to get) *enfadarse*
announce (to) *anunciar*
annoy (to) *molestar*
annulment *anulación*
answer *la respuesta*
answer (to) *atender (door, phone); responder*
antacid *el antácido*
antique *antiguo (adj.)*
  antique shop *tienda de antigüedades*
antiquity *la antigüedad*
any *algún, alguno, alguna*
apartment *el apartamento/apartamiento, el departamento*
appeal *apelación/recurso (legal)*
appeal (to) *apelar/recurrir a (legal)*
appeal to (to) *apetecer*
appearance (to make an) *presentarse*
applaud (to) *aplaudir*
apple *la manzana*
appliance *el aparato eléctrico*

household appliances *aparatos electrodomésticos*
application (for employment) *la solicitud*
appointment *la cita (de negocios)*
 to make an appointment *hacer una cita*
approach (to) *aproximarse a*
April *abril*
area *el área; la zona*
arm *el brazo*
arouse (to) *animar*
arrest (to) *detener, prender*
arrive (to) *llegar, arribar*
 arrival gate *puerta de llegada*
article *el artículo*
as . . . as *tan . . . como*
ask (to) *preguntar*
ask for (to) *pedir*
aspirin *la aspirina*
assign (to) *asignar*
at *a, en*
 at home *en casa*
 at times *a veces*
athlete *el/la atleta, el/la deportista*
attack (to) *atacar*
attempt (to) *intentar*
attend to (to) *atender*
attention *la atención, el cuidado*
 to pay attention *prestar atención*
attractive *guapo (male), atractiva (female), atrayente (abstract)*
 an attractive offer *una oferta atrayente, interesante*
audience *el público*
auditorium *el auditorio*
August *agosto*
aunt *la tía*
automatic *automático, -a*
automobile *el auto, el coche, el carro*
autumn *el otoño*
avenue *la avenida*
avoid (to) *evitar*
awaken (to) *despertar*
 to wake up *despertarse*

B

back *atrás; la espalda (anatomy)*
 back yard *el fondo (de casa/de propiedad)*
bad *mal, malo, -a*
badly *mal*
bag *la bolsa*
baggage *el equipaje*

bakery *la panadería*
balance *el saldo (bank account)*
balcony *la galería*
banana *el guineo; la banana*
"Band-Aid" *el apósito/la "curita"*
bandage *la venda*
bandage (to) *vendar*
bank *el banco*
banker *el banquero, la banquera*
baptism *el bautizo*
bar *el bar*
barber *el barbero, el peluquero, -a*
 barber shop *la barbería, la peluquería*
barley *la cebada*
baseball *el béisbol*
basketball *el baloncesto*
bath *el baño*
bathe (to) *bañar*
bathing suit *el bañador*
bathroom *el baño*
battery *la batería*
 car battery *la batería/el acumulador*
 small battery *la pila*
be (to) *estar; hacer; quedar(se); ser; tener*
 I am well. *Estoy bien.*
 It's warm/cold. *Hace calor/frío.*
 to be right *tener razón*
beach *la playa*
beans *las habichuelas*
beard *la barba*
beautiful *bonito, -a; precioso, -a; guapo, -a*
because *porque*
become (to) *hacerse, llegar a ser, ponerse, volverse*
bed *la cama*
bedroom *el dormitorio*
beef *la carne de res*
beer *la cerveza*
before *antes*
begin (to) *comenzar*
behind *detrás de*
believe (to) *creer, pensar*
bellhop *el/la botones*
beloved *querido, -a*
belt *el cinturón; la zona (area)*
beneath *bajo, -a*
besides *más, además de*
better *mejor*
between *entre*
big *grande*
bill *la cuenta, la factura (business)*

billion *mil millones*
bird *el ave; el pájaro*
birthday *el cumpleaños*
  Happy birthday. *Feliz cumpleaños.*
bit (computer binary digit) *bit/dígito*
    binario
black *negro, -a*
blame *la culpa*
bleach (to) *teñir*
bleachers (stadium) *las gradas*
block (street) *la cuadra*
blond *rubio, -a*
blouse *la blusa*
blue *azul*
boat *el barco*
body *el cuerpo*
boo (to) *abuchear*
book *el libro*
bosom *el pecho*
boss *el jefe/la jefa*
bother (to) *molestar*
boundary *el límite*
box *la caja*
  box office *la billetería, la taquilla*
  safety-deposit box *caja de valores*
boxer *el boxeador, -a*
boxing *el boxeo*
boy *el chico*
boyfriend *el novio*
branch *la sucursal*
brand *la marca*
breakfast *el desayuno*
  to eat breakfast *desayunarse*
bride *la novia*
bring (to) *llevar; traer*
broadcast *la emisión*
broadcast (to) *emitir*
brother *el hermano*
  younger brother *el hermanito*
brother-in-law *el cuñado*
brown *marrón*
brunette *moreno, -a*
brush *el cepillo*
bubble *la burbuja*
buffet *el bufé*
bug (error in computer code) *el error*
build (to) into a wall *empotrar*
building *el edificio*
bullfight *la corrida de toros*
  bullring *plaza de toros*
bullfighter *matador, torero*
bus *el autobús; bus*
  bus station *la estación de autobuses*

business *los negocios*
busy *ocupado, -a*
  The line is busy. *La línea está ocupada.*
busy oneself with (to) *ocuparse de*
but *pero, mas*
butcher shop *la carnicería*
buy (to) *comprar*
by *por*

C

cab *el taxi*
cable *el cable*
  cable TV *la televisión por cable*
cabin *la cabaña*
cactus *el cacto*
  small cactus *la nopal*
CAD (computer-aided design) *el diseño*
    por computadora
cake *la torta*
calculator *la calculadora*
call *la llamada; la visita (visit)*
  collect call *llamada por cobrar*
  long distance call *llamada a larga distancia*
  person to person call *persona a persona*
call (to) *llamar*
CAM (computer-aided
  manufacturing) *la fabricación con*
    ayuda de las computadoras
camera *la cámara*
can (to be able) *poder*
candidate *el candidato*
  to become a candidate *postularse*
canoe *la canoa*
capacity *la capacidad*
capture (to) *prender*
car *el coche, el automóvil, el auto*
  car battery *la batería/el acumulador*
  dining car *el vagón restaurante*
  sleeping car *el coche-cama*
  train car *el vagón*
carbohydrate *el hidrato de carbono/el*
    carbohidrato
carbonated mineral water *la gaseosa*
care *el cuidado, el ojo*
  careful *cuidadoso*
carry (to) *llevar*
card *la tarjeta*
  credit card *tarjeta de crédito*
cart *el carro*
  shopping cart *el carrito*
cartoon *le dibujo animado*

case *la caja*
cash *el efectivo*
cash (to) *cobrar, cambiar*
  to cash a check *cobrar un cheque*
cassette *la audiocinta, el cassette*
  cassette player *el tocacintas*
  cassette recorder *grabadora para cintas*
cast (theater) *el reparto*
cavity *la caries (de dientes)*
cedar *el cedro*
celebrate (to) *celebrar, festejar*
celebration *la celebración*
cent *el centavo/céntimo (Sp.)*
center *el centro*
  shopping centers *centros comerciales*
centigrade *centígrado, -a*
certain *cierto, -a*
challenge *el desafío*
change *el cambio*
change (to) *cambiar*
  to change channels *cambiar el canal*
  to change dollars into pesos *cambiar*
    dólares a/en pesos
channel *el canal*
charge *el cargo*
charge (to) *cobrar, pedir*
charming *encantador, -a*
cheap *barato, -a*
check *el cheque, el talón (Sp.)*
  check book *la chequera, el talonario (Sp.)*
  to cash a check *cobrar un cheque*
  traveler's check *el cheque de viajero*
check (to) *consultar, facturar, revisar,*
  verificar, fijarse en
  check the drawer *fíjate en el cajón*
  check the spelling *revisar/verificar la*
    ortografía
Cheers! *¡Salud!*
chest *el baúl, la caja; el pecho (body)*
chicken *el pollo*
children *los niños; los hijos (progeny)*
chiropractic *la quiropráctica (science)*
chiropractor *el quiropráctico*
choose (to) *escoger/elegir*
chop *la chuleta*
Christmas *las Navidades*
  Merry Christmas! *¡Feliz Navidad!*
  Christmas Eve *la Nochebuena*
cigar *el cigarro*
cigarette *el cigarrillo*
cite (to) *citar*
citizen *el ciudadano*
city *la ciudad*

claim *el derecho*
clap (to) *aplaudir*
class *la clase*
  first class *primera clase*
classified *los clasificados*
clause *la cláusula*
clean (to) *limpiar*
clear *claro, -a*
climate *el clima*
clinic *la clínica*
clock *el reloj*
cloth *la tela*
clothing *la ropa*
club *el centro*
coat *la chaqueta*
codfish *el bacalao*
coffee *el café*
  coffee plant *el cafeto*
coffin *el cajón*
cognate *el cognado*
coin *la moneda*
cold *el frío (weather); el resfriado/resfrío*
  (illness)
collar *el cuello de la camisa*
collect (to) *cobrar*
color *el color; el tinte (dye)*
Columbus Day *Día de la Raza*
column *la columna*
comb *el peine*
comb (to) *peinarse*
come (to) *llegar, venir*
comedy *la comedia*
comics *las cómicas*
  comic strips *tiras cómicas*
communication *la comunicación*
compact disc, CD *el disco compacto/láser*
  compact disc player *aparato de discos*
    compactos
company *la compañía, la empresa*
compare (to) *compararse*
competent *competente*
completely *a fondo*
computation *el cómputo*
compute (to) *computar, calcular*
computer *el computador/la computadora, el*
  ordenador
  computer science *la informática, la*
    computación
  computer program *programa de*
    computación
conceal (to) *esconder, retirar*
concern (to) *tocar (a), concernir*
  concerns *concierne*

conclude (to) *concluir*
condition *la condición*
confusion *la confusión*
congratulate (to) *felicitar*
congressperson *el/la representante/*
  congresista
construe (to) *construir*
continue (to) *continuar, seguir*
contract *el contrato/la contratación (Sp.)*
convene (to) *convenir*
cook (to) *cocinar, cocer (Sp.)*
cool *fresco, -a*
copy *la copia*
corn *el maíz; el choclo (Latin America)*
  corn flour pancake *la tortilla*
corner *la esquina*
  on the corner *en la esquina*
correct *correcto, -a*
cosmetic *el cosmético*
cost (to) *costar, valer*
costume *el traje*
cotton *el algodón*
cough *la tos*
  cough drop *la pastilla para la tos*
  cough syrup *el jarabe para la tos*
count (to) *contar*
country *el país*
countryside *el campo*
course *el curso*
cousin *el primo, -a*
credit *el crédito*
credit (to) *acreditar*
crime *el crimen*
criminal *el/la criminal*
critic *el crítico, -a*
crop *el cultivo*
crossword *el crucigrama*
crowd *la gente*
cry (to) *llorar*
cult *el culto*
culture *la cultura*
cup *la taza*
cure *la cura*
cure (to) *curar*
curl *el rizo*
currency *la divisa*
  currency exchange office *la agencia de*
  cambio
curtain *la cortina, el telón (theater)*
customer *el/la cliente*
customs *la aduana*
  to fill out the customs declaration *llenar la*
  declaración de la aduana

cut (to) *cortar*
cutlet *la chuleta*

D

dagger *el puñal*
dairy store *la lechería*
damage *daño/perjuicio*
damage (to) *dañar/perjudicar*
Damn! *¡Caramba!/¡Caray!*
dance (to) *bailar*
dandruff *la caspa*
date *la cita; la fecha*
  to date, write the date *fechar; poner la*
  fecha
daughter *la hija*
dawn, daybreak *la aurora*
day *el día*
daylight *la luz del día*
deal (to) *dar, tratar*
dear *querido*
December *diciembre*
decorate (to) *adornar*
dedicate oneself to (to) *dedicarse a*
delay *contratiempo, retraso, atraso*
delay (to) *retrasar, atrasar*
delicate *delicado, -a*
deliver (to) *entregar*
delivery *la entrega*
  overnight delivery *entrega nocturna*
democracy *la democracia*
dentist *el/la dentista*
deny (to) *negar*
deodorant *el desodorante*
department *departamento, seccion*
  department store *la tienda, el almacén*
departure *la partida*
  departure gate *puerta de embarque*
deposit *el depósito*
  certificate of deposit *certificado de depósito*
  security deposit *depósito de seguridad*
deposit (to) *depositar*
desire *el deseo*
desire (to) *desear, querer*
despite *a pesar de*
dessert *el postre*
destroy (to) *destruir*
detain (to) *detener*
detective *el/la detective*
develop (to) *desarrollar*
dial (to) *marcar*
dialogue *el diálogo*

dictator *el dictador, -a*
dictatorship *la dictadura*
die (to) *morir(se)*
diet *la dieta, el régimen de alimentos*
different *diferente; distinto, -a*
difficult *difícil*
diminish (to) *disminuir*
dine (to) *cenar*
dining room *el comedor*
dinner *la cena*
diphthongs *diptongos*
direct (to) *dirigir*
direction *la dirección, el lado*
disagreeable *desagradable*
disaster *el desastre*
discount *el descuento, la rebaja*
discuss (to) *tratar*
   Let's discuss that. *Tratemos ese asunto.*
diseased *enfermo, -a*
dish *el plato*
dishwasher *el lavavajillas (machine) (Sp.),*
   el lavaplatos
disinfectant *el desinfectante*
distinguish (to) *distinguir*
diversion *la diversión*
dizziness *el mareo, el vértigo*
   to feel dizzy *sentir vértigo*
do (to) *hacer*
docket *el legajo*
doctor *el doctor, la doctora, el/la médico*
   doctor's office *consultorio del médico*
dollar *el dólar*
doubt *la duda*
   without doubt *sin duda, indudablemente*
doubt (to) *dudar*
downtown *al centro (de la ciudad)*
draw (to) (a figure) *dibujar*
draw (to) (money/funds) *retirar, sacar*
   (dinero/fondos)
dream (to) *soñar*
dress *el vestido*
dressmaker *el/la modista*
drink *la bebida*
   alcoholic drink *bebida alcohólica, el trago*
   soft drink *el refresco*
drink (to) *beber, tomar*
drought *la sequía*
dry (to) *secar*
   dry cleaner *el tintorero, -a*
   dry cleaner's *la tintorería*
   dry clean (to) *lavar a seco*
dryer *el secador; la secadora (clothes dryer)*
dub (to) *doblar*

dubbing *el doblaje*
duck *el pato*
duck (to) *agacharse esquivando*
during *durante*

E

ear (outer) *la oreja*
ear (inner) *el oído*
early *temprano*
   early riser *madrugador, -a*
earn (to) *ganar*
easily *fácilmente*
Easter *Pascuas*
   Easter Sunday *domingo de Pascuas*
   Easter week *Semana Santa*
easy *fácil*
eat (to) *comer, tomar*
   to eat breakfast *desayunar*
   to eat lunch *almorzar*
editorial *el editorial*
effective *efectivo*
effectively *eficazmente*
eight *ocho*
eighteen *dieciocho*
eighth *octavo, -a*
eighty *ochenta*
elect (to) *elegir*
election *la elección*
electricity *la electricidad*
electron *el electrón*
electronic *electrónico, -a*
electronics *la electrónica*
eleven *once*
emergency *la emergencia*
employee *el empleado, -a*
enamel *el esmalte*
end *el final*
endorse (to) *endosar*
engine *el motor*
enjoy (to) *gozar*
enjoy oneself (to) *divertirse*
enough *bastante*
enter (to) *entrar (en)*
entertain (to) *entretener*
entertainment *la diversión*
entrance *la entrada*
environment *el ambiente*
Epiphany *Epifanía*
equipment *el aparato, el equipo*
   electronic equipment *los aparatos*
    electrónicos

music/sound equipment *equipo de música/sonido*
stereo equipment *equipo estereofónico*
video equipment *equipo de video*
errand *el recado, el mandado*
escape (to) *escapar*
eve *la víspera*
evening *la noche*
ever *siempre*
every *todo, -a, -os, -as; cada*
everybody *todo el mundo*
everything *todo*
examine (to) *examinar*
example *ejemplo*
for example *por ejemplo*
excellent *excelente*
exchange *el cambio*
currency exchange office *la agencia de cambio*
exchange student *el/la estudiante de intercambio cultural*
excite (to) *animar*
excitement *la fiebre*
exclude (to) *excluir*
exercise *el ejercicio*
exercise (to) *hacer ejercicios*
exhaust (of a car) *el escape*
exhaust pipe *el caño/tubo de escape*
exhaust (to) *agotar*
to exhaust oneself *agotarse*
exhibition *la muestra, la exhibición*
exist (to) *existir; haber*
exit *la salida*
expense *el gasto*
expensive *caro, -a*
express (to) *representar*
expression *la expresión*
extension *la extensión*
extra *extra; el repuesto (spare part)*
eye *el ojo*
eyeglasses *los anteojos/las gafas (Sp.)*

F

facsimile, fax machine *el telefacsímil, el telefax; el fax*
factory *la fábrica*
factory worker *operario, -a*
fall (season) *el otoño*
family *la familia*
family member *el/la pariente*
family relationship *el parentesco*

fare *el pasaje*
farm *la finca, la estancia*
fashion *la moda*
fat *gordo, -a*
fatigue *la fatiga*
father *el padre*
favor *el favor*
favorite *favorito, -a*
fear (to) *temer*
February *febrero*
fee *la cuota, la tarifa*
feed (to) *dar de comer, cebar (an animal)*
feel (to) *sentir(se)*
I don't feel well! *¡No me siento bien!*
feeling *el sentir*
festival *el festival*
fever *la fiebre*
hayfever *la fiebre del heno*
few *poco, -a, -os, -as*
fewer *menos*
fifteen *quince*
fifth *quinto, -a*
fifty *cincuenta*
fighter *el luchador*
file *el archivo*
file (to) *archivar*
fill (to) *llenar*
filling *el empaste*
film *la película*
film (to) *rodar*
final *final*
finally *al final, ya, ¡por fin! (fam.)*
finance *las rentas públicas, las finanzas*
finance (to) *financiar*
find (to) *encontrar*
fine *la multa*
fine *perfectamente (adv.)*
finger *el dedo*
finish (to) *terminar, acabar*
fireworks *los fuegos artificiales*
first *primer, primero, -a*
fish *el pescado (caught), el pez (alive)*
fishing *la pesca*
deep-sea fishing *la pesca marina*
fit (to) *caber*
This shoe doesn't fit me. *Este zapato no me cabe.*
We don't fit in the car. *No cabemos en el auto.*
fitting *propio, -a*
five *cinco*
five hundred *quinientos, -as*
fix (to) *arreglar*

flat *desinflado, -a*
flight *el vuelo*
floor *el piso*
fog *la niebla*
  light fog *la neblina*
follow (to) *seguir*
food *la comida*
  food and drinks *comidas y bebidas*
foot *el pie*
football *fútbol norteamericano*
for *para, por*
foreigner *el extranjero, la extranjera*
forget (to) *olvidarse*
form *el formulario*
fortunately *felizmente*
forty *cuarenta*
four *cuatro*
fourteen *catorce*
fourth *cuarto, -a*
fowl *el ave*
franc *el franco*
free *gratuito, -a*
freeze (to) *helar*
freezer *el congelador*
frequent *frecuente*
frequently *frecuentemente*
fresh *fresco, -a*
Friday *el viernes*
friend *el amigo, -a*
frighten (to) *asustar*
from *de*
  Where are you from? *¿De dónde es Vd.?*
fruit *la fruta*
  fruit store *la frutería*

G

gain (to) *ganar*
gala *la gala*
garage *el garaje*
garden *el jardín*
gas *el gas*
gasoline *el gasolina*
  gas station *la gasolinera*
  gas tank *el depósito*
  super gasoline *el super*
gate *la puerta*
  arrival gate *puerta de llegada*
  departure gate *puerta de embarque*
general *general (adj.); el general (n.)*
  generally *por lo general*
gentlemen *el señor*

get on (to) *subir a*
get used to (to) *acostumbrarse a*
giant *el gigante*
gift *el regalo*
gigantic *gigante*
girlfriend *la novia*
give (to) *dar, entregar*
  to give birth to *dar a luz, parir*
  to give a gift *regalar*
go (to) *ir; irse*
  go out (to) *salir*
  go up (to) *subir*
golf *el golf*
good-bye *adiós*
gossip *los chismes*
  gossip column *columna de chismes*
governor *el gobernador, la gobernadora*
graceful *bonito, -a*
grammar *la gramática*
grandchild *el nieto, -a*
grandparent *el abuelo, -a*
grateful to (to be) *agradecer*
gray *gris*
greasy *grasoso, -a*
great *gran(de)*
green *verde*
green (vegetable) *las verduras*
greet (to) *dar los buenos días; felicitar*
greeting *la felicitación, el saludo*
groom *el novio*
growth *el aumento*
guarantee *la garantía*
guard (to) *guardar*
guava *la guayaba*
gums (mouth) *las encías*
gun *el revólver*

H

hair *el cabello, el pelo*
haircut *el corte*
hairdo *el peinado*
hairdresser *el peluquero, la peluquera*
  hairdresser's shop *la peluquería*
half *medio, -a*
Halloween *Víspera de Todos los Santos*
ham *el jamón*
hand *la mano*
handkerchief *el pañuelo*
handle *el mango*
handsome *bonito, hermoso, guapo*
hang up (to) *colgar*

happily *felizmente*
happy *contento, -a; feliz*
harm (to) *hacer daño a*
hat *el sombrero*
have (to) *tener, haber*
he *él*
head *la cabeza*
headache *el dolor de cabeza*
headline *el titular*
health *la salud*
heel *el tacón*
Hello! *¡Hola!*
Help! *¡Socorro!*
help *la ayuda*
help (to) *ayudar*
her *la, le, se (object); su (adj.)*
here *aquí*
high *alto, -a*
  first-rate *de alta calidad*
him *lo, le, se*
his *su*
hold (to) *tener*
hole *el agujero*
holiday *el feriado*
  Happy holidays! *¡Felices fiestas!*
home *la casa*
hood *el capó*
hope (to) *esperar*
hospital *la clínica*
hot *caliente*
hotel *el hotel*
house *la casa*
how? *¿cómo? ¿qué?*
how much? how many? *¿cuánto, -a,
  -os, -as?*
however *sin embargo*
humid *húmedo, -a*
humidity *la humedad*
hundred *cien(to)*
  one hundred and one *ciento uno*
hurried *apurado, -a*
hurry *el apuro*
hurry (to) *darse prisa*
husband *el esposo*

I

I *yo*
ice cream *el helado*
idea *la idea*
if *si*
ill *enfermo, -a*

immediate *inmediato, -a*
immediately *en seguida, inmediatamente*
import (to) *importar*
important *importante*
impossible *imposible*
impulse *el impulso*
in *a, en*
  in black and white *en blanco y negro*
  in spite of *a pesar de*
include (to) *incluir*
incorporated *incorporado, -a*
increase *el aumento*
increase (to) *aumentar*
indeed *sí*
indoors *bajo techo, adentro*
ineffective *ineficaz*
information *la información*
inquire (to) *preguntar*
inquiry *la averiguación*
insist (to) *insistir*
inspire (to) *animar*
install (to) *instalar*
instruction *la instrucción*
instructor *el instructor, -a*
insurance *el seguro*
  social security *seguro social*
insure (to) *asegurar*
insured *asegurado, -a*
intelligent *inteligente*
interest *el interés*
interest (to) *interesar*
  to be interested *interesarse*
international *internacional*
intervention *la intervención*
interview *la entrevista*
interview (to) *entrevistar*
introduce (to) *presentar*
invalid *el enfermo, -a*
invitation *la invitación*
invite (to) *invitar*
iron (to) *planchar*
it *lo (m.); la (f.) (obj. pron.)*

J

jacket *la chaqueta*
January *enero*
jeans *el jeans*
job *un trabajo*
jogging *el correr, el jogging*
joke *la broma*
joke (to) *bromear*

juice *el jugo*
July *julio*
June *junio*
justice *la justicia*

K

keep (to) *guardar, mantener*
  to keep in shape *mantenerse en forma*
key *la llave*
keyboard *el teclado*
keyhole *el ojo*
kidney beans *los frijoles*
kill (to) *matar*
kilometer *el kilómetro, el quilómetro*
kind *la clase; el tipo*
kitchen *la cocina*
knife *el puñal*
know (to) *conocer, saber*

L

labor *la obra*
  Labor Day *Día del Trabajo*
lack (to) *faltar, hacer falta*
  to be lacking *faltarle a uno*
lamb *el cordero*
lament (to) *lamentar, sentir*
language *la lengua, idioma (abstract)*
late *tarde*
laugh (to) *reírse*
  to laugh at/about *reírse de*
laundry *el lavado; la lavandería*
  (place)
law *el derecho, la ley*
lawyer *el abogado, -a*
lead (to) *dirigir*
  to lead to *dar a*
learn (to) *aprender*
lease *el arrendamiento*
leave (to) *dejar, partir, salir*
left *izquierdo, -a*
  to the left *a la izquierda*
leg *la pierna*
lend (to) *prestar*
Lent *la Cuaresma*
lessen (to) *disminuirse*
lesson *la lección*
let (to) *permitir, dejar*
letter *la carta*
  letter of complaint *la carta de relamación*

letter of recommendation *la carta de*
  referencia/recomendación
lettuce *la lechuga*
lie down (to) *acostarse, tumbarse*
lifeguard *el/la salvavidas*
lift (to) *levantar, alzar*
light *la luz*
like (to) *gustar, encantarle a uno,*
  querer
liking *el gusto*
limit *el límite*
lip *el labio*
listen (to) *escuchar*
live (to) *vivir*
living room *la sala*
loan *el préstamo*
  to ask for a loan *pedir un préstamo*
lobby *la recepción*
local *local*
long *largo, -a*
look for (to) *buscar*
lose (to) *perder*
lotion *la loción*
  suntan lotion *loción bronceadora*
love *el amor*
  amor mío, cariño *my darling*
love (to) *encantar, querer, amar*
  to fall in love with *enamorarse de*
luck *la suerte*
  Good luck! *¡Buena suerte!*
lunch *el almuerzo*
  to have lunch *almorzar*

M

machine *la máquina*
mail (to) *enviar*
  by air mail *por vía aérea*
mailbox *el buzón*
mailman *el cartero, -a*
maintain (to) *mantener*
majority *la mayoría*
make (to) *hacer*
make-up *el cosmético*
man *el hombre*
management *la dirección*
manager *el/la gerente*
manicure *la manicura*
manner *manera*
many *mucho, -a*
map *el mapa*
March *marzo*

market *el mercado*
  black market *el mercado negro*
marketing *el mercadeo*
marvelous *maravilloso, -a*
material (fabric) *la tela*
May *mayo*
maybe *tal vez*
mayor *el alcalde/la alcadesa*
me *me; mí (prep. obj. pron.)*
meal *la comida*
mean (to) *querer decir*
means *el medio*
measure *la medida, la ley (standard)*
meat *la carne*
media *los medios de comunicación*
meet (to) *encontrar, reunirse*
menu *el menú*
merit *el valor*
meter *el metro, el medidor (electronics)*
middle *el centro*
midnight *la medianoche*
milk *la leche*
milkshake *el batido*
million *millón*
mind *la idea*
minor *menos*
mirror *el espejo*
misfortune *la desgracia*
miss *la señorita*
mist *la neblina*
mistaken (to be) *equivocarse*
mister *el señor*
model *el/la modelo*
modem *el módem (computers)*
modern *moderno, -a*
modernize (to) *actualizar*
moisture *la humedad*
moment *momento*
  Just a moment. One moment. *Momentito.*
Monday *el lunes*
money *el dinero, el efectivo, la moneda*
money order *el giro (postal)*
month *el mes*
moon *la luna*
more *más*
morning *la mañana*
most *la mayor parte*
mother *la madre*
motor *el motor*
moustache *el bigote*
mouse *el ratón (animal), el*
    manejacursores/el "máus" (computers)
mouth *la boca*

mouthwash *el enjuague bucal*
move (to) *mudarse*
movie *el cine, el film, la película*
  movie listings *la cartelera*
  movie theater *el cine*
moviemaker *el/la cineasta*
Mrs., madam *la señora*
much *mucho, -a*
mug (to) *asaltar*
mugger *el/la asaltante*
mugging *el asalto*
murder *el asesinato*
muscle *el músculo*
muscular *musculoso, -a*
music *la música*
  rock music *el rock*
my *mi, mis (poss. adj.)*
myself *me*

N

name *el nombre*
  given name *nombre de pila*
named (to be) *llamarse*
  My name is . . . *Me llamo . . .*
nation *la nación, el pueblo*
national *nacional*
nationality *la nacionalidad*
nature *la naturaleza*
near, nearby *cerca (de)*
necessary *necesario, -a*
neck *el cuello*
necktie *la corbata*
need (to) *necesitar*
neighborhood *el barrio*
nephew *el sobrino*
nervous *nervioso, -a*
network *la red*
never *jamas*
  never mind *note preocupes*
new *nuevo, -a*
  New Year *Año Nuevo*
news *las noticias*
  news broadcast *el noticiero*
newspaper *el periódico*
niece *la sobrina*
night *la noche*
  last night *anoche*
nine *nueve*
nineteen *diecinueve*
ninety *noventa*
ninth *noveno, -a*

no *no*
nobody *nadie*
noise *el ruido*
none *ningún, ninguno, ninguna*
noon *el mediodía*
normal *normal*
normally *normalmente*
nose *la nariz*
not *no*
nothing *nada*
noun *el nombre*
November *noviembre*
now *ahora, ya*
  right now *ahora mismo*
number *el número*

O

obey (to) *obedecer*
obligation *la obligación*
obtain (to) *conseguir*
October *octubre*
of *de*
  of course *claro*
offer *la oferta*
  to make an offer *hacer una oferta*
offer (to) *ofrecer*
office *la oficina*
often *a menudo, asiduamente*
oil *el aceite*
okay *bueno, vale (Sp.)*
old *viejo, -a*
  older *mayor*
on *a, en*
  on board *a bordo*
  on foot *a pie*
on time *a tiempo*
once *una vez*
onion *la cebolla*
open (to) *abrir; estrenarse*
opening *la abertura* (physical); *la apertura*
  (abstract)
opening (show) *el estreno*
operator *el operador, -a*
opinion *el sentir*
  to give an opinion *opinar*
opposite *en frente de*
orange *la naranja, la china (Puerto Rico)*
orchestra *la platea*
  orchestra seat *la butaca de platea*
ostentatious *ostentoso, -a*
other, another *otro, -a, -os, -as*

ourselves *nos*
outdoors *al aire libre, a fuera*
oven *el horno*
overcoat *el abrigo*
owe (to) *deber*
own *propio, -a*

P

package *el paquete*
page *la página*
  first/front page *la primera plana*
pain *el dolor*
pair *el par*
pajamas *el pijama*
pants *los pantalones*
paper *el papel*
parade *el desfile*
park (to) *estacionar, a parcar (Sp.)*
part *la parte; el papel/el rol (role in the*
  theater), la raya (hair)
participate (to) *participar*
party *la fiesta*
Passover *La Pascua Florida*
passport *el pasaporte*
patient *el/la paciente*
pay (to) *pagar*
payment *el pago*
  monthly payments *pagos mensuales*
peanut *el maní*
penalty *la multa*
people *la gente, el pueblo*
peppers *los pimentones*
percent *por ciento*
perfectly *perfectamente*
perform (to) *realizar, representar*
  to perform a role *representar un papel*
performance *el rendimiento (of a product,*
  person, etc,); la representación (theater)
perhaps *puede ser, quizás, tal vez*
permanent *permanente*
permit (to) *permitir*
person *la persona*
personnel *el personal*
  Personnel Department *Departamento de*
  Personal
petition *solicitud*
pharmacist *el farmacéutico, -a*
pharmacy *la botánica (herbs); la farmacia;*
phenomenal *fenomenal*
philosophy *la filosofía*
piano *el piano*

pick up (to) *recoger*
pill *la pastilla*
pin (to) *prender*
pineapple *la piña*
place (to) *poner*
plan *el plan*
plantain *el plátano*
platform *el andén*
play *la pieza*
play (to) *jugar a (game); tocar (musical instrument)*
playhouse *el teatro*
plaza *la plaza*
pleasant *simpático, -a*
please *por favor*
pleasure *el gusto*
plus *más*
police force *la policía*
policeman *el policía*
policewoman *la mujer policía*
policy *la política*
politician *el político, -a*
politics *la política*
pollution *la contaminación*
pool (swimming) *la piscina*
popcorn *las rosetas de maíz*
pork *el puerco*
  roast suckling pig *el lechón*
portable *portátil*
porter *el maletero*
possess (to) *tener*
possible *posible*
postal system *el correo*
  at the post office *en el correo*
  post office box *la casilla de correo*
postcard *la tarjeta postal*
potato *la patata (Sp.), la papa*
pound *la libra*
precious *precioso, -a*
preferable *preferible*
prescribe (to) *recetar*
prescription *la receta*
present *el regalo*
present (to) *presentar*
present oneself (to) *presentarse*
president *el presidente, la presidenta*
press (newspaper) *la prensa*
press (to) *planchar (clothes)*
pretty *bonito, -a*
prevent (to) *impedir*
previous *anterior*
price *el precio*
  price tag *la etiqueta*

printed matter *los impresos*
prison *la cárcel*
prisoner *el preso, -a*
prize *el premio*
problem *el problema*
procedure *el trámite*
produce (to) *producir*
product *el producto*
production *la producción*
program *el programa, el régimen (de un gobierno)*
promise (to) *prometer*
promote (to) *ascender*
promotion *el avance, el ascenso*
prompt *pronto, -a, listo, -a*
  as soon as possible *lo más pronto posible*
pronunciation *la pronunciación*
protect (to) *proteger*
protein *la proteína*
publication *la publicación*
pull out (to) *arrancar*
pump *la bomba*
purse *la bolsa*
pursue (to) *seguir*
put (to) *poner*
put on (to) *ponerse*

Q

quality *la calidad*
quantity *la cantidad*
quarter *cuarto, -a*
quick *pronto, rápidamente*
quiet *quieto, -a*
quiet (to be) *callarse*
quiz *el examen*

R

radio *la radio*
  radio/cassette player *el radio-cassette (para cintas)*
rain (to) *llover*
  It's raining. *Llueve. Está lloviendo.*
raincoat *el impermeable; la garbadina (Sp.)*
raise *el aumento*
raise (to) *levantar*
rally (political) *el acto político*
rape *la violación*
rapid *rápido, -a*
rapidly *rápidamente*

rate *la tasa*
  exchange rate *tasa de cambio*
  interest rate *tasa de interés*
rather *más bien, sino; bastante*
raw *crudo, -a*
  raw materials *materia prima*
reach (to) *llegar*
react (to) *reaccionar*
read (to) *leer*
ready *listo, -a*
real estate *los inmuebles*
  real estate agent *el corredor (-a) de inmuebles*
reality *la realidad*
realize (to) *darse cuenta*
reason *la razón*
receipt *el recibo*
receive (to) *recibir*
reception *la recepción*
receptionist *el/la recepcionista*
recommend (to) *recomendar*
recorder *la grabadora*
record player *el tocadiscos*
red *rojo, -a, tinto (wine)*
redhead *el pelirrojo*
reduce (to) *bajar*
reference *la referencia*
refreshment *el refresco*
refrigerator *el refrigerador; la nevera (Sp.)*
refund *el reembolso, la devolución*
regimen *el régimen*
register (to) *certificar*
registration *la certificación*
regret (to) *lamentar, sentir*
relative *el pariente/la parienta*
remain (to) *permanecer, quedar(se)*
rent *el alquiler, la renta*
rent (to) *alquilar, arrendar*
repair (to) *reparar*
repeat (to) *repetir*
replace (to) *reemplazar*
represent (to) *representar*
request (to) *pedir*
reservation *la reserva, la reservación*
resource *recurso*
responsibility *la obligación*
rest *el descanso*
rest *descansar*
restaurant *el restaurante*
restroom *baño de damas/caballeros*
results *los resultados*
résumé *el resumen*
retail *al por menor*

return (to) *devolver, volver*
review *la reseña (book, film, theater); repaso*
revolver *el revólver*
rice *el arroz*
rich *rico, -a*
right *la derecha; ¡Bien!*
  right there *ahí mismo*
  to be right *tener razón*
  to the right *a la derecha*
ring (to) *sonar; tocar*
rinse (to) *enjuagar*
risk *el riesgo*
river *el río*
rob (to) *asaltar, robar*
robbery *el robo*
rock music *el rock*
role *el papel*
  to perform a role *representar un papel*
room *el cuarto, la habitación*
  room service *el servicio de cuarto*
root *la raíz*
  root canal *el empaste de la raíz*
rose *la rosa*
row *la fila*
run (to) *correr*

S

sad *triste*
safety *la seguridad*
sailboat *el velero*
saint *el santo*
  All Saint's Day *Día de todos los Santos*
salad *la ensalada*
salary *el salario, el sueldo*
sale *la venta*
  retail sale *al por menor*
  sales tag *la etiqueta*
  special sale *venta especial*
  wholesale *al por mayor*
salesperson *el vendedor, -a*
salmon *el salmón*
salon *el salón*
  beauty parlor *el salón de belleza*
sample *la muestra*
sample (to) *tomar/sacar una muestra*
sand *la arena*
sandwich *el bocadillo*
satellite *el satélite*
  by satellite *vía/por satélite*
Saturday *el sábado*

sauce *la salsa*
sausage *el chorizo*
say (to) *decir*
scene *la escena*
schedule *el horario*
scissors *las tijeras*
score *el puntaje, la puntuación, la cuenta
    (fam.) (game)*
screen *la pantalla*
scuba diving *el buceo*
sea *el mar*
seafood *los mariscos*
seamstress *la modista*
seasickness *el mareo*
season *la estación*
seat *el asiento*
second *segundo, -a*
section *la sección*
security *la seguridad*
see (to) *ver*
seem (to) *parecer*
seize (to) *prender*
select (to) *elegir, escoger*
self *propio, -a*
sell (to) *vender, dejar a un precio*
senator *el senador, -a*
send (to) *enviar*
September *septiembre*
serve (to) *servir*
service *el servicio*
seven *siete*
seventeen *diecisiete*
seventh *séptimo, -a*
seventy *setenta*
several *varios, -as*
sew (to) *coser*
shade *la sombra*
shampoo *el champú*
shape *la forma*
    to keep in shape *mantenerse en forma*
shape (to) *formar*
share (to) *participar*
sharp *en punto (on the dot); agudo, -a
    (point, pain)*
shave (to) *afeitarse*
    shaving blade *hoja de afeitar*
    shaving razor *navaja de afeitar*
she *ella*
shelter *el abrigo*
shine (to) *lucir*
shirt *la camisa*
shocking *chocante*
shoe *el zapato*

shoe repair shop *la zapatería*
shoe maker *el zapatero*
shoot (to) *disparar; tirar*
shop (to) *comprar, hacer compras*
    shopping centers *centros comerciales*
short while (a) *un rato*
shoulder *el hombro*
show *espetáculo*
show (to) *exhibir, mostrar, pasar/dar
    (film), presentar*
show up (to) *presentarse*
shower *la ducha*
showing *la función (theater), la exhibición*
showtime (play, film, etc.) *la función, la
    sesión*
shrimp *los camarones*
sick *enfermo, -a*
side *el lado, el costado*
    next to *al lado de, junto a*
sign *el aviso*
sign (to) *firmar*
silk *la seda*
similar *similar*
simple *simple*
sir *el señor*
sister *la hermana*
sister-in-law *la cuñada*
sit down (to) *sentarse*
six *seis*
sixteen *dieciseis*
sixth *sexto, -a*
sixty *sesenta*
skiing *el esquiar*
    water skiing *esquí acuático*
skin *la piel*
skirt *la pollera, la falda (Sp.)*
sleep (to) *dormir*
    to go to sleep *dormirse*
slip (deposit, etc.) *la papeleta, el talón*
small *pequeño, -a*
    smaller *más pequeño*
smell (to) *oler*
smoke (to) *fumar*
    non-smoking section *sección de no fumar*
snack *el bocadillo; las tapas*
snow (to) *nevar*
    It's snowing. *Nieva. Está nevando.*
so *tan*
    so much, many *tantos, -as*
soap *el jabón*
soap opera *la (tele)novela*
soccer *el fútbol*
    soccer player *el/la futbolista*

socks *los calcetines*
soda *la soda, el refresco*
sole (foot) *la planta*
some *algún, alguno, -a*
someone *alguien*
something *algo*
  Something else? *¿Algo más?*
sometimes *algunas/unas veces, a veces*
somewhat *algo; bastante*
son *el hijo*
song *la canción*
sorrow *la pena; el dolor*
Sorry! *¡Lo siento!, ¡Discúlpeme!, ¡Dispense!*
  (Sp.)
soup *la sopa*
space *el espacio*
spare *el repuesto*
speak (to) *hablar*
speaker *el orador, -a (person); el (alto)*
  parlante/ el altavoces (Sp.) (electronics)
special *especial*
specialty *la especialidad*
spectator *el espectador, -a*
spend time (to) *pasar*
  to pass by *pasar por*
spices *las especias*
sponsor (to) *auspiciar*
sport *el deporte*
  water sports *diversiones acuáticas*
spring *la primavera*
square (plaza) *la plaza*
stadium *el estadio*
stain *la mancha*
  to take out a stain *sacar una mancha*
staircase *la escalera*
  to go down/up *abajar/subir*
stall (to) *pararse*
stamp *la estampilla, el sello*
star (performer) *el/la estrella, el/la*
  protagonista
stereo *el estereofónico*
  stereo equipment *el equipo estereofónico*
still *quieto, -a; todavía (adv.)*
stockings *las medias*
stomach *el estómago*
  stomachache *el dolor de estómago*
Stop! *¡Alto!*
stop (to) *detener, pararse*
store *la tienda*
store (to) *guardar*
storey *el piso*
storm *la tormenta*
stout *gordo, -a*

stove *la estufa*
straight *derecho*
  Go straight ahead. *Sigues derecho.*
strawberry *la fresa, la frutilla (Argentina)*
street *la calle*
strong *fuerte*
student *el/la estudiante*
study (to) *estudiar*
style *la moda*
subject *sujeto (of sentence); asignatura,*
  materia (school)
succeed (to) *llegar*
success *el éxito*
sudden *repentino, -a*
  suddenly *de pronto, de repente*
suffer (to) *sufrir*
suggest (to) *sugerir*
suit *el traje*
suitable *propio, -a*
suitcase *la maleta*
sum *la cantidad*
summer *el verano*
sun *el sol*
  to be sunny *hacer sol*
sunbathe (to) *broncearse*
Sunday *el domingo*
supermarket *el supermercado*
supper *la cena*
sure *seguro, -a*
  surely *seguramente*
surfing *el surfe*
  to go surfing *hacer surfe*
surname, last name *el apellido*
swear (to) *jurar*
sweater *el suéter*
sweet banana *el guineo*
swell (to) *hincharse*
swim (to) *nadar*
swimming *la natación*
syrup *el jarabe*

T

table *la mesa*
tablet *la pastilla*
tailor *el sastre*
  tailor's shop *la sastrería*
take (to) *tomar, llevar, quitar*
take care (to) *cuidar*
  to take care of oneself *cuidarse*
take-off *el despegue (plane)*
take off (to) *despegar*

talk (to) *hablar*
tall *alto, -a*
taste *el gusto*
tax *impuesto*
taxi *el taxi*
telephone *el teléfono*
   telephone book *la guía telefónica*
telephone (to) *telefonear*
television *la tele(visión); el televisor*
   (TV set)
teller *el cajero, -a*
   automatic teller machine *cajero automático*
ten *diez*
tennis *el tenis*
   tennis court *la cancha*
   to play tennis *jugar al tenis*
   tennis player *el/la tenista*
terrible *terrible*
test *el examen*
than *que*
thank (to) *agradecer, dar las gracias a*
   thank you *gracias*
Thanksgiving *Día de la Acción de Gracias*
that *ese, esa; aquel, aquella (adj.)*
that one *ése, ésa; aquél, aquélla (pron.)*
theater *el teatro*
them *los (dir. obj.); les*
there *ahí; allí (far away)*
   there is, there are *hay*
   there was, there were *hubo, había*
these *estos, estas (adj.); éstos, éstas*
   (pron.)
they *ellos, ellas*
thief *el ladrón/la ladrona*
thing *la cosa*
think (to) *pensar*
third *tercer, tercero, -a*
thirteen *trece*
thirty *treinta*
this *este, esta (adj.); éste, ésta (pron.)*
those *esos, esas; aquellos, aquellas (adj.);*
   ésos, ésas; aquéllos, aquéllas (pron.)
thousand *mil*
three *tres*
thrilling *emocionante*
through *por*
Thursday *el jueves*
thus *así*
ticket *el boleto, la entrada, el pasaje, el*
   billete
   ticket counter *el mostrador*
   round-trip ticket *pasaje de ida y vuelta*
tie *la corbata*

tie (to) *atar*
time *la hora, la vez*
tire *la llanta*
tire (to) *fatigar, cansar*
to *a*
toast *la tostada (bread); el brindis (salute)*
today *hoy*
toe *el dedo del pie*
together *junto, -a*
   to get together *reunirse*
tomato *el tomate*
tomorrow *la mañana*
   the day after tomorrow *pasado mañana*
tongue *la lengua*
tonight *esta noche*
tooth *el diente, la muela*
   to brush one's teeth *cepillarse*
   toothbrush *el cepillo de dientes*
   toothpaste *la pasta de dientes, el dentífrico*
touch (to) *tocar*
tourism *el turismo*
tourist *el/la turista*
   tourist office *el centro de turismo*
toward *para, hacia*
towel *la toalla*
town *el pueblo*
track (running) *la pista*
trade *las compraventas*
tragedy *la tragedia*
train *el tren*
   train station *la estación ferroviaria/de*
     trenes
transaction *la transacción*
transfer *el transbordo*
translate (to) *traducir*
transportation *el transporte*
travel (to) *viajar*
   travel agency *la agencia de viajes*
   travel sickness *el mareo*
treat (to) *tratar*
trim (to) *cortar un poco*
trip *el viaje*
trunk *el baúl*
truth *la verdad, la realidad*
try (to) *tratar*
Tuesday *el martes*
tuna *el atún*
tune in (to) *sintonizar*
turn (chance) *la vez*
   turn off (to) *apagar*
   turn on (to) *encender*
twelve *doce*
twenty *veinte*

twice *dos veces*
two *dos*
   the two of them, both *los dos, ambos*
type *la clase, el tipo, el género*

U

ugly *feo, -a*
umbrella *el/los paraguas*
   beach umbrella *el parasol*
uncle *el tío*
under *bajo, debajo de*
understand (to) *comprender, entender*
unpleasant *desagradable, antipático, -a*
until *hasta*
update (to) *actualizar*
uproot (to) *arrancar*
us *nos; nosotros, nosotras (obj. pron.)*
usual *común, general*

V

vacancy *habitación libre vacuidad*
   no vacancies *completo*
vacation *las vacaciones*
vaccine *la vacuna*
Valentine's Day *Día de los Enamorados*
value *el valor*
vegetable *la legumbre, la verdura*
vertigo *el vértigo*
very *muy, bien*
victim *el/la víctima*
video *el video/vídeo*
   video equipment *equipo de video*
   video recorder, VCR *la video-grabadora,
      la máquina filmadora*
view *la vista*
village *el pueblo*
visa *la visa*
   tourist visa *visa de turista*
   business visa *visa de negociante*
visit *la visita*
visit (to) *visitar*
vocabulary *el vocabulario*
volleyball *el voleibol*
vote, voting *el voto*
vote (to) *votar*
voter *el/la votante*

W

waist *la cintura*
waiter *el mesero, -a*
walk (to) *caminar, andar*
want (to) *querer*
war *la guerra*
warm *caliente*
warning *la advertencia*
wash (to) *lavar*
   washing and drying *lavado y
      planchado*
wash oneself (to) *lavarse*
washer *la máquina de lavar*
washing *el lavado*
watch *el reloj*
watch (to) *mirar*
   watching TV *mirando la televisión*
water *el agua (f)*
   water skiing *el esquí acuático*
way *el lado*
we *nosotros, nosotras (subj. pron.)*
wear out (to) *agotar*
   to wear oneself out *agotarse*
weariness *la fatiga*
weather *el tiempo*
wedding *la boda*
Wednesday *el miércoles*
week *la semana*
weekend *el fin de semana*
weigh (to) *pesar*
welcome *bienvenido, -a*
   Welcome! *Bienvenido!*
   You're welcome. *De nada.*
well *bien*
   well, well then . . . *pues . . .*
what *¿cómo? ¿cuál? ¿qué?*
where *¿dónde?*
whether *si*
which *que; ¿cuál? ¿qué?*
while *mientras*
whim *el capricho*
white *blanco, -a*
who, whom *que; quien, quienes*
wholesale *al por mayor*
whose? *¿De quién?*
why? *¿Por qué?*
wife *la esposa*
wig *la peluca*
win (to) *ganar*
wind *el aire*
window *la ventanilla*
windy *el viento*

wine *el vino*
  red wine *vino tinto*
  white wine *vino blanco*
wing *el ala (f)*
winner *el ganador, -a*
winter *el invierno*
wish *el deseo*
wish (to) *desear, querer*
with *con*
  with him, her, you, them *consigo*
  with me *conmigo*
  with you *contigo*
withdraw (to) *retirar*
withdrawal *el retiro*
  to make a withdrawal *hacer un
    retiro*
without *sin*
witness *el testigo, -a*
woman *la mujer*
wonderful *maravillosos, -a*
wool *la lana*
word *la palabra*
  word processor *la procesadora de
    palabras*
work *la obra, el trabajo*
work (to) *trabajar*
workdays *los días laborables*
world *el mundo*
worldwide *mundial*
worry (to) *preocuparse*
worse *peor*
worth *el valor*
wound (to) *herir*
wrap (to) *envolver*
wrestler *el luchador*

X

x-ray *la radiografía*
  to take an x-ray *sacar una radiografía*
xenophobia *xenofobia*

Y

year *el año*
  all year long *todo el año*
  Happy New Year! *¡Feliz Año Nuevo!*
  last year *el año pasado*
  New Year *el Año Nuevo*
  New Year's Eve *la Nochevieja*
yearly *por año*
yell (to) *gritar, vociferar*
yellow *amarillo, -a*
yesterday *ayer*
yet *todavía, aún*
  not yet *todavía no*
you *tú, vos (some parts of Latin America)
  usted; vosotros, vosotras (pl. subj. pron.
  Sp.) ustedes; le, la (fml. sg.); les, las, os
  (fml. pl.); te (fam. sg.); ti, sí (prep.)
  (obj. pron.)*
young *joven*
  younger *menor*
youngster *el/la joven*

Z

zero *cero*
zone *la zona*

INDEX